UNFOLDING LIFE

The Evolution of Man's Conception of His Place in Nature

BY

ARTHUR FINDLAY

Honorary Vice-President of the Spiritualists' National Union.
A Founder, and past Chairman of the International Institute for Psychical Research.
Vice-President of the Marylebone Spiritualist Association.
Founder and Vice-President of the Glasgow Society for Psychical Research.
Past President of the London Spiritualist Alliance.
Honorary President of the Essex Federation of Spiritualists.
Honorary President of the Institute of Psychic Writers and Artists.
Vice-President of the Leicester Society for Psychical Research.
Honorary Member of the American Foundation for Psychic Research.
Membro d'Onore Universitaria Accademica Spiritualistica Italiana.
Honorary Member of the Edinburgh Psychic College.
Honorary Member of the Athens Metaphysical Alliance.
Founder of the Quest Club.

"To look upon the soul as going on from strength to strength, to consider that it is to shine forever with new accessions of glory, and brighten to all eternity; that it will be still adding virtue to virtue, and knowledge to knowledge, carries in it something wonderfully agreeable to that ambition which is natural to the mind of man."—
Addison.

First Impression		1935
Second "		1935
Third "		1936
Fourth "		1936
Fifth "		1938

Out of print during the Second World War

Sixth Impression		1949
Seventh "		1950
Eighth "		1950
Ninth "		1959
Tenth "		1959
Eleventh "		1965
Twelfth "		1973
This Edition		1988

ISBN 0 94782 313 1

THE SPIRITUALISTS' NATIONAL UNION was left the copyright to all of Arthur Findlay's books, with the request to keep the titles in print. The SNU is the largest Spiritualist Church organisation in the UK. The SNU also owns the Arthur Findlay College at Stansted Hall.

The SNU is based at Redwoods, Stansted Hall, Stansted Mountfitchet, Essex CM24 8UD.

Two of the foremost publishers in the psychic sphere have combined their talents to produce this most important series. They are:

PSYCHIC PRESS LIMITED. Booksellers, publishers of books and the weekly "PSYCHIC NEWS."
20 Earlham Street, London WC2H 9LW.

THE HEADQUARTERS PUBLISHING COMPANY LIMITED. Booksellers, publishers of books and two Spiritualist monthly magazines "TWO WORLDS" and "HERE AND THERE."
5 Alexandria Road, West Ealing, London W13 0NP.

Printed in Great Britain by
Masterprint, Newport, Essex

THE UNFOLDING UNIVERSE

This book completes the author's trilogy on Spiritualism, and is devoted to an examination of the evolution of humanity's religious and philosophic convictions from the time of primitive man to the present day.

After a study of man as a psychic being, the author gives his opinions as to the nature of the Etheric World, in which we live after death, considering the laws and conditions of life there, as he has been made to understand them from those who communicated with him from that other order of life. Here he shows the naturalness of it all, and how life continues to function after death in a world somewhat similar to the one it has experienced on earth.

He also envisages the future, considering the effect the knowledge of survival and communication will have on the religious, political and social outlook of future generations. The following is a selection of the many Press reviews the book received throughout the English-speaking world.

"*The Unfolding Universe* is Arthur Findlay's greatest book. In it he gives a comprehensive picture of the Universe, as revealed by Spiritualism. His chapter on 'The Age of Superstition' is a masterpiece of reasoning. The book is invigorating and is an oasis of common sense in an arid desert of theology. In his three books he has raised Spiritualism to the level of a science, has disclosed what is false in religion, while emphasising what is true. His philosophy and his psychic experiences must satisfy all human desires as to life and conduct on earth, and our destiny after death. He appeals to reason and knowledge and not to faith, never departing from the scientific method, and the conclusions of modern scientific thought."—*Psychic News.*

"Much is now known about life and conditions after death, and in *The Unfolding Universe* the author has succeeded to a very great extent in making the subject of Spiritualism easily understood by all. It is a volume which is almost certain to become as popular as the author's two previous works."—*Leicester Mail.*

"Mr. Findlay is all for knowledge and against mysteriousness. 'Ignorance and misery,' he says, 'are twin brothers. Spiritualism, which stands for knowledge, lifts the tragedy from life.' *The Unfolding Universe* is informative and a large amount of reading and research have gone to the making of it."—*The Scotsman.*

"Nor can we doubt the attractiveness of the truths so discovered. Mr. Findlay's own success testifies it. I do not doubt that *The Unfolding Universe* will be equally popular."—*The Spectator.*

"Mr. Findlay's book is a brave, able statement of his view. It deserves careful and impartial study."—*The Inquirer.*

"Mr. Findlay has a pungent style and is emphatic in his conclusions. Orthodox Christians will, of course, challenge at least some of his opinions, but his book will appeal to all people who take more than a superficial interest in life in the hereafter."—*Sheffield Telegraph.*

"I have had the privilege of reading Arthur Findlay's new book entitled *The Unfolding Universe*, and I confess that its contents have caused me to think furiously. Mr. Findlay writes convincingly as a man who has discovered something of vital importance."—*Ardrossan & Saltcoats Herald.*

"Mr. Findlay's scheme of a concentric universe of planes of varied vibrations is one of the most clearly conceived we have yet met in Spiritualist literature. *The Unfolding Universe* completes the task he set out to accomplish to make Spiritualism understood by all intelligent people as science, religion and philosophy."—*Cambridge Daily News.*

"Mr. Findlay writes with a facile pen. His arguments are the product of a logical mind and are based on what the author assuredly believes to be facts. *The Unfolding Universe* is written to awaken thought and to stimulate inquiry, and thought and inquiry make for progress."—*Herts & Essex Observer.*

"Mr. Findlay is most honest himself and thoroughgoing. The reading public owe him a debt of gratitude for *The Unfolding Universe.*"—*Belfast Newsletter.*

"This is an arresting book, whether one agrees with Mr. Findlay or disagrees with him. No sincere person can doubt the high motive, the extensive research, and the enthusiastic sincerity of the writer. We thank Mr. Findlay for giving us *The Unfolding Universe.*"—*The Two Worlds.*

"*The Unfolding Universe* is a weighty tome of 475 pages, and our first reaction is to congratulate the writer on the assiduity and zeal displayed in executing this self-imposed task."—*Service.*

"Mr. Findlay writes fearlessly and from conviction reached after careful study, much research and varied experience. By some *The Unfolding Universe* will be accepted, by others condemned, but by all who are interested in an exposition of the sincere belief of a Spiritualist the book will be read with interest."—*Irvine Times.*

"Mr. Arthur Findlay's books have been read because he has always insisted that his readers must exercise their own judgment on the arguments and personal convictions which he stresses. He is frank, as his criticism of the churches makes evident, but his candour makes it all the more easy for the reader to exercise that personal judgment after a study of the author's case. His books on Spiritualism have received more serious consideration than those of any other writer. This week the concluding volume of his trilogy has appeared under the title of *The Unfolding Universe.*"—*Public Opinion.*

"*The Unfolding Universe*, for those who already accept the reality of psychic phenomena, will be read with the profoundest interest. For those who do not accept Spiritualism in all its teachings, we would recommend, in addition to this work, the two former of Mr. Findlay's books, of which this volume forms the last of the trilogy."—*Armchair Science.*

CONTENTS.

	PAGE
Foreword	vii
Introduction	xiii
Chapter I—From Darkness to Light	23
Chapter II—The Age of Superstition	50
Chapter III—The Evolution of Christianity	115
Chapter IV—Jesus or Christ?	164
Chapter V—The Age of Materialism	197
Chapter VI—The New Age of Thought	215
Chapter VII—The Greater World	248
Chapter VIII—Mind is King	308
Chapter IX—The Coming World Religion	326
Chapter X—The Church—Past and Future	370
Chapter XI—Reality Unfolding	423
Chapter XII—The Wider Outlook	457
Index	477

FOREWORD.

ALL who have read Arthur Findlay's two previous books in this Trilogy—*On the Edge of the Etheric* and *The Rock of Truth*—will agree that he has succeeded in making religion and philosophy both intelligible and rational. He has removed religion from the darkness of faith into the light of knowledge, and in this book, *The Unfolding Universe*, the last of the three, the reader is carried forward to the heights where further and enlarged vistas open up. Undoubtedly the credit is due to him for putting Spiritualism on a scientific and realistic basis.

To bring light into dark places, to enlarge the vision and increase humanity's intellectual horizon, has been the aim of many pioneers of the past, and, in the realm of religion and philosophy, Arthur Findlay ranks with the other torch bearers who have carried forward the light of knowledge.

On leaving his preparatory school he went to Fettes College and then to Geneva University. At the age of twenty-five, on the death of his father, he became senior Stockbroking partner of one of the leading Stockbroking and Chartered Accountant firms in Glasgow. After a remarkably successful business career he retired from active business at the age of forty, when he bought the estate of Stansted Hall in Essex, where he and his wife now reside. As a Magistrate for Essex and Ayrshire, and Chairman of Administrative councils in these counties, he has given much of his time to county work.

Arthur Findlay was born in Glasgow in 1883, and comes of a long line of ancestors who have been famous in Scottish history. He is a direct descendant of Allan Fitz Flaand, whose son Walter became first High Steward of Scotland in 1158, founded the Stewart family and gave to Scotland its line of Stewart kings. In the fourteenth century one of Arthur Findlay's ancestors so distinguished himself at the Battle of Bannockburn in 1314 that he was given the Barony and Lordship of Kilmarnock, besides large tracts of land in Ayrshire. The following century, in the reign of James III, one of his ancestors became Lord Chancellor, and Regent during the King's minority.

Ayrshire is his home county, and there his ancestors, in the seventeenth century, played a prominent part in their opposition to being forced to attend the Episcopalian Church, one being hanged in the Grass Market at Edinburgh in 1688, while another was imprisoned, awaiting the same fate, when William of Orange landed and he was pardoned.

Coming to more settled times we find his forbears, over the past two hundred years, prominently connected with the commercial and financial life of Glasgow and the west of Scotland. He is a Freeman of his native city, and during the First World War he was awarded the Order of the British Empire for his organization work in connection with the British Red Cross Society.

Agriculture is one of his many interests, and the improvements he effected, some twenty years ago, in methods of production are generally well known. As chairman of several companies he still retains his interest in finance, on which he has written many articles.

Arthur Findlay, however, is best known to the public through his books and addresses on History, Spiritualism, Philosophy and Religion. As Chairman of Psychic Press Ltd., the proprietors of *Psychic News*, he has taken a prominent part in the furtherance of the knowledge of Spiritualism. He has spoken in the largest halls of most of our great cities and in several of the capitals of Europe, and his books have been read in almost every country throughout the world. He, moreover, took a prominent part in the Church of Scotland enquiry into Spiritualism.

Always a student, and a great reader, he had read many of the standard books on Comparative Religion and Mythology before he was twenty-one years of age, and since then he has made a special study of this branch of science. Readers of his Trilogy will realise how intimately this subject is connected with Spiritualism. How thoroughly he has covered this entire field of thought by these three books will be best realised by turning over the pages of the *Index to the Trilogy*. Here we find nearly sixteen thousand references to their contents, which, in itself, emphasises the amount of labour and research involved in their compilation.

After completing his Trilogy, Arthur Findlay then started to rewrite history from the psychic angle of thought, and in his two monumental books *The Psychic Stream* and *The Curse of Ignorance* (in two volumes) he gave his readers a new interpretation of the past. The former book made rational the origin and growth of the Christian faith, and some day, when the truths of Spiritualism are accepted, it will be recognised as having prepared the way for the removal of the mystery associated with the origin of Christianity and all other supernatural religions.

When *The Psychic Stream* was completed he then turned his attention to the history of mankind, and wrote the two remarkable volumes to which he gave the name *The Curse of Ignorance*, the reason for this title being that so much in history can be traced to ignorance and folly. Herein he recorded the story of mankind from the time of primitive man to the end of the Second World War, and made clear what an important influence psychic phenomena has had on world history. These supernormal occurrences have been responsible for the origin, beliefs, ritual and ceremonial of all religions.

At least half the events of history are shewn to have been caused by religion, a fact which both past and present historians have ignored because they have been unable to explain the cause and origin of religious beliefs. This ignorance of their origin, namely psychic experiences, has caused the influence of religion to be largely passed over, the consequence being that many of the great events of history have been left unexplained.

Slowly but surely the truths that Spiritualism stands for are becoming known, but not until this knowledge increases further will the writings of Arthur Findlay receive their due place in world literature. This, however, I can safely prophesy of them, that a hundred years hence they will be read by a much wider public, with the same intense interest as they are read today by a smaller number of advanced thinkers, because they deal with the vital things of life from the angle of observation and experience, which is the true scientific attitude.

Theological literature, past and present, has confined itself to the realm of faith, and entirely lacked any scientific basis for its assertions, but its day is passing as we are advancing mentally out of the supernatural into the natural, from the age of miracles to the realisation that supernormal happenings do occur, but that these are subject to natural law which dominates both this world and the next.

With religion now raised to the realm of science, and with history now rewritten from the psychic angle of thought, future generations will, in an age of greater enlightenment, look back on the past as a time of theological darkness and historical misinterpretation. The truths of Spiritualism will some day fill the world with intellectual light!

ERNEST THOMPSON,
Former editor of *Two Worlds*.

INTRODUCTION.

This book completes the task I set out to accomplish, which was to make Spiritualism understood by all intelligent people, as a science, religion, and philosophy, so that its teachings might naturally displace the errors which so far have been generally accepted by both orthodox science and religion. I think it is now generally accepted that I succeeded in my first book, *On the Edge of the Etheric*, in my attempt to relate the psychic phenomena I had experienced with known physical laws. Besides this, it was also acknowledged that I had succeeded in scientifically locating the Etheric World and putting it on the map of the Universe. On this basis I commenced to rear the structure in *The Rock of Truth* which followed. This, the third and last book, *The Unfolding Universe*, completes the building.

In *The Rock of Truth* I tried to put forward a new philosophy or religion, based on knowledge and not on faith, in such a clear and rational way that it could be accepted by all unprejudiced people. As our knowledge increases and our minds can grasp more, our philosophy and religion must likewise respond.

In this book I shall complete my attempt to make it possible for all educated people to realise the inherent weakness of the old religions, and the strength of the foundation on which the new religion or philosophy is based. Besides this, I shall try to show what we sentient beings really are, and something of the geography of the real world in which we live; it is much more than merely the world we sense here during our temporary sojourn on earth.

These three books which I have written form a trilogy and should be read as one book. They form, I trust, a trefoil window through which mankind's religious experiences and speculations can be seen. Beyond this a view will be obtained of what awaits us after death, and our destiny in the ages to come. From this extended vision we shall in consequence be able to discard the error in the old, and build up a new philosophy on the basis of our increased knowledge obtained as the result of our enlarged vision.

The opinions expressed in these three books are the result of thirty-four years' study and thought. They represent mature conclusions which have not been reached hastily, but only after prolonged investigation and research.

Because I believe that nothing greater can be done for the happiness and well-being of the human race than to solve this problem of death and the mystery of existence, I have laboured these past seventeen years to find the truth. The result of my discoveries, which are based on unassailable evidence, I have given to the world. This book represents my mature conclusions on the subject of death, and all its implications, and how religious history should be viewed in the light of this knowledge.

We have now entered a new era. The days of faith are passing and the day of knowledge has arrived. Consequently creeds, dogmas, ceremonials and rites must fade away in the light of the new knowledge, which must in time become accepted by all mankind, not by faith but from experience.

Spiritualism, the name which has been given to this new knowledge, will enter more and more into every department of our lives. Nothing will be untouched by it. Our science, religion, politics and social conditions will all be profoundly affected and altered.

Knowledge based on evidence makes men and women free, makes them happy, and makes them respect each other. Ignorance is the enemy of mankind; it causes unrest and want of harmony, leading to political upheavals and war. Logical thinking, and the desire for truth based on evidence, will do more for the future happiness of mankind than people realise. Throughout my books I have always stressed the fact that people should cease to accept what they are told and think for themselves. By this way only can peace and happiness be attained. Past history shows that all the unhappiness and misery our ancestors experienced came from wrong thinking, due to want of knowledge. Knowledge will come when people can think logically, rationally and clearly, and when they base their opinions on facts. When this comes about the human race will develop rapidly, live in harmony and peace, and devote its energies to improving its conditions on earth and not to the purposes of destruction.

Seventy years elapsed from the death of Copernicus before his explanation of the rotation of the planets could be understood, except by the few. It took sixty years for the facts relating to the evolution of the species to become generally accepted. The revolution in thought in consequence of these two great discoveries has been indeed remarkable.

We have only to go back four hundred years and compare the outlook of our ancestors on the universe with our outlook today, to realise the immense change which has taken place in our mental development. If we go back to the middle of last century and examine the writings and sayings of the mid-Victorians, and compare these with the views held today, we can appreciate what a profound effect the knowledge of our ancestry has had on thinking humanity. Great as this has been, it will fade into insignificance when compared with the change which will come about, over the next hundred years, in consequence of the truths of Spiritualism becoming accepted by mankind.

I have not the slightest doubt that these truths for which Spiritualism stands will completely change the outlook of humanity, nor have I the least doubt that Spiritualism will continue to be opposed by all the forces of reaction. Spiritualism is steadily gaining strength, and will continue to do so as the number of mediums increases. The forces of reaction in turn will become weaker as intelligence and knowledge advances.

Those countries called Protestant will undoubtedly lead the world, as we are only now beginning to obtain the real benefit of the reformation of the Christian Church which took place in the 16th century. Looking back on what that event has already accomplished, one can see clearly how inevitable is the end of orthodoxy. The Reformation was the dawn after a long night of Christianity. The Catholic Church was split in two. One half came to the conclusion that only through the Church, as constituted by the early councils, could God's revelation come. The other half decided that only through the Bible did God reveal his will to man.

These momentous decisions were the beginning of freedom in thought, a state of mental liberty which enables truth to be discovered. This right to a free and untrammelled expression of thought and speech has only now been fully conceded in Protestant countries. Roman Catholic countries have not yet reached this position.

The four hundred years which have elapsed since the Reformation have been years of liberation for the Protestant community. Slowly but surely the right of free thought, the right to investigate all questions, the right to question and doubt has become more and more generally conceded. Today, therefore, one can take up a definitely unorthodox attitude and still be a respected and honoured member of society. Intelligence has advanced sufficiently in Protestant countries to make many people realise that truth is too great to be encompassed within the narrow bounds of church creeds and dogmas, or the leaves of an ancient book.

For these reasons Protestant countries will continue to lead the world out of superstition and darkness, but in every country there are some who have broken away from the orthodox religion of their own country and race. These will be the leaders of their people. Free thought, which develops a rational outlook on religion, is making inroads everywhere throughout the world, and no creed is too firmly established to withstand its onslaught.

Orthodox religion, whether under the name of Christianity, Buddhism or Mohammedanism, is gradually weakening everywhere, as it receives fewer and fewer recruits from the younger generations. As orthodoxy weakens, so will the truths of Spiritualism take deeper and deeper root, until a day will come when mankind will have a common religious outlook, though naturally some will have a more developed philosophy than others.

It is just a question of mental evolution. As the mind develops so the universe unfolds. Those most developed mentally will lead in the future, as they have led in the past, the basis of our philosophy tending more and more to become centred on the development of character, and the regarding of this earth as a preparation for a fuller and better life hereafter. "As we sow here so shall we reap hereafter", will become the guiding motto of the human race.

Heretofore it has been "As we believe here so shall we be rewarded", but the creeds, dogmas and ceremonials of the past suited humanity having only a faint intuition of its origin and destiny. Science has taught us our physical origin. Spiritualism is teaching us our psychical origin and our destiny, that we are not merely material creations, but that each one of us has a future undreamed of by the seers of the past.

Orthodoxy suited the race when it was in the nursery stage, when it could not read and write, and required the guidance of authority. It does not suit those who have advanced beyond the nursery stage and can think for themselves. The knowledge we now possess is too vast to permit us to find room in our minds for the childish speculations of supernatural religion. Orthodox religion is not for the cultured and educated mind of today. Gradually humanity will rise beyond the nursery stage, as all children do, and obtain a wider and more developed outlook on life here and hereafter.

This book will not dwell in detail on the evidence which has brought about this greater knowledge. Psychic phenomena were fully considered in *On the Edge of the Etheric*. Our present knowledge of the evolution of all the world religions, and the claims Spiritualism makes to be the coming science, philosophy and religion of mankind, were carefully dealt with in *The Rock of Truth*. When these two books are understood it will be possible for this book, *The Unfolding Universe*, to be appreciated.

This book is not written for the novice, but for those who accept the reality of psychic phenomena, and are prepared seriously to think out its implications, its effect on old ideas, and how it must influence thought in the future. We are only now learning to apply to our lives the great discoveries of physical science, and we must likewise learn to apply to our way of life the discoveries of psychical science.

Attending séances will help us little unless we attract to them Etherians, those denizens of Etheria (the name I give to what heretofore has been called the Spirit World), who will teach us and help us to develop in wisdom and understanding. The séance for the advanced Spiritualist can only be a place for education. Science in the future will increasingly devote itself to the phenomena, and will consequently learn more of the laws of the universe.

We shall learn much from further discoveries, but, once conviction comes, everyone should regard a séance as a means as much for mental development and education as for getting into communication with those who have passed on. The séance room is the nexus between this order of life, which we are now experiencing, and the new order which we shall some day experience. As intelligence advances, what takes place in the séance room will become more and more appreciated, and its real meaning better understood.

When all adopt this attitude, the séance of the future will elevate and develop us mentally and ethically, and, as our mental and ethical development advances, we shall attract Etherians of a higher and higher order. As we advance mentally and ethically, so our understanding increases, and this encourages Etherians of a higher order to communicate with us. The advance is remarkable which has already taken place over the last eighty-six years since the crude Hydesville rappings first made us realise that there were intelligences about us, but beyond our ken. Over the next hundred years the progress should be equally striking, and we should then be receiving instruction and guidance which is beyond our present-day imagination.

Let me now put before you some of the facts we now possess, which will take the place of ancient beliefs, and, after considering these, we shall contemplate the new structure which will take the place of the old. My desire is that this book will make clear what we can safely discard, while emphasising the truth of the fundamentals of religion and philosophy, which can be accepted today and believed in more firmly than ever.

Spiritualists are destined to guide those outgrowing the orthodox creeds and entering into the light of the new knowledge. We have a great responsibility, as on us much of the future happiness and well-being of our race depends. We are the only people who have a religion based on knowledge, on facts and evidence, and more and more those who depend on faith and past tradition will turn to us for guidance. Let us see to it that we are worthy of our great responsibility, that of enlightening the human mind which is slowly coming out of the darkness of ignorance into the light of knowledge.

ARTHUR FINDLAY.

STANSTED HALL,
   ESSEX.
      December 1934.

CHAPTER I.

FROM DARKNESS TO LIGHT.

It is in the nature of man to think, to wonder, and to ponder over the mystery of existence. Since man became a thinking being he has wondered about his origin, and pondered over his destiny. Over the cradle we ask Whence? and over the grave Whither? The mystery of death focuses the mystery of existence. Solve the mystery of death and we have gone far to solve the mystery of existence. Settle once and for all the question as to whether death is, or is not, the end of life, a door or a wall, the opening of wings to fly or the closing of pinions for ever, and the greatest problem which has ever baffled humanity will have been determined.

None of the world's religions will settle this great question, because they all rest on faith and ignore facts. If we examine their claims and assertions, we find that nothing is known about the after-life, and that on this all-important subject they are as ignorant as the savage.

A book has just been published entitled *Our Dead, Where are they?* made up of contributions by six of our leading Christian clergymen, four of them being Doctors of Divinity. The answer of five out of the six is that they cannot say. Even on the subject of survival they write in doubtful terms. They can only express their belief that "the blessed dead are with Christ", a state which only applies to a portion of the human race, even if we include nominal as well as professing Christians. The religious systems can give the enquirer no knowledge, and today rely solely on theological dogmas and ceremonials, just as they have always done.

Primitive man found himself a thinking being in a vast expanse of space, and from his time to this the question uppermost in human minds has been "Whence did I come, and where am I going?" Humanity, however, has always been much more concerned about its destiny than its origin, and, from earliest times to the present day, mankind has given almost as much thought to its future as it has done to its every-day existence. It has been the problem of the theologian, the philosopher and the mystic to try to solve this great question of man's destiny. Much has been written and said on the subject. Countless numbers of religions have come into being in consequence of this insatiable desire to penetrate the future.

Until recent years it seemed that every attempt landed the enquirer against a blank wall, in which there was no door. However, within the last hundred years the door has been found, and our eagerness to learn something of our future is steadily increasing, as we begin to realise that the door is a reality and that it actually exists. All the world religions take the believer as far as the grave and leave him there, he being told that what happens after death is a matter of faith. That state of ignorance relates to the past, as now that we have found the door faith turns to knowledge, the hitherto solid wall between the two worlds having been pierced so successfully that all who wish may learn about this newly discovered land.

For thousands of years this endeavour had been made, and, though some actually succeeded in finding the door, yet, owing to the fact that few could read and write, and printing had not been discovered, the information could only be passed on in so crude a way that the records which have come down to us are relegated to the region of myth and legend by all educated people of today. To satisfy his longing for knowledge of the unknown, man has invented gods and saviours, ceremonials and rites, creeds and dogmas. He has believed in redeemers and mediators, all of whom have comforted and helped him through his earthly pilgrimage. They have acted as a sedative to his longings. They have quieted his burning desire for further information as to his destiny.

By remembering his mistakes, man has advanced and his knowledge has increased. In countless ways he has crawled upwards in intelligence, and the withered pages of history, which cover the track he has trodden, show that his mind has expanded and his knowledge has advanced in proportion to the way he has used and developed his lamp of reason. Looking back, we realise that there is no darkness but ignorance, and that it is the duty of everyone to do what is possible to help to radiate the world with intellectual light. When knowledge comes, faith and fear go. With knowledge comes intellectual contentment.

The intellectual history of man can be divided up into three stages. The first is the age of superstition, which has lasted during the longest period of man's history, and prevails today almost as much as ever, though in countries more intellectually advanced it is less pronounced. The majority of mankind still rely on and believe in ancient superstitions, though some to a lesser degree than formerly. Prior to the Renaissance, except for the philosophical thinkers of Greece and Rome, between the years 600 B.C. and A.D. 200, the world was steeped in superstition. Since the Renaissance intelligence has advanced sufficiently to enable many people to discard the worship of most of these ancient superstitions, but the vast majority still cling to them, though with a loosening grasp.

The cause of this is the influence scientific investigation and scientific thought have exerted on intelligent minds. The scientific age commenced with the discovery by Copernicus (1473-1543) that the sun did not revolve round the earth, but that the earth revolved round the sun, and that day and night were caused by the rotation of the earth on its own axis.[1] He was supported in his opinions by Galileo, Bruno, Leonardo da Vinci and Kepler, the four great scientists who, with Copernicus, ushered in the age of reason. Then followed Newton and Darwin, and slowly it came to be realised that the universe was governed by law and order, that every effect had its cause, and that the workings of nature were not dependent on the caprices of the gods.

The writings of Copernicus were banned by the Church, and denounced by both Catholics and Protestants. In spite of priestly denunciation the knowledge slowly spread that the earth was not flat, but a round globe, that the planets moved round the sun, and that the stars were not lights hung in a dome for the purpose of illuminating the night, but that they

---

[1] Aristarchus, eighteen hundred years earlier, had propounded the same theory, and Heraclitus expressed the opinion that the planets revolved round the sun. These opinions were so ridiculed that they were forgotten

were worlds in themselves at an immense distance from the earth. From the time of Copernicus to the present day the scientific method of investigation has entered more and more into our lives, and gradually the gods have faded from the skies. The discovery that the universe responded to fixed laws naturally had the effect of discrediting entirely the previous beliefs in the gods, and in anything beyond or above what could be proved by the scientific method. Thus we entered the age of materialism which became pronounced in the 19th century.

However, in 1848, a discovery was made which has slowly been bringing thinking people round to the view that the universe does not consist only of what is sensed by the physical eye and ear or by physical touch. In 1848 rappings occurred, in Hydesville in the United States, which could not be accounted for by normal causes. They occurred in the presence of two girls of the name of Fox, and they were reliably recorded and reported at the time. Investigation proved that there was intelligence behind these rappings, and that messages could be spelled out by this means.

Hitherto every abnormal occurrence which took place in the presence of a man or woman was immediately attributed to Satan, and consequently it was thought that the persons concerned in the event were possessed by a devil. They were therefore burned so that this evil influence would be driven out of them This belief still remains in the minds of the ignorant, many foolish priests and ministers of the Christian Church still talking about these abnormal people as being possessed by a devil, and those who take seriously what occurs in their presence as being the servants of the devil.

Witch-burning had ceased at the beginning of the 19th century, and in consequence the Fox sisters were not burned or drowned. For that reason 1848 may be regarded as the year in which Modern Spiritualism was born. If mankind had not been so ignorant as to burn those witches, who, it was thought, were possessed by devils, everyone today would believe in what Spiritualism stands for—in the reality of the after-life, and that communication takes place between this world and the Spirit World, to which I shall always refer as Etheria in the pages which follow. The words Spirit and Spirit World should not be used, as they give the impression of something intangible, whereas a Spirit and the Spirit World are just as tangible as we are ourselves and as is our earth. Vibrations intangible to us are tangible to them and *vice versa*.

John Wesley, a century previous to the happenings at Hydesville, experienced similar occurrences in his own home. These he reported fully but attributed them to Satan, and so lost the great opportunity, which was within his grasp, of being the Father of Modern Spiritualism. He preferred, however, to accept the Biblical view of witches, and stated that to give up the belief in witchcraft meant giving up the Bible.

The history of man is the history of ignorance, the history of folly, the history of mistakes, cruelty and misery, through his misunderstanding the laws of nature. He has relied on the gods and not on himself. He has crawled in worship of the unknown, instead of standing erect and thinking for himself.

The reason of course is that his mind was incapable of anything else, and so history is just the story of man's intellectual development.

The 19th century, in which culminated the age of materialism, also ushered in the age of Spiritualism, and today we are witnessing the claims of Spiritualism being steadily, though slowly, accepted throughout the world.

I have just briefly referred to the three ages of man's intellectual development. This has been a slow process, and so today we still find the world mostly composed of the superstitious on the one hand, and of the materialists—less numerous—on the other. The former are firm believers in the supernatural, and the materialists just as firmly believe that there is nothing above or beyond the physical. Spiritualism takes the middle course. It accepts entirely all the findings of science, but it claims that neither the supernatural nor the materialistic conception explains the universe or man's place in it.

Spiritualism asserts that we physical creatures are endowed with an etheric body, which is an exact duplicate of our physical body. It goes further and says that at death the etheric body, under the control of mind, parts from the physical body, continues its conscious existence in a world of finer matter surrounding this earth, and that, though separated from the physical, it is possible, under certain circumstances, for this etheric being to communicate with us on earth.

This, based as it is on scientific evidence, is a tremendous claim, entirely upsetting the fixed beliefs of the materialists who accept the fact of death as it appears, believing that nothing survives such an event.

Though absolutely discarding all the superstitions of the past, Spiritualists realise that the underlying cause of all the forms, ceremonies and beliefs of all the world religions is the fact that man is constructed as stated above, and that these superstitions are not due, as the materialists say, to vague imaginings, which have no basis but ignorance.

We are thus on the threshold of a new age of thought, which, when accepted, will revolutionise the outlook of humanity to as great an extent as it was changed at the time of Copernicus. No one living today can realise the mental revolution that occurred when it came to be realised that the universe was governed by law and order, that the earth was round, and not flat, and that it circled round the sun and not the sun round the earth. We can only vaguely imagine what a bomb-like effect this must have had on everyone. To be told that something did not happen which they saw happen every day seemed absurd. The sun was seen to rise in the morning and circle round the heavens, and yet our ancestors were told, by apparently sane men, that such a thing did not actually happen as it was none other than an illusion.

From the time of Copernicus onwards, right through the age of science, one new fact after another was proclaimed until people began to wonder if they could believe in anything being as it appeared to be. By the time it was discovered within recent years that matter is not solid, and they had experience from their wireless sets that ether waves penetrated seemingly solid matter, they had reached the state of mind when they were willing to accept almost anything that science had to offer, without expressing astonishment. The bewildering discoveries of science have completely shattered man's old outlook on the universe. Instead of a revolving sun he has now to believe in a revolving earth. Instead of a dome-like heaven he has to believe in endless space. Instead of solid matter he has to believe in electrons and protons, which ultimately resolve themselves into ether waves.

So we arrive at the present day; but, in spite of all these amazing facts, if a census were taken of the beliefs of Christendom at the present time, it would probably be found that the vast majority still accept the superstitions of the past, and a smaller number are atheists or agnostics, believing that nothing can possibly exist except physical matter governed by some blind force. The remainder accept the Spiritualist outlook on life, rejecting the superstitions though believing that the physical is only a minor part of the universe, that the etheric is much the greater part, and that man is a mental-etheric being with a seemingly endless future before him.

The Spiritualist not only goes the entire way with the scientist, but farther, and believes that time must bring the scientist alongside, as the Spiritualist has definite evidence for his belief which the scientist has so far ignored. Thus Spiritualism is the science of the entire universe. Physics, and the other departments of science, consider only the physical and material universe. Spiritualism embraces these and the etheric as well, which it claims to be the real universe, and asserts that to ignore the etheric is to be content with a study of only a part, and not the whole, of natural phenomena.

The superstitions of the past only interest the Spiritualist in so far as they show the inherent instinct in man that he is an etheric being, who, in his ignorance, has adopted beliefs, dogmas, ceremonies, rites and sacrifices which, though based upon and fostered by this instinct, have no real bearing on his destiny. Most of these are symbolic of the truth behind, but their meaning has been lost and forgotten and consequently they are now meaningless.

Taking a broad all-round view of the position, without prejudice, weighing up the pros and cons during the last sixteen years, I have come to accept fully the Spiritualist outlook on life. I have never gone through the age of superstition, as I never could believe what I was taught in childhood and youth, but I have experienced the age of materialism in my mental development. I have never believed in Christianity, though I have always admired Jesus because he bravely died for his convictions. I have never found any basis of truth to make me adopt Christianity, or to accept the creed of any other orthodox religion. I accept all the findings of science, and they do not in the least degree upset the greater knowledge which has come to me through the findings of Spiritualism.

Spiritualism is only an addition to present-day knowledge, and is in no way opposed to it. The only difference between the Spiritualist and the Materialist is that the one accepts an after-life, and an etheric world, while the other does not. The one believes that we are more than physical creations and the other asserts that we are entirely material creatures.

It is, however, interesting to find that the recent

tendency of science is more and more towards accepting the Spiritualist outlook on the universe, and I believe that within another fifty years every scientific man will do so. Then will be ranged, in two opposing camps, the Spiritualist and the Supernaturalist. The age of materialism is passing; it was only a phase, a reaction from the absurd claims of the supernaturalist. The scientist, with his exact methods of investigation, is gradually coming to realise that the universe embraces much that is beyond our physical capacity to appreciate, and that a place must be allotted to another order of life which, though normally un-sensed, is making itself apparent in the séance room in the presence of a super-sensitive individual termed a medium.

The purpose of this book is first of all to review the past religious beliefs of mankind, to examine the claims of the Materialist and then the claims of the Spiritualist. Having done so, it will then picture the world as I anticipate it will be when the facts of Spiritualism are accepted as part of human knowledge. It will attempt to show how our religious beliefs will be changed, how our scientific knowledge will be enlarged, and how this change of outlook will naturally lead to a new social order which will bring increased happiness and contentment to mankind throughout the world.

I shall also try to show how the religious sense can be correctly and scientifically explained without resorting to the materialistic view that it originated in the imaginations of the mind. I hope to make clear how materialism cannot explain all the phenomena of the universe, how Spiritualism can, and further, to emphasise how Spiritualism must supplant in time all the other world religions, Christianity included. Spiritualism is founded on the rock of truth, all other creeds and beliefs on superstition due to ignorance. The creeds of all religions are antagonistic to science, and science is hostile to them. Spiritualism, on the other hand, accepts the findings of science, which in no way disturb its beliefs. Spiritualists have stood for the truth, and only the truth must ultimately prevail.

Spiritualism is not a new sect; it is a world-wide philosophic religion which will be accepted in time by all, whatever may now be their sect and creed. It gives comfort in sorrow, and it makes us understand our origin and destiny in a way that nothing else can do. It has no priestcraft interpreting God's will to man, no holy books, and no holy dogmas. It welcomes investigation, it delights in discovery, it loves facts. It puts the love of man before the love of God and it considers it is more important to love your neighbour than to love an imaginary creation in the heavens.

The love of man for wife, of wife for husband, of parents for children, and of children for parents, makes for happiness and contentment in life. But the adoration and worship of a god or gods, made in the likeness of man, has been the cause of unimaginable cruelties, suffering and misery. It has perpetuated savage beliefs and led to intolerance, wars, cruel superstitions and the degradation of women, because all the gods had a very poor opinion of women, like the men who imagined those gods.

The belief in an anthropomorphic God has been the cause of family disunion, of sects, and of endless quarrels. This idea has supported slavery, torture and every imaginable cruelty in Christendom and elsewhere, because Jehovah and all the Father-gods of the past were savage tyrants. This adoration and worship of one or more gods has been a continual obstruction to the cause of progress. Jehovah, according to his book, the Bible, did not believe in education, investigation or anything which helped towards the advancement of humanity.

W. E. Gladstone stated on one occasion that "the name of Jehovah is encircled in the heart of every believer with the profoundest reverence and love". Why? Because he is the Christian god, and he went on to say that "the Christian religion teaches through the incarnation a personal relation so lofty that it can only be approached in a deep reverential calm". Gladstone was an orthodox Christian, a believer in the creeds and dogmas of the Christian Church, and realised quite clearly that Jehovah is inextricably bound up with the Christian faith.

Jehovah was the god Jesus worshipped, and, according to the Christian belief, though he prayed to him, he was, and still is, part of him. Some Christians today try to ignore Jehovah, but they cannot. Some say that Jesus brought a new revelation which put his father on to a somewhat higher plane. Nevertheless he referred with respect to Jehovah as the only God. He never spoke of him as a tribal god his nation had outgrown, and whose laws should not be obeyed. In the days of Jesus, everything Jehovah was reported as having done and said was considered right, and Jesus supported this view of Jehovah, whose laws, he said, he had come to fulfil.

Christianity is the greatest assembly of illogical ideas that has ever come together in the world's history. They are all fixed together by bands of error, any one of which can be broken by logical thought, bringing the entire fabric to pieces. Jehovah must for ever remain the Christian God, whose son Jesus was part of himself, together with the Holy Ghost. Christians cannot deny the God accepted by Jesus, as to do so is to admit that Jesus was mistaken on this vital matter. It would shatter the Trinity, the central dogma of their religion. Jesus never once condemns the cruelty of Jehovah, so naturally Christians considered, when Christendom was really Christian, that they were right in following Jehovah's commands.

Jehovah is the God of Great Britain, the Bible is his book, and that is why a copy is in every Protestant church in this country. That is why it is referred to as "The Word of God" and "The Holy Scriptures" and "The Holy Bible". Christians believe Jehovah wrote it by inspiring holy men with his ideas. This has been fervently and devoutly believed by all Christian people throughout the Christian era. The commands, injunctions and laws laid down in the Bible have been followed by Christendom throughout the Christian era, and Jehovah has received the worship and adoration of all who call themselves Christians.

It is because of this worship of Jehovah that the world is in the position it is in today. Jehovah was a god of war, and the Bible is a book which supports war, slavery and other wrongdoing. The Christian

Church has always supported war and never once raised its voice in protest against a war. Christianity and war go together, and, if we are to get away from war, we must get away from Christianity and the belief that all the commands in the Bible came from a divine source for the ordering of our daily life.

It is unreasonable to quote the good passages from the Bible, from the sayings of Jesus, and to ignore the bad. They must have come from the same source, both the good and bad, if the Bible is the Word of God. If they have not, and the Bible is just a patchwork of good and bad, its authority vanishes. If they do not all come from one definite authority superior to man, what is the good of quoting the best as superior to the sayings of the good and wise throughout the ages?

What we want is a new ideal, a new religion, something new to inspire us to greater heights and greater efforts. This can never be found in Christianity, which is a religion which worships the dead past. We do not want a religion which worships the past; we want a philosophy which will inspire us in the present, comfort us in sorrow, and point out to us plainly our destiny.

The old orthodox religions of creeds and dogmas have had their day, and suited the world before the advent of the scientific age. Christianity cannot be made to fit in to our age of scientific thought. It has opposed science in every direction. It has opposed investigation into the unseen in every conceivable way, and now it must retire into oblivion and give place to science, which is making our lives on earth better and happier. It must give way to Spiritualism, which has demonstrated a new world around us, and proved that we are etheric beings in physical bodies who can communicate direct with the unseen, and not through intermediary priests, whose messages from the gods are the result of the false claims made by their predecessors.

The ancients peopled the heavens with angels, and the underworld with demons, whom they worshipped or feared, an assembly of fantastic ideas which goes under the name of mythology. Spiritualism is mythology rationalised, just as Astronomy is Astrology rationalised. Christianity borrowed this mythology, called it history and preached as fact what was just legend and myth. It materialised the immaterial and thus made a mockery of nature's revelation by introducing miracles, or something contrary to nature, to explain what was natural psychic phenomena.

Spiritualism is Religion, the religion of humanity. It is not *a* religion. It is religion and science combined in one harmonious whole. It stresses that only character counts, and that belief in creeds is only for the ignorant, not for the present-day intelligent man or woman. The development of our character, it insists, should be our great object in life, and Spiritualists do not believe that this can take place through the repetition of creeds or the acceptance of theological dogmas. As we sow here, so shall we reap hereafter.

Some day, when the truths of Spiritualism are accepted and understood by mankind, all the creeds of orthodox religions will fade away. The name Spiritualism itself may be forgotten, as one natural religion will then be universal, making our lives better and happier on earth, and giving us definite knowledge of our destiny. History makes clear that religious creeds have never raised humanity ethically. They have given comfort but never acted as an urge to higher attainments or to improved social conditions.

The ethical basis of Spiritualism is right conduct, which is helped and strengthened under the guidance of the knowledge that we are destined for a great hereafter. It is, moreover, based on facts, not on faith. Spiritualists know that death is only a bend in the road of life. Our friends come back to tell us they are still alive, and, with their greater knowledge, they guide us to loftier heights and greater wisdom. Christianity teaches nothing of any value about the other world, and never refers to the possibility of communication with it. Its idea of death and resurrection was borrowed from the Egyptians. It is the influence of Spiritualism which is now making Christian people have a more natural and rational outlook on death and the hereafter.

Fear of the orthodox Christian god has made life to millions a misery, and still does so amongst the ignorant. Increasingly large numbers are unable to find in Christianity any proofs of an after-life, only vague promises of some far-off fantastic heaven for believers in impossible dogmas and doctrines, combined with threats of everlasting torment for all who deny them. This doctrine of Hell is the blackest spot in Christianity, and the misery it has caused balances all the comfort the religion has given to those who could not think for themselves.

Slowly people are coming to realise the ghastly trail of cruelty and misery which has followed in the wake of Christianity over the last nineteen centuries. Those who listened to the tragedy recently broadcast, entitled "Grissel Jaffray", must have had the fact brought home to them, in a way that no amount of reading would do, that our ancestors were ignorant savage brutes. This reproduction of an historical event was broadcast by The British Broadcasting Corporation, and it is a sign of the times that such was possible, because some years ago the Church would have been strong enough to prevent it.

This dreadful tragedy was the reproduction of the arrest, trial and burning of an old woman who lived a respectable life with her husband in Dundee in Protestant Scotland in the year 1669. She was accused by the Parish Church parson of seeing and conversing with the spirits of the dead and curing people by touch; in other words she was a medium and her crime was witchcraft. The parson was the principal villain of the piece throughout. He accused her of the crime and then submitted her to torture by thumb-screw and other fiendish devices.

Listeners were harrowed by the screams of the victim, her yells and her groans. The parson then conducted the religious service at the trial and again at the stake. He offered up sanctimonious prayers in the unctuous voice cultivated by the profession, and he led the people in the singing of the Psalms at the trial and at the stake. This self-styled man of God then read quotations from the Bible to justify the torture and the sentence of death, and throughout it all listeners were distressed by the shrieks and wailing voice of poor Grissel Jaffray.

These laws against witchcraft are still in force in this country.[1] They have never been repealed, and mediums are still liable to persecution and prosecution. Spiritualism is the only religion which is illegal in this country, and Spiritualists are denied the rights possessed by all other religions. The feeling against Spiritualism, though modified from what it was, still exists. Our ignorant ancestors, basing their laws on quotations from the Bible, have kept the people from knowing that communication can take place between the two worlds, and that nature intended sensitive people called mediums to be the avenue through which the two worlds are joined.

When people come to realise that the universe is governed by law and order, that the findings of science are much more reliable than the inspired Bible, that every cause has an effect and every effect a cause, they are relieved of an enormous incubus. When they realise that the Heaven and the Hell of the Christian religion developed out of the ignorant imaginings of our savage ancestors, and that those who do what is right here to the best of their ability have no reason to fear, they begin to feel the joy of living.

To be master of our own destiny, to be free to investigate, to be free to live up to our own ideals, to be free to decide and determine for oneself, and to be no longer a slave to a heavenly tyrant, is to escape from the dungeon of superstition into the full light of liberty. This freedom enables us to read

[1] In 1950 a law was passed in the British Parliament making genuine mediums safe from arrest and punishment.

and enjoy the writings of the great and the good of all lands, of all faiths, and of all times. It enables us to study untrammelled past history and the Bibles of the other world religions.

We consequently find delight in studying the writings of the great and noble thinkers of Greece and Rome, whose philosophy was on an infinitely higher and grander level than those ignorant of it can possibly imagine. Unfortunately their teachings were obliterated by Christianity, and their arts and crafts destroyed by Christian fanatics. Had this not been so the world would be a better and happier place than it is after nineteen hundred years of Christian superstition.

We can now judge the past justly and not through the spectacles of prejudice and ignorance. We can now realise that the claim made by Christians that Jesus was "The Light of the World" is unfair to the other great teachers and thinkers who lived before him, who taught greater wisdom and suffered and died in their attempts to raise the people of their time. It would be more correct to describe him as "A Light to the World".

We now realise that to claim that Christianity raised the Pagan world is ridiculous, and not borne out by history, and that Jesus contributed nothing to the world's knowledge of the after-life, as everything he is reported to have taught was borrowed from the Greek and Egyptian religions. We have further discovered that what is called Christianity was borrowed from the Pagans, and that it is just a continuation of the superstitions the great philosophers of Greece and Rome tried to raise the people above and beyond.

Our minds develop by the study of the noble thoughts of Socrates, one of the wisest of men, and of Plato, his biographer, himself a king of thought. They expand in contemplation of the thoughts expressed by the slave philosopher Epictetus, who taught that in each one of us lies the impregnable fortress of the soul, and in the philosophic writings of Epicurus, whose noble ideals and spotless life of service to others place him amongst the world's greatest benefactors.

An impartial study of the history of their times proves that their civilisation was higher, their laws were better, and learning was on a higher level than was the case during the ages when Christianity ruled supreme. The worst of the old was preserved in Christianity, the best obliterated, and this religion is responsible for having plunged Europe into a sea of stagnant superstition. Enlightenment came to Christendom only when the writings of Aristotle, the supreme thinker of his time, came to be read after being banned for a thousand years.

Our laws, our civilisation, our standard of justice, and our ideals came from Rome and Athens, and it is utterly false to claim that all we are today is due to Christianity, as Christians say. This religion, when it had the power, kept from Europe the civilising influence of the literature of Rome and Greece, and only when printing was discovered, and the Church could not prevent the spread of knowledge, did Europe become civilised, due to the circulation of Greek and Roman writings on science, ethics and culture.

When we are able to absorb this greater knowledge

we realise that what are termed religious beliefs consist of creeds and dogmas which are only a crutch for the ignorant. It is philosophy that sustains the intelligent. We realise that the greatest thing on earth is to think right and to do right, to think honestly and to act honestly. When we reach that conclusion we realise that Christianity is not fitted for our present-day civilisation, that we have progressed beyond and above it, and that, if the human race continues to develop, Christianity cannot last much longer.

We are living at a time when this superstition, which has caused so much sorrow, misery and suffering, so much intolerance, so many sects and divisions, is dying, when the foundation of the Christian Church is crumbling, its walls are cracking, its pillars leaning, and its dome toppling for a fall. Its power to prevent progress and human enlightenment in Protestant countries has gone, and in Catholic countries is going. It is only a question of time, a little more mental development, until it is dead, buried and forgotten. This is obvious from the declining number who are communicants of the Church of England. According to the Bishop of Durham (*The Times*, 22nd September, 1934), when consideration is given to the increase in the population the number today is only one-ninth of what it was three hundred years ago.

What is the cause behind this coming collapse of an ancient institution? The answer is the advance which has taken place in scientific knowledge, and the proofs that Spiritualism can give of another life and another world. When we obtain the definite proof that life continues after death, when we receive evidence to our own satisfaction that we enter another world after we leave this one, and that as we live here so shall we live there, our minds expand, our thoughts develop, and the longing to be in tune with the Infinite becomes satisfied.

Our minds reach out in gratitude to the great thinkers of the past, who have helped to enlighten the world and free us from the orthodoxy born in the days of ignorance. Our thoughts go out in thankfulness to those super-sensitive people we term mediums, because they act as a nexus between this order of existence and the next. They have brought to mankind the realisation of this great fact, and, in spite of torture, burning, imprisonment and the jeers of the ignorant, they have helped to establish communication with our friends who were considered to be dead.

Those whose minds have thus expanded to absorb all this new knowledge cannot but realise that it will fill the world with intellectual light, and bring happiness and consolation to millions yet unborn. We are living to witness the death of a religion which has propagated ideas so crude and revolting that the intelligent person of the present day turns from them in disgust. In the place of the old a new religion is arising freed from all these absurdities, based on facts and evidence which can appeal to the present-day educated and intelligent individual.

Our duty then is to help to liberate those who are still living in the dungeons of superstition, and thus enable them to throw off their chains of creeds and dogmas, to quit their prison of ignorance, and reach the light of day. When they have discarded those fetters, we shall point them to the land beyond this world of ours which one and all will reach without the necessity for a passport in the form of a belief. Then they will realise that death is not a curse inflicted on mankind by God, but a natural event like birth, and that there is no sin other than selfishness. We are all destined, irrespective of race, creed or church, to reach some day this new-found land, where our place is determined, not by what creeds we believe on earth, but by our ideals and our conduct towards our fellow men.

No believer in the old theology likes to be told of the errors he has accepted without question. I realise the strength of the opposition behind any reform movement, especially when that opposition has nineteen hundred years of tradition behind its beliefs. Instinctively the orthodox dislike having their ideas disturbed. They have inherited the beliefs of their ancestors, and have not given them considered thought.[1]

Fortunately intolerance in Protestant countries is fast disappearing. Tolerance and freedom of thought, the right of everyone to express his honest thoughts, is now much more freely exercised. Life therefore for the reformer, the teacher of something new and strange, is not unpleasant now as formerly. The prison, rack, and stake have given place to abuse

---

[1] *Psychic News* in September 1933 issued a challenge to all the Protestant clergymen in Great Britain and Ireland (28,630 altogether). The challenge was that they should reply to the statements made in *The Rock of Truth* with regard to the origin of Christianity, and expose any errors or misstatements made therein. So that each clergyman would be sure of reading this challenge, a copy of that newspaper was sent to each one individually and their attention was prominently drawn to the challenge on the front page. Over fifteen years have now passed, and no reply has been made, so that it can only be concluded that no reply can be made because the statements made in *The Rock of Truth* are accurate and cannot be disputed.

and criticism, but "the man of independent mind, he looks and laughs at a' that".

Some say that attacking the Church, or exposing the errors of the priesthood, is not the best way to spread the truths of Spiritualism. These timid critics believe that I shall offend the Church and the clergy, and that if I offend them I shall keep back the acceptance of the new knowledge. How can the exposure of error keep back truth and knowledge? Today the great majority of the clergy are against the truths of Spiritualism; I cannot make them more against them than they already are.

Some say that the clergy are just on the point of coming round to Spiritualism. Even supposing that this is true, which it is not, how can they be kept from coming round to Spiritualism because I tell the truth about Christianity and the truth about Spiritualism? If they are coming round it is because they see the error in Christianity and the truth in Spiritualism. In any case all who destroy weeds in the garden of the mind are benefactors to the race. Space formerly occupied by thistles can then be planted with the flowers of knowledge.

I am told again that I shall keep Christian people from becoming Spiritualists by telling the truth about the Bible and about Christianity. Christian people will only become Spiritualists if they think. By thinking they will come to realise the truth of my assertions. They will come to realise that Christianity is a broken reed, and that Spiritualism must take its place, because Spiritualism rests on truth and evidence.

What I want to do is to make the people think,

and the more they think the more the truths of Spiritualism will be accepted. I do not want the people to become Spiritualists without thinking. Those who do not wish to think, and are quite satisfied with their beliefs, would be wiser to ignore the subject entirely.

Christians, however, send missionaries to the heathen to convert them to what they claim is a better religion. Spiritualists do not believe in thus replacing one superstition by another, but surely they have the same right as Christians claim to have. If Spiritualists see error in Christianity they have the right to expose it, just as Christians have the right to expose the error they see in other religions. Christians would never argue that by their missionaries exposing these errors they are unable to convert those they term the heathen. Only by first destroying error can you clear the foundation on which to build the edifice of Truth.

I am therefore doing no more than Christians are doing, and the assertion sometimes made that I am taking away the comfort of Christianity is equally true of Christian missionaries, who take away from the "heathen" the comfort of the religion into which they were born. Christians will reply that they are trying to give those misguided people something better. Spiritualists have therefore equal liberty to try to give Christians something that they consider is better than Christianity.

Things being as they are, let us now look back and find the source of all this error in orthodox religion. Let us then weigh up the knowledge we now possess, and then look forward and envisage what the world will be like when the Universe has further unfolded and the truths of Spiritualism have conquered the error born in the past. Nothing remains stationary. We must either advance or go back, but the mind of man tends to go forward if the necessary environment exists.

In my belief the environment is tending more and more to enable intelligence to develop. The movement of human thought today points to the possibility that our descendants will be on a higher level from a religious, moral and social point of view than we are at present, in consequence of this new knowledge which has now come to the few, and which will ultimately spread to the many.

CHAPTER II.

THE AGE OF SUPERSTITION.

The relation of God, or many gods, to the universe has been the constant study of mankind throughout the ages, from the ignorant savage to the wisest philosophers of Greece and Rome. They have one and all tried to explain the universe, and, in their explaining of the phenomena of nature, God, or the gods, have always found a place. Until the age of Materialism, which was a reaction from the age of Superstition, every philosophic teacher found a place for one or more gods governing the universe. They could not imagine the universe without directive thought.

All kinds of deities have therefore found the most prominent place in man's religious and philosophic thoughts. Just as the idea of the universe has changed, so has the idea of Infinite Intelligence. As the mind of man has unfolded, so has the universe. So also has what is termed the Infinite. To the savage the Infinite is of small dimensions. By the present-day philosopher the Infinite is realised to be beyond human capacity to understand.

What is it that strikes the enquirer when studying history? Surely the ignorance of humanity. All the mistakes of the past, the cruelty, savagery, wars, misery and bloodshed were due to ignorance, just as they are due to ignorance at the present time. Ignorance lives by night and intelligence by day. An ignorant man is like one who travels by night without a light, compass or road to guide him. He stumbles and falls, he suffers and fears. The intelligent man is like one who travels by day, who grasps his surroundings, realises where he will place his next step, then walks in confidence, fearless and without danger.

What this chapter recounts is fact, and it is not written for the purpose of scoffing at the ignorance of the past. Such an attitude I would never take up, as what has helped and comforted our ancestors, who knew no better, should always be respected. Living, however, as we do in the present day of greater enlightenment, one can but regret the fact that the organisations which stand for religion in this country, and throughout the world, should remain wedded to those ancient superstitions which satisfied the world when it was young. One regrets this all the more because the people could receive so much more comfort and satisfaction from the knowledge that nature itself can give them, without their having to wrap this precious knowledge round with ancient legends and myths so that the truth is well-nigh smothered.

A study of the past reveals the terrible mistakes and follies, the unimaginable cruelties, the wars and sufferings which have accompanied man in his struggle upwards from the level of the beast. The savage is little better than an animal, and we all have in us evidence of this ancestry. Dwelling in his cave the savage is struck with terror by natural phenomena. Living on roots, and the chance of the chase, he is in daily fear of tomorrow and the unknown. Thunder and lightning, hurricane, earthquake, and the unknown land which stretches before him, make him realise his insignificance. He cannot trace the end or the source of the mighty river. To him the ever-surging onward stream is without beginning and without end. The sea is a limitless expanse with but one single shore.

In that long night of savagery, in that constant fight against the forces of nature, the seeds of superstition were sown in the human mind, and this fetishism is still part of our inheritance from the past. Fear comes to those who are not able to comprehend the laws of nature. As intelligence develops it enables us to appreciate that we live in an ordered universe. Then fear departs. As we understand nature better we fear it less. By intelligence we can guard ourselves against its terrors, and thus rise superior to our surroundings.

The savage, on the other hand, surrounded without by wild beasts stronger than himself, by rain and hail, thunder and lightning, earthquake and volcano, and within by disease, pain and sickness, prostrates himself in very terror to the ground, pleading protection from some unknown power. Herein lies the difference between the savage and the beast. From this consciousness of a power outside of himself, which he thought he could placate by flattery or by prayer, just as he himself could be placated, the savage developed the faculty of worship, and the forces of nature became his gods. Good forces were good gods and evil forces evil gods.

An accompanying development was the belief that the gods were persons in the likeness of man and that they were like man himself in their desires and passions.

This was doubtless the outcome of seeing apparitions, besides experiencing poltergeist phenomenon and what happened when a medium was in trance. So it was believed that the gods came to earth and walked with men. They were the fathers of human children. Virgins, we find from the study of mythology, were the special favourites of the gods, and often the claim was made, not by those so-called virgins, but at a later date, that their children were the result of their contact with the gods, and that in consequence they had brought forth god-men. If we could trace their origin far enough back it would be found that every god or goddess was once a man or woman who had lived on earth as such.

Moreover, because the various phenomena of nature were attributed to the gods, they were given nature names such as Red Cloud, High Wind, Running Water and so on. Consequently many controls of present-day mediums still retain these names which in the first place were given to their predecessors by primitive man.

Much labour has been devoted by eminent men,[1] who have studied the various world religions, to find the reason for the belief in gods in the image of man, but only Spiritualists can rationally explain the problem. As just mentioned the explanation is that, then as now, the people of the other world were seen, and at times conversed with, the only difference between then and now being that we do not regard them as gods ruling the universe but as men and women like

---

[1] Further information on this subject will be found in *The Principles of Sociology* by Herbert Spencer, *The Golden Bough* by Sir James Frazer, *The Evolution of the Idea of God* by Grant Allen, and *Encyclopædia Britannica* under "Apparitions".

ourselves who once lived on earth. Primitive man believed that the apparitions of the dead were divine beings and that they were behind all the forces of nature. This belief continued throughout historical times up to the present day, and even cultured people like the Greeks and Romans performed a sacrificial ritual to the gods such as is still practised by savages.

The origin of the anthropomorphic God, or the God in the likeness of man, was this belief regarding apparitions, out of which grew ancestor worship. When the family was a unit the deceased parents were worshipped. When families became a tribe the dead chief was worshipped, and when the tribe became a nation the national heroes became gods. For ages the sky was filled with gods, but time has brought about a wonderful culling from the heavens. Greece and Rome had many gods. In Athens an altar was discovered in 1934 dedicated "To the twelve gods". Christianity reduced them to three gods, one goddess and many saints. Finally a camel driver, Mohammed, disgusted at the image worship of the Christians, declared in favour of one only. If we except Jews and Moslems, who believe in only one God, and the Buddhists who are atheists, the believers in most of the other world religions are polytheists. It is not the number of gods worshipped that we are now considering; it is the belief in one or more personal gods that has dominated all religions and all creeds from the days of primitive man to the present time.

Cicero and Plato both refer to the spirits of the dead as gods, and this belief has been world-wide. The appearance of the dead to the living is the origin of the belief in a God, or gods, in the likeness of man, and this idea runs back throughout the ages. Such apparitions were seen only occasionally, so primitive man kept himself in remembrance of them by carving wood and stone in many weird and crude ways into their likeness. Image worship, therefore, became a part of all religions and is still of many, even to this day, though its origin is forgotten.

Epicurus, the noble Greek, who lived three hundred years before Jesus, endeavoured to free his contemporaries in Athens from their craven fear of the gods, and taught that they had their own duties to attend to and did not worry about the earth. Consequently, he argued, it is useless waste to sacrifice to them, and folly to fear them. Far better, he said, for everyone to seek goodness, nobility and purity, not to please the gods, but because these qualities were essential to the dignity, welfare and happiness of mankind.

This was the level to which the great thinkers of the golden age of Greece tried to raise the people, who, however, remained wedded to their gods, saviours and superstitions. The world has had to wait for over two thousand years before mankind was sufficiently advanced to be able to appreciate the high and noble thoughts of those great teachers.

The origin of the altar, which has occupied a place in most religions, from the earliest times to the present day, is the boulder stone over the grave of the dead chief or tribal leader. On this altar primitive man sacrificed to his departed chief in order to feed him with the etheric bodies of the slain victims. The chief, in the other world, became one of his gods who, it was believed, still watched over and protected the tribe he had once ruled. However, his friendship could only be kept by generous hospitality, and in consequence a regular supply of victims was slain in order to supply him with their etheric bodies. On the spot of this primitive altar arose the cromlech or tumulus, and later it became a roofed-over place of worship to which the name of temple was given.

William Simpson, who probably visited a larger number of ancient places of worship all over the world than any other traveller, in his publication *The Worship of Death* points out that the origin of almost every such place he visited could be traced to a tomb or burial ground. Thus on the site of the tomb arose the place of worship, but the church of primitive man was no better than a mud or wooden hut or cave, in which was the altar and in which he kept his sacred images. Therein also sat the tribe's medium, through whom spoke the voice of the medium's control who was looked upon as a god to be consulted by the priests.

In the Catacombs at Rome at intervals are shrines and altars, and their use was continued in Christian churches when the Christians had freedom and liberty to worship openly. Out of this worship of the dead arose the adoration of the saints, at whose grave prayers were offered, and relics were deposited.

This veneration of their dead by Christians came from Egypt, where the dead body was preserved pending a physical resurrection by the return of the soul. The Romans burned their dead, as they did not accept this belief, which was the principal innovation Christianity brought to the Roman world, but it was only adopted by degrees.

Though man has developed sufficiently to have acquired the art of building beautiful cathedrals, temples, mosques and pagodas in the place of mud huts, yet he has not advanced intellectually to enable him to alter his form of worship, which is still directed to one or more personal gods, and is surrounded by all the superstitions of the savage age.[1] Sacrifice is one of the earliest of religious rites, at which it was believed the gods attended because, like Jehovah, they appreciated the smell of the sweet savour of the victim whose etheric body was being released by death for them to eat.

The altar of sacrifice became the Holy of Holies, and the ceremonial and ritual still performed by priests at the altar originated in the incantations over the body of the dead chief. Nowadays these take place before the bread and wine representing the body and blood of a god-man. Religious ceremonials have changed little since the days of savagery, but their origin is forgotten or unknown by all except a few who have studied the question.

The altar of sacrifice became sacred ground, and before the images of his gods man prostrated himself in humble supplication for his wants. This was the beginning of worship and prayer. Here we are at the beginning of sacrifice and altars, of holy things and sacred rites. Here do we find the reason for temples and churches, and from this worship of the spirits of the dead has sprung idolatry and superstition. This worship of the denizens of Etheria in material form is still enacted at the present time in

---

[1] "If we could trace the whole course of religious development we might find that the chain which links our ideas of the godhead with that of the savage is one and unbroken."—Sir James Frazer in *The Golden Bough*.

Roman Catholic churches, as this Church adheres to the findings of the Council of Nice, held in 787, which decreed that the worship of images is lawful.

Then the savage found that by rubbing two sticks together he could produce fire by friction. This new wonder he worshipped as a god, and fire in time became the symbol of life. As far back as it is possible to trace the old religions of mankind one finds fire as an object of worship, and virgin priestesses an important adjunct to the prevailing worship. Vestal virgins, as an organised cult in Rome, date from 715 B.C. and continued for one thousand years. They occupied a prominent part in the religion of Rome, and are the ancestors of the sisterhoods of nuns of the Christian Church. However, the beginning of this worship of the god of fire is to be found thousands of years back, when its powers for good and evil became recognised. It was a thing of wonder which needed not only worship but protection, this task being entrusted to the purest and the most exalted virgins of the time.

This new god, man also imaged and worshipped in the form of two sticks, one across the other, in the form of a cross. The cross in time became the symbol of life and sacrifice, and has been venerated by millions for thousands of years. It is to be found carved on the stone slabs placed over the graves of some of the most ancient of people.

In Egypt, Assyria, Persia, India, Mexico and Scandinavia the cross occupied a prominent place in religious worship. Constantine, it is said, adopted it as the symbol of the Christian faith from the solar wheel, the spokes of which formed a cross, which was a symbol used by his legionaries from Gaul in their religion of sun worship. Whether this be so or not, what Christ and the Cross stand for has meant much the same for thousands of years, so that the Christian symbol is of far greater antiquity than the religion it now represents.

As primitive man grew more civilised, and a little less fearful, he employed someone to protect the holy hut and holy images while he himself was out hunting, and thus the priesthood originated. This class, who were looked on as holy men in charge of the holy place and sacred images, became sufficiently numerous, sufficiently revered, and sufficiently feared to dominate and order the lives of the rest of the community. They came to be looked on as superior to the rest of the people, and consequently refused to do manual work. As their time was spent in appeasing the gods, they were supported out of the labour of the tribe.

From those early times up to the present day priests have been just as all men are, the products of their times. To record their crimes, mistakes and follies is what I now propose to do, not for the purpose of making them out to be worse than their contemporaries, but to record facts as matters of history. In so doing let me make clear that it would be unjust not to remember the self-sacrificing lives led by many priests, both past and present, and that countless millions have been comforted by their ministrations.

Their power was only slight to begin with, but, as the tribe increased in number, so did the duties of the priests. The rise in the power of the priesthood is thus described by Grant Allen in his book *The Evolution of the Idea of God*:—

> The temple attendants, endowed for the purpose of performing sacred rites for the ghost or god, have grown into priests, who knew the habits of the unseen denizen of the shrine. Bit by bit prescriptions have arisen; customs and rituals have developed; and the priests have become the depositories of the divine traditions. They alone know how to approach the god; they alone can read the hidden signs of his pleasure and displeasure. As intermediaries between worshipper and deity, they are themselves half sacred. Without them no votary can rightly approach the shrine of his patron. Thus at last they rise into importance far above their origin; priestcraft comes into being; and by magnifying their god the members of the hierarchy magnify at the same time their own office and function.

Thus the priesthood originated, and it has been for long claimed by this class that its members act as intermediaries, or middlemen, between the gods and man, that they take messages for man, interpreting and conveying them to the people as the mouthpiece of the gods. This claim has been made by the priests since early times in all countries no matter to what race the people belong, or what they profess to believe.

To begin with this assertion was true, because they were originally the protectors of the tribe's mediums, and passed on to the chief, or the people, what the controlling spirits had to say. Gradually, however, by fraud and mimicry they found that they could beguile the people by themselves pretending to be mediums. By what is called magic they were able to delude the people any time, whereas the genuine medium could say nothing until moved by the spirit

In this way magic took the place of mediumship and the genuine medium fell into disrepute.

Fortunately, after centuries of fraud and deceit on the part of the priesthood, the genuine medium is coming to be recognised in our time as the only intermediary between the two worlds. The deceptions and follies of the priesthood have been uncovered, and the only hope of the survival of this class of men is that they return to their original calling, namely the protectors and transmitters of the communications which come through mediumship. The time may some day come when our orthodox churches will again be filled, because the priests have returned to their old rôle, and preach to the people from the vast Spiritualist literature now available. Then, with the medium again replaced in the position he or she occupied in the early Apostolic Church, the form of service and the beliefs of the present-day Christian Church will have come into line with that of the Spiritualist Church, a service giving satisfaction and contentment without theology or superstition.

Acting as they do contrary to nature, the priests have worked against the intellectual development of mankind. Whether they call themselves priests, parsons, or ministers of the gospel in Christendom, or pongyis, mullahs, or whatever name they adopt elsewhere to differentiate themselves from the rest of mankind, they hate facts and love mystery, and in every possible way they have frightened and discouraged any attempt to get into touch with the etheric world through mediumship. Though in some religions the priests have encouraged the art of reading, it has always been for the purpose of advancing theological doctrines and superstitions—never science, never facts. The Christian Church ruled Europe intellectually from the 4th century to our own times, yet the great majority of the people, as late as 1870, could neither read nor write after fifteen hundred years of Christian rule. If mental development had not progressed, the people would still be illiterate, but fortunately the power of the mind broke the reactionary omnipotence of both Church and State, so much so that as political strength passed over to the people last century education increased and Christianity decreased.

At the end of the 18th century Joseph Lancaster started schools for the poor of England, who were steeped in ignorance. He was one of the first to advocate that the people should be educated, and he travelled throughout the country setting up primitive schools. He established about fifty such schools and taught some of his own pupils to become teachers. In these schools no creeds or dogmas were taught, the teaching being ethical, non-sectarian and educational. This so alarmed the Church authorities that they started rival schools for the purpose of incorporating Christian doctrines in their teaching. Not the desire for education, but its own preservation, was the reason for Church schools. Otherwise they would never have been started.

Just as the priesthood have discouraged humanity from acquiring general knowledge, so have they obstructed by every possible means the gaining of psychic knowledge through mediumship. In pre-Christian days this knowledge was confined to the priesthood, but throughout the Christian era ignorance took its place, and the policy of the Christian Church has always been to discourage psychic knowledge amongst both priests and people. The Roman Catholic Church elevated certain eminent mediums after death to a position next to the gods, but the Protestant Church has always severely condemned even this recognition of mediumship. Both organisations, when they had the power, destroyed all who were endowed with psychic gifts and never allowed the subject to be investigated.

Naturally it must be against the interests of any religious organisation to have the people getting into touch with the next order of existence. The whole idea behind those institutions is to supply a nexus between this order and the next—to act as middlemen between the gods and humanity. So it must be evident to everyone that if the people make contact with Etheria there is no need for the priesthood. The medium, the Church realised from early times, is the great competitor of the priest, and consequently the medium has been kept under, kept down, and was if necessary destroyed.

The official religious organisation has, therefore, been working against nature. From early times nature has been producing mediums who could reveal Etheria to us humans. The Church, on the other hand, has been destroying what nature produced, so as to protect itself against this competition. Spiritualism is a far greater danger to orthodox religion than is Materialism. The innate instinct of the majority would always support the religious organisation against the materialist, but in the most advanced countries the Church is fighting a losing battle against nature, which has decreed that the opening through to Etheria is by means of the medium and not through the Church.

Everyone, in bygone days, called mediums by the name of witches, unfortunate creatures who were feared and avoided by everyone, to be denounced, tortured, burned or drowned, the claim being made by the clergy that they had instructions from the gods that no witch should ever be allowed to live. The priests of Christendom do not look upon themselves as teachers but preachers, whose declarations come from the three Christian gods and must be accepted without question. They maintain, especially in Catholic countries, that it is not the privilege of the people to think for themselves on religious subjects, but that they must accept what is taught them by their appointed spiritual leaders, whose duty it is to interpret the revelation of the gods to mankind. This false claim is now accepted only by those who feel incapable of thinking out the deeper problems of life for themselves, and it will sooner or later have to be abandoned when education increases, and when the truths of Spiritualism become known to all mankind.

When the people were ignorant, the Church could use its authority to destroy mediums, and it is estimated that some 250,000 innocent people were thus cruelly murdered throughout the Christian era. Today the Church cannot do such deeds, and the clergy have to stand by and witness a steady erosion taking place in the foundations of their organisation. They can do nothing against this disintegration except abuse and misrepresent the cause. They will not come alongside Spiritualism because that would be admitting defeat.

So they will hold the fort against it for as long as possible and gradually be obliterated by it, just as a sand castle is gradually demolished by the oncoming waves.

The average educated person of today is ripe for guidance and is yearning for a lead. The minds of the majority are ready to unfold further before the enlarged universe science now presents to us, but the clergy still stand in the pulpit of tradition and ignore the advance that has taken place in knowledge. Thus they can give no lead to the people. They continue to repeat the phraseology which appealed to our grandfathers and grandmothers in the early Victorian age, before the people were able to read or think for themselves. The human mind must advance and develop, and as it does so it discards the old and reaches out for what is new. So it has been throughout the ages of the past.

What a noble profession it would have been if the priesthood had been the teachers of humanity, and had always striven to raise mankind to a higher mental and moral level! Unfortunately history teaches the very reverse. When this class had the power the mind of humanity was stifled and battened down by religious dogmas. Everything new which was contrary to their teaching was termed blasphemy, and immediately suppressed. All who still bow to authority in religion are mental slaves, who can only think as their masters the priests instruct them.

Socrates, Plato and Aristotle laid the foundation of a philosophy of life which illumined mankind, and made possible the civilisation we today enjoy. They were followed by a galaxy of men of intellectual splendour whose sayings and writings will glorify humanity for ever. The Greeks were the first to establish schools for learning, as distinct from theological seminaries.

Learning and Christianity could not live together, and Simplicius in the 6th century was the last philosopher and thinker to brave its deadening influence. Just as its grip tightened the bounds of scholarship narrowed. Only in Athens, Alexandria and Constantinople were there in his day any libraries. Only in Athens were philosophy and law then taught. In 529, under Justinian, the Church became everywhere supreme, all libraries were closed, as were also the Empire schools, every schoolmaster being banished or liquidated.

The Dark Ages thus commenced. All the remaining philosophers, Simplicius included, were expelled from Europe because they would not accept Christianity, and they had to seek refuge in Persia. Everyone who put learning before Christianity was murdered or exiled, until the thinkers and scholars were exterminated, and Europe was dominated by hordes of Christian barbarians, ignorant and superstitious, who believed that all knowledge was sinful.

Pomp and circumstance, when Christianity ruled, were purchased at the price of liberty and happiness. For every cathedral built there was a dungeon. The clang of the fetters filled the air along with the music of the choir, and the hand that lit the taper on the altar lit the faggot at the stake. For every cross there was a sword, for every blessing a curse, and the cries of the damned mingled with the hallelujahs of the saved.

Only scholars and historians can know, in view of the way history has been distorted under the influence of the Church, the blight Christianity has been, and how much better the world would have been if it had never been known. If the numerous schools of learning and of philosophy, in existence before Christianity reigned supreme, had remained open to shed their light over Europe and the world, what might we not have been today! Everything certainly points to the probability that we would have been at least a thousand years in advance of what we now are.[1]

At the Reformation the most intelligent part of Europe threw over this deadening organisation, and formed a new one, which enabled progress to be made, but still the theological mind of the reformed Church remained much the same as that of the Church from which it came. In Protestant countries the parson is still a priest in his mental outlook. He still has the same priestly mind. Enormous progress has been made in Protestant countries since the Reformation, but that progress has always been made in face of the opposition of the clergy.

The attitude of the clergy in Protestant countries makes sorry history, and there is scarcely a reform that has been carried in the British Parliament that has not received the strong united opposition of the bishops in the House of Lords. Laws for the good of the people in this country, for the abolition of slavery and child labour, for the increased happiness of the people,

---

[1] I can recommend the student of religious history to read *The History of the Conflict between Religion and Science* and *History of the Intellectual Development of Europe* by John William Draper; *The Martyrdom of Man* by Winwood Reade; and the 15th and 16th Chapters in *The Decline and Fall of the Roman Empire* by Gibbon, published in "The Thinker's Library", Series No. 11.

their comfort and well-being, besides many discoveries in medicine and science, have encountered the opposition of the Protestant clergy of Great Britain. To them progress was not the will of the Christian gods, and was not supported by the Christian Bible.

Thus we find today the almost unanimous opposition of the Christian Church in this country to any enquiry into the life beyond. It is in the interest of the clergy to keep this a mystery, because, so long as it remains a mystery, they can rely on the support of the ignorant to their own worn-out theology. The attitude of Dr. Temple, when Archbishop of York, is typical of that of the Christian Church towards our having evidence of our destiny. In *The Times* of 2nd March, 1934, he is reported as stating in his Third Gifford lecture:—

> Except as implied in the righteousness and love of God, immortality is not a religious interest at all. It is therefore positively undesirable that there should be experimental proof of man's survival of death.

How characteristically priestly! How typically theological in expression and ambiguity! How exactly in accordance with the history of his craft throughout the ages! The Archbishop, representing the Christian Church, speaks words with which the historian is very familiar. Nothing has ever been desirable to the priests if it has been contrary to the creeds of their organisation, even if it were for the good of humanity.

When Spiritualists succeed in their effort to educate the world in the belief that as we sow here we shall reap hereafter, that the theological heaven and hell do not exist, and that man is his own saviour, then will fade away all the creeds and dogmas of every religion and the priests who preach them.

Hence to the clergy it is much more desirable that the people should remain ignorant on the vital question of the hereafter, because, so long as they do so, the priesthood is supported out of the labour of the workers. Ignorance is better than knowledge, as the more ignorant the people are the greater is the hold the Church has over them, and the more it can get from them.

To the laity intellectual honesty in the affairs of every-day life is the peak of wisdom, in all business dealings sincerity and candour are sword and shield, but in the case of the priesthood the reverse is the case. From the theological seminary onwards, honest thinking, candour and sincerity are resolutely avoided. In their place we find equivocation, fear of straightforward thinking, dissembling, and the distorting of truth to those still simple enough to be thus deceived.

From the Pope downwards in Roman Catholic countries, and in this country from the Archbishops downwards, the clergy find that it is undesirable for the people to know about the hereafter. All progress and reform, and everything for the cultural and intellectual advance of the people, has likewise in the past been undesirable, and only when the masses overcame the determined opposition of the upper classes, and secured the vote last century, did education commence and Church influence decline.

Only the ignorant and uneducated would think of consulting a priest about the deeper things of life, and few will question the Bishop of Bristol's opinion, as expressed in the same issue of *The Times* just referred to, that the clergy do not now belong to the learned professions. One has only to listen to the average sermon to realise that the bishop's statement is only too true, but the clergy have themselves to blame. Stagnation means moral and intellectual retrogression, and in that word is summed up the history of the priesthood.

Throughout the world tens of thousands of men are being trained, not educated, in the world's theological colleges. For what purpose? Not for the purpose of investigating the phenomena of nature or for accumulating knowledge obtained by evidence. No, for quite the reverse. The purpose is to train them to defend and propagate opinions formed by ignorant men in the ages when the world was mentally young, when our ancestors had minds of children and could express only childish ideas which have come down to us as myth and legend.

These misguided theological students believe that those simple unformed ideas they are learning to propagate will give more comfort to people than the knowledge we have at the present time. Nevertheless many people are still so ignorant that they devote their wealth and energy to supporting, not only the prospective priests of every world religion, but also those presently in office.

Nature is the mother of us all, and, if we understood her better, we would find greater comfort from her present-day revelations than can be found in the past, when, through lack of knowledge, her ways were not understood. The man or woman appreciates a parent's training better when grown up than in childhood, and we do not expect to obtain from the child in the nursery a true appreciation of its early education. Why, therefore, be guided by the simple ideas of our childish ancestors, except to profit by their mistakes? Why be guided by those who worship the past, whose duty it is to exalt the past at the expense of the present, whose minds are either so dishonest or so simple and undeveloped that they devote their lives to preaching the errors of the past, and ignore the great discoveries of the present?

In Christendom these men are paid by the community to tell the people that God revealed himself on only two occasions, first to the Hebrews and then to the Christians, all the rest of mankind being left as outcasts in utter darkness. That untruth they live by, and live on, and so long as they can keep the people believing it they are content. Fortunately it is becoming clear that the people themselves are thinking, and the bishops and clergy are beginning to wonder about their future.

The priesthood has never been an order of teachers. Learning, to them, in the past consisted of copying and illuminating the sacred scriptures, and preaching the religion to which they belonged. They never taught the world facts, only superstition, which is the science of priest-craft, and this is as true today as it has ever been. They excited wonder, emphasised the miraculous and the supernatural, but never tried to understand or explain the forces of nature. They always accepted appearances and never tried to account for them. They always denounced scientific enquiry and investigation. They always endeavoured to keep the mind of man from thinking, as the less their supporters thought the more secure was their position.

They stood with arms outstretched before the unknown, or prostrated themselves in worship before an imaginary god. When they had the power to do so they murdered the thinker, the enquirer and the investigator, and all who strove to enlighten the world. Priestcraft has been the greatest force known to history against the progress of humanity.

Of course humanity got only what it was mentally fitted to receive. The majority of the priests of the past doubtless believed that what they taught was true, that they had a privileged position given them by the gods, and that it was the duty of their followers to accept and not to enquire. Humanity was, and is still in many countries, mentally fitted only for this. Otherwise it would not have submitted to it in the past or still continue to do so.

In order to maintain their power, the priesthood claimed that certain instructions had been received by them which they said had come from the gods. After writing was discovered they claimed that some of these writings had been directly inspired by the gods and must be accepted as verbally true and consequently believed without question.

When the ignorant multitude was in terror over some natural phenomenon, the priests insisted on the necessity for some sacrifice being made to feed the gods, and thus restore friendly relations between heaven and earth. The sacrifice, to begin with, took the form of a human victim, the greatest offering man could make. The story of Jephtha, and other similar horrible records, fill some of the pages of the Christian Bible. Later, when mankind ceased being cannibals, and consequently imagined that the gods had done likewise, animals took the place of the human victims.

Sacrifice was the outcome of the belief in wrongdoing, the beginning of the orthodox idea of sin, which is an offence against the dictates of the gods, and out of this developed the atonement. Sacrifice thus became an offering to the imagined offended deity, it being a world-wide idea that sin could be transferred to a human or an animal, just as it was believed that disease could be cured by this means. Thus sinners obtained the pardon for their offences and sinful man again appeased his god. This *rapprochement* was given the name of at-onement, or atonement.

The reason humans and animals were sacrificed to placate the gods was for the purpose of releasing the etheric duplicate of the victims to satisfy their imagined hunger. When men were cannibals they thought their gods were also cannibals, and enjoyed eating the duplicate bodies which were offered to them and which in substance were akin to the gods. This can be discovered when reading old literature on sacrifice, the chapters in *Genesis*, *Exodus* and *Leviticus* being particularly illuminating on this question, but when reading them we should always remember that the words "the Lord" and "God" should be read "the gods", as originally written. This idea of sacrifice, and the ceremonies attached to it, constitute the most primitive form of man's attempt to be on friendly terms with the gods, those omnipotent beings who controlled the course of nature, but in time everything became more complicated.

This came about by the introduction of the belief in a saviour-god, and it is very interesting to remember the origin of this idea. We first read of a saviour-god when someone in Egypt, who came to be called Osiris, in the 18th century B.C., was deified as such. His sacrifice may have been an important occasion when the people desired to give to the gods their very best. So he may have been the son of a king, as the gods were believed to prefer the bodies of the highest in the land. Again he may have been a reformer who had angered the priests, but whoever he was he suffered and died to be seen again as an apparition after death.

This reappearing in his etheric body was taken as a sign that the gods had allowed the victim to live, were no longer angry with mankind, and had removed the curse which the priests said was laid on mankind because of his wickedness. Consequently the reappearance of the victim after death was taken to mean that he had conquered death and opened up heaven to believers. Thus Osiris "humbled himself, becoming obedient even unto death", as Paul expressed it seventeen hundred years later about Jesus. This being so Osiris came to be known as the Saviour, Redeemer and Mediator, to receive all the love and adoration his grateful worshippers could bestow.

Thus began an idea which was copied by other nations as they gave up ancestor worship and became believers in a saviour-god. Finally the mass of theology and mythology surrounding this belief culminated in Christianity, which was the last of the saviour-god religions, but it incorporated in its beliefs all those that had gone before, right back into antiquity.

The beliefs, rites and ceremonies surrounding sacrifice, and its development from early times, is given in much greater detail in my book devoted to the origin and growth of the Christian Faith entitled *The Psychic Stream*, but sufficient has here been written to explain how a human victim was finally transformed into a god in heaven, the final development being the belief that this god had incarnated on earth to become the sacrifice for the sins of humanity.

This belief is to be found during the ages in many religions, which taught, as Sir James Frazer says, that "The accumulated misfortunes of the whole people are sometimes laid on the dying god, who is supposed to bear them away for ever, leaving the people innocent and happy". Christianity adopted its belief in the atonement from Greek thought, the belief in a god-man sacrificed for the sins of the world being a Grecian idea, to be found in the writings of Hesiod, Plato and other Greek writers.

Hesiod, the Greek poet, who lived two thousand eight hundred years ago, before a book of the Bible was written, tells the story of the atonement which was handed down to become incorporated into Christianity and centre round Jesus. Hesiod tells how early man fell from innocence. The Greek Adam, called Epimetheus, was tempted by the Greek Eve named Pandora and fell. Thus sin came into the world which Zeus, the Greek Jehovah, decided to destroy. This he did by means of a flood. Only a few escaped, and as they continued to sin Zeus decided that only by the sacrifice of a god-man could his wrath be appeased.

Prometheus, the Greek Christ, offered himself as the sacrifice in place of humanity and suffered death bound to a rock. Thus was the anger of Zeus appeased and Prometheus was worshipped as the Saviour of humanity. At his death the earth shook, the rocks were rent, and the dead came out of their graves when the Saviour gave up the ghost. The Passion play depicting the death of Prometheus, his burial, resurrection and ascension, was performed in Greece five hundred years before the Christian era. A similar performance takes place today at Oberammergau, the only difference being that the god-man is now known by another name.

The word Christ stands for this ancient belief. Jesus, during his time on earth, was never known as Christ, which is a Greek name adopted by those who accepted Paul's opinion that Jesus was the Christ or Christos. This divine name conveyed to the Pagans similar ideas as the word Messiah did to the Jews, and the Greek word Logos stands for the same idea. The name Jesus stands for the man who went about doing good, who was probably an Essene, and, according to tradition, taught his followers to believe in the fatherhood of God and the brotherhood of man.

The word Christ stands for a sacrificed saviour-god and all that is Pagan in Christianity. It should never be associated with Jesus by intelligent people. Similarly the Christian religion is not the religion of Jesus. Paul founded Christianity, his preaching and writings being based on the Paganism he had learned at Tarsus, where the Pagan god Dionysus was worshipped. Much of what was believed about this beloved Greek saviour-god, Paul draped round Jesus, and those who call themselves Christians should ponder carefully over this fact, as it is all important.

The belief in the sacrifice of a god for the sins of humanity was held, as we have seen, in pre-Christian times, but it is not accepted by some of the other leading world religions. The Jews, Buddhists and Mohammedans do not countenance this idea of divine sacrifice, and the great majority in Christendom, who still believe it, do so because the idea was instilled into them from infancy before they could think logically, and they have never given serious thought to the subject since then. What is taught to a child is seldom forgotten.

The idea of one of the gods, as in the case of Christianity, suffering himself for man's misdeeds has been the cause of crimes and wickednesses without number amongst all who have believed this doctrine. The believer, having been taught that his sins had been pardoned through this sacrifice, did not feel responsible for his own misdeeds. Consequently this doctrine that the shedding of blood by another absolved the believer from his mistakes took away the urge to live a better life, and men and women gave way freely to their passions, comforted by the belief that through the sacrifice of another they were safe for eternity.[1] Anyone who was intelligent enough to doubt this doctrine was branded as an infidel, an atheist or as a blasphemer, and, up till the 17th century, murdered, so that he would not contaminate others with his heresies. The wonder is that mankind ever advanced at all.

The first infidel who managed to live was respon-

---

[1] His own self bare our sins in his own body on the tree, that we, being dead to sins, should live unto righteousness: by whose stripes ye were healed.
(1. *Peter* ii, 24)

sible for the first step made in the march of progress. He was denounced and hated by the orthodox, but he was the first survivor of those who had character enough to think for themselves, and risk death rather than be unfaithful to their honest thoughts. Perhaps this primitive infidel was the first to make a stand against one of his children being sacrified, offering an animal instead. Thus in time animal sacrifice took the place of human sacrifice.

Again, at a much later date, some thinker or infidel grudged and protested against this waste of animal life, and so the priests, with animals getting short, resorted to the idea that one of the gods became man and was sacrificed for the sins of the world. As the cross represented life eternal, the story came to be believed that he was crucified on a cross. Similar tales are told of the sixteen saviour-gods before the time of Jesus. The story of their lives on earth, from virgin birth to death and resurrection, are all similar, one religion copying from another earlier religion. These stories can all be traced back to sun worship and the romances told of the sun in its apparent daily and annual journey in the heavens.[1]

The story of Calvary originated in sun worship. To the sun thousands of victims were offered. The holocaust increased when an eclipse of the sun occurred.[2] Then it was thought that the sun god was angry and had withdrawn from his people. Ancient stories tell how the victim prior to the eclipse was

---

[1] The standard books on this subject are Frazer's *The Golden Bough*; Robertson's *Christianity and Mythology* and *Pagan Christs*; Massey's *The Beginnings* and *Ancient Egypt*.

[2] According to Matthew's gospel, chapter xxvii, darkness descended when Jesus was crucified and an earthquake occurred at the moment of death, besides other miraculous wonders.

bound or nailed to a cross which was placed on an altar. Over him oil was poured and he was anointed prior to satisfying the deity's anger. During the eclipse he was set alight and prayers were offered. The eclipse passed and it was believed that the victim, often one of the most important men of the tribe, had saved his people. He was their saviour and became their Christ, the anointed one, a god-man who had taken on himself the people's punishment.

From this source came the story of the crucifixion of Jesus and all the drama with which it is surrounded. From the sixth hour there was darkness over all the land till the ninth hour, we are told, when Jesus was crucified. Thus his death (which the Jewish *Talmud* says occurred by his being stoned, his body being afterwards hung on a tree) came to be surrounded with the rites and beliefs of the ancients which they carried out for the purpose of appeasing the sun god during an eclipse.

The people required some material expression of these sacrifices, so the Eucharist was instituted, and they were told that by eating a specially-prepared barley cake, or wafer, they were eating the flesh of a sacrificed god, and that the wine was his blood. In Rome the slain god was termed "Hostia", the Latin for a sacrificial victim, whence is derived the word "Host" which represents the consecrated bread of the Roman Catholic Eucharist. In the 9th century developed the belief in "The Real Presence", when also the Pagan wafer was displaced and bread was substituted.

The belief in "The Real Presence" goes back to early times, and can be traced to what we now call a séance, where it was realised that an invisible being was present and communicated through the medium. This being was looked on as a god and in pre-Christian times was called the Divine Spirit, from which developed the belief in the Holy Spirit of the early Apostolic Church, the early Jesuians believing that at their séances Jesus used the medium's control, called the Divine Spirit, to communicate with his followers on earth. However, when mediums in the fourth Christian century were forbidden to exercise their gifts in a church, the belief in the Holy Spirit became a vague idea and few Christians, if any, know its origin.

The eating of consecrated bread comes from the days when it was believed that the flesh of a sacrificed victim had life-giving properties to be called *mana* by the Greeks. So the king, his courtiers and chief priests ate the victim's flesh and drank his blood, but, as there was not sufficient for the common people, the priests deluded them into the belief that they had transferred the victim's *mana* into the bread and wine, the result being that the people ate and drank this consecrated bread and wine believing that it was the body and blood of the victim. So we find in Mexico that one or more victims were crucified each year after being consecrated as sin bearers in a temple. When ready for the sacrifice they were looked on as gods, their bodies being eaten and their blood drunk by the aristocracy, the humble people being satisfied with the consecrated bread and wine.

This ancient rite of eating consecrated bread and drinking wine is practised by every sect in Christendom, though most Protestants believe that the feast is one of remembrance of the sacrifice, and that they do not eat the body of God or drink his blood, as is believed by the Catholic section of the Christian Church. This idea of the bread and wine developed from the ritual surrounding the worship of the ancient corn and wine gods. Thus we find in many ancient religions throughout the world that the cake was eaten and the wine drunk in the belief that by this act sin would be pardoned and salvation secured.

Gradually the priesthood became so powerful that it ordered the lives of every man and woman from birth to death. It decreed, in order to obtain its influence at the earliest possible age, that the child must be baptized in infancy or it would be damned. Its priests told the people that the streets of hell were paved with the skulls of unbaptized children. Not only was it told to Christians by their priests, but to those of other religions by their priests. This belief that a child unbaptized goes to hell still prevails throughout much of Christendom, and has caused incalculable misery to Christian parents since the 4th century, when Christianity adopted the sacrament of baptism from Paganism.

The child was required also to be confirmed when it attained adolescence, to make it a member and supporter of the religious organisation. When the child became man or woman it was necessary that it should attend certain ceremonies, and hold certain beliefs, so as to ensure salvation. If this individual did all that he was told to do, and believed all that he was told to believe by the Church authorities of his day, he was considered a good member of society. If he objected, and demanded the freedom of his own thoughts, he was considered an infidel, an evil influence, a heretic, and painfully murdered. Thus these representatives of the gods performed ceremonies and propounded doctrines which came to be believed naturally and as part of the every-day life of the community. Certain days were holy days, and in Christendom when the Church was supreme nearly every second day was a holy day.

Very early in history we find that the people celebrated the birthday of one of the gods on or about 25th December, as the original god to be worshipped was the sun. This date was chosen because about that time the northern hemisphere of the earth commences to incline towards the sun and thus gets more heat and light. Different holy days were set apart for special festivals, and they were determined by the different positions of the earth in relation to the sun in the heavens throughout the year. The legends told of the sun then became intertwined with the lives of the gods who were believed to have visited the earth from time to time.

The priests also turned the ancient contract of marriage into a religious rite and sacrament, and the Christian priests described marriage as a mystical union, comparing it with the mystical union of Christ with his Church. There is of course no resemblance between the two, but it was the only thing they could think of to give them the necessary power over an ignorant and illiterate people. A signed contract was impossible in past times, but the fear of God made many a marriage permanent which otherwise would have been dissolved. Considering the number of alterations and additions the Church authorities have made to the original writings composing the New Testament, it shows great laxity on the part of the early prelates that they did not attribute to Jesus some saying empowering the Christian Church to interfere in regard to marriage. However, those who followed received inspiration enough to alight on this idea of the mystical union of Christ with his Church, and up to now it has been accepted by the faithful.

Thus the priests ordered the lives of their subjects from the cradle to the grave, and, when the Church funds were running low, they told stories about the rich going to hell and the poor to heaven. We are all familiar with the Christian story of Dives and Lazarus. Another story of a different kind, but produced for the same purpose, is that of Ananias and Sapphira, which was added to the other stories about the early Church so as to prevent the faithful pleading poverty when poverty did not exist. It is a cruel story, and is still taught to our children as an example of the dealings of God with the wicked.

Moreover, the writings in the New Testament emphasising the difficulty of the rich in entering heaven, praising poverty, and denouncing wealth, are also interpolations, inserted in the early days when the documents now comprising our New Testament were added to, and curtailed, just as the early Church authorities considered right. These texts, and those denouncing usury, retarded the progress of Europe for more than one thousand years. The priests wanted the people's money, and did not wish them to save or lend it.

For centuries those texts against usury were used as a pretext for the persecution of the Jews, the financiers of Europe. In the Dark Ages the Church refused to sanction its supporters lending out money at interest, and persecuted all who did so. The acquisition of wealth, except by the Church, was considered a sin, and poverty was elevated to such a degree that Europe became populated by a race of mendicants. Gorgeous churches were built while the people could only afford to live in hovels, and their savings were directed into the coffers of the Church, which owned half the cultivated land in Europe and tens of thousands of serfs and slaves. What took place in Europe has happened also in India, China and other eastern countries. Monasteries and convents throughout Europe and Asia were occupied by the pious idle, who scorned the sons of toil working for their maintenance.

Besides obtaining money for their organisation by deluding the people, the priests made the faithful fear them by relating how discourtesy towards any of their class was always punished by death. The Jewish priesthood, for example, told their ignorant followers how angry Jehovah would be if his priests were ever slighted or made to look ridiculous. Even children in those days, being human, were amused at the sight of a tonsured priest, and, to prevent uncomplimentary remarks being passed on their class, the priests told stories of how wicked it was, and how angry Jehovah would be to hear such blasphemy. One of the stories handed down to us tells how one of Jehovah's priests cursed some little children in the name of Jehovah, because they called after him "Go up, thou bald head", and that two bears came out of a wood and destroyed forty-two of them.

This wicked priest, we are told, then proceeded on his way quite unconcerned at the misery and suffering Jehovah had wrought at his request, and our children are taught that this man Elisha was a man of God, and one of Jehovah's prophets revealing his will to mankind. This is only one of many similar barbarous tales taught by the Christian Church as part of God's revelation to man in his inspired book, termed "The Word of God", "The Holy Bible", or "The Holy Scriptures".

Little wonder that the history of Christianity is one of cruelty, savagery and crime. Its god is a cruel, unscrupulous and unjust tyrant, and, as their god is, so are the people until education raises them to a higher level, because everyone makes his god as he imagines God should be.

The kings of the past controlled the bodies of their subjects and the priests their minds. Just as the kings were above and beyond the law of the land, so the priests in time became so powerful that they placed themselves not only above the law but at times above the kings. The kings terrorised their subjects by fear of consequences on earth, but they in turn were terrorised by the priests, who frightened them with the danger of incurring the wrath of the gods if they did not carry out the wishes of the priests.

This was so in every country, no matter what religion was professed. In Christendom no Cardinal-Bishop could be convicted unless 72 witnesses supported the charge. Before a Cardinal-Presbyter could be convicted 44 were required. To secure the conviction of a Cardinal-Deacon 24 were required, and 7 to secure the conviction of a Sub-Deacon. Some of the most inhuman laws in England, now fortunately amended or abolished, were taken from the canon law of the Catholic Church. These laws were conceived in savage minds and can be traced back to the savage in his cave, with a dug-out tree-trunk as his only transport, a club his only weapon, and his wife and children as his chattels and property. Natural phenomena, and the ghosts of his ancestors, were his gods, and fear the basis of his worship.

In Christendom slavery was upheld and practised till the 19th century. Death was the penalty for the smallest crime, and cruelty reigned everywhere. Drunkenness prevailed in all classes of society. Until the 18th century torture and fiendish devices were used against criminals and heretics. If we go a hundred years farther back to the 17th century we find that our Christian ancestors were not satisfied with first torturing and then hanging their victims, but before death mercifully intervened they were castrated and their internals gouged out.

The misery caused by Christians persecuting each other, and those they termed heretics, no one will ever be able to describe. In Spain alone the Inquisition put to death 32,000 people by cruel torture, and this continued until it was stopped by the soldiers of Napoleon who, in fury at what they saw, put the persecutors through the same misery as they were inflicting on their victims. Throughout Europe 25,000,000 innocent people[1] suffered death by torture or massacre at the hands of both Catholics and Protestants, and when we consider the relatively small

---

[1] How this number of victims is arrived at will be found in greater detail in the author's book *The Curse of Ignorance*.

population of Europe in those days, these figures are appalling. When the Catholics were in power many Pagans, Protestants and heretics were put to death by torture, and wherever Protestants dominated the Catholics and heretics were similarly treated, but the Protestants went further—they put each other to death. In Scotland between 1661 and 1688 the Episcopalians put to death 28,000 Presbyterians because they would not conform to the Episcopalian form of worship. In England the Puritans likewise suffered for the same reason.

In England it was a common practice to whip publicly through the streets all Catholics who did not attend service at the Protestant churches. Catholic priests were hanged who performed a marriage between a Catholic and a Protestant, and any bookseller who sold a book which was condemned by the Protestant Church was put to death. This state of affairs continued until the 19th century, and was the aftermath of the Renaissance.

Copernicus, Galileo, Bruno, Kepler and Newton blew up the whole edifice of superstition in the 16th and 17th centuries, and their followers were the victims of the falling debris. The Christian Church fought hard to maintain its authority, but its edifice was shattered beyond repair. For three hundred years, in its dying agony, victims fell in its struggle for life, and in its downfall it inflicted cruelty, suffering and misery beyond imagination.

We are fortunately now living to witness the shattered edifice from which no further harm need be expected. On the road which Truth pursued, as it arose phœnix-like out of error, are the bodies of countless martyrs strewn on either side. As each one fell the road became easier for Truth to walk on, and as time passed the dangers became fewer and the sufferings less. In democratic lands the barriers to the progress of truth are now almost all swept away, but in others tyranny too often reigns supreme. In Spain in 1935 the editor of a newspaper was sentenced to two months' imprisonment and a fine of £13 because he was bold enough to throw doubt on the teaching of the Catholic Church. Elsewhere political dictatorships have taken the place of Church domination, with the same disastrous results to the intellectual freedom of the individual.

The roots of our heredity strike deep down into the past, and draw from the ages of ignorance the sap that fills our minds today. True the sap is growing weaker as the roots are growing longer, but still a large majority of mankind worships and prays as the result of fear. Many think that thereby their lives will be easier, their happiness will be increased, and their contentment will be greater. By likening their god's nature to their own, they think that he will deal more kindly with them through flattery, praise and worship.

The origin of worship, of mankind's continuous effort to placate the gods, can be traced back to primitive man living in fear of natural phenomena. Moreover, he believed that he was surrounded by etheric beings, both good and bad, and he treated them as his friends or enemies. One especially was his friend and he carved his image out of wood as best he could. In this he believed the invisible being dwelt, and he told the image his desires and fears. This is the origin of prayer. Thus these early men and women bowed themselves down to wood and sometimes to images of stone, and before their idols they pleaded for their desires, but the gods were silent. Little did our primitive ancestors realise that prayer does not alter the unbroken law of cause and effect, which has been for all time, and will be for all eternity.

Prayer to be of help must not be directed to the purpose of trying to alter the course of nature, or to obtaining the gratification of some selfish desire. Prayer to be of personal value must have for its motive the increase of our charity for others, some being thus helped by this mental exercise in their desire to increase in kindness and consideration towards others. Consequently, those who get help from prayer should always direct their prayers towards this goal, but never for the gratification of some selfish desire.

Prayer should be the tuning-in of the human mind with the Infinite, the reaching out of our thoughts towards the divine in nature. Knowledge gives strength to carry life's burdens, and those who have trained themselves philosophically gain strength and fortitude, and may at times reach to greater heights through contemplation, or meditation, on the deeper things of life than can be done by others through prayer alone. Many ways lead to the Infinite and are trodden by minds of different degree. Prayer and contemplation are the means used by humanity to gain touch, and retain contact, with the source of our existence, with the Divine Mind of which we each are part.

I believe that as we grow in intelligence contemplation will more and more take the place of prayer. It is the highest form of prayer because it is quite unselfish. Until fear, however, is eradicated from the human mind, prayer, as it exists today amongst the faithful and the fearful, will continue. Fear and uncertainty with regard to the unknown, the future, and our destiny, besides the belief that God is a person who answers requests, form the basis of all the prayers of the orthodox.

The whole of the Christian system of worship is based on this instinctive fear of the unknown. Fear imprisons the mind; it is the father of superstition which flourishes in the garden of ignorance. The Church of England litany was written from fear, and is sung or read today by the fearful who are taught that "The fear of God is the beginning of wisdom". The people think that it is pleasing to God that they should call themselves miserable sinners, and what is said of the litany can be said of most of the other set prayers of the Christian Church.

Their origin is fear, and they are repeated, or listened to, by those who think that their happiness will be increased here and hereafter by thus humbling themselves before Almighty God. Prayer comes naturally, and, like a tonic, it gives strength and encouragement to those who do not realise the unbroken law of cause and effect. Mankind therefore throughout the ages has been immensely helped by prayer. For thousands of years men and women have been making supplication to the gods. They have asked aid from the gods and told them all their troubles. With reverent outstretched hands and closed eyes they have worshipped the men and women of the other world who were imagined as omnipotent and omniscient gods. As the years passed the number of gods has become fewer, the most civilised races of today being satisfied with one or at the most three.

Believing, as primitive man did, that invisible beings ordered the heavens and the earth, it was but natural that he should allot them the stars and planets in the heavens as their dwelling-place. In time this idea was materialised and the sun, the moon and the planets came to be looked upon as gods instead of the habitation of the gods. The sun and moon were the two principal gods, the first a good god because it gave light, comfort and growth, and because it shone by day. The other was evil, because it gave no heat, light or growth to the earth and shone by night. The sun represented the divine or mysterious in nature.

The god-men, and the saviours of the ancients, were often sun gods, as the stories attributed to the sun were wound round their lives, just as they were with Jesus. They were pictured with the sun behind their heads, which is the origin of the halo, and to the sun has been directed billions of prayers. Then there were the gods of thunder, wind and rain, a god for each force in nature and the produce of the earth, such as corn gods and wine gods. Beasts were turned into gods and made sacred. Serpents even were worshipped as the representatives of those higher powers. To those gods our ancestors built altars, and to them they erected temples, where they sacrificed both man and beast.

The history of mythology makes clear to us how much religion entered into the lives of the ancients. Each nation had one or more gods, and in every case those gods had the faults and failings of the nation over which they reigned. Those gods were cruel and treacherous, and hated the nations who were the enemies of their chosen people. The gods were vain and loved flattery, praise and worship. Nothing delighted them more than sacrifice. The shedding of blood gave them especial pleasure. The minds of our ancestors imagined gods of all kinds, and some had several heads. Brahma, the Hindu god, we are told, is one god with four heads, whereas the Christian god is three gods in one godhead.

Mythology tells us of all the saviour-gods who came to earth as the saviours of humanity. They chose virgins for their mothers, so we find the virgin and child venerated in pre-Christian religions. In Egypt the saviour-god was Osiris. Isis was the mother of the god Horus. In India, Devaki was the virgin mother of the god Krishna. All those gods when on earth lived similar lives, just as they all had similar births. Their lives teemed with the miraculous and they all experienced similar violent deaths, rose again from the dead, and ascended into heaven, the victors of death, all of which legends were originally told of the sun. Some gods went in pairs. Others were triplets like Brahma, Vishnu and Siva of the Hindus. The Persians worshipped Mithra, but, with the incorporation into their religion of the philosophy of Zoroaster, Mithra took second place, and the Persian Trinity of Ormuzd, Mithra and Vohu Mano came into being. In Egypt the Trinity was Osiris, Isis and Horus, who were the forerunners of the Father, Son and Holy Ghost of Christianity.

Whether the gods were single, double, treble or quadruple, there is one thing common about them all. They were all very ignorant, and knew no more than the people over whom they ruled. They did not even know the shape of the world they had created. They did not know about the vastness of space or the movements of the planets, and that our planetary system circled round the sun. We read of one god Jehovah who thought that the sun circled round the earth, and that by stopping it the day would be lengthened, he being quite ignorant of the fact that the reason for day and night is the earth turning on its axis, and not the sun circling round the world.

To the ancients the gods always revealed how they had created the heavens and the earth. The baked clay tablets found in Nineveh recall this story as it was revealed to the Sumerians, Babylonians and the Assyrians. These tablets were discovered between 1866 and 1870 by Sir A. H. Layard and others, who were excavating on behalf of the British Museum. The record tells how the gods created man and woman, the beasts of the field, the grass and vegetation, the plants and the trees. It is somewhat similar to the account as given in *Genesis*.

The gods of the Sumerians—Anu, Enlil, Enurta, Ennugi and Ninigiku Ea—decided that all the people on earth must be drowned. The Hebrews at a later date attributed this decision to their god Jehovah, having learned the story when they were in captivity. The cuneiform tablets found in Nineveh, which are four thousand years old, give a description of what we now know was no more than a local disaster. They tell of a man, by name Uta-Napishtim, who, with his family, was singled out to be saved, how he built a boat and collected therein the various animals, and when the rain began to descend he entered the boat with his wife and family.

Then the land was submerged and only water could be seen. First of all he sent out a dove which came back, and then a swallow which came back, and then a raven which did not come back because the waters had subsided. Finally the ship rested on the top of a mountain called Nisir, when the Babylonian Noah left his ship with his family and offered up a sacrifice in gratitude for his escape.

The generally accepted view held by Assyriologists is that the story records a disaster which happened to some cities near the head of the Persian Gulf. The sea since then has receded, but in the days of the Deluge these cities were nearer the sea and were overwhelmed by a tidal wave accompanied by a cyclone. The story was handed down and ultimately became written in the Babylonian cuneiform characters, on tablets of clay, discovered by George Smith in 1873, who assisted Sir Henry Rawlinson in discovering and translating the past history of Babylon inscribed in stone. Another Babylonian tablet tells what it is lawful to do on the seventh day, which was called Sabatu, and means "The day of rest for the heart". On this tablet, dating from the 17th century B.C., we find laws similar to those found in the Bible, and attributed to Jehovah.

Though no tablet has been discovered relating to the Tower of Babel, this story undoubtedly comes from Babylon, and, like the Jews, the Greeks have a similar legend recording the attempt that was made to reach the dwelling-place of the Greek god Zeus. It is now believed that such towers were built in those days as astronomical observatories, to which the priests objected, and they consequently incited the people to destroy them.

Throughout the entire Old Testament two gods are referred to in the original text, one Jehovah and the other Elohim (a plural name probably signifying a trinity), but from our translation it is impossible to tell to whom credit or discredit should be given in connection with the different Old Testament records of their doings. However, what the Babylonian gods claim to have done in the way of the creation of the earth and heavens was also claimed by Elohim, and the explanation of this similarity is because the Jews attributed to this god what they learned when they were captives in Babylon. All the Babylonian tablets are much older than any book of the Bible, the Pentateuch, the name given to the first five books of the Bible, being written about the year 450 B.C., just after the Jews returned from Babylon, whereas these tablets go back to at least two thousand years before the time of Jesus.

What is termed "The Book of the Dead" tells us wondrous stories of the doings of the Egyptian gods. This title is given to the great collection of funerary texts which the ancient Egyptian scribes composed. These consist of spells and incantations, hymns, litanies and prayers, and they are found cut or painted on the walls of the pyramids and tombs, or painted on coffins and sarcophagi and rolls of papyrus. They go back to 2800 B.C. It was believed that they were inspired by one of the Egyptian gods named Thoth. This is the oldest Bible in the world. It was to the Egyptians what Homer was to the Greeks, and shows that the early dwellers on the Nile delta believed in a future existence. At that time they did not consider it necessary to embalm the body, as they looked on it as useless after death.

"The Book of the Dead" covers a long period, and, as we proceed, we find that the dead body gets more and more respect, to be mummified because by then had come the belief in the resurrection of the physical body. The dead body had to be preserved for the habitation of its former occupant, and this being so great precautions were taken for its safety. Both the mummified body, and the spirit which had inhabited it on earth, required protection from a multitude of devils and fiends. These powers of evil had hideous and terrifying shapes and forms, and infested the region through which the spirit had to pass before it reached the Kingdom of Osiris.

The Biblical text in *Genesis*, believed by Christians to refer to Christ, "It (the woman's seed) shall bruise thy head and thou (the serpent) shall bruise his heel", originated in Egypt. War existed between Rā, the Sun god, and Aapep, the devil, and we have illustrations of Rā spearing the head of a serpent, which represented the devil, just as it does in Christian literature. The serpent, to the Egyptians, represented the powers of evil warring against God, while in Greece we have the story about the vulnerable heel of Achilles. As happened in the case of the Old and New Testaments of the Christian Bible, so also in Egypt, as time went on, additions were made to the holy papyri

The Age of Superstition

by the priests, and these interpolations can be discovered just as they have been discovered in the Bible.

The Egyptian religion follows much the same course as the Christian religion. In the early days, Rā, the Sun god, was worshipped just as Jehovah was worshipped. Then came Osiris through whose suffering, death and resurrection believers were saved. These at death reached what the Egyptians called the world just bordering the visible world, or what we would call today the Astral plane, over which Osiris was the ruling deity. Just as Christianity succeeded Judaism, so the worship of Osiris developed out of the worship of the Sun god Rā, the Egyptians coming to prefer the hymns and litanies, which dealt with his suffering, death and resurrection, to the stern judgments and laws of Rā.

Osiris came to be looked on as the one and only giver of everlasting life. He was the God of Truth and Justice who had died for the sins of humanity and risen again. Osiris was the Christ of the Egyptians. It was believed that he had lived on earth as a godman and had conquered death, after having been tempted by Set, termed "The liar", who, after the triumph of Osiris over death, was bound with cords and hacked to pieces.

The Egyptians hated death and loved life, and when the belief gained ground among them that Osiris, the God of the dead, had himself risen from the dead, and had the power to "make man and woman to be born again" because of his truth and righteousness, they came to regard him as the judge as well as the god of the dead. Then developed the belief in the resurrection of the body, and for this reason it was not destroyed. Christians borrowed the idea of a bodily resurrection from Egypt, and this explains why they buried the dead body and did not burn it as did the Romans. So it has been found, when all the facts are put together, that the Egyptian religion from Rā to Osiris corresponds very closely with the development of the Jewish-Christian religion from Jehovah to Christ.

As time went on, and moral and religious ideas developed, the Egyptians became certain that only those who believed in Osiris, and satisfied his ideals of truth and justice, could hope for admission into his kingdom. One of the prayers in the "Book of the Dead", which could be said by Christians today, reads as follows:—

> Wash away my sins, Lord of Truth, destroy my transgressions, wickedness and iniquity, O God of Truth. May this God be at peace with me. Destroy the things that are obstacles between us. Give me peace, and remove all dissatisfaction from my heart in respect of thee.

Thus we find that for nearly two thousand years before the Christian religion, the same beliefs were held by the Egyptians as have been held for the last nineteen hundred years by Christians.[1] The history of Christianity shows how the beliefs regarding the man Jesus went through the same theological change as did those held about Osiris. These, as regards Jesus, culminated in Nicaea in A.D. 325 under the influence

---

[1] The authorities of the British Museum have compiled three interesting brochures entitled *The Book of the Dead*, *The Babylonian story of the Deluge*, *The Babylonian Legends of the Creation*, which give photographs of the original Babylonian tablets and illustrations of Egyptian art, as well as word for word translations from the originals.

of the prelates of Alexandria, who managed to bring the theology of Egypt into the doctrines of the new religion. Thus Egypt added its quota to the total of ideas which resulted in Christianity as we now know it.

Christianity, as shown in *The Rock of Truth*, is a combination of Judaic, Babylonian, Egyptian, Greek and Mithraic theology, as these five religions contributed to make Christianity what it became in the 4th century. In Alexandria, at the commencement of the Christian era, was the world's greatest theological school. There all the various religious beliefs centred. In this atmosphere Christianity was nurtured to become the official religion of Rome at Nicaea three hundred years later, it having accumulated during this time something from all five of the religions mentioned. This medley of beliefs became orthodox at Nicaea under the name of Christianity, to receive the backing of the Emperor Constantine and become the State religion of the Roman Empire.

When Egypt was supreme, its gods were the overruling world deities, and so also were the gods of Babylon, Greece and Rome when each in turn ruled the then known world. The greatest nations had the greatest and most powerful gods, and each god promised through his faithful priests happiness hereafter to all who abjectly bowed down and worshipped him. To those who would not, and disobeyed his priests, he threatened eternal punishment. Everything would be forgiven, all the crimes on earth would be pardoned so long as man did not commit the greatest crime of all—that of disbelieving in the existence and commands of his country's deity, and that a sacrifice had been made on his behalf by one of the gods or some other scape-goat, man or animal.

Just as each nation had its gods whom it supplicated and worshipped, so also it had one or more devils, the bad gods whom it feared; but these devils were much superior to the gods, though they were termed fallen gods. They were more humane, and we do not find them giving instructions which would disgrace a savage, such as we are told were given by the gods the people worshipped. In the Old Testament we find the god of the Jews giving his chosen people the most barbarous and savage instructions as to how they should deal with their enemies.

Nowhere is it found that the devils ever gave such instructions to mankind. It was always the gods who brought about famine, pestilence and war. The devils of the past were much more respectable in their behaviour. The gods were always cruel, treacherous, cunning and vain in the extreme. No devil is reported as having drowned everyone with the exception of eight people.

All these ideas concerning gods and devils occurred in the mind of man, as man made god in his own image, and the more cruel man was the more cruel was his god. The Jews were cruel and Jehovah was likewise cruel.

The Greeks imagined their gods as men of perfect Greek stature, and Jupiter, the supreme deity of the Romans, is depicted by them as an exemplary citizen. The gods of the Egyptians resembled the Egyptians themselves, dignified and placid, and in the northern countries they were clad in warm clothing. Where the country was mountainous and rocky they had hammers with which they broke the mountains in pieces. The gods of the Africans had curly hair and black skins, those of the Chinese had yellow skins and almond-shaped eyes, and the Semites could not imagine a god without a beard. To those masters of the heavens men built altars, shrines and temples. They reddened their altars with the blood of their dearest. Nothing could be done without consulting the gods, whose opinions were given through their authorised priests.

These priests were at times magicians, and bewildered the people with their magic and cunning. In Egypt a visitor today will be shown a recess where in the old days a priest sat. This communicated with the mouth of a crocodile of stone, through which the priest spoke. When the people wanted to know the will of the gods they knelt before the beast in abject wonder because it could speak.

In Rome the priests bewildered and mystified the people by employing steam and hydraulic power to create illusions. Excavations have revealed such aids to this imposture. Steam pipes leading to secret recesses under the images of the gods have been disclosed, and frescoes have been found picturing balloons (probably filled with hot air) floating over the heads of the gods. Evidently these were manipulated in such a way as to cause the people to think that they were in contact with the supernatural.

A learned contributor to an old edition of *Chambers' Encyclopedia* writes that

The hold which the secrecy of these meetings, together with their extraordinary worship, must naturally have taken upon minds, more fresh and childlike than our advanced age can boast of, was increased by all the mechanical contrivances of the effects of light and sound which the priests could command. Mysterious voices were heard singing, whispering and sighing all round; lights gleamed in manifold colours from above and below, figures appeared and disappeared. All the arts were taxed to the very utmost to make these performances (the nearest approach to which in this country is furnished by transformation scenes, or sensation dramas in general) as attractive and profitable to the priests as could be.

The foregoing devices, however, must not be attributed to the Greeks in the days of their splendour, as it is generally believed that in the Greek mystery temples genuine psychic phenomena occurred. Their imitation elsewhere was effected by trickery so as to keep up the old traditions. There is little doubt that what later was the result of fraud was originally genuine psychic phenomena. The Vedic mysteries of India, the Mithraic of Persia and those of the Chaldeans, Egyptians and Greeks doubtless commenced with genuine psychic phenomena, but degenerated, through the weakness of human nature, to fraudulent imitations, when the psychic power was lacking. As one could always rely on producing the imitation, and not always on obtaining the genuine phenomena, the imitation took the place of the genuine, the people being too ignorant to appreciate the difference.

Just as the origin of Christianity can be traced back to psychic phenomena, so can the beginning of other religions be likewise ascribed. From the knowledge we now have it seems evident that these sporadic revelations from the other world were responsible for the origin of all the other world religions, which became debased through the fraudulent practices of the priests.

Moreover, out of the genuine phenomena developed what we now call magic. We have an example of this in the story of the wonderful performances of Moses before the Egyptian priests. To Moses genuine phenomena are attributed to the help of the god of Israel, but, in the case of the Egyptian priests, their performance is put down to magic. If the writer had been an Egyptian it would have been the other way round.

The origin of magic is therefore found in psychic phenomena, and we have even in our day magicians duplicating by illusion what occurs in the séance room. Some leading magicians have nevertheless been forced to accept the reality of psychic phenomena because they find that they cannot duplicate them in every instance. This has brought them to the position that the only other explanation must be one of a supernormal nature.

As man became more civilised so did his gods, the Old Testament, for instance, being just a record of the mental development of the Hebrews, their advance in social, political and religious wisdom being noticeable as their experience accumulated. Man cannot conceive the Infinite other than as his mind is capable of so doing. No matter to what race he belongs, or how high his culture, the power that rules the universe is always imagined according to the capacity of each individual mind. As his mentality develops so does his religion, and the freer it is of superstitious beliefs the more will philosophy take the place of supernatural religion.

Every world religion without exception has the same roots extending back to sun worship, the same ideas, the same aspirations, hopes and fears, the same kind of gods, the same kind of teachings, the same mistakes, the same follies, and the same priesthood. Be it under the name of Christian, Hindu, or Mohammedan, supernatural religion today still stands for the worship of imaginary beings who delight in prayers and supplications, they having decreed that the only road to heaven is through the gates of belief in that particular religion of which they are the patron gods. Though each has brought comfort, consolation and happiness to untold millions throughout the world, yet one and all have been used to support what is cruel in human nature.

I can imagine the misery of the dying victims lying on the smoking altars, encircled by priests prostrating themselves before some imaginary tyrant who demanded this sacrifice or burnt offering. I see the cromlechs, the stonehenges and the broken altars, which still remain as relics of this ghastly practice of human sacrifice. Let our minds travel where they will, to Mexico or Peru, Assyria or Palestine, into Persia or India, and we always find the same dreadful story in the monuments and records of our savage ancestors. It is difficult to imagine the depraved state of the human mind during those primitive ages, which were followed, after human sacrifice had been abandoned, by the torture, imprisonment and burning of the thinkers and all who tried to make the world a better and happier place for humanity.

In every department of life, except that of orthodox religion, the ideas of the people throughout the world have advanced. Supernatural religion, however, still professes the same beliefs as prevailed in the days of savagery. Christianity is based on sacrifice and the shedding of blood, without which we are told there is no remission of sins. Christianity is based on this vicarious atonement, this offering up of a sacrifice to satisfy the wrath of God. This barbarous idea is derived from the practices and beliefs of our ignorant and savage ancestors, and yet, in this so-called enlightened age, it remains the basis of the Christian creed.

In commerce, science, politics, medicine, navigation and transport, and in every other direction, mankind has advanced enormously since the days of primitive man. Theology alone stands still; theology still preaches the religion of the savage. The theological mind can think only of the past, it can worship only the gods of the past and their inspired writings.

What stands for religion today differs little from what it has stood for right back into antiquity. Each tribe and nation had its own particular gods, possessing the weaknesses and passions, as well as the good qualities, of the people who imagined them. We read of the Israelites carrying out the cruel and barbarous laws of Jehovah, as given by his priests. We learn of the Assyrians singing praises to Rimmon and Anu the illustrious, of the Chaldeans making their sacrifices to Bel, the Hindus to Brahma and Vishnu, and the Egyptians to Rā. We find the Greeks erecting gorgeous temples to Zeus and Athena, the Romans likewise honouring Jupiter and Bacchus, and the

Christians living in hovels yet building magnificent temples to Christ as God. We look back and see the wealth of the world sacrificed to those imaginary creations. History teaches us that the Christian Church has grown rich and powerful on the simplicity of its supporters.

This long night of ignorance has been lightened from time to time by teachers who rose above the level of their contemporaries. These more enlightened ones preached that love for, and service to, mankind, not sacrifice, appealed to God, who had no particular nation on which he showered his favours. The ignorant multitudes spurned most of these teachers, murdered them, and afterwards worshipped at their graves, twisting in turn their words and sayings into the very dogmas against which they had protested. So the teacher Jesus is worshipped as the god-man Christ, and the simple Gautama as the god-man Buddha, their distorted sayings being made the foundation of a priesthood, a caste they so freely condemned.

Why, it may be asked, is this possible? Because it is the nature of ignorance to think of God in the form of man, who demands obedience and flattery, with desires which can be expressed only in certain cast-iron words. Only when man becomes intelligent can he stand erect, refusing to bow the knee to false creations of the mind. Just as the intelligent individual does not himself wish to be worshipped and be the master of slaves, so he cannot conceive his God to be one who delights in worship, sacrifice and self-abnegation.

Were all the world temples and churches therefore

built in vain? Were all the sacrifices of the past instituted for no purpose whatever? Assuredly not. They met the innermost craving of man's soul that there is something, some power, greater than himself in the universe. Only vaguely did the worshipper realise that he himself was part of this directing intelligence, this omnipotent, omniscient, omnipresent Mind, and that, like a magnet, it was slowly drawing him over the ages to a true realisation of his destiny and his relationship to it, the Divine Mind of the Universe. The fact that he is part of this Cosmic Mind made him long and yearn to get into greater harmony with it.

All the religions of the past are historically false and so also are their holy books and relics. Their creeds and dogmas are but the imaginations of the mind, though running through them is an underlying truth which is nearly obliterated by the false. These errors which man received in exchange for the produce of his toil have nevertheless accomplished a great purpose. They have made it possible for humanity, ignorant of its destiny, to live in mental peace, and they have made it possible for mankind to face death. Why were these crutches needed? Because man is an etheric being, his real home is not on earth, but in Etheria, as "here have we no continuing city, but we seek one to come". (*Hebrews* xiii, 14.)

Early man's ideas of God, of prayer and of the after-life were very crude. He made his gods in his own image, and treated them as if they were to be appeased by supplications and prayer. He thought that if he asked in the prescribed manner his desires would be granted. This religious sense, which mankind has apart from the animals, is one outstanding difference between the two creations. Though we all have our animal ancestry, yet the superiority of even the lowest type of man is appreciable in comparison with the animal. That which is termed the religious sense is one of the most striking differences between man and animal, and it is in every human being, though in some it is developed much more than in others.

This religious sense, however, has its limitations. For this reason one or more gods are imagined in the likeness of man. No man has the capacity to think of something he has not some way or other experienced on earth. He cannot create in his imagination either a god or another world that has not some resemblance to things seen on earth. Man has the capacity to combine, to add together, to take away from, to divide. In his imagination he can build mind images of his own creations, but all are limited to his personal experience. No one can think of a colour, sound or taste he has not experienced. No one can think of a shape or form that does not resemble a shape or a form on earth. We can imagine greater and smaller things than we have experienced, but still they are based on our earth experiences of colour, taste, sound and form.

The writer of the first chapter of the book of *Genesis* stated that God[1] made man in his own image, but it would be more correct to say that man made God in his own image. The God of the savage is a savage God. The after-life of the savage is a happy hunting-ground. If this belief had developed along these lines, how happy the people on earth would have

---

[1] The correct translation is "the gods".

been! The fear of hell, which has been the torment of many sensitive minds, would never have developed. Unfortunately our ancestors were very cruel, and lust and hatred were the companions of love and kindness.

The good gods lived in some good place beyond, but, as nature is both kind and cruel, it was natural that evil gods had to be imagined as well, and they required a habitation. The heavens above were reserved for the good, and hell below for the bad. When priest-craft came into being the good were the people who supported the Church of the time and consequently went to heaven, and those who were not orthodox, and thought for themselves, were consigned to hell. As man left the open spaces, the forests and the fields, and came to live in towns, the happy hunting-ground became a new Jerusalem, a new Athens or Rome, a city paved with gold.

In time the gods of our ancestors, and likewise the priests, became fewer until today, in most civilised countries, the number of priests compared with the population is less than ever it was. This is due to our being in the scientific age, and it is most noticeable in Protestant countries, but in Roman Catholic countries priests, monks and nuns are still numerous and the people are poorer in consequence. We have still to reach the time when the people will be intelligent enough not to require priests, and when that day comes they will have ceased to worship a god in human form.

Some day they will realise that Infinite Intelligence, or the Cosmic Mind of the Universe, is not a personal god with the passions of humanity, but the great directing and controlling influence of the universe.

As knowledge increases so will fade away the belief in a personal god or a trinity of personal gods, in miracles, and anything contrary to nature. When people cease conceiving a personal god, they will no longer worship as they do at present and carpet the floors of the churches with their knees. Just as the belief in a personal devil has vanished from the minds of intelligent people, so will depart the idea of a personal god in the likeness of man.

Contemplation of the divine in nature will then take the place of worship. When all reach this stage the occupation of the theologian will have ceased, and we shall have passed through and left behind the age of superstition. This will come about through our increasing in physical and psychic knowledge, by our advance in wisdom, and our increased appreciation of the unseen world around us, which will bring home to everyone the true meaning of religion.

Surely what must strike every intelligent man and woman is the extreme simplicity and childishness of most people, even amongst the so-called educated. In Protestant countries their religious orbit is studded round with a few well-chosen Biblical texts which specially appeal to them. All argument, everything debatable, finds an answer in an appropriate quotation which to them is final. The texts expressing quite the contrary are ignored. Who wrote their quotations, when they were written, what caused them to be written, and whether they have been correctly recorded over the centuries since they were composed, is never considered. To those simple minds they came from God by means of his chosen scribes.

In Roman Catholic countries equal simplicity is

to be observed. Instead of a holy book which Protestants worship, we find a holy church full of images, pictures, jewels and relics which are worshipped and revered. I have attended many religious services in various parts of the world, and the same simple minds of the worshippers are noticeable everywhere. East or west, north or south the mentality is similar—one which accepts and never reasons, believes and never doubts.

I have stood watching the faithful solemnly kissing the toe of a Pagan statue of Jupiter, in Saint Peter's at Rome, which they accept as a representation of the apostle Peter because the priests have told them it is so. The toe of the right foot has been kissed so frequently that all resemblance to a toe has disappeared. I have seen them worship dolls, dressed in beautiful silks, lace and priceless jewels, as images of the infant Jesus. I have observed the devout bow down before a piece of wood they believed was part of the cross on which Jesus suffered. I have seen what I was told were the footprints of Saint Peter when he visited Rome, and also his tomb, a gorgeous shrine in which it is believed his body lies buried, but for which claim there is not an iota of evidence.

I have wandered round the catacombs in Rome, those early Christian places of burial, and heard the priests tell, and seen the people accept, how on the last day the dead bodies of those early Christians (which have now become dust, have mingled with the soil, and become part of the vegetation, and in turn part of other living bodies) will all come together again and become the habitation of the spirits which once used them as earthly vehicles.

I have witnessed the veneration of the people for the Pope, how they bowed down and worshipped him. I have heard him claim to be the chosen representative of Christ on earth. I have stood before him in the Vatican Palace to receive his blessing, while he was seated on his throne surrounded by soldiers dressed in medieval uniforms, armed with the weapons of the Middle Ages—battleaxes, spears and lances. Around me was all the pomp and ceremony the mind of man could imagine. About me everywhere was fabulous wealth in the form of magnificent statues, priceless marbles, pictures, golden, silver and bronze ornaments.

Go where you will, travel anywhere on earth, and you find the same accumulation of wealth, the same worship of the material in the name of religion by all the religious organisations representing the world's orthodox faiths. In Burma's picturesque pagodas, in India's temples and shrines, images and relics, vestments, jewels and all that is precious are gathered together to satisfy mankind's passion for the worship of the unknown God in material form. In Protestant countries we find the same worship of the material, and the same simplicity of the worshippers is apparent but in a different form.

To the ignorant what is new never appeals. It is the old that incites worship. An old book, an old piece of wood, or an ancient image receives from the faithful much more reverence than objective proof that we survive death. One hundred thousand pounds has been paid to Russia for an old book known as the *Codex Sinaiticus*. It is not of the least value to anyone because few can read it. It tells us nothing of importance. If it were translated, the orthodox, many of whom have helped to pay for it by their church collections, would be terribly shocked because it greatly differs from the books of our Bible, of which it is supposed to be a 5th-century copy of previous early copies of other early copies. It is not the original of the New Testament, as many think it is, and we shall find in the next chapter that very little is known about the original books comprising the New Testament.

Nevertheless £100,000 was paid for this old relic, and people stand before it in the British Museum and gaze at it in veneration, just as they look at the *Codex Vaticanus*, another 5th-century copy which is housed in the Vatican in Rome. These so-called priceless relics, the gorgeous churches, temples and pagodas excite wonder and reverence, which the world's religious organisations encourage, but they add nothing to the well-being of mankind.

They doubtless give comfort to the uneducated, but if the money spent on their maintenance and protection were used for the purpose of developing the minds of the people, for making them intelligent, thoughtful and logical, how much wiser and prosperous mankind would become. If the £100,000 used for the purchase of the *Codex Sinaiticus* had been devoted to investigating and developing mediums, what an advance would have been made in our knowledge of our psychic make-up and of the after-life! If the money spent in maintaining places of worship and priests throughout the world were devoted to the mental development of the community, to teaching them to think correctly, how quickly the truths and findings of Spiritualism would be accepted, and how quickly the people would grow in knowledge and wisdom!

The reason these truths are becoming accepted so slowly is not for want of evidence, which is already more than ample, but for want of the people being trained and educated to enable them to accept what is real and true, and leave aside what is false. Their minds are not capable of accepting the truth, and so long as priest-craft has any say in the matter they never will be. Priest-craft hangs like a pall over the mental world, and the rays of intelligence can only slowly pierce the gloom.

Over the last three hundred years the rays have been strengthening, and each year their strength increases. The age of superstition is still with us, but the sun of truth is more and more breaking through the mist of ignorance, so much so that some day the world will rejoice in the full light of positive knowledge which will take the place of blind faith.

CHAPTER III.

THE EVOLUTION OF CHRISTIANITY.

In the last chapter I considered the origin of the belief in one or more personal gods, the origin of sacrifice, rites and ceremonials, and the cause behind prayer and worship, all of which combine to make up orthodox religion, under whatever name it is known. As, however, most of the readers of this book were born and brought up in the Christian faith, it is not out of place to devote a chapter exclusively to the basis for Christianity, under which name all its beliefs and acts are grouped.

The forms, ceremonies, worship and prayer of all peoples are much the same, except that their gods are called by different names, and, in the case of saviour-gods, they were supposed to have lived on earth at different times. Thus the various schemes of salvation were believed to have been revealed to different nations by different gods, and this revelation became incorporated in different books, in different ways, in different languages, and at different dates.

What, however, interests Christendom is the Christian religion. Christians agree that all the other religions are founded on error, based on superstition, and that only Christians have the true revelation. This being so, there is no need to discuss all the other world religions. Let us then examine the Christian faith, probe its foundations, and find if its assertions and beliefs rest on a solid foundation, or if, like those of all the other world religions, they are based on sand.

Let us find the reason for the arrogant assertion which expresses the beliefs of Protestants and Catholics alike that

> Whosoever will be saved, before all things it is necessary that he hold the Catholic faith, which faith except everyone do keep whole and undefiled, without doubt he shall perish everlastingly.

A religion making such a tremendous assertion and such a fearful threat, the worst that man can make to man, must surely be based on a foundation so firm that its dogmas and doctrines are absolutely unchallengeable. If they are not, then to raise such an alarm is the most dreadful crime it is possible to perpetrate, and all those who support the organisation which is guilty of such a criminal offence are also in a measure guilty.

That the fundamentals of Christianity, as contained in the creeds of the Christian Church, are accepted by the Church authorities was emphasised only a few months ago by the archbishops and bishops of the Church of England. So they are still adhered to, and Christians of a more tolerant outlook need not charge me with whipping a dead horse. The Christian creeds cannot be abandoned by the Christian Church. If they ever are, Christianity will immediately collapse. On creeds it was founded, on creeds it was maintained, and on creeds it is today sustained and will be preserved until its final extinction by apathy and neglect.

Let us now examine the basis of Christianity, and follow its evolution from its earliest days until it became a full-fledged State religion, keeping always in mind its terrible threats and its uncompromising assertions.

In *The Rock of Truth* I devoted a considerable amount of space to tracing the beliefs of all religions, Christianity included, to sun worship. Therein I showed that the beliefs held by the various world religions could be traced back to this source, and that most of the ceremonials and rites originated in sun worship. I also explained how one religion developed out of one or more earlier religions, that each new religion was the child of those preceding it, and that Christianity was only another name for an accumulation of beliefs taken from the religions of Judea, Babylon, Egypt, Greece and Rome.

I tried also to show that Alexandria in Egypt was the centre where Christianity evolved, as there gathered from all parts theological students who attended its school of theology, the greatest of its day. I then proceeded to explain how Paul became imbued with the ideas of this school of thought, and thus laid the foundation for the religion called Christianity, which was born a fully-developed child at the Council of Nicaea in A.D. 325, under the patronage of the Emperor Constantine, with all the backing of Imperial Rome behind it.

Though all religions have common parents, each has an individual origin, an individual seed, round which has grown the beliefs, ceremonials and rites common to all. To each is attributed a founder, a god-man, who is believed to have propounded the doctrines, instituted the ceremonies and rites of that religion. That these are similar in all religions is true, but it is also true that each religion believes in an individual founder, who was the cause behind the various effects which followed his life on earth.

To find the source of Christianity one must therefore find Jesus, not Christ, a name adopted later. If Jesus had never lived on earth there would have been no Paul. If there had been no Paul there would have been no Christ. Without Christ there would have been no Christianity. Jesus was behind Paul, just as Paul was behind Christianity. Can Jesus be found? That is the great question and one that has exercised the thoughts of scholars from the time of Erasmus (1466–1536), who was the first to study the Bible in an intelligent and thoughtful manner. He was the father of what is today termed the School of Higher Criticism, being the first to attempt to reach a better understanding of the documents comprising the New Testament, by comparing all the old manuscripts he could obtain. This work he carried through against the strong opposition of the Church, which, from his time onwards, has opposed all such methods of intelligent study.

An immense amount of time and thought, since the time of Erasmus, has been devoted to this question. It has attracted scholars by the hundreds not only in this country, but in the United States of America, in Germany and France. It has been a magnet, which has drawn earnest and thoughtful men into the enquiry, the quest for the historical Jesus. The literature on the subject is consequently immense, so great in fact that it is impossible for any individual to cover the entire ground which has been explored.[1]

Bit by bit, however, the search has narrowed, and gradually scholars are approaching unanimity on certain definite conclusions. These conclusions are, firstly, that a man named Jesus did live about the time commonly accepted, that he was probably born some years prior to 4 B.C., as Herod died in that year. Secondly, it is agreed that nothing is known of his life until he was about thirty years of age, that for just under two years he wandered about a narrow strip of country in Palestine, preaching and healing. The sayings attributed to him can be traced to earlier teachers or documents, and there is no evidence that he ever said them. Finally he was arrested and slain by the authorities.[2]

Five names are associated with fundamental changes in the world of thought, Krishna, Buddha, Confucius, Socrates and Jesus, and yet none of these men left any writings of their own, their thoughts being left to later generations to record. Consequently, to find the historical Jesus it is necessary to discover one or more trustworthy documents, and therein lies the difficulty. If there is no document to be trusted, everything resolves itself into mist and cloud. To find the truth about an event of the past we must have a trustworthy written document. Tradition is of no value. A document which is

---

[1] For those who wish to pursue this study further I would recommend *Jesus Christ, an Historical Outline*, and *The Earliest Sources for the life of Jesus*, both by F. C. Burkitt; *The Four Gospels, a study of origin*, by B. H. Streeter; *Jesus*, by Bultmann; *The Historical Christ*, and *Myth, Magic and Morals*, both by F. C. Conybeare.

[2] Much of the elaboration surrounding the story of the crucifixion undoubtedly came from Babylon where the same story was told about the god Bel. For further details see *The Rock of Truth* and *The Psychic Stream*.

genuine, and not a forgery, that has survived the course of time, without the copyists having added to it, or taken from it, must be discovered. Otherwise we can obtain no record of the event which is of any value.

It must be obvious to anyone that no original document relating to the life of Jesus has survived. Do we, however, know of any faithful copies of an original document or documents relating to his life? No, we do not, as none exist.

Jesus is not an historical character, and the critics who assert that he never lived are logical, up to a point. Those who take up this line of thought, however, overlook two very important matters, the first and most important being that the Christian cult did start nineteen hundred years ago. Therefore someone must have started it, and it is an historical fact that in the first Christian century this someone had followers who believed that this person lived and died. The second point is the fact that Paul is accepted as an historical character, and that some of his writings or epistles are accepted as more or less genuine.

The Gospel records are not considered historical records. The earliest, namely *Mark*, originated in simple form, about the year 70. *Luke* likewise began between the years 80 and 95, and *Matthew* about the year 100. The Gospel according to *John*, which came into existence about 110, is considered to be of so little veridical value that is not worth discussing. Its contents are believed to be based largely on the imagination of the writer.

In his recently published translation of the Gospels from the Aramaic Eastern Version, Dr. George M.

Lamsa, the Aramaic scholar, points out in his introduction that very many errors have been handed down in the Western Version owing to mistranslation. Because of its small vocabulary, Aramaic being one of the world's most ancient languages, the same words have often from six to seven different meanings.

Moreover the misplacement of a dot over a word by the copyist entirely altered its meaning. This was done to such an extent that the meaning the original writer intended to convey was misunderstood by the first translators of the original Aramaic into Greek, who have throughout mistranslated the meaning of the original sayings and stories. This has been done to such an extent that in places the translation, on which the Christian Church has always relied, has distorted the original meaning beyond all recognition. In the light of modern knowledge nothing recorded in the Gospels should be taken seriously, or be attributed to Jesus or his disciples.

The first three gospels, termed Synoptic, are believed to be copies of another or other documents of earlier date, and scholars, by a careful study of these three gospels, have been at great trouble to find this common source. This original does not now exist, but all are agreed that it once existed, and that from it the first three gospels slowly grew in the course of years to what they are today.

I shall now consider the bases for Christianity in the correct order. The first is the evidence of Paul. The opinion of Paul is taken first, as this is the earliest evidence we have of Jesus, his writings being about a generation earlier than the Gospel of *Mark*. Here surely we should find some details of the life of Jesus.

Though he knew him not, yet he was a contemporary and was acquainted with Peter, James and John. He, however, tells us next to nothing.

Paul mentions that "we preach Christ crucified", that Jesus was naturally born of the seed of David, thus accepting a human father, and that Jesus was a Jew, sharing human weaknesses and infirmities. This is all that this enthusiast for the cause thinks necessary to tell the Gentiles about the earth life of Jesus, who, according to Paul, died for our sins and thus became the Christ.

Now to get an explanation of this extraordinary neglect on the part of Paul to provide his readers with any particulars of Jesus, we must bear this in mind or confusion will follow. There is behind everything in the gospels and epistles the natural human Jesus, and intertwined with him is the theological Christ, brought into being by the enthusiasm of Paul.

Let us see how it all developed. Paul, as Saul, persecuted the early followers of Jesus. Then on that fateful day going to Damascus he had what he termed a heavenly vision which changed his entire life, and laid the seed for his belief in Jesus being the crucified Saviour of humanity, which belief has profoundly affected the course of history and the evolution of a large part of the human race.

Such an event must surely be one of the greatest in history, because it had a tremendous effect on the lives of all future generations of a large section of the human race. It was not unique, as such experiences are recorded as happening before that time and since, especially of recent years. Its importance rests on the consequences which followed the event.

Paul, as I say, had a vision and heard a voice which said "Saul, Saul, why persecutest thou me?" to which he replied "Who art thou, Lord?" and the reply came back "I am Jesus whom thou persecutest." Whether it was Jesus or not no one can say. There is no evidence that it was, but Paul accepted it without question. Moreover it changed his entire life, which burned from that time onwards with the fierce heat of missionary zeal. He never claims to have seen Jesus in the flesh, and yet this incident, reported in the *Acts of the Apostles*, is referred to by him in a general way on various occasions in his epistles. Though we need not accept the details as accurate, a supernormal occurrence seems to have taken place which so changed his outlook that he sacrificed everything to proclaim a theological dogma which he built around this experience.

Paul was evidently strongly psychic, and what we would term clairvoyant, as he recalls various supernormal experiences, but this one on the road to Damascus was probably his first as he never mentions any before this event. I have already stated in the previous chapter that in those days an apparition was looked on as a god, and Paul doubtless accepted the current view without question. The death of Jesus had occurred but recently; he was aware of it, and may have heard that others who knew him had seen him in his etheric body after death. As Paul was persecuting the followers of Jesus, the latter must have been in his mind. In his speech before King Agrippa, Paul stated that he saw a vision or what we would term nowadays an apparition. This he accepted as Jesus in his etheric body, and after considering the matter he came to the conclusion that as Jesus had the power to appear after death he must be a god.

Why such a jump from the natural to the supernatural? There can be only one answer, which is that Paul naturally accepted the opinion of his age that an apparition was a god. In those days the natural and the supernatural were closely intertwined, and nothing was known about the laws of nature. Everything inexplicable was attributed to a god.

After this the earth-life of Jesus mattered nothing to Paul. The revelation had come to him, and on him Jesus had cast his mantle. He would not desert the cause for which he now believed Jesus had died. So we can imagine that he remembered his days in Tarsus where another saviour-god, Dionysus, was worshipped. Was Jesus not the beloved Dionysus once more returned to earth to fulfil his mission and redeem mankind? Consequently, to Paul the death of Jesus is everything, and his life on earth of little importance. So he makes little or no reference, in his letters to his converts, to what Jesus said or did and dwells unceasingly on his death.

Paul's writings so encompass what was believed about the Greek saviour-god Dionysus, that it is evident he came to believe Jesus to be none other than this god returned to earth a second time. Dionysus, like Jesus, was believed to have performed wonderful deeds when on earth—miracles, they were called— and, moreover, Dionysus was the god of Tarsus, Paul's home town. So we need not be surprised that Paul knew much about the beliefs surrounding this famous Greek god, and that he attached to Jesus some of the mystical phraseology connected with the worship of Dionysus, the heavenly being, born on earth to a virgin impregnated by Zeus, who suffered and died for mankind, a divine creation from all eternity who had humbled himself to save humanity. Dionysus was represented by his statues as radiant, triumphant and glorious, and above his head were the words "I am Life, Death and Resurrection, I hold the winged crown", the crown which Paul believed he would receive at the end of his career from him he called the Christ, who had become to him the symbol of the resurrection and the life.

Paul's experience is not unique. Many have had similar experiences. Others besides Paul have had their lives changed by seeing an apparition which they termed Christ. I know several devout people who are clairvoyant, and I have heard of others, who are convinced that they have seen Christ. I know of some who believe that they are continually guided by Christ. It is noticeable that the word they use in connection with these apparitions is always Christ, never Jesus, which shows the influence Paul's experience has had on their minds.

Though I have pointed out to them that Christ is a name to denote a theological dogma, yet they are firmly convinced that they have seen a god, and are in touch with a god. Reason seems not to influence them, as they never seem to wonder how they can be so sure of whom they have seen, having never seen the being in the flesh. Like Paul, again, the flesh being means nothing to them; it is the shining apparition which can be none other than a god.

Just as my friends today believe that they have seen a god, whom they call Christ, so also did Paul, whose mind was doubtless imbued with the belief in the coming of a Messiah, a Hebrew word meaning Christ. It would be well if these clairvoyant people, who jump to such a tremendous assumption without any evidence whatever, would be more realistic and admit that they had seen only an etheric being, a man or woman of the other world. Etherians, clothed in radiant light, can show themselves to clairvoyants on earth, and what to the orthodox seems a special revelation by a god, whom Christians term Christ, is a common enough experience with clairvoyants, and accepted by Spiritualists as quite a natural event. Spiritualists would certainly never think of relating it to the supernatural, as to them the supernatural does not exist—only the supernormal.

All apparitions are today understood by Spiritualists to be the return to earth vibrations of human beings like ourselves, who have died, and whose faster vibrations affect the clairvoyant as radiant light. Hundreds of times have I heard clairvoyants describe beings in radiant light who gave their names and messages to their friends on earth. Nowadays, however, only those imbued with the ideas of Paul would look upon them as gods and build on those experiences theological doctrines such as Paul did, the reason being that we now know more about Etheria, its inhabitants, and their visits to earth, than did Paul.

After his conversion, or psychic experience, Paul retired to Arabia, to think out this wonderful mission he believed had been entrusted to him. He was an educated man, and doubtless knew something of the various saviours of the past, as in Tarsus, his home, which was a great seat of learning, lived numerous

Pagans. Gamaliel, his teacher, had surely also taught him the theological beliefs expounded in Alexandria, including the belief in the Christos, the coming world-saviour.

Saint John's Gospel represents the views which developed out of Paul's belief that Jesus was the Christ or Logos, and that is why the doctrines of that gospel vary so much from those of the synoptic gospels which more nearly represented, before the miraculous element was added, the opinions of the disciples. Saint John's Gospel and the Epistles of Paul have much more in common, and the reason is that in Alexandria, where Greek thought predominated, the seed was produced which Paul planted. Paul's ideas and beliefs came from Alexandria.

Philo, the Alexandrian Jew, used many expressions in his writings similar to those used by Paul and the writer of Saint John's Gospel, but without any reference to Jesus. In Philo's day the Alexandrian theory of the Logos or Christos was well known and discussed by the theologically-minded. This school of thought contained all the speculations, philosophic and mystical, which were then current, and were known under the name Hellenistic. What Paul did was to make use of them. No need, said he, to speculate further; the Logos, the Christos, has come and died, and laid on me the duty of proclaiming this gospel of glad tidings to the world.

Thus the school of Alexandria provided Paul with his doctrine, and so at Alexandria what became Christianity was conceived from the inflow of the ideas centering round the other world religions. There they ripened and produced the basis for the religion which came to be known as Christianity. There also the Christian Trinity was conceived, the Neo-Platonists assuming the existence of three gods, of which the Logos was one. Later, the Trinity was developed by the Greek-Egyptian Athanasius in the 4th century into a definite statute of Christian belief. Alexandria was the connecting link between Judaic-Hellenic philosophy and the Egyptian religion, with its love for the mystical trinity of gods which were but one, a trinity in unity.

Many deeply religious Pagans and Jews in Paul's day were speculating about the Messiah, the Christos, or the Logos. Forty years before the birth of Jesus, Virgil foretold the coming of the Christ and how the golden age would begin on earth, when war, poverty and hardship would disappear and the whole world would be ruled by equity, love and justice. The question in Paul's day was whether the redemption of man would be achieved by the expiatory sacrifice of a redeemer, or, on the other hand, whether redemption would be achieved through knowledge of God's plan of salvation (Gnosis) brought to earth by the coming of a Christ, the Son of God. This coming Christ was termed the Word of God (Logos) and Wisdom (Sophia). He would be killed by the supernatural powers opposed to God, not as a sacrifice, but because they foresaw that their influence over mankind was about to be terminated.

Nowhere in the Hebrew Book of the Law, now known as the Old Testament, is the Messiah referred to as one with God or part of God, as Christianity now claims for Jesus. In fact, except for rare occasions, Jehovah reigned supreme. All other gods were wicked impostors, and when the Hebrews deserted him from time to time to worship Baal (Bel), the Babylonian saviour-god, he was very wrathful. Here indeed is a strange paradox. Jehovah denounces Baal, the second member of the Babylonian trinity, as he had no use for trinities, there being only one God who created and sustained the heavens and the earth, and that was Jehovah. Nevertheless, if the Christian doctrine be true, Jehovah at this time was the father-god of a trinity of gods, because the Christian trinity is not limited to the Christian era and is claimed to have been from all time. Why then did Jehovah denounce the belief in a trinity of gods, a doctrine which was to become the central belief in the coming Christian faith, about which he must have been aware if what is claimed for him is true?

Nevertheless, as time went on, and because of the strong Greek influence over the Jews which took place in the 2nd century B.C., the belief grew in strength that Jehovah would some day reveal himself through a Messiah or Christ, and the study of the writings of Philo, the famous Alexandrian Jewish theologian, makes clear how Paul's doctrine was in no way new. Paul only used the speculations of Alexandrian thought and attributed these to Jesus, just as at a later date, from the same source, came the adoration and sanctification of his mother, which developed from the cult of the Egyptian goddess Isis with Horus her child nestled in her arms.

Down the ages Messiahs have come and gone. Mithra was the Christ of the Persians, and Osiris the Christ of the Egyptians. What is today called the "Christ spirit" was believed to have animated great religious teachers from time to time, but now we know that these men became great because of their reappearance after death, when it was thought that their suffering at the hands of the priests, and their reappearance, had broken the curse of death to open up heaven to mankind. So it was believed that after long intervals the "Christ spirit" returned to earth, a belief that originated in sun worship, the sun returning each morning after its disappearance, to be hailed as the saviour of the world.

Philo represented this school of thought, which was surely known to Paul. Philo was born in Alexandria about 25 B.C. He is recognised as the most important exponent of philosophic thought of his day, which was a combination taken from that of Greece and Judea and is known as Alexandrian, because in Alexandria it reached its highest development. Philo's philosophy was founded on the Hebrew Law, Plato, Pythagoras and the philosophy of the Stoics, but he absorbed the teachings of the latter so thoroughly that he is regarded rather as a Greek than a Jewish philosopher. His writings can briefly be summarised as follows.

Philo attributes to God absolute sovereignty over the world, to be worshipped, not as an individual, but as representing the essence of perfection, goodness, truth and purity. God fills and encompasses all things with his being. God is made manifest to mankind by divine forces which are identical with the Demons (spirits) of the Greeks and the Angels of the Jews. These are today called Spirits of the Dead, and to Philo they were messengers of God to earth.

God, to Philo, is revealed to man by what he calls

ideas, the totality of which is the Reason of God. Philo regards these as personified in the Logos which is the highest mediator between God and the world, the first-born son of God, the archangel who is the vehicle of all revelation, and the High Priest who stands before God on behalf of the world. Through him the world was created, and he terms this divine being the Word of God, the mediator between God and man.

Philo's doctrine of man is dualistic and mainly derived from Plato. Man is a two fold being with a higher and a lower nature. The higher is due to his being an incarnation of a spirit taking the human form. The lower is due to his earthly desires and passions. The body is therefore a prison of the incarnated spirit which seeks to return whence it came. Consequently man must free himself from all carnal lusts, and reach out to God who will help all those who make the effort. Without God's help man is a captive and unable of himself to reach true wisdom and virtue.

Man's duty is to reach fellowship with God, and this is the goal he should set before himself. Thus the truly wise and virtuous seeker is lifted above his earth desires and enjoys in ecstasy the vision of God, his own consciousness sinking and disappearing in the Divine Light. Then to the righteous at death comes the entire liberation from the body, and the return of the soul to its original condition. It came from God and to God it must return.

The foregoing only briefly summarises the teachings of Philo, the representative of Alexandrian thought at the time of Paul. In this atmosphere Paul was doubtless nurtured, and on these speculations he must have often dwelt. They were not revealed to him by the Lord, as he would make his readers believe. That was his way of putting his views before his hearers and readers. The opinions which he so boldly expounds were those current in his own day, and all he contributed to the world was the associating of them with the simple Jesus of Nazareth, the psychic healer and teacher. Why? Because he had experienced a vision of an angel, a messenger, whom we would term an Etherian, but who was to him none other than a god. Just as an apparition was a god to Plato, Cicero and Socrates, to Paul the god was Jesus just dead. If he were not a god how could he appear after death, and who else could he be but Jesus who had recently been seen by his followers after his death?

Paul was deeply religious and longed for the anticipated Messiah. He was a mystic, an enthusiast, a man of strong character, and his belief that he had been entrusted by Jesus to tell the world that he was the Christ was enough to make him burn with enthusiasm and dedicate the rest of his life to preaching Christ crucified. No matter to him that Jesus was born of human parents, and had lived like other men. It was enough that Jesus was now a god, and had entrusted to him the revelation that he was the longed-for Messiah. As his ideas developed, they changed from the belief that Jesus was the Messiah to his being the Christ, the world's Saviour, who had died for the sins of humanity.

Such an idea is difficult to imagine by present-day intelligent people, but it is quite understandable in the irrational emotional religious atmosphere prevalent in Paul's day, when the gods meant far more to everyone ("as there are gods many", 1 *Cor.* viii, 5), and were believed to be much more closely in touch with human beings, than was ever the case throughout the Christian era. Only by remembering this is it possible to understand the extraordinary sequence of events which followed.

So satisfied was Paul that he was now the chosen exponent of Christ crucified for the sins of humanity that he refused to consort with the other disciples, or discuss with them the meaning of the mission of Jesus. To Paul, Jesus had become a heavenly being, second only to Jehovah, who, like Prometheus five hundred years earlier, had descended to earth from sitting at the right hand of God, in the likeness of sinful flesh, and had died a cruel death in order to conciliate the wrath of a revengeful deity. Thus Jesus acted as the mediator, the world's saviour, not of the Jews alone, but of humanity, and thereby fulfilled his destiny ordained from the beginning of the world.

Paul established the Christian Eucharist.[1] The words attributed to him in 1 *Corinthians* xi, 23-25, were copied later by Matthew, Mark and Luke. The Eucharist, as practised by Christians, was not established by Jesus but by Paul, who never knew Jesus. He says he received it from the Lord, not from those who were supposed to have partaken of the Last Supper with Jesus. He does not say how he received it, where or when, but just that it came to him from God; and on this worthless basis the Church has established its principal and most sacred rite.

If the Eucharist had been instituted by Jesus, one

---

[1] Some scholars think that the account of the Last Supper, as recorded in the Epistle to the Corinthians, is an interpolation by a copyist at a later date, to be afterwards copied into the gospels.

would have expected Paul to have got the account from those who had been present on that occasion; but no, it is the other way about. Paul starts the story, attributing it to Jesus, and those who wrote the gospels of Matthew, Mark and Luke copied Paul's words many years later. John just refers to the "supper being ended" and no more.

Paul, or someone else, copied the Eucharist feast ritual from Paganism and made it to centre round Jesus. The Pagans were devoutly attached to this ceremony of communion with the gods, and believed that these divine beings participated with them in the sacrificial meal. Porphyry (A.D. 233–306) the Neo-platonist tells us that the spirits sit beside the worshippers, and we find from an inscription addressed to the god Hercules, discovered in Kos, a description of the ritual performed at the Eucharist to his memory. Drawings have also been discovered of chalices used in the Eucharistic service to Mithra. Through these sacrificial rites it was believed that at-onement was established between the gods and their worshippers, just as is believed today by Christians, the Presbyterians still adopting the Pagan expressions of the Lord's table and the Table of the Lord.

Paul put Jesus, whom he called Christ, in place of the other gods in commemoration of whose death the people celebrated the Eucharist, and he tells his readers that the other gods are devils. "Ye cannot drink the cup of the Lord and the cup of the devils, ye cannot partake of the table of the Lord, and of the table of the devils." Cicero, in *The Nature of the Gods*, makes it quite evident whence Paul copied the Christian Eucharist or Holy Communion, and

Christians all these centuries have just been continuing a Pagan ceremony under the impression that it was instituted by Jesus, whereas Paul, or someone else, adopted it from Paganism and grafted it on to the other Pagan beliefs he incorporated in his teaching about Jesus.

Jesus never instituted the Eucharist; Paul did so, and all his philosophical and mystical writings relate to current religious opinions of those days, into which he introduces his imaginary Christ. The idea of a divine body broken, and divine blood shed, can be traced back for thousands of years. Atonement, the ancients believed, was attained by these sacramental meals, the immortality their god had attained being transferred to the communicants by their eating and drinking bread and wine the priests had turned into his flesh and blood. Few Pagans ever neglected this rite, thus reinforcing themselves with the immortal properties which they believed came from this ceremony. In return the first fruits of the herds and fields were consecrated to the gods for them to eat their etheric counterparts.

Such, then, was the revelation evolved in the mind of Paul, and the fact that it had been believed in times past that other gods had suffered and died for the sins of humanity was the basis on which he worked up his new conception of Jesus. This evolved and expanded until Jesus became, by the 4th century, just another of the many Christs who were believed to have died for the sins of humanity.

There is nothing mysterious in all this. It had been done before, and it was done after Paul's time. Luther, for instance, forged out of the old Christian religion a new interpretation. Paul's basis was

Judaism and Paganism. Luther's was Catholicism. The change in thought brought about by the enthusiasm of Paul was no greater than that brought about by Luther. Luther did not produce a new religion. Neither did Paul. They both struck when the people were ready for the change, and the change in both cases meant only an altered outlook on the same subject. Just as Luther was opposed by his brother priests, so was Paul, as his views did not appeal to the disciples of Jesus.

What did the disciples of Jesus, those who knew him on earth, think of all these new ideas? They thoroughly disapproved, and could see no justification for them. Jesus had preached to the Jews only, and they resented Paul carrying his message to the Gentiles who would not conform to the Jewish law. They believed that Paul was preaching heresy, which was nothing more than his own invention. They scoffed at him, and asked on what authority he preached it. His only reply was that he had seen the living Christ, but, as they had known the real Jesus, the rift developed and for a time they drew apart.

At a later date they agreed that he should carry the gospel to the Gentiles, while they remained to preach to the Jews what Jesus had taught them. Paul's gaze, however, remained steadily fixed on heaven, and he goes his way with only Barnabas. He never refers to the moral and ethical teaching of Jesus; he lives under the spell of this first experience, and writes as if he were in regular *rapport* with the risen Lord. He is consequently quite indifferent to the opinion of Peter and James, whose teaching and his were at variance.

It is quite evident that Paul most earnestly believed that his revelation was to him alone, and had no connection with the beliefs of the immediate followers of Jesus. They, for their part, could see no resemblance between the teaching of the Master and that of the enthusiastic Paul of a doctrine about which they knew nothing, and about which Jesus had been silent. Consequently there was this division amongst them, and it remained long after this great champion of Christ, and the followers of the teacher Jesus, had passed away.

Thus was laid the first stratum of Christian theology, the beginning of the deification of Jesus, and all the transcendental speculations about him which ultimately crystallised into the dogmas, creeds, rites and ceremonials of the Christian Church in 325, at Nicaea. Thus was Jesus, who lived and died a man, a Jew, raised, through an apparition, from being one of the human family, to be a god and the saviour of all mankind, the bearer of a name above every name, before whom all the angels in heaven and the demons in hell must prostrate themselves in reverent submission.

How different it would all have been had Paul known Jesus on earth! He could never have imagined what he did had he heard Jesus and his simple words. How history throughout the ages has been changed by seeming trifles! How profoundly ignorant we are of the effect our actions will have! Deeds which seem to us insignificant may lead to most important results.

So it came about that one of the world's greatest missionaries passed from earth in old age, quite unaware of the comfort his doctrine would give to millions, and equally profoundly ignorant of how it would be used against the thinkers, the great, the good and the noble, who saw the impossibility of it all. Little did he realise that it would plunge Europe into a midnight of superstition which would last for nineteen hundred years, and from which the world is only now gradually emerging. Little did he appreciate that the gentle Jesus, whom he turned into a god, would be used as an incitement to war, crime, torture, imprisonment and every imaginable cruelty, and that to many his time on earth would prove a curse, and not a blessing.

It must not be thought that scholars think that all the dogmas and doctrines contained in the Pauline epistles originated in the mind of Paul. Rather it is believed that he started the idea that Jesus was the Christ, and Saviour of the world, and that round this idea the Christian Faith developed by slow degrees. Just as the original gospels were added to, and taken from, so were the epistles of Paul.

The foregoing survey of Paul's mental evolution therefore represents what scholars and students consider helped to form the ideas contained in the original letters of Paul to his various flocks. It is by no means certain and conclusive, as his writings have been so tampered with, but rather a reasonable explanation of the cause which led this visionary and epileptic to adopt the course he pursued with such vigour and with such effect throughout his life.[1]

In concluding his masterly treatise entitled *A*

---

[1] Marcion in the second century complained of the way the text of St. Paul's epistles and the Gospels had been tampered with and mutilated by the Church authorities.

Critical Analysis of the four chief Pauline Epistles, the author, L. Gordon Rylands, writes as follows:

A rigorous analysis of the Pauline epistles, and of other available sources, reduces considerably the number of facts which we can claim to know about Paul. Yet the figure which remains, though sketched with fewer lines, is greater and more pleasing than the extraordinary mass of contradictions hitherto presented to us as a portrait. The man who was at once harsh, domineering, and overflowing with love; arrogant, boastful, and yet modest, the propagator of doctrines so fundamentally irreconcilable that they cannot possibly have originated in one mind, is a monstrous fiction.

Theological critics have begun to perceive that the very inconsistent opinions attributed to Jesus do not form a homogeneous body of doctrine, proceeding from a single mind. It really is time that they realized the highly composite character of the Pauline doctrine. . . . Doctrines which must be repulsive to every wholesome mind are shown not to have originated from, nor even to have been taught by him. If we have any of his original writings, they are the two early gnostic epistles reproduced in this book; and they are of such a character as to lead one to form a high opinion of the man who wrote them. They may not be the work of a very deep thinker; but they show us a mind whose religious and ethical conceptions were high and noble, and whose quality was sober, broad and tolerant. . . .

There was no Christianity before Paul, using the word Christianity in its modern sense. The best evidence we have leads to the opinion that the Church at Jerusalem was Ebionitish. . . . Without the universalistic propaganda of Paul, and his coadjutors, Christianity would not have broken the bonds of Judaism. The Christ Jesus of Paul was not a Jewish Messiah, nor the son of David according to the flesh. . . . He was a supernatural being, the son of the Supreme God of the Universe, who appeared among men "in the likeness of flesh" in order to reveal to them the true God. . . .

Theologians admit now that there was a somewhat important and widely-spread Gnosticism just before the Christian era. It has been proved that some of the pre-Christian Gnostics revered a Son of God under the name of "Christos" or "Chrestos". . . . Surely it ought not to be difficult to see that there must have been some connecting link between the pre-Christian and the highly elaborated Christian Gnosticism of the second century. . . . Now that it has been demonstrated that Pauline Christianity was Gnostic, the connecting link is found. Pauline Christianity was evidently a development from the pre-Christian Gnosticism.

I have now given a brief sketch of the origin of the Christian doctrines, but we have still to find the historical Jesus, the first cause of the Christian faith, the cause behind this contradictory mass of ideas which followed his life on earth. Can the real Jesus be found, and, if so, where? Our only source for this information is in the Gospels. No scholar, however, will accept the Jesus as presented to us in the four gospels of the New Testament. It is too clearly realised that over the life of the real Jesus has been laid layer after layer of interpolations, which makes the quest extremely difficult but not impossible. In fact, it is now accepted that a very satisfactory reconstruction has been made of the source from which much of the material given in *Matthew* and *Luke* was obtained, but this needs some explanation.

No scholar takes the gospel according to John seriously. It inverts the sequence of the ministry of Jesus, as given in the other three gospels, and it changes his teaching beyond recognition. Further, it pictures Jesus in an entirely different light, that of the Logos, the Christ, which developed from the speculations of Paul.

The *Encyclopædia Britannica* under "Gospels" says that either the Gospel of Saint John is inaccurate or the synoptic gospels are, as both cannot be correct, and remarks on its "accumulation of obviously inconsistent statements" and how "contradictions" meet the reader. F. C. Conybeare, who made the subject a life study, describes this gospel as a romance, full of exaggerations, and not worthy of any consideration by those who wish to find the true Jesus. F. C. Burkitt, Professor of Divinity at Cambridge University, in his book published in 1932 entitled *Jesus Christ, An Historical Outline,* remarks as follows about this gospel:—

> The contents of the Gospel of John do not seem historical at all. . . . I do not think the writer distinguished in his own consciousness between what he remembered, or had derived from the reminiscences of others, and what he felt must have been true, and I greatly doubt whether we can distinguish often in that gospel what is derived from tradition and what is derived from imagination.

This, then, is the opinion of one of the greatest authorities on the subject and must be respected. If the fourth gospel is derived from the imagination of the writer it seems waste of time to consider it, as it does not help us to get back to the real Jesus. This being so, we shall give our attention only to the first three gospels.

The first three agree more or less in style and contents, containing as they do traditional stories of the life of Jesus. Further, it will be found that *Matthew* and *Luke* are so much in verbal agreement with *Mark*, that if you strike out from *Mark* every verse repeated in *Matthew* and *Luke*, very little will be left in *Mark*. *Matthew* and *Luke*, in other words, independently copied from *Mark*, abridging and altering here and there. This was the common practice in those days.

Let us now take the next step. After eliminating all the matter Matthew and Luke copied from Mark, there is much left over in these two gospels which is not included in *Mark*. Here again Matthew and Luke copied from another source to obtain this information, as Matthew and Luke tell the same stories and repeat sayings in much the same words. They must therefore have obtained this information from a common source. Unfortunately this source is lost, but it can be reconstructed from what Matthew and Luke have preserved. The name given to this document is "Quelle", from the German, meaning the source.

We therefore find that Matthew and Luke compiled their narratives from two sources, the one being *Mark*, which we know, and the other called "Quelle", which is lost. By eliminating all that Matthew and Luke copied from Mark, which was in fact most of *Mark*, we have this residue left over, and Professor Harnack, one of the greatest of Biblical scholars, reconstructed it in the form of a narrative, omitting some portions which were not common to *Matthew* and *Luke*. The orthodox view that the gospels are independent records written under inspiration finds no confirmation, and it is evident that they were put together bit by bit over a considerable period of time.

It is now important that we should give some consideration to *Mark*, as it formed, along with "Quelle", the basis of *Matthew* and *Luke*. One of the first things to strike the careful reader is how the writer repeats himself. If *Mark* were an original gospel these repetitions would not occur, so the conclusion is that the writer, like Matthew and Luke, used earlier documents. As *Mark* is full of Aramaic phrases and idioms, it is now accepted that the documents from which the writer of this gospel copied were translations into Greek of Aramaic originals. *Mark* is composed of different layers, and, like the other gospels, stratum was laid on stratum. First came the oral story, which was written down. Then some scribe added another version of the same story, which in time came to be taken as a separate episode.

It will be seen that *Mark*, as we now know it, though the oldest of the gospels, is no more reliable as history than the others. All three are copies of earlier originals, and to get anywhere near to the real life of Jesus it is better to rely on the reconstructed "Quelle" gospel as being the least inaccurate and the nearest in date to the times to which it refers, and consequently the most likely to give us the most reliable picture of Jesus.

I shall now give this "Quelle" document as reconstructed by Professor Harnack.[1] Several scholars besides Harnack have carried out the task of reconstructing this additional source used by Matthew and Luke, and these separate attempts vary little from each other.

The Quelle Reconstructed Manuscript.

All the region round about Jordan . . . John saw many . . . coming to baptism, and said of them, Offspring of vipers, who warned you to flee from the impending wrath?

---

[1] I am indebted to the Rationalist Press Association, the publishers of *Myth, Magic and Morals*, by F. Cornwallis Conybeare, for their kind permission to reproduce this document from that concise and lucid work.

Produce therefore fruit worthy of repentance. And think not to say in yourselves, We have as father Abraham. For I tell you, that God is able out of these stones to raise up children to Abraham. And already the axe is laid at the root of the trees. Every tree then not producing good fruit is cut down and thrown into the fire. I indeed baptise you in water unto repentance; but he that comes after me is stronger than I, whose shoes I am not worthy to carry. He shall baptise you in fire, whose winnowing fan is in his hand, and he shall purge out his threshing-floor, and shall gather his grain into his barn; but the chaff he will burn up in fire unquenchable.

Jesus was led up into the desert by the Spirit to be tempted by the devil; and, having fasted forty days and forty nights, he afterwards hungered. And the tempter said to him, An thou art Son of God, bid these stones to become bread. And he answered, It is written, Not upon bread alone shall man live. So he taketh him with him to Jerusalem, and he stood him on the pinnacle of the temple; and saith he to him, An thou art Son of God, throw thyself down; for it is written that he will give his angels charge concerning thee, and on their hands they shall bear thee up, lest ever thou dash against a stone thy foot. Jesus said to him, Likewise is it written, Thou shalt not tempt the Lord thy God. Again he taketh him with him into a mountain exceedingly high, and shows him all the kingdoms of the world and their glory. And he said to him, All this I will give thee, if thou wilt fall down and worship me. And Jesus said to him: It is written, The Lord thy God shalt thou worship, and him alone shalt thou serve. And the devil leaveth him.

... Multitudes ... he taught the disciples, saying ... Blessed are the poor, for theirs is the kingdom of God.

Blessed are the sorrowers, for they shall be comforted.

Blessed are the hungry, for they shall be filled.

Blessed are ye, whenever they revile and persecute you, and say all that is evil against you falsely.

Rejoice and exult, because your reward is great in heaven; for even so they persecuted the prophets who were before you.

Whoever smites thee on thy cheek, turn to him also the other. And to one who would go to law with thee and take thy shirt, give up to him also thy coat.

To one who asks of thee, give; and from one who would borrow of thee, turn not away.

I say to you, Love your enemies and pray for them that persecute you, in order that ye may become sons of your father, for he causes his sun to rise upon the wicked and the good. For if ye love those who love you, what reward have ye? Do not the tax-farmers do this very thing? And if ye love your brethren alone, what that is extraordinary do ye do? Do not the Gentiles also do as much? Ye shall therefore be merciful as your father is merciful.

All things whatsoever ye desire that men should do unto you, even so do ye unto them.

Judge not, that ye be not judged; for with whatsoever judgment ye judge, shall ye be judged; and with that measure wherewith ye measure, shall it be measured unto you. And why markest thou the mote in thy brother's eye, but perceivest not the beam in thine own eye? or how shalt thou say to thy brother, Let me cast the mote out of thine eye, while the beam is in thine own eye? Hypocrite, first cast the beam out of thine own eye, and then shalt thou see clearly how to cast the mote out of thy brother's eye.

If a blind man lead a blind, they will both fall into a ditch.

A disciple is not above his teacher, nor a servant above his master. Let it suffice for the disciple to be as his teacher, and for the servant to be as his master.

By its fruit the tree is known. They surely do not gather grapes off thorns or figs off thistles? Even so, every good tree produces good fruit, but the rotten tree produces bad fruit. A good tree cannot bear bad fruit, nor a rotten tree produce good fruit.

Not everyone who saith to me, Lord, Lord, shall enter the kingdom of God, but he who doeth the will of my father. Everyone then that listens to these words and doeth them shall be likened to a man who builded his house on the rock. And the rain came down, and the rivers came, and the winds blew, and fell upon that house, and it fell not; for it was founded on the rock. And everyone who listens to these my words, but doeth them not, shall be likened to a man who builded his house on the sand. And the rain came down, and the rivers came, and the winds blew, and smote upon that house, and it fell, and great was the fall thereof.

He entered Capernaum, and there approached him a centurion, calling on him and saying, Master, my child lies at home struck down by paralysis, suffering dreadfully. He said to him, I will come and heal him. But the centurion answered and said, Lord, I am not worthy that you should enter under my roof; but only say a word, and my child will be healed. For I am a man in authority, having under me soldiers; and I say to this one, Go, and he goeth, and to another, Come, and he cometh; and to my servant, Do this, and he doeth it. But Jesus heard and wondered, and said to them who followed, Verily, I tell you, not even in Israel have I found so much faith.

But John, hearing in the prison the works of Jesus, sent by his disciples and said to him, Art thou he that is to come, or must we expect another? And he answered and said to them, Go ye, and report to John what ye hear and see. The blind see anew and the lame walk, lepers are cleansed and deaf hear, and dead men are raised and poor receive good tidings. And blessed is he who is not scandalised in me. But as they walked along he began to talk to the multitudes about John: What went ye out into the wilderness to see? A reed shaken by the wind? But what went ye out to see? A man clothed in soft raiment? Lo, they who wear soft raiment are in the houses of kings. Then why went ye out? To see a prophet? Nay, I tell you, one even greater than a prophet. For he it is of whom it is written, Lo, I send my angel before thy face, who shall prepare thy path before thee. Verily, I tell you that among those born of women there hath been raised up none greater than John the Baptist; yet the least in the kingdom of God is greater than he.

To what shall I liken this generation, and what is it like? It is like to children sitting in the public square, which address the others and say: We have piped to you, and ye danced not. We sang dirges, and ye mourned not. For John came neither eating nor drinking, and they say, He hath a devil. The Son of Man came eating and drinking, and they say, Behold a man, a glutton and a wine-bibber, friend of publicans and sinners. And wisdom is justified of her children.

Go ye and proclaim, saying that the kingdom of God is at hand.

One said to him, I will follow thee whithersoever thou goest. And Jesus answered him: The foxes have burrows and the birds of heaven nests; but the Son of Man hath not where to lay his head. But another one said to him: Permit me first to go away and bury my father. But he answered him: Follow me, and let the dead bury their dead.

He saith to his disciples: The harvest is abundant, but the workers few. Beseech, then, the lord of the harvest to send forth workers for his harvest.

Behold, I send you forth as sheep amidst wolves.

But when ye enter into the house, give it greeting. And if the house be worthy, let your peace descend upon it. But if it be not worthy, let your peace return unto you.

For the worker is worthy of his food.

Verily, I tell you, it shall be more tolerable for the land of Sodom and Gomorrah in that day than for that city.

Woe to thee, Chorazin; woe to thee, Bethsaida. For had the works of power which have been wrought in you been wrought in Tyre and Sidon, they would long ago have repented in sackcloth and ashes. But I tell you, it shall be more tolerable for Tyre and Sidon in the day of judgment than for you. And thou, Capernaum, instead of being exalted to heaven, shall go down unto hell.

In that season he said: I give thee thanks, Father, Lord of heaven and earth, that thou hast hidden these things from the wise and clever, and hast revealed them to infants. Yea, O Father, for so it was thy good will before thee. All things have been made over to me by the father, and no one hath known.

Blessed are your eyes, because they see, and your ears, because they hear. For verily I say to you, that many prophets and kings desired to see what ye see, and saw not, and to hear what you hear, and heard not.

Father, give us this day our daily bread, and forgive us our debts, even as we have forgiven our debtors, and lead us not into temptation.

Ask, and it shall be given to you; seek, and ye shall find; knock, and it shall be opened to you. For everyone who asks receiveth; and who seeks finds; and to the knocker it shall be opened. Or is there any one of you, of whom his son shall ask for bread, he will surely not give him a stone? Or if he ask for a fish, he will surely not tender him a viper? If, then, ye, being sinners, know how to give good gifts to your children, how much more shall your father from heaven give good things to them that ask him?

He healed one possessed by a devil, dumb, so that the dumb one spake, and all the multitudes were astonished . . . Every kingdom divided against itself is made desolate . . . And if I through Beelzebub cast out devils, through whom do your own sons cast them out? Therefore shall they be your judges. But if I by the spirit of God cast out demons, then indeed hath the kingdom of God hastened to come upon you . . . Unless a man is with me, he is against me; and he who gathers not in with me, scatters . . . Whensoever the unclean spirit quits a man, he passes through dry places seeking rest, and finds none. Then he says, I will return into the house whence I went forth. And he goes, and finds it vacant and swept and adorned Then he goes and takes with him seven spirits more evil than himself, and they enter and dwell there. And the last state of that man is worse than the first.

They said, We wish to see a sign wrought by thee. But he said, An evil and adulterous generation seeks for a sign, and a sign shall not be given to it, except the sign of Jonah. For as Jonah was a sign to the Ninevites, so shall be the Son of Man to this generation. The men of Nineveh shall rise up in the judgment with this generation, and shall condemn it; for they repented at the preaching of Jonah, and behold more than Jonah is here. The Queen of the South shall rise up in judgment with this generation and condemn it, for she came from the ends of the earth to listen to the wisdom of Solomon, and behold more than Solomon is here.

They light not a candle and set it under the bushel, but on the candlestick, and it lights all who are in the house.

The light of the body is thine eye; if, then, thine eye be simple, thine whole body will be full of light. But if thine eye be wicked, thy whole body will be dark. If, then, the light within thee is darkness, how great the darkness!

They bind up heavy burdens, and lay them on the shoulders of men; but they themselves would not move them with their little finger.

Woe to you Pharisees, because ye shut up the kingdom of God before men's faces. For ye enter not yourselves, nor permit them to enter who would do so.

Woe to you Pharisees, for ye tithe mint and anise and cummin; but have left undone the weightier parts of the law, judgment and mercy.

Now, ye Pharisees, ye cleanse the outside of the cup and platter, but within they are full of robbery and licence.

Woe to you, for ye are like graves unseen, and men who walk over them recognise them not.

Woe to you, because ye build the tombs of the prophets and say, Had we been in the days of our fathers, we would not have been sharers with them in the blood of the prophets. So that ye bear witness that ye are sons of them that slew the prophets. And ye fill up the measure of your fathers.

Therefore the Wisdom of God said: I send unto you prophets and wise men and scribes. Some of them ye will slay and persecute, that there may come on you all the blood shed on earth, from that of Abel until that of Zacharias, whom ye slew between the shrine and the altar. Verily I say to you, All these things shall come on this generation.

Nothing is hidden which shall not be revealed, or secret which shall not be known. What I speak to you in darkness, do ye speak in the light; and what ye hear in a whisper, proclaim ye on the house-tops. And fear ye not them that slay the body, but have no power to slay the soul. But fear rather him that is able to destroy soul and body in Gehenna. Are not two sparrows sold for one penny? And one of them shall not fall to the ground without God's will. And of your heads the very hairs are numbered. Fear not then. Ye are of far more account than sparrows. Everyone then who shall make confession of me before men shall the Son of Man also make confession of before the angels of God. But whosoever denies me before men, I also will deny him before the angels of God.

And whoever speaketh ill of

the Son of Man, it shall be forgiven him; but whoever speaketh ill of the Holy Spirit[1] it shall not be forgiven him.

Therefore I say unto you, feel no concern for your life, what ye shall eat, nor for your body, what ye shall put on. Is not the life more than food, and the body than raiment? Look at the crows, how they sow not nor reap nor gather into barns, yet God feedeth them. Are ye not of more account than they? And who of you by fussing can add to his stature one cubit? And about raiment why fuss thee? Mark the lilies how they grow. They labour not, nor do they spin. Yet I say to you, not even Solomon in all his glory was clad as one of these. But if God so dresses the weed which is today in the field and tomorrow is cast into a furnace, how much more you, O ye of little faith? Therefore ye shall not worry and say: What shall we eat? or what shall we drink? or what shall we wear? For all these things are in quest for the Gentiles. For your father knows that ye are in need of all these. But seek ye his kingdom, and all these things shall be added to you.

Treasure not up for yourselves treasures on earth, where the moth and rust deform, and where thieves break through and steal. But treasure up for yourselves treasures in heaven, where neither moth nor rust deform, and where thieves neither break through nor steal. For wherever your treasure is, there will be also your heart.

But this know ye, that if the householder knew in what hour the thief cometh, he would keep awake and not allow his house to be broken into. Who, then, is the faithful servant and thoughtful, whom the master set over his household to give its members food in season? Blessed is that servant whom the master shall find so doing when he comes. Verily I tell you that he will set him over all that belong to him. But if that servant say in his heart: My master delays, and begins to beat his fellow-servants, and eats and drinks with drunkards,

---

[1] According to the second-century book entitled *The Shepherd of Hermas*, in which is recorded an untampered account of early Jesuism, we find that the holy spirit, or divine spirit as he was sometimes called, is the medium's control who used his medium to speak through. This divine being was held in great respect in the early Apostolic Church.

the master of that servant shall come in a day when he expects him not and in an hour of which he is not aware, and shall cut him in two and set his portion together with the hypocrites.

Think ye that I came to shed peace upon the land? I came not to shed peace, but a sword. For I came to part asunder a man against his father and a daughter against her mother, and a daughter-in-law against her mother-in-law. And a man's foes are those of his own household.

Be reconciled with thine adversary quickly, whilst thou art still with him in the street; lest the adversary deliver thee to the judge, and the judge to the officer, and thou be cast into prison. Verily, I tell you, thou shalt not depart thence until thou hast paid the last farthing.

And again he said: To what shall I liken the kingdom of God? It is like leaven which a woman took and hid in three measures of meal, until the whole was leavened.

Enter ye through the narrow gate. For wide and broad the road, which leads to ruin, and many are they that pass in along it. For narrow is the gate and worn the road which leads unto life, and few are they who find it.

I tell you that from East and West they shall come and lie down with Abraham and Isaac and Jacob in the kingdom of God, but the children of the kingdom shall be cast out. There shall be wailing and gnashing of teeth.

Jerusalem, Jerusalem, thou that killest the prophets and stonest them that have been sent unto thee! How many times have I wished to gather together thy children, as a bird gathers her nestlings under her wings, and ye would not have it. Behold, your house is abandoned unto you desolate. For I tell you, ye shall not see me henceforth until you shall say: Blessed he who cometh in the name of the Lord.

Whosoever shall lift himself up shall be abased, and whosoever shall abase himself shall be lifted up.

He that takes not up his cross and follows me is not worthy of me.

Ye are the salt; but if the salt be spoiled, wherewith shall it be salted? It is useful for nothing any more, except to be cast outside and trodden under foot by men.

What think ye? If a man should have a hundred sheep,

and one of them lose its way, would he not leave the ninety-nine on the mountains, and go and seek the lost one? And if so be he find it, I say unto you that he rejoiceth over it more than over the ninety-nine that lost not their way.

No one can serve two masters. For either he will hate the one and love the other, or he will adhere to the one and despise the other. Ye cannot serve God and mammon.

The prophets and the law lasted until John. From then till now the kingdom of God is being wrested by force, and men of violence snatch at it.

Verily I tell you, until heaven and earth pass away not one jot or tittle shall pass away of the law.

I tell you, everyone who divorces his wife causes her to commit adultery; and whoever shall marry a divorced woman commits adultery.

It must be that scandals come, but woe to the man through whom the scandal comes.

If thy brother sin, rebuke him; if he listens to thee, thou hast won thy brother to thy gain . . . How often shall my brother sin against me and I forgive him? Until seven times? Jesus said to him: I tell thee, not until seven times, but until seventy times seven.

If ye have faith as a grain of mustard, ye shall say to this mountain, Get thee hence, and it shall be removed.

If, then, they say to you, Lo, he is in the wilderness, go ye not out. Lo, in the storerooms, believe them not. For as the lightning quits the east and flashes across to the west, so shall be the coming of the Son of Man. Wheresoever is the corpse, there shall the eagles be gathered together.

As were the days of Noah, so shall be the coming of the Son of Man. For as they were, in those days which preceded the flood, eating and drinking, marrying and giving in marriage, until the day when Noah entered the ark, and as they knew not until the flood came and swept them all away, so shall be the coming of the Son of Man. There shall be two in the field, one is taken and the other left; two women grinding in the mill, the one is taken and the other left.

He that finds his life shall lose it, and he that loses his life shall find it.

To everyone who has shall be given, and in abundance; but from him who has not, even

what he has shall be taken from him.
 Ye who have followed me shall sit upon twelve thrones, judging the twelve tribes of Israel.

The foregoing, then, was the second document which, together with Mark's gospel, was made use of by the writers of the first and third gospels. We notice the first trace of the mythical element in the story of the forty days hunger and temptation in the desert, and of Jesus being taken to a mountain by the devil and again tempted. The first is similar to the story told about Buddha, and the second like the story of the temptation of Jupiter by Pan, the Pagan devil with hoofs and tail who was incorporated into Christianity.

As to the contents of this reconstructed document, it will be noticed that nothing miraculous is reported, and Jesus is pictured as a teacher, a healer, and as a man. This is as near to the original Jesus as it is likely we shall ever get. He will never be an historical character such as Socrates, whose words were taken down at the time, and whose biographers, Xenophon and Plato, acted much in the same way to him as did Boswell to Dr. Johnson. Can this be considered a sound basis on which to build up a true religion? This series of opinions, sayings and teachings, which are similar to those found in other ancient books, cannot be the basis for religion. Nothing is to be found to support the tremendous supernatural claims made by Christianity. The basis of Christianity is Paganism. Jesus had nothing in common with the religion which claims him falsely as its founder.

What we learn, however, from all this patient

research is how to unravel the tangled mass of contradictions which has come down to us under the name of Christianity. The name Christian is appropriated by everyone who wishes to bear that name, but, in time, as education increases, it will be realised that those only are entitled to the name who accept the Pagan doctrines which Paul linked up with Jesus, and which grew round his name over the centuries, until they were crystallised and consolidated at Nicaea.

Those who claim to be Christians, because they try to follow Jesus, are misusing the name, because he was not a Christian and never would have been. There was nothing Pagan about his teachings. Those who discard the Paganism and wish to call themselves by a name associated with Jesus should call themselves Jesuians. It is very unfortunate that so many people make use of the name Christian, which stands for something quite different from their ideals, but it is just another illustration of the fact that few give the subject of religion serious thought, and are too often guided only by their emotions, by what the priest or minister says, or by common usage.

The original Jesus, it is surely unnecessary to emphasise, was a human being who was born, lived and died like every other man. The theological Christ is quite another matter. The fact that Paul felt that it was necessary to drag in the theological Christ, to drape a mantle of theology over the man Jesus, and associate Jesus with the Christs of Paganism caused immediate divisions in the early Church. These two opposing views, the belief in the human psychic healer and teacher, and the belief in Jesus as the Christ and Saviour, continued for three hundred years to disrupt the early Church. Consequently we read of the various heresies, the different sects, and the discordant divisions which disturbed the early life of Christianity.

Constantine, for ever receiving appeals to settle these differences between the Jesuians and the Christians of his empire, called together various councils, made up of high-ranking priests, and an agreement was ultimately reached at Nicaea after a vote was taken to determine whether Jesus was equal with, or subordinate to, Jehovah. By a large majority the voting went in favour of his being equal to Jehovah, and, to stop the quarrels and dissensions which had become so common, Constantine lost no time, as there and then he forced the majority to settle on what became known as the Nicene Creed. This everyone from now onwards was expected to believe, those who did not being excommunicated from the Church and regarded as heretics. Consequently Arius, the leader of the minority, was exiled and many of his followers were either banished, imprisoned, tortured or murdered.

It will be seen from this how the idea, first started by Paul, and added to over a period of three hundred years, was finally accepted by the Church as the basis of Christianity. From the time of Nicaea dates the beginning of Christian persecution, but another fifty years elapsed before the new religion was strong enough to persecute those of other faiths. Until then its history is a record of persecution of those who, prior to the adoption of the Nicene Creed, were the followers of Jesus.

Owing to the influence of Paul, the Christ idea,

by appealing to the Gentiles, grew and gathered more and more adherents. Consequently the early writings of the life of Jesus, of which we have an example in the "Quelle" gospel, were gradually added to until finally they made him into a supernatural creation, and the Saviour of the World. These accretions gathered slowly, just as the idea gained force. The idea in itself was not new; what was new was the attributing of it to Jesus.

All the miraculous, mythical and mystical writings which have found their way into the New Testament were in those days generally accepted in relation to the other gods, who once were likewise human when on earth, to be deified when seen as apparitions after death. The early history of Christianity is the story of the miraculous and mythical being gradually applied to Jesus. Just as there is nothing new in the sayings of Jesus, all of which were said by teachers and writers before his day, so the mystical, mythical and legendary part of Christianity was likewise not new. In fact it formed the basis of the beliefs of other religions of the then civilised world. It is doubtful if there is a single new idea in Christianity differing from what was in vogue in pre-Christian days, except the change of name of the god the Christians worshipped.

All that Christianity did was to change the name of the god, and Jesus took the place of Osiris, Bel, Dionysus and others, as the world's saviour. So the mystical theological ideas expressed in Paul's epistles were not new, and had been written before his time about the other gods the people worshipped or anticipated would come to earth. The only thing new was that to Paul the god was Jesus.

· · · · ·

This strange drama called Christianity which took three hundred years to produce has taken three hundred years to understand. Scholars during these last three centuries have been trying to unravel the threads of truth, contradiction and falsehood which the early Church fathers so tangled up during their efforts to magnify their Christ at the expense of those saviours hitherto accepted by the people.

They, and the converted Pagan priests who supported them in grafting their new ideas on to the old religions of Rome and Greece, were opposed to the Greek philosophy which was making steady headway along the coast of the Mediterranean, but they saw that if it were to be defeated a compromise was needed. Christianity was the compromise. Conditions then were like conditions now. Philosophy then, as Science now is doing, was killing superstition, and consequently the Pagan priesthood opposed it just as the Christian priesthood opposed all new knowledge. Science has conquered because it had behind it the printing press which philosophy lacked.

The people then were turning away from the ancient religions, the temples were neglected, and the gods were not worshipped as of old. Something had to be done to preserve the power of the priesthood. Something new, but yet the same, had to be given to the people to satisfy their longings. Constantine, on reaching the throne, saw how events were moving within his domain, especially in Rome, and he decided that the then little known cult, Christianity, suited best the needs of the people, provided its differences could be settled and it was brought more into line with Pagan thought.

Eusebius and Athanasius produced the necessary structure, the former the Nicene Creed and the latter the ideas which ultimately developed into the Athanasian Creed. Moreover Eusebius, Jerome and the other Church fathers admitted in their own writings that they had made the necessary alterations in the gospels and epistles to bring them into line with the creeds they produced. Honesty and accuracy, as we understand these words, did not exist in those days.

For three hundred years prior to Nicaea no historical records existed, so there was no great difficulty in deluding the people as to the past story of the cult. Anything could be added to, or subtracted from, its past beliefs without undue comment. What the Church fathers decided the people should know and believe became the creeds and doctrines of the new state religion. Those who, like Arius, objected, were cast out, and all who held opinions contrary to what Eusebius and the majority of the priests decided became outcasts. Behind it all was Constantine, and Eusebius was his trusted henchman.

All this superstition which accumulated around Jesus was the result of slow growth, to culminate in the reign of Constantine. It was a fight between Greek philosophy and Paganism, and out of this developed Christianity. Valentinus and Clement of Alexandria contributed to this fusion of thought, Valentinus being the first man in Christendom who set to work to bring together Greek philosophy and the Pagan beliefs which, by the 2nd century, had come to surround Jesus. He was a man of singular gifts and his writings are marked by originality and depth of thought. So he worked Jesus in as the keystone in the great structure of thought which Greek philosophy had reared, thus blending philosophy and superstition into what is now known as Christianity. Likewise Clement, in the 3rd century, continued this work of compromise by his attempt to reconcile the teachings of philosophy with those of the sacrificial religions. Origen was one of his pupils, and thus the assimilation proceeded, each succeeding generation adding some fresh ideas.

To mix philosophy and superstition was quite impossible. One or the other had to go. Unfortunately it was philosophy. So we find after Nicaea that philosophy, which was making men free and making them think, was abandoned, its schools everywhere throughout the Empire were closed, and Christendom entered its dark night of superstition which was to last for more than fifteen hundred years. Had it not been for Christianity, philosophy might have conquered Paganism and lit all Europe, and in time the world, with intellectual light.

If printing and paper had been in use in the days of the Greek philosophers, and if everyone had been able to read and think in an intelligent way, it is impossible to imagine Christianity ever coming into being. Because philosophy was confined to the towns, where schools were established, and it could thus influence only those minds with which it was in direct contact, the great mass of humanity was ignorant and illiterate. If it had been educated and had read the literature of Greece and Rome, had studied the philosophy of Zeno and Epicurus, had been familiar with the writings of Cicero, Seneca, Plato and Aristotle, there would have been no soil on which the seeds of Christian superstition could have taken root, grown and flourished.

This polluted soil of error and compromise in which Christianity was nurtured was the cause of all the sects and divisions throughout Christendom from its infancy. Considering the various influences which brought about its birth, nothing otherwise could have been expected. Its pre-natal influences were many and varied, and at birth it displayed them all, though its nurses did their best to prevent them from appearing on the surface as far as possible. All its life its bad heredity has been making itself felt, to the discomfiture of its supporters. Could this be otherwise, considering its history?

Christianity was conceived at Alexandria, born at Nicaea and cradled at Rome. Paul was its father, and Constantine and his mother Helena its guardians. Its two principal nurses were Eusebius and Athanasius. Under the care of these, and its other attendants, it grew and flourished, protected by all the wealth and power of the Roman Court. After the death of its guardians it experienced only one slight set-back during the short reign of Julian. Except for this its progress to manhood was steady, so much so that fifty years after its birth at Nicaea it was adopting the role of persecutor and destroying all who stood in its way.

From the 5th century till the Reformation the Church wielded its authority with a firm and iron hand, excommunicating in the 11th century what became the Greek Church, owing to a difference of opinion about the Trinity. Few were intelligent enough to doubt, so as the Church defined Christianity it was accepted and believed without question. The invention of printing and the circulation of the classics brought about the Renaissance, and this in turn brought about the Reformation. From that time Western Christianity broke up into numerous sects and divisions, just as the original cult had broken up prior to the hand of authority taking a firm grasp from the time of Nicaea onwards.

If the reformers had just been intelligent enough to cut off entirely, instead of to prune, the Paganism in their religion, what a difference it would have made to the world. Unfortunately the people were not ready, and in consequence the pruning was only half done. It is regrettable that Calvin and Luther were followed instead of Servetus and Bruno. Bruno fell a victim to the old and Servetus to the new dispensation, and, because they put what they considered true before creeds and dogmas, they met their death by burning at the stake. Each died a martyr's death, but they lit the lamp that neither Catholicism nor Protestantism has been able to extinguish.

At the Reformation the most conservative preferred to remain under the old authority, but the split which caused a break-away from authority was the beginning of the end of Christianity. Some centuries hence, when the history of Christianity is written, the Reformation will be recognised as the cause which led to its death, it being a religion which could live only under authority, as when the people thought about it for themselves everyone formed a different opinion. From the time of the Reformation those who did not accept the authority of the Roman Church began to take different views, and quote from different passages in the Old and New Testaments, just as these were suited to their opinions.

Thus the historian of the future will find that the cause behind the death of Christianity was authority giving way to freedom of thought, because it could flourish only in ignorance and amongst people who could not think for themselves. As they increased in intelligence and thought more, Christianity gradually faded from their minds, until it took its place with all the other dead superstitions of the past. The world survived the loss of Jupiter, which no one thought possible nineteen hundred years ago. It will likewise survive the loss of Christ and be the better for the loss, just as it was the better for the loss of Jupiter.

Protestant Christians will generally admit that Jesus stands for their religious ideal, and they are often at a loss to identify the teachings of their Church with those of Jesus. The Roman Catholic section overcomes the difficulty by basing all its beliefs on the findings of the early Church fathers, and this view the Anglo-Catholics of the Church of England also adopt.

Christianity is becoming increasingly divided on this point, and Protestants will more and more draw away from the rest of Christendom, by putting Jesus before Christ, while Roman and Anglo-Catholics will continue for some time longer to worship the theological Christ, and ignore Jesus. Protestants, I believe, will be the first to cease to be Christians, and come to accept Jesus as he was before he became misrepresented by the Christian Church.

In the next chapter we shall consider for what

exactly Jesus stands, and for what Christ stands, and, when this is presented clearly and logically, many who now find difficulty in reconciling two opposite opinions will have their minds cleared, and their doubts removed, to their lasting comfort and contentment.

CHAPTER IV.

JESUS OR CHRIST?

Those who call themselves Christians must, as the Universe unfolds before them, decide whether they intend to base their religious beliefs on the teachings of Jesus or on those of the Christian Church. They cannot honestly serve both Jesus and Christ, because the one is diametrically opposed to the other. All Christian people who wish to be intellectually honest must, in view of the greater knowledge we now possess, take the decision and face the position fearlessly. Jesus and Christ cannot both be worshipped. One or the other must be discarded, as what is attributed to Jesus is flatly contradicted by what is ascribed to Christ, and what is imputed to Christ is equally contradicted by what is attributed to Jesus.

Throughout the entire New Testament run two diametrically opposite opinions, the one the opinion of Jesus about himself and his relationship to God and humanity, and the other the opinion of the writers about Christ. One is the teaching and preaching of a reformer and healer, and the other is the doctrine of a crucified saviour for the redemption of the world, through whose sacrifice an angry deity was appeased.

Christians may continue to ignore Jesus, just as Paul did, and thus continue the worship of Christ, or they may see that Christ is nothing more than the creation of Paul and the Christian Church fathers, an idea which, like other man-made things, must perish.

They may, on the other hand, try to follow many of the teachings of Jesus, and base on these their religion and philosophy. Some of the remarks attributed to him will stand for all time, as they are above and beyond theology, creeds and dogmas, being part of the ethical code of humanity. These moralisings are found in all the leading world religions, and they were expressed hundreds of years before the time of Jesus. Jesus either said them because he had learned them, or they were attributed to him by his biographers so as to heighten the belief in his wisdom.

At the beginning of his ministry, according to Luke's gospel, Jesus made quite clear what was his purpose in life. Entering the Synagogue, he read from the book of Isaiah:—

> The Spirit of the Lord is upon me because he hath anointed me to preach the gospel to the poor, he hath sent me to heal the broken hearted, to preach deliverance to the captives and recovering of sight to the blind. To set at liberty them that are bruised, to preach the acceptable year of the Lord.

After finishing this reading he sat down and said:—

> This day is this scripture fulfilled in your ears.

Could anything be clearer or more definite, could any words be put together to produce a more human impression than those with which Jesus associated himself? Could any words be less easily interpreted into meaning that Jesus considered himself God, and the second member of a trinity of gods? Christians must choose one or the other, Jesus the man, or Christ the God. They cannot have both.

Jesus was the son of Joseph, according to Matthew's gospel before the story of his birth was tampered with by the priests, and his genealogical descent is given right back to David. Christ is a virgin-born god having no relationship whatever to Joseph. The fact that his descent through Joseph is given in *Matthew* shows that the idea of his being a virgin-born god was an after-thought.

Jesus said, "Why callest thou me good, there is none good but one, that is God." And again, when in the hour of his agony he felt as if all that he had worked for had been in vain, he piteously cried out aloud, "My God, my God, why hast thou forsaken me," but it was Christ who said, "He that believeth and is baptised shall be saved, but he that believeth not shall be damned."

All that is natural in the gospels comprised the basis, the original, the foundation of a record of a man who, as the centuries passed, came to be looked on as a god. Jesus, the Jew, over a period of three hundred years, became just another Pagan Christ, being officially added to the pantheon of sacrificed god-men at Nicaea. Just as this came about, so was attributed to him what was attributed to the god-men worshipped by the religions surrounding Palestine. Thus throughout the entire New Testament we have the man Jesus, who is referred to seventy-six times as the son of man, and intertwined with him is the god Christ, who, in course of time, became interwoven with Jesus. The result is that we have a composite portrait made up of the original and an entirely different one painted over it. In places the man obliterates the god, while in others the god obliterates the man, so much so that the original portrait of the man is well-nigh impossible to discover. Jesus is indeed a misty figure in history.

In the pages which follow I shall try to disentangle the two, and relate side by side what we may reasonably believe the name of Jesus stands for, and what the Christ of Saint Paul and the Christian Church stands for.

Jesus stands for the friend of the poor, the healer of the sick by means of his psychic power, the comforter of those in sorrow, and the preacher of glad tidings to all mankind. Jesus foretold happiness in the life hereafter to all who tried to live aright on earth. Christ on the other hand stands for the damnation of all who do not accept the creeds of the Christian Church, for all who do not believe in his virgin birth, his miracles, his death as a sacrifice, his physical resurrection and ascension, that Christ and God are one, and that they together with the Holy Spirit form the trinity of the Christian pantheon.

Jesus stands for the friend of sinners, he is the advocate of free thought and the one who saw the errors of the religion of his time. He taught that as we lived on earth so would be our place hereafter. Christ stands for the Church, for orthodoxy, and salvation through belief and faith.

Jesus stands for the man of sorrows who could find no resting-place, because of the intolerance and bigotry of the prevailing religion which made him a wanderer from place to place. Christ stands for God, for a name above every name at which every knee must bow.

Jesus stands for a martyr, a reformer, and for one

who suffered for his convictions. Christ stands for a crucified saviour-god, who took the sins of the world and suffered in the place of humanity.

Jesus taught us to look on God as our Father in Heaven, who pities us, and cares for us as a father does his children. Christ stands for original sin and the need for a saviour, a mediator between an angry God and sinful man, who had to be sacrificed and suffer to satisfy the wrath and vengeance of God.

Jesus taught the brotherhood of man, and that we should not judge others unjustly because we ourselves wish to be justly judged. Christ stands for a god of injustice, a tyrant, who has consigned practically every one of his creation to eternal hell, "where their worm dieth not and the fire is not quenched". Jesus stands for peace, harmony and international brotherhood; Christ for war, Christianity having been the cause of many of the wars of Europe up to the 18th century.

Jesus taught love, charitableness, loving-kindness and long suffering. Christ stands for intrigue, intolerance, persecution, torture, murder and imprisonment, all of which have followed his Church since the year 377 when its power increased sufficiently to suppress by force its former rival, Mithraism, from which it had copied all its forms, ceremonials and ritual, and its priests their vestments.

The name Jesus is related to harmony, humility, kindness and the relief of suffering. Christ is responsible for the saying "But those mine enemies, which would not that I reign over them, bring hither and slay them before me," one of the texts which brought the Inquisition into being.

Jesus stands for unity, Christ for dissension, sects and divisions which have kept Europe divided since the 11th century because of different opinions held about the Trinity and other doctrines. The history of Ireland is an example of how two sects of Christians hate each other because they cannot agree as to the meaning of the dogma for which Christ stands.

Jesus taught a simple religion of love and service which required no priest to interpret. Christ is responsible for saying, "Depart from me, ye cursed, into everlasting fire prepared for the devil and his angels." This and other similar sayings were the cause behind all the persecutions which have followed his name during the age of Christendom. Dungeons were built because of these sayings. They lighted the faggots of the stake and stimulated fiends to invent the thumbscrew, the contracting boot and the rack to mangle the bodies of those who differed in their interpretation of Christ from the opinions held by the Christian sect in power for the time being.

Jesus lived a Jew and died a Jew. He never founded a Church or a religion. Christ stands for the Church, theological colleges, monasteries, convents, and also for priests, clergymen, ministers of the gospel, who all claim to be his representatives on earth for the purpose of revealing to man an ecclesiastical scheme of salvation.

Jesus possessed neither riches nor honours. His life was one of poverty and great simplicity. Christ represents papal crowns and mitres sparkling with precious stones, processions, crucifixes, images, pomp, ceremony and the vast wealth owned by his Church.

Jesus is reported as having partaken before his

death of a simple meal of farewell with his disciples, which has been turned into the mystical ceremony of the Eucharist, representing Christ's body and blood transformed into the bread and wine partaken of at the ceremony.

Jesus taught that the Kingdom of Heaven is within us. Christ stands for an immense organisation which claims him as the corner stone. Jesus taught that as we live on earth so shall our place be hereafter. Christ, on the other hand, is represented as the only way of salvation.

God's love towards us, and our love towards God and our neighbour is what Jesus stands for. He showed his contempt for the priesthood, because then as now it spread false doctrines. Christ stands for dogma, doctrine, baptism, the confessional, confirmation, the churching of women, the marriage and burial services, and the doctrine that whoever his Church binds on earth shall be bound in heaven.

Jesus stands for a man like ourselves, who expressly stated that he was not God and that there was only one God, our Father in Heaven. He shared with us human failings and weaknesses. He went about doing good and preached the gospel of repentance and hope. Christ stands for the very God of very God, who is coming in his glory to judge the world:—

> In whom we have redemption through his blood, even the forgiveness of sins. Who is the image of the invisible God, the first born of every creature. For by him were all things created that are in heaven and that are in earth, visible and invisible, whether they be thrones or dominions or principalities or powers, all things were created by him and for him. (*Colossians* i, 14–16.)

To Jesus is attributed the words "Honour thy father and thy mother." Christ is responsible for the statement "He who hates not his father and mother, and wife and children, and brethren, yea and his own life also, cannot be my disciple."

Christianity stands for what Christ stands for. Spiritualism stands for what Jesus stands for, for what he preached, and for what he suffered and died.

What Spiritualists are trying to do is to show that what caused Christianity, namely Paul's vision, was a natural occurrence, because visions and apparitions occur today. They assert that Paul, in his ignorance, built up on his psychic experience a theology for which there is no basis in fact, and that the error he established has been added to, enlarged, and developed until its final form has no more resemblance to the teaching of Jesus than night has to day.

Spiritualists are trying to bring Christians back to Jesus, to show them that they have misrepresented and maligned this man for nineteen hundred years. The Church lifted this sublime man out of his setting after his death, made him its possession and emblem, and its priests paraded him about the world, attributing to him what its early theologians had invented. By cunningly distorting and misrepresenting his mission in life it has amassed great wealth, which its followers have contributed in fear, and this keeps in being an immense black-coated clerical army for the express purpose of preaching the false doctrines its founders so subtly borrowed from Pagan sources.

One of the many extraordinary things about this conglomeration of diverse opinions is that what started Christianity, and what gave Paul his beliefs and faith to preach Christ crucified, was a natural psychic phenomenon, denied by orthodox Christians as occurring today. To them it was something unique which happened once and has never happened since.

Because the early Church put man-made doctrines and dogmas in place of natural phenomena, it had no firm basis on which to rear a structure. By the force of imperial power the Catholic Church, as it came to be called, won its greatest victory against the Arians. Thus, by Constantine's help, the Trinitarians won and the Arians, today called Unitarians, were turned away as outcasts. So, for a time after that, the Catholic Church presented one united front, and, though a large slice of it was torn from it by Islam, yet it nevertheless maintained outward solidarity until the 11th century.

Then happened one of the most stupid things that has ever occurred in history, if we are to judge by the effects. Had the Catholic priests not started interfering with the Creed this unity of front might have been maintained until the Reformation, in fact there might have been no Reformation at all. In 1054, after different councils had been held in Western Christendom, the Pope, Leo IX, decided to add the word *Filioque*, meaning "and from the Son", to the Creed. Because of this uncalled-for addition to the original Nicene Creed, for which there was not a scrap of authority or justification, the Christian Church split in two and from that time onwards the Eastern and Western Church have not been in fellowship. Because the Eastern Church would not agree to this alteration Leo IX excommunicated all Eastern Christians, and from that day to this the Popes of the west and the

Patriarchs of the east have hated and reviled each other with an intense bitterness.

From 1054 onwards the Eastern Orthodox Church has gone its own way, denouncing and despising the west. An iron curtain fell between the east and the west, and it has not been lifted to this day. Likewise the Western Church pursued its own aims until the time came when its corruption was so great that a split occurred at the time now called the Reformation. Western Europe was thus divided in two by those who preferred to remain with the old Church and those who accepted the Bible as their authority in place of the Church. Then arose the Unitarians, for the first time since their ejection as Arians from the Catholic Church in the 4th century, and, though a small religious body, they have had an influence for good out of all proportion to their size. Not bound by creeds, doctrines and dogmas they have been able to fashion a religion divorced from the grossest of Christianity's superstitions.

At the Reformation the Unitarians refused to ally themselves with the Protestants, holding that the Reformation was not thorough enough, and that what was Pagan should be entirely cut out. Jesus, they declared, should be looked upon as a human being. The Protestants at the Reformation accepted much of the Paganism which constituted Christianity. Instead, however, of worshipping images they worshipped a book which was the outcome of printing and of people learning to read. The Protestants, taking over the doctrine of the Trinity, kept outside their fold the Unitarians, the survivors of the Arians, who could not understand why this, like image-worshipping, should not also be discarded along with the other Pagan beliefs rejected by the Protestants. Though exercising little political or religious influence, their beliefs have been accepted over the last three hundred years by many of the thinking people of Europe.

Lastly there are the mystical Christians, those who are quite unorthodox, and who reject as literally true the ideas expressed in the creeds. They believe, however, in what they term the "Christ Spirit" or the "Cosmic Christ", and consider that Christianity is a mystical religion and can be looked on only as such. These mystics call themselves Christians, but really their beliefs are those held by many religiously-minded Pagans of old.

They do not accept Christianity as a new revelation, but as only a continuation of the mystery religions of Egypt, Greece and Rome. To them, as to Paul, the historical Jesus means nothing. To them, the creeps are only crude attempts to put into words something which words cannot encompass. To them, all that happened nineteen hundred years ago was that the ancient mysteries received a new name, and, instead of worshipping at the shrine of Osiris, Isis, Dionysus, Orpheus, Adonis or Mithra, the people worshipped at the shrine of Jesus, who was given the mystical name of Christ, so as to associate him more closely with the mysteries of the past. Thus are perpetuated the beliefs of the Gnostics of the 2nd century.

Everywhere throughout the ancient world, temples existed for those to whom religion was a mystical union with the divine, through the death of a god-man who appeased the wrath of an angry deity. They were the temples of the Mysteries, or Mystery Temples, a name which aptly describes what was taught in them. Therein assembled those who sought, by means of sacrificed saviours and god-men, to get more into tune with the Infinite. Those who were content with the phenomena caused by the interaction of the two worlds consulted the Oracles, but the mystics attended the Mysteries, seeking after mystic truths, undergoing lengthy and severe trials of personal fortitude and endurance, thinking that by sacrificing the flesh they would understand better the divine mysteries.

Within these Mystery temples were enacted Cosmic dramas, the main scenes in the lives, deaths and resurrections of the various gods of the past, and Christians carried these on in the early Church, the new god Christ taking the place of those who had been dethroned. From this source Christians continued the terms and phraseology still so widely used, such as "being born again", "salvation through faith", "washed in the blood of the Lamb", and numerous others. To these "Stewards of the Mysteries", as Paul termed them, the legends about the gods were taught, but, as was said by Sallust:—

If the truth about the gods were taught to all, the unintelligent would disdain it, from not understanding it, and the more capable would make light of it. But if the truth is given in mystical veil, it is assured against contempt, and serves as a stimulus to philosophic thinking.

Just as the Egyptians used to repeat "As truly as Osiris lives so shall I live. As truly as Osiris is not dead shall I not die," so the early Christians adopted the same phraseology, using the name of Christ instead of the name of Osiris. Symbolic dramas were enacted in all the pre-Christian mystery temples in order to commemorate the death, resurrection and ascension of their respective deities.

When Jesus, now called Christ, was added to the pantheon of saviour-gods, it does not surprise us to find that all the stories told of the previous saviour-gods were likewise told of him. Thus we have the legends and myths surrounding the life of Jesus, from the virgin birth to his bodily resurrection and ascension. The Christian story of the trial, death, resurrection and ascension of Jesus is only the drama enacted in the mystery temples put into words, and made to centre round Jesus instead of Osiris, Bel, Prometheus, or one of the other gods.

Christianity then was not new or unique, and the story of Calvary culminates all the mysteries of antiquity. At the back of all the creeds, dogmas, and ceremonials of Christianity is this mystical conception of union with the deity through the vicarious sacrifice of a god-man for the purpose of appeasing divine wrath. Christianity is consequently just another link in the chain which can be traced back to early sun worship, and the story of its victim's sacrifice has in it the early rudiments of sun worship, Matthew's gospel telling us of a solar eclipse at the time of the crucifixion.

Some accept this ancient lineage, while others are shocked that such suggestions should be made, because, to the majority, Christianity is the only divine revelation and came to the world nineteen hundred years ago, fresh and free, to replace heathenism and the worship of gods of wood and stone.

I trust that these thoughts may make clear what to most people is obscure, and that I have succeeded in explaining and unravelling the contradictions of the Christian religion. Once they are disentangled and understood, the claim made by Christian people that Christianity is a special revelation given to mankind nineteen hundred years ago, and that the Church is a divinely appointed institution for its propagation, is no longer tenable. Much as it is in the interests of the priests to keep this illusion in the minds of the people for as long as possible, sooner or later the truth must prevail and the error be discarded.

The foregoing is a fair summary of the different views held by those who do not belong to either the Roman Catholic or Greek Churches. The Orthodox take the Bible and creeds more or less literally; the Unitarians do not accept the creeds or take the Bible literally, but believe in one personal God. The Mystics read into the Christian creeds the mysticism of the past, and believe that all the old sacrificial religions were just mysticism materialised so as to make it understood by the people.

The orthodox amongst the Pagans held views similar to those of orthodox Christians, only their gods were called by other names, and to each his religion was the one and only revelation from the gods to man. To the mystical this need not be so, as to them religion is the tuning-in with the Infinite, a psychic state of mind which some are able to reach, though it is beyond the understanding of most practical people.

The heresy of Marcion of the 2nd century, the writings of Philo, Clement of Alexandria, Origen, Eusebius and Augustine show that Christianity was just the outcome of the Mystery religions of the Pagans. This can be accepted as an historical fact, but why do present-day mystics call themselves Christians, when supernatural Christianity stands for a spontaneous divine revelation which came to the world nineteen hundred years ago, since when all revelation of the unseen has ceased? Natural religion, as I have previously said, includes this reaching out to the divine, but why should the mystics of today, who call themselves Christians, wish to be associated with Christianity, the child of Paganism, which, with its creeds and dogmas, is based upon the death and suffering of a saviour-god?

Why do they not cut adrift from this material expression of a mystical symbolism, and all the superstitions attached to it, which we should by now have outgrown? Surely we can have mysticism without Christianity, whose record and beliefs have degraded the word religion in the minds of all thinking people. The reaching out after the Infinite is the basis of religion, but needs no label. Rather let us place all orthodox religions, including Christianity, in the only category for which they are fitted—as representing the attempts of our ignorant ancestors to express their religious instinct in a tangible way.

Their ignorance was so profound that their way of salvation was in consequence crude, cruel and repulsive, so much so that it can appeal only to the uneducated. These simple uncritical people leave their religious thinking in the keeping of an organisation which is maintained today, as in the past, for those who cannot think out the deeper problems of existence for themselves, and require some recognised authority to specify for them what they must believe in order to be saved.

Through all the sacrificial religions of the past runs the same thread (the very foundation of Christianity and clearly emphasised throughout both the Old and New Testaments), that without the shedding of blood there is no remission of sins. This is the religion of the savage, and all the religions based on this doctrine are savage religions. They have been the cause of unimaginable cruelty, misery and suffering. This is the central theme of Christianity, from which it can never be disentangled. This is Christianity, just as it was Paganism under whatever name it flourished. This was not the teaching of Jesus, though it was attributed to him at a later date. It is false, and it has no divine authority behind it. It is debasing, and, just in proportion as the people have come to discard it, so has the world advanced both mentally and morally.

Just as fear has lessened in the mind of man, has he given more thought to his material well-being, which has resulted in the increased comfort and happiness of the human race. Still this doctrine of sacrifice is regularly preached throughout Christendom, and the British Broadcasting Corporation reserves Sunday for its propagation, all other unorthodox religious beliefs being banned, the reason the Corporation gives for Spiritualism being excluded is that it does not come within the mainstream of Christian tradition.

Sunday is still reserved for the propagation of these ancient speculations, as it has always been down the ages since early sun worship, it being the day

of the week on which the sun was worshipped.
Christianity borrowed this holy day from Mithraism,
which was called by the Mithraists "The Lord's Day",
and it draped round Jesus all the legends which surrounded sun worship and were incorporated with the
lives of the saviour-gods of the past.

The orthodox never grasp the fact that Jesus
contributed nothing to Christianity. He was worked
into the new religion and used by the organisation
which came to be called the Christian Church. Fifty
years after his death he would not have recognised
what was being preached in his name. The definition
of the Trinity, which was added to Christianity
in the 8th century, by some unknown person, at
some unknown date, at some unknown place, and
called the Athanasian Creed, would have been considered by him as a string of crazy meaningless words.

Up till the beginning of the 3rd century, before the
moss of error had grown over the rock of fact, the
majority of Christians were Unitarians, believing in one
God only, and that Jesus was a prophet, a healer and
a teacher. The Trinitarians were in a decided minority.
There was constant disputing between these two sects,
but it was not till the end of the 8th century that the
doctrine of the Trinity was officially accepted, at the
Council of Friuli in 796, after which date it became
recognised as one of the fundamental doctrines of
Christianity. As the result of this decision the
Athanasian Creed made its appearance, and was
attributed to this early Church father so as to
increase its authority.[1]

---

[1] For further information on this subject see *Encyclopædia Britannica* under "Creeds".

Jesus never referred to his virgin birth, because he always considered that he was naturally born, and so did everyone until one hundred years after his death when the legend was added to the record of his life. He did not know that he was God, and distinctly said he was not. His physical body never rose from the dead and ascended into heaven, as reported in the New Testament. The earliest document relating to his life does not mention this stupendous event, or that he was crucified for the sins of the world, as when it was written no one held such ideas. Everything that has been added to the natural life of Jesus has come from various sources. His simple teachings and sayings came from Essenism, and all that is miraculous was copied from Paganism, the resurrection story having been superimposed on an earlier one to the effect that he was seen after death as an apparition.

The life of Jesus was a natural one. He was born in a natural way. He lived and taught like other teachers of his time. Both before his time and after it thousands have done far more for humanity than he did, as his life of service lasted only about two years at the most. From this acorn of a simple life of service and self-sacrifice has sprung the enormous oak of superstition termed Christianity. It was planted in an age of ignorance, and watered by ignorant and superstitious men. Its childhood was an age when few could read or write, and, like a mushroom, it flourished best in darkness.

Thus it extended its growth throughout Europe and the Americas during the time in history now called the Dark Ages. Its corruption was great. Its evil influence everywhere was so pronounced that when Mohammed arose he took from the Christian faith about half its followers. In disgust many of his supporters turned from the image-worshipping of Christianity, and vowed that no image would ever be worshipped by them.

His followers also took from Christendom its most precious possessions: Palestine, with all its sacred associations, Asia Minor, where its first churches were established, Egypt, whence originated the doctrine of the Trinity, Carthage, famous for its Church councils, and Constantinople, the first Christian city. Before this time the chief seats of Christendom were Rome, Constantinople, Antioch and Alexandria. Only Rome remained.

The history of Christianity from the 4th century onwards for fifteen hundred years is revolting in the extreme. Its popes, bishops, patriarchs and primates were mixed up in all the evil doings of the time, and devoted their energies to excommunicating and cursing their enemies. Assassinations, poisonings, immoralities, torture, murder, riots, treason and the lust for domination and power are associated with the lives of the leaders of Christianity. Amidst these atrocities and crimes Mohammed appeared in the 7th century, denouncing it all as evil and repellent.

Then, five hundred years later, followed the Crusades, when Christendom fought to recapture the Holy Land. For two hundred years this fruitless effort kept Europe in a turmoil, wretched and poor. The people were in misery, yet everything was diverted towards this one aim, the recovery of the Church's lost possessions. The history of the Crusades

Jesus or Christ?

is one of the blackest spots in Christian history. Treachery, cruelty and lust were rampant everywhere as a result of this inter-religious war. Millions of lives and vast wealth were sacrificed. On both sides the fiercest passions were roused and kept aflame to such a degree that the worst barbarities and atrocities ever recorded in history took place under the flags of Christ and Islam.

Christianity has undoubtedly comforted its followers in the past and does so today, but, on the other hand, there is no crime known which its followers have not committed in its name and under the authority of the inspired *Holy Bible*. This religion has supported every villainy, every cruelty, every lust, and every crime that ever entered the mind of man, and a Bible text was readily found in support of each. Yet the word Christian is used today as if it stood for all that is good. People talk of "Christian charity", "Christian ethics", and "Christian ideals". No word in the English language is so misapplied.

Paul may have written in favour of charity, but he founded a religion based on doctrines in which this quality never existed and never can exist. A religion whose God is a monster, who consigns all unbelievers to hell, is the antithesis of charity. If we talked of "Jesuian charity", "Jesuian ideals" and "Jesuian ethics", these words would more correctly represent what idealists today mean to express, but certainly the words cannot be associated with the Christian religion. Christianity advocates both good and bad. It has made Jesus responsible for saying words of kindness and cruelty, of forgiveness and eternal damnation, of wisdom and folly, and during the night of Christianity full use was made of all that is bad, and only few followed the good.

One thing emerges above all others, and should never be lost sight of. Jesus was not a Christian, and would have scorned to bear that name. From what little we know of him we can imagine that one of his temperament, his humanity, his compassion, his breadth of thought, his kindness and charity, could never have brought his mind into the small compass necessary to accept the creeds and dogmas of the religion that is falsely attributed to him. He was too unorthodox towards Judaism to be responsible for another hide-bound religion. There are no two ideologies more diametrically opposite than those of Jesuism and Christianity.

If I were asked to give an impartial description, in a few words, of what Jesus was on earth, I would say that he approached more nearly in his beliefs and teachings to the seven principles of Spiritualism than to anything else I know. The nearer you get to the real Jesus, the more clearly it becomes evident that he accepted and acted up to the truths of Spiritualism, and lived according to the principles of this religion. Spiritualists do not worship Jesus, but they admire him. Spiritualists do not accept Jesus as God, or as their Saviour, but they look on him as one who in his short public life did what he could to heal the sick with his psychic power, showed his followers that as we live here so shall we live hereafter, and taught that this earth is a preparation for another and better life for all who live up to the best that is in them.

Jesus was not responsible for the religion which does not even bear his name, and to refer to him as

Jesus Christ is entirely wrong—the adding to the common Hebrew name of Jeshuah a Greek name associated only with theology. To those who knew him he was a teacher and healer, who taught a simple belief in the fatherhood of God and the brotherhood of man.

Under the garments of ignorance and cruelty which have been placed on his back, behind the theological Christ, behind all the lies and frauds of Christianity, behind all the Christian churches, images and altars erected in his name, behind the creeds and dogmas manufactured out of the Pagan religions of a superstitious age, behind all the popes, cardinals, bishops, priests, clergymen and ministers of the gospel, whose business in life is to propagate the mistakes and falsehoods of the early Church fathers, I see the real man, the man of sorrows acquainted with grief, who went about doing good, healing the sick with his psychic power, raising the fallen, and endeavouring to reform and uplift the people and their religion, within a narrow strip of territory a few miles at the most.

For the man Jesus I have infinite respect, but I am repelled by the theological Christ, maintained and sustained by all the wealth of a powerful organisation, employing its army of priests and parsons to propagate error and denounce the truth as proclaimed by Spiritualism. This mighty organisation of superstition called the Christian Church has its tentacles in every country in the world, disseminating lies about Jesus and his life on earth, misleading the people, and diverting their earnings into its greedy coffers.

It is considered one of the worst of crimes to libel a man after his death, to tell lies about him, to portray him as different from what he really was. This is what Christians are guilty of every time they repeat the Creed, every time they listen, without protest, to an orthodox sermon and every time they bring the name of Jesus into their religion. This man's name since his death has been dragged through the mud of nineteen Christian centuries, has been employed in connection with every known crime mankind is capable of inventing, and has been used to support every lie, tyranny, cruelty and crime that could shape itself in the human mind. All in the name of religion!

Those who protested against this greatest of all crimes, this defaming of a good man's name, were denounced, cursed, excommunicated and banned from society, if they were fortunate enough to escape imprisonment, torture and being burned at the stake. They were preached against, and denounced by the army of preachers Christians keep in being to propagate their lies about Jesus, an army that takes millions upon millions each year from honest toil, and has battened, bivouacked and camped on the fairest soil of Christendom for the past sixteen hundred years.

In the name of Jesus they have obstructed social and educational progress. Superstition was elevated, facts were treated with scorn and they have doped the minds of all they could reach from childhood to old age. Not content with that, they have prophesied, in the name of one whose life, we imagine, was filled with forgiveness, gentleness and love, a future filled with eternal pain for all who did not misrepresent his life on earth, and use his name to support their lies and crimes. Such is the record of the Christian priesthood whose doings make up the history of Christianity from the days of the Church fathers.

What I am trying to do is to protect the fair name of Jesus from further misrepresentation. All I say is true, every word, but the people do not like being told the truth because they are ignorant of the facts and cannot think logically. Ninety-nine per cent. of the population of this country are muddle-headed, illogical thinkers and unable to think clearly and rationally. Because of this they allow their religious beliefs to be made for them by the organisation of the sect to which they belong. Accepting is so much easier than thinking!

All I am anxious to do is to make the people think and face the truth, and if they face it honestly they will accept it. What I wish to do is to stop the name of Jesus being dragged into Christian superstition and associated with Paganism, which is just what every priest and parson is employed to do with the support of the Christian community. I am trying to put the position fairly and honestly before every thinking man and woman, and explain to them how they have been misled by those whose interest it is to mislead, and leave it at that.

I know that when the position has been put fairly and truthfully before them, the drapings of superstition which have been wound around Jesus will be discarded, and he will come to be revered and respected as the man he was, and not as he has been misrepresented these past nineteen hundred years.

There is no possible connection between Christianity and Spiritualism, as some who term themselves Christian Spiritualists try to make out. Christianity for nineteen hundred years has stood, and must always stand, for what is contained in its creeds. Once it discards a part or the whole of these its doom is sealed, and those who support this organisation will stand for the creeds of the Church to the last.

When it sinks out of sight it will sink entirely, with the flag of Christ flying at the masthead. Its supporters must hold to the fundamentals or perish. Its death will come about through its gaining fewer and fewer adherents. The Roman Catholic Church is right in insisting on *Semper idem*. Either the Church is right in whole, or it is not right at all. It cannot support one doctrine or dogma and discard another.

Christianity stands for baptism into the Church, salvation by faith, the belief in three personal gods, of whom Jesus is one. It stands, moreover, for the miraculous life of Jesus as recorded in the New Testament. It stands for the inspiration and accuracy of the *Holy Bible*, because if you do away with Adam you do away with Christ. Christianity is summed up in the words of Paul, "As in Adam all die, so in Christ shall all be made alive." It stands for a heaven for believers and a hell for unbelievers, and asserts that God, through his Holy Word, revealed his scheme of salvation to man, first to the Jews and then to the Christians. This scheme centred round the death of Jesus, one of the three gods of the Christian trinity, to satisfy the wrath and just indignation of Jehovah, the first god in the Trinity, because of the sins of mankind. That is Christianity, which includes much more but nothing less. Nothing less can be Christianity.

I am told by some that as Christianity stands for

an after-life, as does Spiritualism, this link must join the two religions. The belief in an after-life is far older than Christianity. Round this belief have been coiled all the superstitions of the world's religions. When these superstitions have been uncoiled it will be found that what is accepted by Spiritualism remains. It might as well be said that because the Egyptians believed in an after-life, Spiritualism and the worship of Osiris, with all the superstitions attached to it, could be linked up.

The belief in an after-life is not peculiar to Christianity, and is in fact much more feebly expressed in this religion than in many another. This link will not join the two religions, because Christianity stands for what our present-day knowledge proves to be untrue and Spiritualism stands for what we know to be true. Spiritualism and Christianity are such poles apart that they can no more come together than oil and water can mix. Spiritualism stands for the central truth found in all religions, but utterly discards the drapings, the theological clothes, which have been put on to all religions. These may have been necessary, and doubtless were, when the mind of man was young, but they cannot possibly be accepted to-day by intelligent people. No Spiritualist can therefore be a Christian, any more than he can be a Pagan.

I am surprised at the ignorant and slipshod way people write in Spiritualist journals, as Spiritualists should know better. One does not expect to find truth or accuracy in Christian publications, but it should certainly be found in those devoted to Spiritualism. An example of what I mean appeared in a

Spiritualist journal a few months ago. It is just a sample, but I could give many similar extracts.

> A Christian is one brought up in the knowledge and love of Jesus Christ. The Christianity taught by Christ and his Apostles was plain, pure and primitive. A Christian is one who follows Christ, Christianity is a life to be lived.

All this is untrue, a pandering to an ancient name, a misusing and distorting of a name that stands for something completely different. This attempt to apologise for and whitewash the name Christian is futile, and, as education grows, must be abandoned, because to reason thus is to argue against the facts of history, against every fact known by scholars about Christianity.

In any case there is nothing to be proud of about the name Christian. Christianity was perhaps an improvement on Druidism, which it displaced in this country, as it believed that Jesus was the sacrifice for sin, and consequently Christianity was never guilty of human sacrifice. Its record of murder, however, out-did Druidism so far as the sacrifice of life is concerned. A religion of human sacrifice could not have had more victims than the 25,000,000 who were sacrificed on the altar of Christianity, during the fifteen hundred years after Nicaea when it held the reins of power in its hands.

Throughout the night of Christianity prisoners were treated like beasts. Death was the penalty for nearly every offence. The conditions of the poor were appalling, and cruelty to man, woman, child and beast reigned everywhere. Both the body and mind of man were in slavery. There was no liberty of thought, and slavery was supported everywhere. The rich lorded it over the poor, and the Church domineered and interfered in everything in connection with the individual and the state.

Over the past hundred years, as people became intelligent enough to doubt the principles on which this religion was founded, we have become more civilised and more humane. As we become less Christian we become less cruel, less bigoted and less intolerant. When Europe was in the Dark Ages of Christianity, the Moslems were encouraging science, building hospitals and investigating the art of healing. From them, during the Crusades, Christendom took the idea of hospitals for the sick, just as it copied its monastic life from Buddhism. Before the monasteries and convents became corrupt in the Middle Ages any charity or mercy exercised in those cruel times centred in these institutions.

Christians recall many individuals of their own faith who did works of charity and mercy. They cannot, however, go back much more than one hundred years, during which time the individual conscience was quickening owing to the growth of knowledge. Then, even more than now, nearly everyone termed himself a Christian, so naturally the religion takes the credit for their good works though it had nothing to do with them. If it had, why was it left till the 19th century for what is called Christian charity to develop? Why was it dead for eighteen hundred years? Our culture has increased as our education has advanced, and what we are today is due to education and increased knowledge, and nothing more. Today the works of charity and mercy are supported by people of all beliefs, and all shades of religious opinion.

The claim was generally made in past years by Christians, and still is by some, that Christianity only is responsible for the charitable organisations in this country. This claim is untrue. Belief in Church creeds and dogmas has nothing to do with love for humanity, and both believers and non-believers in Christianity have done their share in helping to raise humanity to a higher level, and to relieve suffering.

Putting aside the scientists, the doctors, and all who by their work and labour added to the happiness of mankind, let me mention just a few of the philanthropists and reformers who were not Christian people. Richard Carlile last century suffered and achieved more for the liberty of the press than any other Englishman. John Stuart Mill, the Utilitarian philosopher, by his writings helped to raise humanity; Thomas Firmin founded St. Thomas' Hospital in London; Thomas Cogan founded the Royal Humane Society; John Pounds founded the Ragged Schools; Joseph Tuckerman founded the Domestic Missions for the Poor in England and America.

The Ten Hours Bill was introduced by John Fielden who pleaded that it should be the Eight Hours Bill. Catherine Wilkinson originated public washhouses and public baths; S. G. Howe took a leading part in bringing education to the blind and deaf; Mary Carpenter founded the Industrial Reformatory Schools for Girls; Dorothea Dix brought about better treatment for lunatics; William Rathbone founded the District Nursing Associations; Frances Cobbe did much to prevent cruelty to animals; George Jacob Holyoake founded the Co-operative movement; Passmore Edwards founded Institutes and free libraries for working men.

Thomas Paine was the first man in Christendom to advocate the abolition of slavery and the rights of women. Voltaire stopped the Inquisition in France and, by his writings, brought in an era of political and religious liberty in Europe. Last but by no means least we must remember Florence Nightingale, who gave her life to nursing the wounded and the sick.

These, and many others, who worked for the uplifting of mankind and the relief of suffering, did not profess the Christian faith, but this in no way dimmed their love for humanity, which shone as brightly in their lives as it did in the lives of many Christian philanthropists. This short recital makes it clear that the belief in creeds is unnecessary for human progress, and history proves that when people become less superstitious they become more humane.

I do not wish in the least degree to pass over the unselfish work done for humanity by many professing Christians. The desire to save from destruction the souls of those who did not accept Christ as their saviour has stimulated self-sacrifice in the lives of many Christian people. Many have given up all that was most dear to them to further the knowledge of the Gospel message. In their enthusiasm they have penetrated all parts of the earth. Self-sacrifice and the dedication of lives to Christ, as is the saying, is written on the pages of Christian history. This urge has raised many to heights of unselfishness, just as it has been the cause of intolerable cruelty caused by the fear of hell.

The desire to save souls has produced both self-sacrifice and cruelty in equal measure. Persuasion and force have been used by fervent Christians, who believed intensely in the promises and threats contained in the Bible and in the creeds of their religion, and who divided humanity up as either the saved or the damned, of which the latter largely predominated.

Charlemagne was undoubtedly Christianity's greatest missionary. North-western Europe, which now comprises the Netherlands, France, Germany, Denmark, Norway and Sweden, was an arena of bitter conflict between the new and the old religion. He carried the cross and sword in his ravages through Western Europe, slaying all who would not accept the Gospel message. Not satisfied with this his zeal took him down the Adriatic coast and also past the Pyrenees. For his great work in establishing Christianity in Europe he was crowned by the Pope in Rome as Caesar and Augustus, and thus commenced, on this foundation of bloodshed, the Holy Roman Empire which was to be the cause of wars and crimes for a thousand years.

From early times the Church launched crusades against all who would not accept its doctrines, and "Saint" Dominic, the founder of the order which bears his name, slaughtered thousands he could not convert. The same zeal was displayed, at the instigation of the Church, by the Spanish conquerors in South America, and by many Christian kings and princes throughout the Christian era, resulting in the slaughter of multitudes of innocent people.

What has been done by Christians has been likewise done by the enthusiasts of all religions. Just as much self-sacrifice and cruelty has accompanied the missionary work of the Moslems. Buddhists have shown the same zeal without the cruelty which has accompanied both Christianity and Mohammedanism. This zeal, displayed everywhere down the ages by the fanatics of all religions, does not in any way prove that what they preached and believed was true. It only demonstrates a phase of mental emotion which makes possible much kindness on the one hand or, on the other, abominable cruelty for the purpose of influencing those the zealots believed were on the road to destruction.

Now that Spiritualism tells us what in reality happens to us after death, and as our future is no longer a matter of speculation, this missionary zeal will become directed into more useful channels, such as educating, healing and uplifting humanity. By thus improving their minds and bodies, those helped are fitted to live better lives, both here and hereafter, without having their minds clogged with needless superstitions which have no bearing on life here or in Etheria.

Spiritualism stands for the complete overthrow of superstition throughout the world. Those who call themselves Christian Spiritualists have adopted the name, but they are not Spiritualists. They try to have a foot in both camps. They are glad to obtain the assurance of another life, through mediumship, but they do not wish to give up the superstitions of their childhood. Perhaps this half-way house is necessary, as the cutting of ties formed in childhood is very difficult. Christian Spiritualists in time will become Spiritualists, and so Spiritualism will grow and gather strength at the expense of Christianity which will gradually, as the years pass, mean less and less to the people until finally it expires and is forgotten.

What is vaguely in the minds of most people today is how unsatisfying supernatural religion is. The reason for this is because religion to them means orthodox Christianity. Supernatural religion is dying, but not so natural religion which does not consist in believing the impossible. As the truths of Spiritualism become more and more known, so will the hunger of the human mind become ever more satisfied.

In spite of all the magnificent edifices belonging to the world's orthodox religions, whether they are termed cathedrals, churches, temples, mosques or pagodas; in spite of all the theological schools and seminaries built for the purpose of twisting the minds of priests and ministers to enable them to go out and spread the superstitions attached to the faith they profess, orthodox religions are doomed to die, and all those great material assets will avail them nothing. The mind of man is forever seeking after truth, and truth will be sought wherever it can be found.

Natural religion does not depend on gorgeous buildings, magnificent edifices, robed priests or ecclesiastical wealth. Behind Spiritualism, and its material poverty, are ranged the hosts of Etherians slowly breaking down the dividing wall. They will not be diverted from their task. For that reason Spiritualism, which stands for truth and truth only, its one priceless asset, will conquer the world, and give intellectual and spiritual light to all mankind.

CHAPTER V.

THE AGE OF MATERIALISM.

The age of materialism followed the age of superstition. When educated people found that the supernatural gods had flown from the sky, and that the universe was not run by caprice, a reaction from the supernatural was inevitable.

Many great and outstanding names come floating through one's mind, of men who were responsible for raising the intellectual outlook of Europe from that of barbarism, and starting it on the path which has led humanity to the position it has reached today. Though they were not all materialists, as now understood, their discoveries laid the foundation for this age of thought. Bruno the philosopher, one of the most charming of men, who was burned at the stake in Rome after seven years' imprisonment, is one of the first to come to mind. Copernicus and Galileo between them shook the powers of superstition to their foundations.

Leonardo da Vinci, one of the most remarkable men the human race has produced, whose mind could turn to and master almost any subject, was undoubtedly the most outstanding figure of the Renaissance. Another, less known to fame, was Tycho Brahe, the master of Kepler, whose pupil became far more famous than did his teacher, because he brought to victory the idea that originated in the mind of Copernicus. In the same year, 1642, in which Galileo died, the illustrious scientist Isaac Newton was born.

By this time the place and movement of the earth in the solar system was established. The science which has penetrated into the depths of space had survived its birth in a hostile world, and the foundations of that temple of knowledge had been well and truly laid. Kepler and Newton formulated the laws of motion, the latter establishing with mathematical precision the law of the attraction of gravity, and won from the poet Pope these immortal words:—

> Nature and Nature's laws lay hid in night:
> God said, Let Newton be! and all was light.

This galaxy of names covers the men who brought light to the world, and raised it from the darkness of ignorance into the glorious light of knowledge. They were followed by Franklin, who discovered that lightning and electricity are one and the same thing, and he prepared the way for the work Faraday accomplished one hundred years later.

Michael Faraday laid the foundation of the scientific method of investigation, and he was the father of electricity. Harvey did likewise for the science of medicine, as did Priestley and Lavoisier for chemistry. Darwin and Wallace traced back our ancestry, and Huxley spent his life trying to make the people understand their discoveries. Lamarck, fifty years before Darwin, had attempted to establish the same theory, but he failed to convince the biologists through the lack of positive evidence. Humboldt, Clerk-Maxwell, Helmholtz and Kelvin laid the foundations of physics, and made it possible for us to comprehend the nature of substance.

Others in their way were just as great, and to one and all our gratitude should be extended because they added to the health, wealth and happiness of the human race. By their discoveries they banished from the minds of all thinking people the superstition which had kept man in a state of ignorance, poverty and fear throughout the ages, and had made him a slave of the gods and their servants the priests.

The ancients had always a place for the gods in their science and philosophy, and for that reason their knowledge was slight. When the gods were brought in as an explanation for everything not understood, knowledge could not accumulate. When the God idea passed from the minds of men, they naturally turned their thoughts to find another explanation for natural phenomena.

What, then, was the primary reason for the God idea being abandoned? It was the invention of the telescope, or the instrument of the devil, as it was termed by the Christian Church. The telescope enabled us to explore the sky, just as the compass enabled us to explore the world. The telescope proved the vastness of space, the enormous distances between the stars and planets, that our globe circled on its own axis, and made its annual journey round the sun. The compass enabled us to circumnavigate the earth, and prove it to be round.

These discoveries were the most profound, the most important, and the most far-reaching in the history of man, since they made him think, reason, wonder and doubt. The more he thought and reasoned, the more he wondered at the greatness and the vastness of the universe. The more he reasoned, the more he doubted the revelation from God, as proclaimed by the Church. When it was found that every effect had a cause, and every cause produced in turn an effect, there was no room for the gods. Another explanation for natural phenomena had been found which fitted in with experience and with facts. Law and order took the place of the gods, and when it came to be realised that the universe was a machine, and that every part performed its own function mechanically, nothing was left for the gods to perform. Thus they faded into oblivion.

In this new age only what could be seen, handled and calculated was considered. Anything outside of that did not exist. The universe consisted of matter, force, law and order, nothing more and nothing less. This view of the universe came slowly, commencing as it did in the 16th century and reaching its height in the 19th century. It took three centuries before the age of materialism reached its zenith, and when this time arrived science had a full and satisfactory explanation to give for all that occurred on this planet and in the heavens.

Let us now examine the contentions of the materialist. This chapter is devoted to recording these—neither agreeing with them nor refuting them. As this book proceeds, the universe as it appears to me will be expounded in the light of all the knowledge we possess. I shall not ignore the discoveries made in the realm of psychic science, as do the materialists. I shall try to encompass the entire boundary of our present-day knowledge, ignoring nothing for which we possess evidence. On this firm basis is built up the new science which today only a very few advanced thinkers, who have the knowledge and courage, are expounding to an ignorant and hostile world.

The age of materialism was the natural consequence of the long night of superstition. Up to within the last three hundred years everything that happened was attributed to the gods or to God. Consequently, learning was at a standstill and mankind made no mental advance. What was there to learn? Storms and hail, thunder and lightning, earthquake and tempest, heat and growth, were all expressions of the power of the gods. Everything was understood, and for everything there was an explanation. There was nothing to learn.

The Church had a complete explanation for all the phenomena of nature, and this institution governed mankind. As diseases were caused by devils, the priests exorcised the devils, and so the priests were the doctors. All natural phenomena were just the expression of the pleasure or anger of the gods, so the priests were the scientists. All government was through the divinely-appointed representatives of the gods, as approved by the Church, so the Pope and his cardinals were the divine autocrats of Europe, holding all governments in their hands, and kings as their vassals. Thus to our ancestors, up to within the last three hundred years, the gods and devils were the rulers of this earth, and the cause of all that happened. The Church consequently had an iron grip of the people, body, soul and spirit, from birth till death, and too often used its power for its own greedy ends.

The discovery, in the 15th century, of how to make

paper and print on it, the invention of the telescope in the 17th century, and the use made of the compass, an idea which came from China, created a mental revolution in Europe. It is difficult for us today to envisage the consternation caused by these discoveries. Copernicus dropped such a bomb into the minds of Europe that its repercussion is still being felt. For a time it paralysed men with fear of the revenge of the gods, and only slowly did this terror depart. This great astronomer died in 1543, quite unaware of the mental havoc he had caused, as he did not dare to publish his discoveries until he was on his deathbed. But it took another three hundred years before the illusions and delusions caused by theology began to pass away, and these are still with us even at the present day.

Before the time of the discovery of the scientific method of acquiring knowledge, little advance in intelligence had occurred over thousands of years. During the golden age of Greece and Rome, the arts and philosophy received more consideration than the application of rational investigation, and only after the adoption of the scientific method, of learning from observation and experience, did progress commence. Hitherto no one had given thought to progress, a word which was meaningless to our ancestors prior to the Renaissance. With the desire for progress came cruel persecution, and the more the people thought and wondered the more intense became their distress.

Then it was that our present-day political labels, Conservative and Liberal, came to have a meaning, and over the last four hundred years the fight between these two different types of mind has been constant and bitter. Nevertheless, mental development continued, and nearly every country in the world has had its standard of life raised, some more, some less, in consequence of the impetus given to discovery and the acquisition of knowledge which was set in motion by the great Copernicus. Though increased knowledge has been used for both good and bad purposes, his great discovery set the wheels of progress in motion, so much so that every year since his time their momentum has increased, and today everything points to humanity being carried in consequence to further new heights of knowledge which can only be envisaged in flights of imagination.

Progress was very halting in the early days of awakening. Only slowly did astronomers begin to obtain a grasp of the magnitude of the universe and map out the heavens. Only gradually did our ancestors come to realise the size, velocity and weight of the stars and planets. Just as these discoveries were made so it came to be realised how insignificant in size is this earth—no more than a grain of sand on the shore of the universal ocean. Consequently all thinking people came to comprehend the absurdity of the claim that all the starry hosts of heaven had been created to give light at night to mankind, and that this earth was the only creation of importance in the universe.

From the study of astronomy, men then directed their minds to the investigation of geology. They found the results of the action of fire, ice, water, wind and rain, and how they had been responsible for the formation of continents and islands. By exploring the depths of the earth they found how stratum had been laid on stratum, and how the crust of the earth had been built up. They grouped these strata into igneous and sedimentary formations, and discovered how the igneous rocks had been forced up through fissures and cracks from the furnace of lava within the crust of the earth. Then they observed how the sedimentary rocks had been laid down by erosion through the action of rivers and seas.

Gradually it came to be realised that every cause had an effect, and that all these discoveries proved conclusively that this iron law worked remorselessly and had been in operation, mechanically and devoid of feeling, for millions of years. Up to then everyone had been taught that God had created the world in six days, and the reaction, when this was found to be untrue, was terrific. Finally, everything outside the material was thrown over by many scientists, and the universe was explained in material terms as if the physical was everything and nothing else existed. Scientists were so dazzled by their successes, so hypnotised by their new discoveries, that all the psychic phenomena of the past, which had been the cause of religion and had occupied the pages of much ancient literature, were ignored or forgotten. Thus the world entered the materialistic age, and the door began to close on the age of ignorance and superstition.

So it came about that the geologists examined the effects of sea, river, volcano and glacier, and from these they told the story of the formation of the crust of the earth. Then they began to calculate, only to discover that the earth's crust had taken hundreds of millions of years to solidify. One branch of knowledge after another was taken up, and to it was applied the same methods, namely observation, experience and experiment. When all that we experience had been subjected to this scientific scrutiny, the bewildered people had to adjust themselves to a new outlook on life, though it took several hundred years before even the most thoughtful could come to realise that the beautiful theological picture built up in the past was now shattered beyond repair.

With the study of geology went the study of biology, and this included the increased knowledge of ourselves and the animals. Knowing now something of the age of the different strata of the earth's crust, our explorers into the past found it hard to believe what they now discovered. Every religion so far had taught that life on this planet went back not much further than six thousand years. This belief was not confined to Christianity but was world-wide, and now the biologists proclaimed that life had existed for millions of years, away back to the time when the Laurentian rocks were formed, and had continued evolving ever since. They had examined the rocks and found fossils, imprints, skeletons and remains of life, as far back as the time when the crust of the earth was in its early stage of formation.

Amazed, enthusiastic and zealous in their quest for truth, these pioneers into a new world followed life right through from the amoeba to the fish and on to the mammal until they reached man and the way his development had proceeded up to the present time. Instead of the immediate creation of life, as everyone had so far believed, it was discovered that life had been evolving for all these millions of years to the time when it was taken up by the anthropologists and historians who traced it through the stone age, the bronze age, and the iron age, through the ages of pre-history until history began, on to the present day. When all this was summed up it was discovered that our ancestors' preconceived ideas about themselves, the earth, its inhabitants and the universe had to be revised, and it came to be accepted that the roots of the human family tree went back to the days when the earth was still relatively old, and yet millions of years younger than it is today.

Then men began to study the phenomena of nature, to try to find out the causes behind the effects, the reason for the attraction and repulsion of the substances and forces which make up the universe. In their research they found that nothing basic could be created, nothing destroyed, and that all that happened was a change of form. Consequently these chemists and physicists adopted the logical conclusion that if nothing can be created or destroyed the physical universe must be eternal. Therefore matter in its different shapes and forms has been from all time, and will be for all eternity. This being so, there is no creator.

It was also discovered that force and matter were inseparable, that force, like matter, is indestructible and therefore eternal. If eternal, then both force and matter have been from all time and will be for all time. You can change motion into heat and heat back into motion, but never destroy this inherent force in matter. So it was argued that there is no directing intelligence in the universe, all is mechanical, all governed by law and order, all the result of cause following effect, and all explainable by the laws laid down by Newton. Consequently the conclusion

The Age of Materialism

reached was to the effect that it is more logical to say that force and matter are eternal than to imagine God as the creator, a personal being who in turn must have been created.

Then it was considered that mind, the producer of thought, was likewise material and a vitally inherent part of matter. Thought and matter were thus inseparable. Outside of matter, and its attribute force, there was therefore nothing. Consequently matter and force constitute the universe, nothing more, nothing less. They were never created, they cannot be destroyed, they must have been from eternity, and must last throughout eternity. Napoleon, when he heard this reasoning, asked the great scientist Laplace, "And what about God?" To this question Laplace answered, "Sire, I have no need for that unfounded hypothesis," and this answer, based as it was on the foregoing argument, can be understood and accepted as logical and reasonable.

It is now generally accepted that even the most advanced organism of all, namely man, was not brought into being by one creative act, but developed slowly from a long series of mammal ancestors, our nearest animal relation being the anthropoid ape. Much controversy raged during the 19th century over this suggestion, when Darwin sent out his challenge in his great work, *Origin of Species*, published in 1859. He was derided by the Church and Science, and not until towards the end of the last century did his theory, with certain modifications, win general consent.

The other discoveries of science had banished the gods from the universe. Many believed that this new discovery turned man himself into a material creation, minus a soul, his term of conscious life being limited to the short span from the cradle to the grave. Materialism had thus an answer for everything. There was no God, and there was no soul in man. Nothing existed apart from matter. Matter was all and in all, omnipresent, omnipotent and omniscient. Matter was the universe, and nothing existed beyond our sense perceptions.

In terms of evolution scientists drew the picture of the development of earth and man. The forces of nature were forever changing the surface of the earth. Charles Lyell, the famous geologist, in 1831, explained how all this happened, how mountains and land were formed, how deposits of coal and iron occurred, and all the minerals were laid down slowly over the ages. Then came the plants, to be followed by animal life which occupied a period of more than a hundred million years.

Ernest Haeckel then pursued the task Darwin had commenced, and propounded his conclusion that the whole cosmogony could be expressed in one word "Monism", and that man himself was just a material unit. He published various standard books, his first being *Evolution of Man*, advocating this view.

In his opinion it is a delusion to believe that the soul in man is a separate entity, an independent individuality, which dwells for a time only in the mortal frame, leaving it, and living on after death. The personal soul has a beginning to its existence, which beginning can be determined to the moment, namely when the male and female cells coalesce. Consequently, the souls of men or animals have not pre-existed, because they are bound up with the chemical constitution of the plasm. What has not pre-existed cannot be termed immortal. The soul is not a special immaterial entity, but the sum total of a number of connected functions of the brain. When the brain dies the soul also dies.

Haeckel has a large following today, who consider, as he did, that the belief in a life after death is wholly inconsistent with the facts of evolution and of physiology. They argue that each one of us was at the beginning of our existence a simple globule of protoplasm in which there is no place for the soul, that all organisms descend from possibly a single primitive form, and this developed out of lifeless matter by spontaneous generation.

The creed of monistic philosophy can best be summed up in the words of Haeckel. They are found at the end of his last pronouncement entitled *Last Words on Evolution*, which followed his two famous books, *The Riddle of the Universe* and *The Wonders of Life*. What follows must be considered the mature conclusion of this great man.

> Our Monistic God, the all-embracing essence of the world, the nature God of Spinoza and Goethe, is identical with the eternal, all-inspiring energy, and is one in eternal and infinite substance with space-filling matter. It lives and moves in all things. And as we see that the law of substance is universal, that the conservation of matter and of energy is inseparably connected, and that the ceaseless development of this substance follows the same eternal iron laws, we find God in natural law itself. The will of God is at work in every falling drop of rain and every growing crystal, in the scent of the rose, and the spirit of man.

In *The Riddle of the Universe* Haeckel definitely

pronounced against the idea that man survived death, in the following words:—

> The belief in the immortality of the soul is a dogma in hopeless contradiction with the most solid empirical truths of modern science.

Professor Tyndall considered the belief in an afterlife a "base delusion", and Huxley thought that the subject was not even worth discussing, as about it "we do know nothing and can know nothing". Sir Arthur Keith, the well-known anatomist and anthropologist, is quite clear and definite when advocating his materialistic beliefs. In one of his lectures he spoke as follows:—

> Every fact known to them (medical men) compels the inference that mind, spirit and soul are the manifestations of a living brain, just as flame is the manifest spirit of a burning candle. At the moment of extinction both flame and spirit cease to have a separate existence. However much this mode of explaining man's mentality may run counter to long and deeply-cherished beliefs, medical men cannot think otherwise if they are to believe the evidence of their senses.

The question which divides the Materialist from the Spiritualist relates to the survival of the soul after death. Thus the Materialist challenges the Spiritualist because he thinks that proof of survival does not exist, and that nothing can be believed without evidence. To talk about the mind as if it were an independent entity directing the body requires evidence, and no proof exists for such an assertion. Everything comes from matter, and mind is no exception. The universe, in other words, can be described in terms of physics and chemistry. It is impossible to dissociate the mind from the brain. When the brain is diseased the mind ceases to function. Therefore the mind is not independent of the brain, but depends on the brain. Destroy the brain and you destroy the mind.

Thus, to the Materialist, religion resolves itself into a question of ethics, of the duty of each one to his neighbour. The fact that the life of a Materialist is as good as that of a non-materialist proves that it is not a question of belief in the supernatural, or in gods, that makes one good or bad. To the Materialist the love of righteousness is in itself a sufficient incentive, as experience proves that happiness can best be attained by treating our neighbour as we ourselves wish to be treated.

In the words of Vivian Phelips, in his recently published book *Modern Knowledge and Old Beliefs*:—

> We militant Rationalists are inspired, as indeed you are well aware, with that very love of the good and the true and the beautiful. . . . You have no right to imply that we are not guided by the same high motive you claim for yourself.

Again, as Samuel Laing says in *Modern Science and Modern Thought*:—

> Rightly considered, self reverence, self knowledge and self control are the three pillars which support the edifice of a wise and well ordered practical life.

I think I have given a fair statement in the foregoing pages of the outlook on life of the Materialist, and this can be summed up in a few words. The universe is guided by unbroken law. We are individual material creatures, and life is a material expression which lasts only during our conscious existence on earth. The supernatural does not exist, and all supernatural religion is due to man's ignorance of universal laws. A world beyond the physical is a figment of the imagination, and it is just as false to imagine such a state as it is to believe that God or the gods order the universe. Matter, or what we see and handle, exists; nothing else. Believing this, however, in no way affects our duty to our neighbour, and we believe that all should do their utmost to make our sojourn on earth as happy as possible, help the helpless, comfort the sorrowing, and give a helping hand wherever possible to those less fortunate than ourselves.

Let us not, however, confuse the word Materialist with the word Rationalist. A Rationalist need not be a Materialist. It is a word which to the orthodox means one who is against religion, because the Rationalist uses his reason and thinks for himself. He will not rely on authority and must have a satisfactory reason behind his beliefs and actions. *The New English Dictionary* defines Rationalism as (1) the practice of explaining in a manner agreeable to reason whatever is apparently supernatural in the records of sacred history; (2) the principle of regarding reason as the chief or only guide in matters of religion.

On that definition I take my stand as a Rationalist. Because I used my reason, because I thought, and because I would not allow sentiment to sway my judgment from pursuing the road to the goal of truth, I am a Spiritualist. For the same reason I have discarded the supernatural in religion, and I now put forward a rational religion discarding the supernatural but embracing the supernormal. For the supernormal there is ample evidence, but there is none for the supernatural, and on the supernatural all orthodox religions are based.

Reason is our only guide. It is the compass of life. Each one of us is an individual mind and that mind makes decisions. If we take no account of evidence and experience in making our decisions we are not rational beings; we are irrational. Everyone should therefore aim at being a Rationalist and be proud to claim the name, because once reason is dethroned the flood-gates are opened for the in-flow of superstition, to be followed by intolerance and misery. The more we have used our reason, in like proportion has our happiness and well-being increased.

As this book proceeds we shall see how far I, a Rationalist and a Spiritualist, consider the Materialist is right, and wherein I think he errs. That he is right in much is undoubted, but in my opinion he has only part of the truth. When he knows more, much that is obscure to him will become clear, because materialism alone cannot explain the universe on the basis of all the facts we now possess. An addition to his knowledge must come in time, and when that day comes he will not have to abandon his present knowledge but rather add to it.

It is what the Materialist lacks that the Spiritualist perceives. What the Materialist already knows is accepted by intelligent Spiritualists as proved by evidence. What they desire is to extend the bounds of knowledge of the Materialist. The gulf between the Materialist and the Spiritualist lies entirely in the belief of the latter that he has the proof that man has a mind and etheric body which survive death, and that what the Materialist describes as the directing force of the universe is Mind, which is behind the causes and effects we perceive.

Instead of matter constituting the universe, the evidence of the séance room proves without a doubt to the Spiritualist that matter is only one expression of reality in the universe. Spiritualists have found reality expressed through a different substance from physical matter, and one which is much more under the control of the discarnate mind than is physical matter under the control of the mind encased in flesh. This will be made clear in the chapter which follows.

CHAPTER VI.

THE NEW AGE OF THOUGHT.

Now I wish to focus all I have so far written. Until this is done it is useless to proceed further. This book is not for the purpose of destroying what is true in religion, but only that which is false. Only after the chaff has been separated from the grain, and been discarded, is it possible to bring religion and science into harmony. Science in turn must put aside certain prejudices engendered by the folly, intolerance and ignorance of those who have supported orthodox religion.

Because the belief in survival, and the existence of another order of life than this one on earth is the central theme of religion, science, in consequence of the mistakes which have been linked with religion, has consigned it, as well as the rubbish, to the waste heap of superstition. In this respect science must change, and in fact is changing slowly.

Let us now undrape from religion all the garments of superstition on the one hand, and be really and truly scientific on the other. Let us adopt the scientific attitude to religion, and accept only that for which there is evidence. Let us also adopt the scientific attitude to all natural phenomena, and accept all that nature reveals to us. Let us discard only what is untrue and not shut our eyes to that which is true. If we withdraw from religion all that is false, and retain what is true, and if we accept as true all that nature reveals to us, it will be found that science and religion today are in complete harmony. In fact they are one, and have always been one. Only ignorance on both sides has separated them and kept them apart.

I shall deal first of all with religion. The word in the minds of most unthinking people stands for superstition, the belief in the miraculous, in gods and demons, saviours, sacrifice, forms, ceremonies, rites, god-written books and all the foolish drapings which have come to surround it. Religion is a word which comes from the Latin *re legare* and means "to bind again", it being the link between the etheric and physical orders. This link has been so encrusted with error that before I start its cleaning I must first of all clear away many misconceptions. The first is the belief that the gods are divine potentates ordering the world; the second, that sacrifice was ever a divine institution; and the third, that a special revelation came from God, or the gods, to a privileged group of people, no matter what name they go by, Christian, Jew or Mohammedan.

How did all these errors creep into religion? The cause is not difficult to trace, and lies entirely in the misconception of the word "God". For thousands of years this word has been mistranslated, misapplied and misused. The word originally meant "Spirit". "God is a Spirit," says the *Scottish Shorter Catechism*, but no other four words in the English language have been more misunderstood and misquoted.

The word "God" is the name given by the ancients to a Spirit, one who has lived on earth and died, or, as I term this being, an Etherian, an inhabitant of the

Spirit World, or the Etheric World, or Etheria, whichever term you prefer. The word "Gods" refers to the Spirits, to those who have lived on earth and now inhabit Etheria. Cicero makes this quite clear in the following passage: "Those whose minds scorn the limitations of the body are honoured with the frequent appearance of the gods." If this is rendered into modern English it means that those who have the gift of clairvoyance can frequently see spirits. That is the plain English of the phrase. Many other old quotations similar to this could be given to prove that when the Jews, Romans, Greeks and others used the word God, they meant a Spirit, an Etherian.

Now I have reached one of the most important parts of this book. If I cannot make myself understood it is impossible for me to get focussed in the minds of the reader what has gone before. I shall be as clear as possible, but every word must be carefully followed.

When reading ancient literature in future, substitute the words "other-world man" for God and "other-world woman" for Goddess, and, when the gods or goddesses are referred to, use the words "other-world men" or "other-world women". I prefer, as do so many of my friends in Etheria, the word "Etherian" as they are solid, not vaporous, beings, but that does not affect the argument. That is how the words god or gods should be read, but, as the word "spirit" is the one commonly used and best understood, I shall use it in this chapter.

Besides doing this, remember also the next time you read the Bible that throughout the Old Testament the words "God", or "the Lord", have been frequently mistranslated and should read "the gods". The Jewish records in the original Hebrew contain two different words, one singular and the other plural, Yahveh meaning God, and Elohim meaning the gods. They both probably originated in Egypt. Elohim occurs more than two thousand times in the Old Testament, and should not have been translated "God" but "the gods".

That, however, is only one mistake the translators made. When I say the translators I do not necessarily mean those who translated the Bible into English, but those who made the translation from the originals. Another mistake is that they often used the singular word God, or the Lord, throughout instead of the word spirit or spirits. Now read the Bible with this in mind, substituting the words spirit, or the spirits, for the words God or the Lord. What then do we find? That the ancients believed that they were in contact with the spirits of the dead, not with some potentate of the sky, who had created the heavens and the earth, and who gave his commandments to mankind. The word God, meaning Infinite Intelligence, need seldom be applied, though doubtless the priests tried to convey this idea to the people when the original meaning of the word God or gods was forgotten.

Again, when reading ancient literature, the Greek or Roman classics, or the Babylonian and Egyptian records, use the word spirit or spirits for God, or the gods, and you will obtain the correct meaning of these ancient writings. This mistranslation of God, or the gods, is the root cause of all the difficulties with which devout people are faced today. The orthodox take everything literally in their sacred writings and forget that over the ages the meaning of words has changed, and that the documents they think infallible have passed through many hands, been tampered with, altered, and mistranslated for thousands of years.

Hence the Bible gives a different meaning to words and sayings from that which was originally intended, and so expresses religious beliefs which no intelligent person can accept. When, however, the meaning of the word God to the ancients is understood, there will be no necessity to be troubled by trying to justify all the cruel and barbaric teaching, attributed to Infinite Intelligence, as recorded in the Bible. It came largely from the cruel imagination of the priests. Originally it purported to be derived from the spirits, but it was interpreted as the priests desired. What occurs in the Bible occurs in all ancient literature, the Greek classics for instance, in which the gods or spirits are made to speak like men.

Every god was once a man who lived on earth, and every goddess a woman. Primitive man, when he saw an apparition, termed it a god. It is quite understandable that he should do so, as it was something beyond the physical. I have already explained in a previous chapter how these apparitions were the origin, and became the basis, of the supernatural in religion. On this foundation the supernatural in all religions is based. On this natural basis has been reared all the superstitions surrounding all religions, Christianity included.

The mystical nature of the individual, not content with the simple fact that those who had died appeared on earth from time to time in their etheric bodies, to be seen by those who had clairvoyant sight, made it necessary to weave round this natural occurrence draping after draping of symbolic beliefs and ritual, until they had completely obscured the natural by the supernatural. Religion thus became entwined with supernatural words, symbols and rites, and only now are some intelligent enough to see the wood for the trees.

We now have taken the first step, namely the substituting for the word God the word Spirit. Let us now take the next. What do the drapings mean? There are hidden meanings for each, but hardly anyone knows what they are. They are lost in the ages of antiquity. We must undrape this ancient mummy bit by bit, and examine each cloth to find the reason for it being wrapped round the body of the underlying truth.

In most religions the people worshipped many gods, because clairvoyance revealed many spirits, each in turn being deified. Greek literature tells us that séances were held, at which the gods appeared. They materialised just as spirits materialise today in the presence of a medium. In Greece and Asia Minor mediums were attached to certain temples, and there the people resorted to communicate with the gods. To these holy places came deputations from all over Greece and neighbouring countries, to ask advice of the gods upon all subjects from politics to religion.

Most of the great law-givers and sages in pre-Christian days, during the height of Greek and Roman civilisation, made contact with the gods, particularly by means of the Delphic oracle. We are at a loss to know how genuine this method of communication was, but Plutarch tells us that no fraud was ever found to be associated with the medium at Delphi. Genuine psychic phenomena was doubtless mixed up with much that came from the sub-conscious minds of the mediums. But this we know, that nearly every great thinker and ruler of these times held mediums, or oracles, in high regard and considered their utterances as sacred messages from another order of existence.

The belief that the gods communicated with man through mediums goes back into the far distant past, and what the priests learned about the nature of man, and the after-life, they expressed in terms of symbolism, which came to be accepted literally. Thus we have the symbol of the Trinity, found in many religions. In Egypt it was represented by an equilateral triangle. This is composed of three equal lines, forming three similar angles. It was a unity in itself, made up of three lines and angles, a trinity in unity. This symbol represented man, who is body, soul and spirit, and from this fact developed the doctrine of the Trinity.

As the people could not think of God other than in the form of a man, who is the highest creation we know, they symbolised God in the form of a god-man, born of a human mother after contact with a god or spirit. This god-man revealed God to man, but God likewise was symbolised as a trinity, and the god-man was looked on as a member of this trinity. The Deity was thus divided up into a trinity, just as is man himself. So we find the Deity represented as three persons, but one God. The first member in this trinity of gods was the principal god, who was called the Father God. He represented mind in man. The god-man represented the flesh body of man and he was the Son. The third god of this trinity was termed the

Holy Spirit or Holy Ghost, symbolical of man's etheric body, which returned to earth to commune with its inhabitants, and was termed the Comforter. Thus was the Deity symbolised in the likeness of man. A trinity in unity, each part separate in itself but forming one whole.

Just as the conception of God was symbolised in the likeness of man, so death was symbolised by the experiences attributed to the god-men who came to be looked on as saviours who suffered, died, rose again and ascended into heaven. These episodes in the lives of all the world-saviours have, down the ages, been terribly mutilated in their telling, but we can disengage the false from the true. It is simply the story of what befalls man at death. He suffers, dies and rises in his etheric body into the etheric world. His flesh body is figuratively crucified by illness before death.

His mind—the Father God—can no longer keep in contact with the earth through the flesh, and, because of being displaced, is depicted as angry with the flesh man. Death, however, is not the end, just as Calvary was not the end. The empty tomb symbolises death conquered by the released spirit. The spirit then enters Hades, or the Astral Plane, and returns to earth to comfort those who are left behind, after which comes its ascension into glory, when it passes through the Astral to Heaven, or the plane above the Astral. All the death and resurrection stories of the various world-saviours are just embellished anecdotes of the greatest event in the life of everyone. The appearance after death was important for the purpose of keeping the people in mind that life continues after death.

These ideas formed the basis of a very ancient religious drama, a god-man being the hero, and the people were told its meaning by the priests. It is still enacted at the present time at Oberammergau. These dramas, thousands of years old, were held at various times of the year, in different countries, when the earth entered various phases of its annual journey round the sun. This is a relic from sun-worship. The people could understand the deeper things of life only by being taught them in parables, which was the method adopted by Jesus, and all teachers, in the days when the world was young. As the sun rose each day, so man rose from the dead, and another old parable likens death and life to vegetation which dies to come again to life. This method of presentation is needed even today, as otherwise the simple-minded could not understand. A saviour can be understood by the masses, but the knowledge Spiritualists possess can be understood only by those of deeper intelligence.

The origin of the Eucharist can now also be understood. The story of the god-man's death was not enough. The people required something more tangible than an ancient story. Hence the Eucharist, which is a ceremony at which the priests turn bread and wine into the saviour's body and blood. By consuming these the partakers gain eternal life, as the victim, who has survived death, bestows this divine gift through transmuting the bread and wine which becomes his body and blood. No Roman Catholic will die without receiving the last rites, because he believes, as did his ancestors for thousands of years back, that by partaking of the body and blood he becomes immortal, as his saviour is immortal. This is a very old delusion handed down from early man, and believed in by all Christians in one form or another.

I shall now leave this subject of symbolism for the reader to think out further, because once on the right track it is not difficult to give an underlying meaning to all the forms and ceremonies of all religions. They are just drapings which, when the world was young, were wound round the central truth of man's survival after death, for the purpose of enabling him to get a faint idea of a great reality. They are retained today by the priesthood, which extols the old and despises the truths Spiritualism proclaims to the world, because they are the custodians of the drapings. When the truth is known the drapings are no longer required and their work is at an end.

What surprises one is that in the light of modern knowledge the people continue to support the priests, who cannot now plead ignorance as could their brothers in the days prior to the Renaissance. In those days the priests no doubt honestly believed what they preached, but today it cannot be so. After four hundred years of growing knowledge, it is difficult to believe that any priest in Christendom can honestly believe that what he preaches is true. If he does, it can only be by shutting himself entirely from the world, and reading no other book than the Bible or some other devotional literature.

If this is true about the priests, it is also true about the orthodox laity. Consequently orthodoxy still worships the drapings, and thinks little about what is underneath. The drapings have hidden the truth about the after-life from its eyes, but they must be retained at all costs because, if they were discarded, the custodians would be without employment. The drapings are so old that the priests themselves have forgotten their meaning. They perform their ceremonials in connection with them as a custom, as a routine, but they do not know what they mean.

I have asked dozens of priests and ministers of the Christian religion to explain to me the underlying meaning of the forms, symbols and ceremonials of Christianity, but not one has been able to do so. They are quite ignorant of the world's ancient religions which preceded Christianity, and the only way any honest-minded parson can continue his work is by remaining ignorant. Otherwise there would be a battle between his profession and his honesty. This battle has doubtless often been fought, and every subterfuge employed to make it possible for him to support his Church and at the same time satisfy his reason.

The knowledge of what these symbols mean creates an intelligent interest in mankind's religious activities, but what is also important is to realise that the gods have not vanished from the sky, that they fill the heavens, that instead of being one, or a dozen, there are billions of them, and that all who have lived on earth and died are none other than the gods. The word "God" has been wrongly used to denote a being superior to man, a personal god, who has his habitation in the heavens and governs the earth through his chosen priests.

That is what the priests have always made the people believe and still do, and that is why they hate

Spiritualism, because, when one accepts what Spiritualism teaches, he has no need for a priest. That is also the reason why the Christian Church burned or drowned a quarter of a million mediums, as its leaders realised that the medium is the rival to the priests, the medium being able to reveal the other world to the people without the aid of the symbolism of the priests. It was very cunning of the Hebrew priests to put into the mouth of Jehovah the command "Thou shalt not suffer a witch to live." It is a good sample of priestly inspiration, and the Christian Church made full use of it when it had the power to enforce its will.

Thus we see how, though all the orthodox gods have perished, Spiritualism proves that we ourselves are gods, that in each one of us is the divine mind which survives death and may well be immortal. Instead of being slaves of the gods, we have before us what appears to be an endless future, which will be to each one as he wills it. We have all the attributes of the gods. We have risen now mentally to the position of being able to appreciate the fact that each one of us has latent within us what the ancients ascribed to the gods.

We are all potential gods and goddesses. This has always been man's destiny, but only now does he know it, as the result of direct evidence and not by faith alone. Just as we gain a fuller knowledge of our destiny, so do we rise in self-respect. As heirs to a glorious heritage, we cease to cringe and worship, and consequently we leave old superstitions far behind us. Man, the only known personal God, can now stand erect, and face the future without fear, armed with the knowledge gained through the only revelation that has come from heaven to earth, to be known in our day as Spiritualism.

We must not, however, forget the Materialist. I have in my previous books made clear that the claims made by Spiritualism rest on a solid scientific basis. Can the same be said of those of the Materialist? Like the priests at the time of Galileo who refused to make use of his telescope and see the planets and stars, the Materialist declines to make use of the telescope of clairvoyance and the telephone of clairaudience and learn from our clairvoyants and clairaudients what they have to tell us about the world of finer matter, without and within this earth of ours.

He refuses to attend séances, and thus make contact with this very real world, which in the presence of a medium can be made apparent to all. He refuses to listen to the voices of those he considers dead, and is most unscientific in his attitude towards phenomena which he will not trouble to investigate. The orthodox believe too much, but the Materialist believes too little.

Let us now consider the basis the Materialists have for their negative attitude. I think I shall be able to show that they have no grounds for their assertions, and when evidence is lacking definite pronouncements should not be made. They accept the existence only of the visible and the tangible, and deny that more than this exists.

Man's soul, the Materialist believes, is not a separate entity, a unique independent individuality, which controls for a time only the mortal frame, leaving it and living on as a thinking individual body after death. On what evidence is this view based? None whatever. The laws of physics, the Materialist believes, control the life of the soul just as absolutely as they do the phenomena of inorganic nature. If the soul is part of the material body, and life and physical matter are inseparable, this is a natural inference, but, if it is not, then the laws of physics do not operate. The whole question resolves itself into whether the soul is or is not part of the material body. The belief of the Materialist that plasm is a chemical compound of carbon, and that it alone accomplishes the various processes of life and thought, is one for which there is no evidence.

Because the stem cell divides and subdivides rapidly into a number of simple cells, the Materialist does not accept Mind as the explanation, but rather he terms it the unconscious memory of the plasm, which is part of the plasm. He points to a damaged brain, and from it draws the conclusion that mind and brain are one and the same, and that brain changes and mental processes are similar. Until recently it was heresy to argue that the brain was like a piano, the mind being compared to the player, and that if the instrument became damaged the player could not function. It is all a question of evidence as to whether the brain performs the duties of both player and instrument or is the instrument only. The Materialist will not face the evidence which proves that mind is not a part of the brain, and that it leaves the physical brain at death to function through the etheric duplicate brain which passes from the body along with the mind at death.

Another argument the Materialist uses against survival is that the beginning of personality can be traced to conception, which is a physical event. This argument carries no weight with the Spiritualist who believes that we continue to exist after death, once personality and individuality are established, and that is what happens at conception. If the parents have souls which survive death, have they not the power to transmit part of their souls to their progeny? It all sums itself up into the question of monism or dualism in relation to man.

Then the Materialist will refer you to the development of the brain. The more intelligence develops, the larger, the more voluminous, and the more specialised does the cerebrum become. The grey matter, or cortex of the cerebrum, which is its most important part, attains only in the higher mammals the degree of quantitative and qualitative development that qualifies it to be the organ of mind. Hence, as there is no seat for the mind in the lower animals, it follows that mind has evolved, so they argue, just like the body, and that it dies with the body.

Though the higher mammals have an organised seat for the mind it does not follow, the Spiritualist believes, that a less developed mind does not exist in the lower animals. It can be equally well contended that, as mind gets more and more control of its organism, it develops a localised seat for its special habitation. The gulf then between the savage and a savant, or between a worm and a dog, is all a question of mental development, and mental development means the faculty of making clearer mental images and relating these to each other in an orderly and intelligent manner.

It is a question of the quality and fertility of the mind acting on the physical substance, and, though we witness evolving mind, this is no argument that it and the physical are one. There is solid ground for believing that developing mind has caused the physical to evolve and is the cause of evolution. It has directed the evolution of the physical, but it is no permanent part of the physical.

All that divides the Materialist from the Spiritualist is this question as to whether man is a dual or a single organism. Neither physics nor chemistry can give the answer. Because they cannot answer the problem it does not follow that the Materialist has a right to assert that man is a material monism. Fifty years ago physical science was ignorant of the fact that ether waves existed. If somebody last century had asked if such phenomena as ether waves existed, science would have replied in the negative, because science knew nothing about ether waves.

Science never invents phenomena, it only discovers what is hidden in nature's storehouse. Now we know that ether waves not only exist, but can be produced at will, and that they can be turned into sound by means of the transformer termed our radio set. The radio set therefore proves that something unseen exists, just as in the time of Galileo the telescope proved the vastness of space. In other words, when the medium for the expression of a phenomenon is discovered, that which is unseen and unsensed can be expressed.

Each physical body is a medium for the expression of mind, just as our radio set is the medium for the expression of unsensed ether waves. Mind, in contact with matter, means life. Matter devoid of mind is something dead. Mind is normally unsensed by physical beings apart from physical substance, but, when conditions are suitable, a discarnate mind can use physical substance to express itself, and this physical substance we term a medium, a person who can lend to a discarnate mind his or her body, or part of his or her body, to enable this mind to express itself.

This discarnate mind asserts that it once used a physical body of its own to express itself on earth, that at death it was severed from this physical body and now functions in a finer body. This finer body, we are told, when on earth was woven into the texture of the physical body which was no more than its physical envelope. The physical is like a copper electric wire through which electricity expresses itself. Both brain and body are only conduits for the life force which is generated by the mind, each physical cell being connected to the mind by an etheric duplicate cell which all together make up the etheric brain and body.

Infra-red photography proves that sensitive plates can be affected by vibrations without the assistance of ordinary light. Psychic photography proves that sensitive plates can be affected by etheric substance outside our range of vision. In some of Dr. Osty's experiments with Rudi Schneider it was proved that this medium externalised a force or substance which, by obstructing or occulting a beam of infra-red light, absolutely proves its real existence. This externalised force or substance can move objects, and show intelligence, even to the extent of tying a knot in a handkerchief. The points that Dr. Osty's experiments bring out beyond all criticism are:—

(1) The real existence of the substance, without any possible normal effort of any human being, the arrangements being such as to preclude the physical possibility of fraud, and,

(2) That the substance, though invisible, has physical power and can be directed by, or through, the mind of the medium.

This is a proved fact of science, but only when we had the medium could we experience it, and that is the point of the whole matter. Spiritualists know that in the presence of mediums phenomena occur which cannot happen beyond their presence. The medium in this case performs the same function as does our radio set, making manifest some force or intelligence which we do not experience in our normal life.

What is this force or intelligence? That it exists there is no doubt, and the question is just how to explain it. The Materialist denies its existence. Thus, like an ostrich, he is hiding his head in the sand, because this discovery upsets his pre-conceived theory that man is a monism. If man is a material monism, how can he explain the Rudi Schneider phenomena? I agree that it does not prove survival of death, but it proves that the individual has extended faculties which are ignored by the Materialist.

For fifty years men with scientific minds have been devoting themselves to psychic science, and coming more and more to the conclusion that mind is something apart from the physical organism. Last century the number of scientific men who held this view was notably small, but today the number is steadily increasing. If the Spiritualist contention is wrong, men of science would never have pursued the investigation, but because the Spiritualist contention is right more and more scientists are coming over to the Spiritualist belief, and accepting it as the only explanation of what are termed supernormal occurrences.

Nothing I have said so far proves survival. Normal trance in my opinion does not definitely prove survival, though the latest scientific experiments with trance mediums may do so as they develop. The recent experiments of Dr. Adolph Meyers with Mrs. Garrett certainly go far to prove that another personality is using her organism. Dr. Meyers is chief of the department of Psychiatry at Johns Hopkins University, U.S.A. He had a series of sixteen sittings with this medium, and by means of the "association test" found that normally she reacted differently from what she did in trance.

Mrs. Garrett was given this test, which comprised a series of words which she had to answer according to the association which each word evoked. The test hung on what is called the association of ideas. For instance, if someone is asked of what the colour blue makes him think, the reply would probably be the sky. Mrs. Garrett was given a large number of these words, when normal, and the way she associated them was duly noted. In trance, however, when the same questions were asked, quite different answers were given. On comparing the results Dr. Meyers found that the reactions differed as widely as they would in the case of different independent personalities. Tests were also made with the Galvanometer held by her normally, and in trance. Here again the reaction to words or phrases was quite different in the two states.

Clairvoyance, clairaudience and psychic photography do prove survival. If there were only one clairvoyant and only one clairaudient medium, and only one psychic photographic medium in the world, I would be very chary in expressing an opinion as to the cause behind the results obtained. When, however, there are thousands of clairvoyants and clairaudients, and scores of photographic mediums throughout the world in whose presence photographs of deceased people appear on ordinary negatives, the cumulative evidence which has been gathered as the result of their mediumship, in my opinion, proves survival.

These clairvoyants and clairaudients see and hear something beyond the normal range of sight and hearing, or otherwise they could not receive the evidential messages which daily come through them as instruments. The messages from, and the descriptions they give of, people called dead, are too realistic to allow those who have had experience of them to doubt that these messages and descriptions are other than what they profess to be.

The evidence in favour of clairvoyance and clairaudience is so comprehensive, exhaustive and complete, that if we had nothing but this to guide us we would have sufficient to prove survival. In time, as psychic photographic mediums increase, it will become as common to get photographs of the departed as it is now for our friends abroad to send us their photographs.

A pencil writing on a sheet of paper in full light, without visible material contact, and moreover writing in the style of the deceased person who claims to be present, is very difficult to explain unless we believe that the individual who once lived on earth and wrote in a handwriting of similar style, and signed his or her name in exactly the same manner, is present and is moving the pencil in the manner all can see.

Furthermore how are we to explain the Direct Voice, a voice speaking in the presence of the medium, but quite apart from his vocal organs, and often several yards away from them? These voices will answer questions, and make intelligent remarks. Each voice will speak as its professed owner did when on earth. When this phenomenon is at its best the voice can easily be recognised as the one belonging to the deceased person who is purporting to speak. It is emphatic always that the personality behind the voice once lived on earth, and was called on earth by the name the personality is still known by.

This phenomenon, in my opinion, definitely proves survival. How it is produced by the discarnate speaker I have fully explained in my book *On the Edge of the Etheric*, and therein I have also given some of the information I have received through these voices speaking in space quite apart from the medium. In my investigations of this phenomenon, which extended over five years, I took all the precautions necessary to prevent the medium speaking, and I was quite satisfied that when the voice was speaking it was not produced by the medium or any other earth person.

The Direct Voice has been heard in daylight as well

as in the dark, and the infra-red telescope, which is now in use, proves that the voices we hear do not come from the vocal organs of either the medium or the sitters. The direct voice has been heard by hundreds of people at the same time. It cannot be put down to hallucination, as it has been often recorded on gramophone records. Its largest audience was on the occasion when Walter, the deceased brother of Margery Crandon, the famous American medium, broadcast his voice over the wireless, and it was heard not only in America but in this country as well.

Lastly, we come to the best evidence we have for survival, namely the complete materialisation which can be recognised as the figure of the deceased person. These materialisations have been recorded under strictly scientific test conditions. Each materialised figure takes the form and features of the individual as he appeared on earth. Each talks and hears and shows memory, emotion, affection, and moves about the room like an ordinary individual.

These materialised figures claim to have lived on earth, and survived death. They explain that they make their presence seen and felt by us by borrowing ectoplasm from the medium, which makes them visible and enables their voices to vibrate our atmosphere. These materialisations have occurred on thousands of occasions and have been reliably recorded. This phenomenon proves survival.

We have therefore six different classes of phenomena which in themselves prove survival abundantly. The first is clairvoyance, the second clairaudience, the third psychic photography, the fourth pencil writing, the fifth Direct Voice, and the sixth materialisation. Taken in conjunction with these six, trance phenomenon deserves to be taken seriously, though it may remain the least impressive and convincing evidence of survival. The difficulty with trance phenomenon is just to know when the influence of the mind of the communicator takes the place of the mind of the medium, and how much the medium's mind influences the communications.

The foregoing are the outstanding classes of phenomena the Spiritualist relies on to prove his contention that mind survives death. There are, however, other supernormal occurrences which, when taken together, strengthen this conviction, such as messages spelt out by a tilting table, apports, automatic writing, apparitions, hauntings, and various other experiences which seem to prove that discarnate intelligences are behind and responsible for what occurs.

All my assertions are based on evidence and experience. What, therefore, does it matter to the Spiritualist if the scientist cannot find the soul in plasm? What does it matter to the Spiritualist if the Materialist says that, because he cannot see or weigh an immaterial soul, no soul exists? He might as well argue that because he cannot weigh and see the ether no ether waves exist. He, however, postulates an invisible ether, because he cannot account for the sounds which come from his radio set in any other way. Similarly, the Spiritualists cannot account for psychic phenomena except on the basis that mind and personality exist after the change called death.

It is not as if the Spiritualist is propounding something new, as he is doing no more than give specific evidence in support of a belief that has been accepted by mankind throughout the ages. It is the Materialist who, over the last three hundred years, has drawn the red herring across the trail, and it is for the Materialist to prove by evidence that his assertions are right. If he cannot do so, his assertions count for nothing.

Materialism is based on unevidential assertions. Materialism relies for its beliefs on only what it sees and feels. All recent scientific discoveries are tending more and more to show us that the universe includes unsensed forces, which in turn operate on unsensed substance, and that the universe is infinitely greater than our physical senses can comprehend.

It is not physical matter that is the sovereign power of the universe, but some unseen force which is responsible for the vibrations which produce matter, or physical substance, on the one hand and etheric substance on the other. This unseen, yet very real force, I term Mind, because it performs the functions which we relate to mind. Mind is King of the Universe, and the universe can be explained and understood only in terms of mind. It might be more correct to term man a monism of mind than a monism of matter, but this needs qualification.

Mind expresses itself in all degrees from physical matter to etheric substance, and we individuals are composed of this mind substance which appreciates, and the matter substance which is appreciated. In other words we are a dualism, made up of body and mind. On earth, however, we are a trinity, as we are composed of mind the guiding substance, besides the etheric body—the substance acted upon by mind—and lastly physical matter which is the covering for this etheric body during our time on earth. We pass on to our descendants this trinity, and what the Materialists call the monism of plasm is in reality a trinity made up of these three ranges of vibrations—mind, etheric body and physical covering.

If we can best express the universe in terms of mind, then the mind which guides each individual must be part of the thinking substance of the universe which has become individualised in each individual. Apart from mind it is impossible to imagine the universe, and it is equally impossible for us to imagine the universe without substance on which mind can act. Only by thinking of the universe as Mind, the cause of the numerous vibrations, and by remembering that mind is behind every appearance, can the universe be understood. Mind on earth cannot be seen but only its effect. Mind is super-physical and super-etheric. It is the thinking substance of the universe, always changing, always developing, never still. Mind is the moulding power in nature and it is the cause of growth, development, form and feature.

When mind in man is freed from its physical instrument, and attains full freedom in the finest ranges of etheric substance, then time and distance will cease for that mind. To Mind there is no distance and no time. The furthest distance is here, and the longest time is now. Mind is omnipresent, omnipotent and omniscient. It orders and it governs the universe, it is the cause behind every effect, which effect becomes a cause and that cause an effect. Mind causes the cause, and responds in the effect. Cause and effect are but words to denote different states of vibration, and behind each vibration is mind. The univeser is a gigantic scale of vibrations, and mind is the cause. Without mind there would be no vibration. Without vibration there would be no universe.

Mind, the highest scale of vibration, expresses itself through the lower scales. To conceive of anything higher than mind is impossible. It is now, always was, and ever shall be. Mind uses the physical vibrations to become individualised, and mind in man bounds the limit of our knowledge.

That there are individual minds outside the physical has been realised throughout the ages, but they are never other than men, super-men perhaps, but always men, with men's mind and ideas. No one can imagine a being higher than man. Consequently all the gods of the past have been created in the image of man, with his qualities and failings. Because he has realised this activity both outside and within himself, he could attribute it only to a man-like God, somewhat bigger and greater than himself, but with all man's qualities.

In error our ancestors placed the gods outside the universe, governing it as something apart from themselves. Only some advanced thinkers are as yet able to realise that mind dominates the universe, and that without mind there would be no universe. So, if we term God-Mind, or Mind-God, it matters little, so long as we understand that God and Mind both stand for that life-giving power which keeps the universe alive and in motion. It is behind all phenomena, and is the guiding intelligence in which we live, move and have our being. Mind, or God, with infinite arms embraces all that ever was, all that is, and all that ever shall be.

I am now using the word God correctly, and not relating it to the spirit of a dead man. The history of man is the story of his mistakes in trying to discover his relationship with this thinking power of the universe. Thus we find that from savagery to civilised man, from the stone age to the present day, humanity has been making overtures to this unseen power, to this unexplained force, through the medium of the gods or spirits. Thus has religion developed from early sun worship to the beliefs, forms and ceremonials of the present time.

From earliest times it was believed that the gods were either good or bad. The good were termed gods and the evil devils. One by one they were reduced in number until the last religion, Mohammedanism, retained one God only. One Devil was also left. Christians, however, still worship three gods, though some religions have more, and a few, such as Buddhism, none at all.

Humanity lived, and still lives to some extent, under the shadow of gods and devils. These beings are still held to be the cause of all the good or ill in life, of happiness or misery, of health or disease, of good or bad harvests, and it is still believed that our attitude to them determines our happiness here and hereafter. Each religion has its own particular gods, and the devout follower of the tenets of a religion expects to be rewarded here and hereafter. To attain the merit he so ardently desires he must follow carefully the particular customs and ceremonies attached to that religion, and accept without question the dogmas its priests expound as the divine revelation, which the gods have given through them to mankind for his acceptance.

If this had added to the happiness of mankind, had increased his peace, and made his death a joyous and glorious sunset, his ignorance of the universe would have done him little harm, but history tells a different story. Unfortunately, so as to placate the gods, no horror has been omitted and no crime has been left undone. For them churches were built, and for the thinkers dungeons. Verily the history of man is a record of ignorance, cruelty, savagery, murder, rapine and war, which evil doing was too often engaged in for no other reason than to please the gods.

In this more enlightened age we can still learn a wonderful lesson from the past, and can get confirmation of a great underlying truth. Cruel and barbarous as have been our ancestors, they were more than animals. That they were once animals, if we go far enough back, is true, but when man came to realise a force, a power in the universe to which he was related, however crude the idea of that relationship was and still is to many, man showed himself superior to the beasts. Not much superior very often, but yet superior, and this distinction became more and more marked as he developed in intelligence.

The animals can conceive of no power greater than man. Man, however, can conceive of a directing power in nature above and beyond his limited intelligence, which he worshipped and to which he offered his sacrificed victims. This groping after the Infinite, these attempts to get into closer and happier relationship with this divine intelligence, however much he likened it to himself, clearly shows the superiority of man, that he is something more than an animal, and has a higher type of mind than that with which the animal is endowed.

We can go even further and say that only when this realisation of the Infinite appears does man change from being an animal to become a man. That this did come about far back in history is true. Then some animal brain became fitted during the course of evolution to be the habitation of a more developed mind than that of any other animal of its time. Once this finer mind appeared it developed and expanded, and, as it did so, the universe unfolded, the history of man being just the record of this developing, expanding mind.

Thus today we find some minds so refined and developed that they have ceased to look on this earth with content. They have that urge which intensifies the desire for closer contact with the divine mind of which they are part, and this accounts for Religion, Philosophy and Mysticism. This more embracing mind possessed by man shows in other ways its difference from that of animals, in that right down the ages humanity has instinctively felt that death was but the door to another life. This idea the animals do not entertain, so far as our evidence goes, and this may be because they are not immortal as man may be, though the higher animals do retain their personality after death for a limited time.

The belief that man is an immortal being has ebbed and flowed like the sea. It has beaten in countless waves on the shore of time carrying both hope and fear. As human affection grew, hope and fear increased and developed into a systematic form of religion. Its priests made full use of these emotions, working on the love of man for woman, and woman for man, of parents for child, promising happiness to the supporters of their organisation, and misery for those who ignored their promises and claims.

Thus the fear of the unknown has kept a great organisation in being throughout the ages, under the names of different religions, all of which claim to have been revealed by God. All rivalry was suppressed, and none but the priests had access to the world unseen. Honest mediumship was sometimes employed, but, when the power failed, as it did so often, magic and fraud were substituted, which accounts for the magicians and the priests of old having so much in common. All mediumship outside the organisation was suppressed, and the people were taught that it was of the devil. When, however, it was made use of by the priests, then it was of God, and mediums were his oracles.

Mediumship seems to be a natural development of the human race, and, as it developed apart from the priesthood, every brutal method was employed by the priests to suppress it, so much so that it was almost stamped out. Materialism was the natural result. Millions of innocent people have been destroyed so that the power of priest-craft could prevail, and, in the case of mediumship, the idea that mediums were possessed of devils was fostered until even the victims themselves often believed it.

They were accused of being the cause of storm, disease, famine and everything that was not wanted.

Once accused they entered a quicksand from which they could not escape, and a tragic and violent death, accompanied often by torture, inevitably followed. Only by mental development have some evolved beyond this fear of the unknown, but it still dominates the lives of the majority.

History makes it clear that contact with the unseen, through mediumship, has existed right back into the distant past, and that the unseen and the unknown exerted a profound influence on our ancestors. They shaped the past story of nations, kingdoms and individuals. It is not religion that has civilised humanity but humanity that has civilised religion, and, as man developed mentally and morally, so his gods likewise improved.

When the mind of man develops sufficiently to grasp what this and my other books have to tell, there will be no further need of supernatural religion to keep society together as in the past, or to keep the people law-abiding by fear of divine punishment. Increased knowledge, and a sane understanding of our destiny, will in themselves act as the necessary safeguards against the frailties and instabilities of mankind, to produce a character so strong that it can overcome the way of life inherited from jungle ancestors.

Fear made man afraid to think. Fear made ignorance honoured, knowledge denounced, and to think or to question a crime. Every step in the path of progress has been taken over the dead bodies of those who had prepared the way for the advance, at the sacrifice of their lives and happiness. We are what we are today because some dared to question, to doubt and to challenge the authority of king and priest. These are the real heroes of the past, the thinkers, the inventors, the social reformers and the infidels. They paved the way for our present-day comforts and luxuries, for government by the people, and for the freedom enjoyed in some countries where honest thoughts can be expressed whether or not they are approved of by the government or church in power.

This freedom of thought has brought with it countless blessings to all who experience it. Unfortunately it is not recognised everywhere, and both Church and State still dominate many individual consciences. Fortunately in Britain we have now no cause for complaint. Complete freedom of thought and its expression is permitted, and this has resulted in a mighty quickening of intellectual development to the happiness of all. This advance has brought about a much truer realisation of our relationship to the rest of the universe, and, instead of cringing, we can now stand erect. Instead of fearing the future we can go forward, with the confident knowledge that if we do our best, seek righteousness and avoid that which is evil, our happiness here and hereafter is assured.

All that we need demand of ourselves is that we do our utmost for ourselves and others, because, by helping others, we likewise help ourselves and fit ourselves for the life to come. Increased happiness will be experienced hereafter in proportion as we have developed our minds on earth. Each one of us can rise by raising others, and to stoop to raise the fallen develops character, self-reliance and charity in all. If we have lived for ourselves alone, then we shall find a place ready for us in Etheria, and it will be a lonely one. On the other hand, if we have given thought to others, and have lived an unselfish life on earth, then our future abode will be bright and pleasant. The art of living and thinking aright is the essence of science, religion and philosophy.

My aim is to make people look below the surface of things, not just to accept what is generally believed, as the more deeply they think so does the universe unfold before them. The thinkers live in an unfolding universe, to their great joy and happiness. Those who always accept current opinions and never think deeply unfortunately miss much, for, as the mind is, so is the condition. This being so on earth, it will be much more pronounced hereafter, as in Etheria our thoughts condition our happiness and environment much more definitely than on earth.

There is a good reason for this. We reach the place in Etheria for which we are mentally fitted, because as the mind is so will be our surroundings. We mentally gravitate to the surroundings our minds are capable of appreciating, for as we think there so we are. There, mind can accommodate itself much more easily than it can on earth, as there to think is to be.

Let us therefore give more and more thought to our mental development, because, as the mind is, so is our happiness or our unhappiness. In Etheria we can mould our surroundings much more in accordance with our thoughts than we can on earth. There mind is a most potent force. Without mind there is nothing, and as the mind is so are we. Mind is King, mind in all states of development is the universe. We are all fragments of this over-ruling mind, which is everywhere, and in everything, has been from all eternity, and will be for all eternity.

CHAPTER VII.

THE GREATER WORLD.

THE previous chapters of this book are just the story of the attempt of mankind to meet an innate longing. We eat and sleep to meet a desire, and for the same reason we formulate beliefs, ideas and opinions about our destiny and what will happen to us after death. These go under the name of Religion. We also formulate opinions about the directive force or Mind which governs and orders the universe of which each of us is a part. This we also embrace under the term Religion, but it is also covered by the word Philosophy. Why are such words in use? Why are the words religion and philosophy found in our vocabulary?

For one reason only. Because there is another order of existence, into which we shall enter at death. To most people this is a subconscious idea and it prevails throughout the whole human race, irrespective of what intellectual opinions the individual may have on the subject. Outwardly the individual may deny this subconscious feeling, but even the most dogmatic materialist experiences it at times, and inwardly hates the thought of extinction.

As there are different orders of existence which it is our destiny to experience, it follows that there are different orders of substance in which they function. So far as our own world is concerned, as apart from the other worlds of the universe, this functioning takes place in what I term the Greater World, which is the subject of this chapter and the kernel of this book. If there had been no Greater World the foregoing chapters could never have been written, as history would not have supplied the necessary material.

Our ancestors would have had no religion and no philosophy, because they would have made no speculations as to their destiny. There would have been no prayers, worship, sacrifices, martyrs, religious beliefs, dogmas, rites, ceremonials, holy books, priests, mosques, temples, pagodas or churches. If there were no life for us beyond the grave, and no other world for us except this earth, half the history of humanity, as we now have it, would not have been. Half our story of the human race would not have been recorded, as it would never have occurred.[1] This being so, we have now come to the central theme in our consideration of the Unfolding Universe.

The Greater World has been scientifically discovered within the last century. It is no more a speculation; it is an actual fact, and some are now able to grasp it in its true setting because of our increased understanding and knowledge, our greater intelligence resulting from our minds being more developed than those of our ancestors. The universe during our time has consequently unfolded itself further, because mind in man has itself unfolded further, and is able to envisage and encompass this greater world. This being the case, let us now consider how much we now know of it, and what our future home is really like.

I can only enlarge in this book on what I said in

---

[1] This I have made clear in my book *The Curse of Ignorance*, a history of mankind, in two volumes.

On the Edge of the Etheric and *The Rock of Truth*, wherein I attempted to give an idea of the real world in which we live. In the following pages I have put together the information I have gathered from time to time from my informants in Etheria, when I was conversing with them on the causes which are behind appearances in Etheria, and on this I have developed the structure of the Greater World as I visualise it. We on earth, when dealing with another order of existence, are like blind people, who have to visualise their surroundings from what they are told. We have not even the capacity of touch possessed by the blind, and moreover we have to rely on information which reaches us only through a supernormal channel.

My endeavour has always been to relate the new knowledge to what we already know about the universe. Unless this can be done, it is impossible to grasp or visualise the complete picture. We must build only on a sound scientific basis. If this is possible, the Greater World can become comprehensible.

The immensity of the universe overwhelms us, because we regard the cosmos only from the physical point of view, from the material aspect. When, however, we remember that the physical is but one phase we realise that we are considering only the part and not the whole. Here on earth the material is everything to us, but after death we experience a new outlook on the same universe, the physical being replaced to our senses by the etheric. One range of vibrations takes the place of another. So death presents us with a new range of thoughts of the same universe, and until we can encompass the entire scope of universal vibrations the riddle of the universe will remain unsolved.

In *On the Edge of the Etheric* I think I succeeded in relating psychic phenomena, as experienced in the séance room, to physical science. On this occasion I shall attempt to relate what we are told about the Greater World, by those who communicate with us, to our present knowledge of the physical universe. If I succeed I shall have achieved my purpose of relating psychic science to physical science, of joining physics and psychics and making them one harmonious whole. In other words, I shall have been able to enlarge our bounds of knowledge on a strictly scientific basis.

I do not expect that what I have to say will be accepted by the scientific world, because it knows very little about what takes place at séances. It is only just beginning to awaken to the fact that supernormal phenomena take place at a séance, and it is far from accepting that this is caused by extra-terrestrial intelligences. This being so, our orthodox scientists have not yet arrived even at the threshold of obtaining further knowledge of the universe from super-physical intelligences. That will come in time, but it will only come slowly.

How few people really give serious thought to the meaning of existence! Most of them just take everything as a matter of course, and life consists of accepting conditions as they arrive. To our ancestors the earth was flat, enclosed in a dome, round which the sun circled. To them the universe was a very small place. As we grow mentally it enlarges, but it is still the same universe. Only now we look at it differently from the way our ancestors did. The universe is solely what mind interprets it to be, and the past is just the story of man's interpretation and ideas of the earth and the universe.

The universe can never be more and never less to us than the mind can grasp. Therefore, as mind is, so is the universe. Mind conditions the universe. Therefore the universe can be described and understood only in terms of mind. Just as the mind expands the universe expands. To many people today the earth means more than it meant to our parents, and it means much more to us than it meant to our ancestors of only a few hundred years ago.

Life is made up of experiences. Life is nothing more than a series of experiences. If we never experienced anything, we would not be conscious beings. Consequently there must be something to experience these experiences, and that something is our mind. Our conscious life therefore consists of our mind, which is our self, imaging the experiences that it, namely we, experience. These experiences all come from our surroundings, but as the mind expands it experiences more and more.

As all that exists has always been, it follows that our experiencing more is due to the fact that our minds are becoming more developed, and capable of a greater appreciation. Our ancestors had not the capacity to grasp the universe as we can today. Their minds were not sufficiently developed to enable them to realise their relationship to their surroundings as we now can do, and they had not the capacity to produce the instruments and implements necessary for the development of their understanding.

Everything is very different to each succeeding generation. It is all a question of expanding mind. If this is so, where lies the end? We have sufficient proof today to know that mind does not die, but continues functioning under different circumstances. We have now sufficient information to make us realise that mind persists in a new state after death and continues the expanding process. This process seems to continue indefinitely.

During its time on earth mind makes use of, and dominates, physical substance which it uses for demonstration purposes, to achieve in matter the materialisation of its immaterial pictures. Mind and matter are two completely different substances, and to correlate thought to matter or matter to thinking is wrong, because the brain is a mass of pulpy stuff, a purely physical creation, whereas the mind is something vastly different.

From our first conscious thought mind has expanded. It develops, I believe, through becoming more and more attuned with the faster vibrations of the mind-substance of the universe. The vibrations of the universal mind-substance are of different degrees. The expanding individual mind absorbs those beyond its normal orbit. Our minds are therefore a growing and expanding substance, increasingly capable of absorbing more and more of this finer mind-substance of the universe. It follows therefore that the universe is a great assembly of developing thoughts or ideas.

I am told by my informants in Etheria that the individual mind reaches ultimately a state of pure thought, wherein to think is to be. Then time and space, as we understand time and space, cease to exist, and the universe, when that stage is reached, will be looked on from an entirely different angle to that of our present-day line of vision.

Let us, however, concentrate our thoughts on mind, the image maker, and not allow ourselves to be bewildered by the vast distances of space, and the myriads of worlds which the telescope reveals. These are transient problems in which mankind is presently absorbed, but in reality they mean nothing of value to eternal mind, and that is what each one of us is. Sir James Jeans has just concluded a series of masterly articles in the *Sunday Express*, entitled "Through Space and Time," with the following words:—

> Only a few minutes back on the astronomical clock man emerges, and starts gradually and slowly to climb the long, steep ladder of civilization. Yet only within the last few ticks of this clock has he concerned himself with the meaning of the mighty pageant of the sky.
> Then Egyptians, Chinese, Babylonians and Greeks began in turn to wonder what it all meant. Only one tick ago the telescope was invented and gave us the means of finding out. Within that one tick almost all I have told you has been discovered, and many thousands of times as much besides. And with our knowledge of the skies increasing at its present rate who shall say what strange surprises the next tick of the clock may have in store for us?

He has taken his readers through billions and billions of miles of space, and told them about millions and millions of stars, about the nebulae, and the time light takes to reach us from these most distant known stars. Then we are told that our sun is but a grain of sand on this universal desert, and that this earth is not more than a millionth part of this grain. Hundreds of years are reduced to a tick of the astronomical clock, and the individual life on earth to the merest fraction of a tick. How insignificant it makes us feel, and yet, for all that, we are gods, we are divine because we think.

These vast incomprehensible astronomical figures should leave the Spiritualist cold. The Materialist may ponder and wonder about our seeming insignificance. Not so the Spiritualist. Just as our life on earth is but a fraction of a tick astronomically, so do we realise that it is but a tick of the clock of life, and that as our mind develops it is able to grasp and encompass the universe, not as envisaged from the physical viewpoint, but from the mental. To the mind the universe must ever remain boundless and timeless, because mind cannot conceive boundaries or be confined within time.

Astronomical science has devoted itself to the things seen from a material aspect. It has given us facts and figures which reduce the individual to such insignificance that we become no more than microbes in universal space. Science has devoted itself to the things seen, but neglected the real thing which sees and thinks. Science has concentrated on the universe as seen, but ignored the universe unseen. If these articles by Sir James Jeans are ever read by the inhabitants of Etheria, which they can do if they wish, what reaction would these facts and figures have on their minds? They would find them of no special interest because the physical universe means little to them.

These facts deal with only one narrow range in the

vast gamut of universal vibrations. We on earth live within this insignificant range of vibrations, which seem to us to be the universe. Etherians, however, live within other ranges, and what is of interest to us does not particularly interest them. Nevertheless, and this is all important, they have the same minds there as they had when here on earth, and we in turn will have the same minds there as we have here. The physical is temporal, the mind is eternal.

To concentrate on the temporal and ignore the eternal, which science does, is a great mistake, and until science reverses its attitude and always thinks the other way about, putting mind first, and the things mind sees second, it will never be able to get a correct grasp of the universe, or discover Reality.

We thus see that mind is the only permanency and that the physical is but a passing phase to us, a tick of our clock of life. This being so, what does it matter to us if we are but material microbes living on a tiny speck of dust, circling round a grain of sand? What really matters is our thoughts. As these are, so is the universe to each of us. Each mind is an individual universe, and, though it settles for a fraction of a tick on the physical earth, passing on to different stages in the etheric, these are but passing conditions and experiences to eternal mind and nothing more. Mind alone is permanent, its various temporary habitations being transient.

This being so, science must now turn its attention from the temporal to the eternal. Long enough has it ignored the unseen for the seen, the eternal for the temporal. If the physical universe ultimately turns out to be ten, or a thousand, or a million, times the size astronomers now think it is, it matters nothing. Any figures greater than we have at present cannot leave us colder, nor more indifferent, than do those already supplied to us. What interests us is this greater world of ours which has far more wonders to unfold to humanity than nebulae a hundred and thirty-five million light years distant from us.[1]

Let scientists now start and fish for knowledge in home waters, and they will find that the facts Spiritualism stands for, which they have so far ignored, will reveal to them the true universe. The discoveries they make in this direction will be of intense interest and importance to humanity, and will really help the human race to obtain a better understanding of its destiny. This will not be discovered one hundred and thirty-five million light years from here, but round and about this speck of dust we term the earth.

Sir James Jeans anticipates some strange surprises for science in these far off distant spaces. They will not be found there so much as they will be found here at home, and the sooner scientists realise their mistake in ignoring the facts of nature, which reveal the etheric world about and around us, the sooner will they re-establish their position as the leaders of human thought. This leadership is held today by Spiritualists and those in sympathy with their aims and objects. We have now entered this new era of psychic thought, just as four hundred years ago we entered the era of physical science, and slowly the mind of man will adjust itself to the new knowledge.

---

[1] Light travels at the speed of one hundred and eighty-six thousand miles a second, which is termed a light second. A light year is that figure multiplied by the number of seconds in a year and represents a distance of just under six million million miles.

We are gradually changing our conception of the universe, and this is due to our obtaining more and more evidence of what the universe really is. The more our minds expand the more evidence they can accumulate. Four hundred years ago the greatest awakening that ever happened in the history of man took place. When it was discovered that our relationship to the other bodies of the heavens was entirely different from what it seemed to be, humanity entered a new age of thought and this has been responsible for all we are and have today.

This knowledge has brought to mankind material comforts and increased happiness on the one hand, but, on the other, increased power for destruction and added misery. True happiness will not be attained on earth until physical science also embraces psychic science, and mind's true place in the universe is acknowledged. When this is done mankind will be sufficiently developed to handle the forces science has placed in his hands, and to use them only for good and not for evil purposes as is done today.

We are today at the opening of a new phase in our outlook on the universe, the psychic vista, just as were our ancestors four hundred years ago to the physical prospect, but now we have a new problem to solve. We have to determine the meaning of the great discovery that took place at Hydesville one hundred years ago. Then as great a discovery took place as occurred in 1543, when Copernicus made his famous proclamation to the world.

It has taken all these years since 1848 for a few of us to grasp what the occurrences at Hydesville really mean to mankind, because they mean something very great. So much indeed that I think the year 1848 will come in time to be looked on as just as important as the year 1543 when Copernicus made his great discovery. These will be two of the greatest dates in the history of man. The one revealed the physical universe and the other revealed the etheric universe. With these two important events before us let us try to build up the Greater World, as we are now capable of visualising it.

Before we can be conscious of our surroundings by sight we require five things to make up our conscious existence. These are as follows:—
(1) A Mind, the image maker.
(2) Brain substance in which it functions, and through which it is expressed. This brain substance like all else in our body is dual, physical and etheric.
(3) An eye, or opening, first to focus, and then to admit the vibrations of our surroundings to our brain, which houses the image maker.
(4) Substance, to cause vibrations which make the the mental image.
(5) Light, the name given to the vibrations, which causes substance to be seen by their reflection from it to our eyes, and through them to our brain, and thence to our mind.

Now when all these are present we are conscious of our surroundings or, as we term it, we can see. Let me make this quite clear by Diagram No. 1 on the next page. It is important that everyone should know exactly the process of seeing on earth, as until

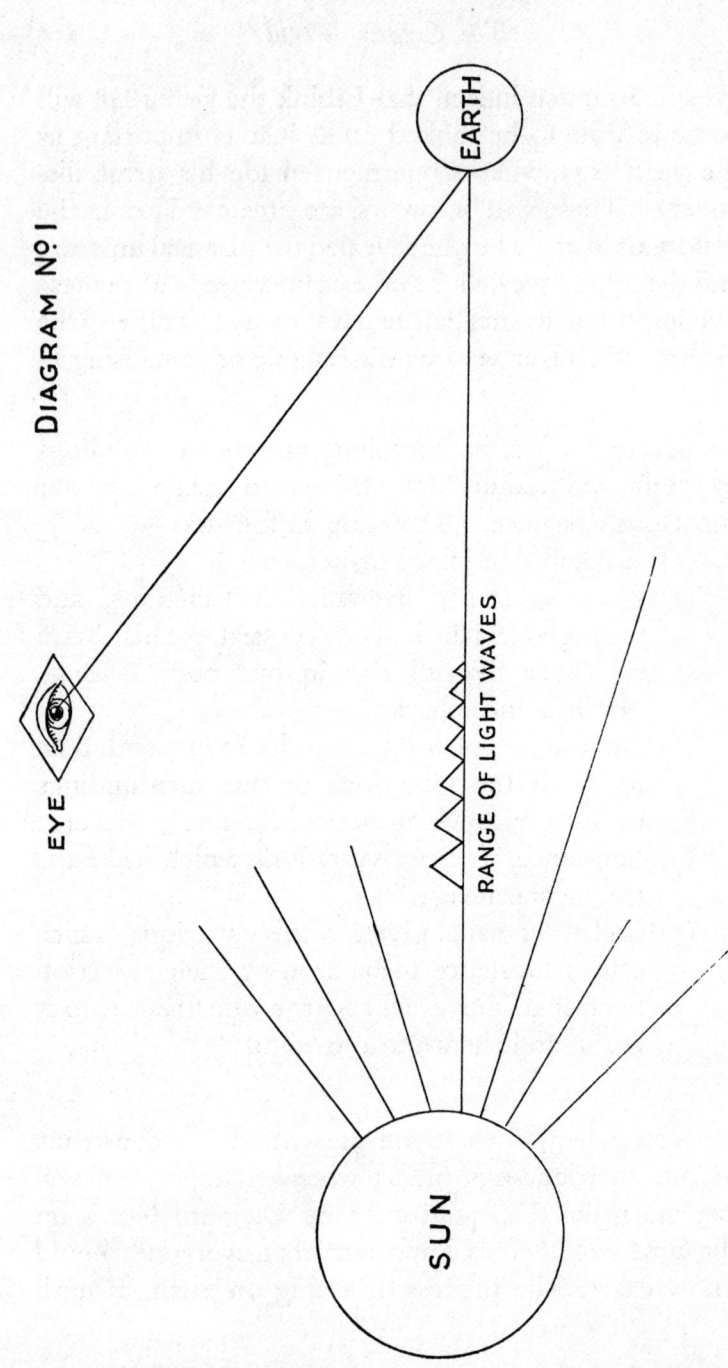

this is understood I cannot expect my picture of the Greater World to be appreciated.

The larger circle marked "Sun" represents the sun, and the smaller one the earth. Neither the distance they are shown to be apart, nor their relative sizes, represent reality. The sun is more than a million times larger than the earth, and the distance between them is 93,000,000 miles. The sun is constantly radiating light in the form of waves or rays. These waves vary in size; 34,000 of the longest would occupy an inch, and 64,000 of the shortest would occupy the same space.

As all these waves travel at a speed of 186,000 miles a second, it follows that four hundred billions of the longest would pass a given point in a second, while seven hundred and fifty billions of the shorte would pass the same point in a second. The straight line in the diagram represents an imaginary line of these waves, but it will be realised that they radiate from the sun in all directions and by far the greater number of them miss our earth altogether. The earth intercepts a minute fraction of the waves of light emitted by the sun.

Let us follow this imaginary line. The entire range of these waves, from 34,000 to 64,000 an inch, is radiated from the sun, and those which follow our imaginary line strike, let us say, a red brick of a house. What happens? Well, before I can tell you that, I must explain that each different substance on earth is vibrating in harmony with one or other of these waves. In my previous books I dwelt at some length on the properties of matter, so that I shall only make a passing reference to them on this occasion.

What we term matter is composed of atoms, and these atoms consist of electrons and protons. The electrons determine the substance and the protons the weight. We shall consider the protons later on. It is the electrons which interest us at the moment, as they give us what we term colour. According to the speed at which the electrons revolve in the atom so is the colour. The electrons in each substance are revolving at different speeds, and it is the speed at which they are revolving that determines colour.

The electrons in a substance which make a rapid journey around a small orbit will reflect the short waves of light and give back waves which we call violet. Other electrons which revolve more slowly around their larger orbits will reflect the light waves which we call red. In orbits between these two extremes are the electrons which reflect the other colours from the light rays.

A good simile is that of tuning-forks placed upright on a board. If we cause one fork to vibrate by drawing a violin bow across it we shall probably find another of the forks will also vibrate, because it is attuned to the same atmospheric waves as those to which the fork vibrated is attuned. The fork which is vibrated by the first fork will then set up air waves of its own. There is similar harmony between the different electrons composing earth substance and the electrons composing the sun. The waves produced by the electrons which make up the sun are called light, and this light is the cause of colour, as I shall now explain.

We arrived at the point when a range of light waves struck a red brick, and I asked what then happened.

Well, this is what happens. All the waves of the range at a higher frequency than that at which the brick is vibrating are spent or absorbed, so to speak. They do not affect our observation in regard to the brick. Only the slowest vibrations of the entire range are noticed, by the following process.

The slowest vibrations are reflected to our eye. The electrons in the atoms which make up the red brick stop the waves of the same degree as themselves, and when these waves strike the brick they are converted into another series of waves, which are thrown out in all directions. Some of these strike the eye and vibrate the retina, these vibrations passing down the optic nerve to our brain, and thence to our mind which images the brick in the colour to which we have given the name red. We give the name red to this range of vibrations. All the colours we see are produced as colour by our mind, so when the light vibrations are reflected from substance our mind picture of it is of such a nature that it receives the name of the colour we associate with its particular vibrations.

Now the entire range of light waves from the sun are affected in like manner as the one we have just considered. The waves, giving us the impression of red, vibrate with the least frequency of all the light waves, and, when striking a substance at the same frequency of vibration, they always give us the impression of red. Those next in the scale, that is those of greater frequency than the ones which give us the impression of red, give us the impression of what we term orange, and so on through yellow, green, blue, indigo and violet, which last is the colour produced by those of the greatest frequency.

Thus we see that a ray of light from the sun contains a range of waves, the entire gamut of which makes up the staple colours. These in turn can be blended into all the other colours, by the merging of the reflected rays. White light is simply a combination of all the colours of the rainbow. The combined rays make up the white light of a sunbeam.

Sir Isaac Newton made this discovery by means of a prism. This he fixed in a dark room, into which he admitted a sunbeam through a hole in the shutter. He placed the prism so that the ray passed through it. As it did so it was broken up by the prism into its constituent parts, which we call Red, Orange, Yellow, Green, Blue, Indigo and Violet, all of which are termed the spectrum of the spectroscope, the instrument into which is fitted the prism. He, however, thought of light as something material, composed of infinitely small particles, but now we know that it is a certain wave-motion in the ether.

Before leaving this subject let me fix it in your mind by means of Diagram No. 2. Here we see what represents a segment of the sun emitting rays, some of which strike a house on earth at which we are looking. The bricks reflect the red rays, the orange-coloured flowers the orange, a yellow creeper on the house the yellow, the green window-frame the green, the blue tiles on the roof the blue, the indigo-painted door the indigo, and the violet window-blinds the violet. Those rays which are stopped by the substance vibrating in harmony are reflected to our eyes. All the other rays striking the red bricks are spent and never return to us, only the red rays, and so on with all the different substances which make up the house.

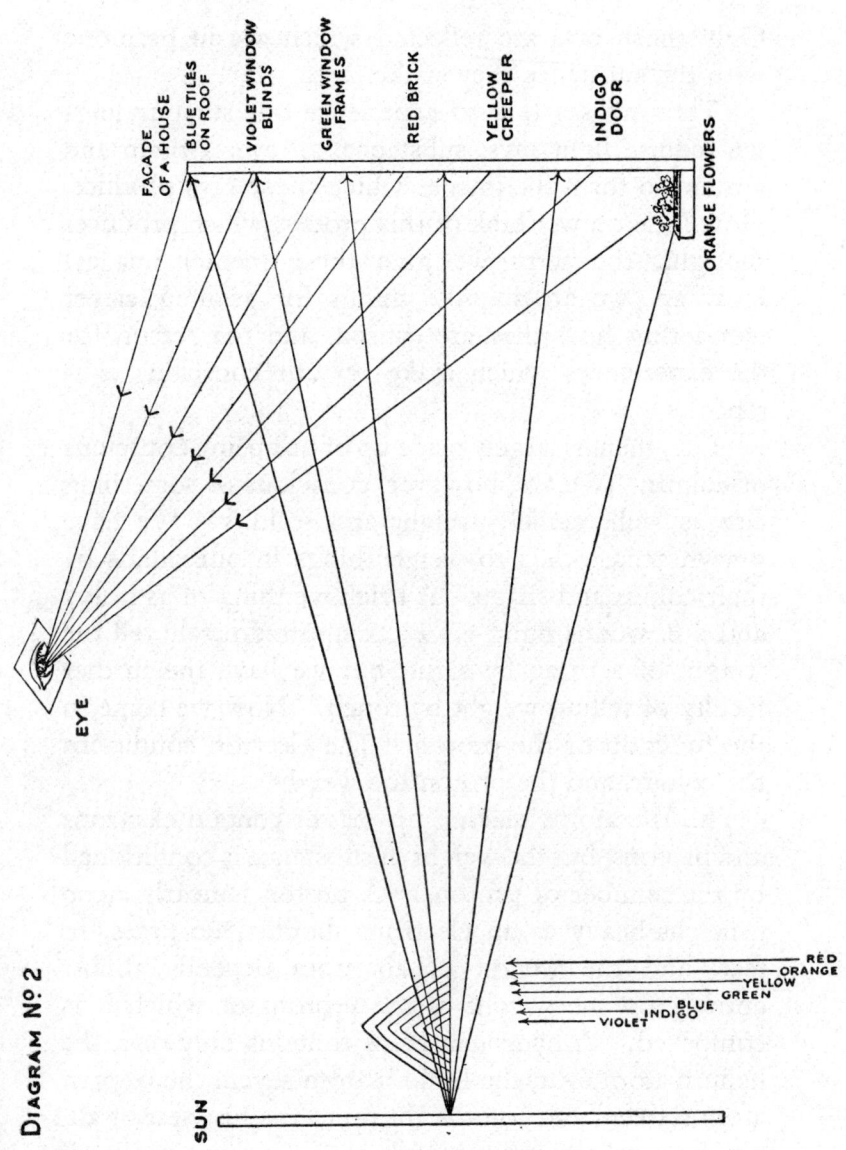

Only those rays are reflected which are in harmony with the substance they strike.

Thus we see that to experience our surroundings we require light rays, substance, an eye, a brain and a mind to form the images which those rays produce. How little do we think of this process which produces thought, the term we give these mental images! How apt we are to take things for granted, never wondering how they are caused, and the reason for the experiences which make up our conscious existence!

Life, then, is largely made up of our being conscious of colour. We are, however, conscious of something else as well, namely weight and solidity. We have grown accustomed to weigh things in our minds by their colour and shape. A brick we think of as heavy and a flower as light. We can approximately tell the weight of a thing by sight, but we have the further faculty of telling weight by touch. Now we come to the function of the proton. The electron conditions the colour, and the proton the weight.

All the atoms making up matter contain electrons and protons, but the weight of substance is conditioned by the number of protons. A proton is nearly 2,000 times as heavy as an electron, about 1,840 times, in fact, and the weight of an atom depends almost entirely on the weight of the protons of which it is composed. A hydrogen atom contains only one, the helium atom four, the lithium atom seven, the oxygen atom sixteen, and so on right up to the heaviest of all, uranium, which contains 238.

Thus the proton gives a substance weight, and according to the number and grouping of the electrons are the different chemical elements constituted. The electron and proton are two oppositely charged particles of electricity, the electron being the negative and the proton the positive. Thus matter appeals to us by the effect these electrons and protons have on our sight and touch. Just as in sight, so the protons, through our nerves, create mental images which give us the impression of weight, and thus by touch we image whether something is light or heavy.

To bring it all down to reality, sight and touch are just words to record, in the case of the former, the effect which the vibrations, set up in the ether by the electrons, have on our eyes and, in the case of the latter, the registering of the gravitational pull of the earth on the protons. As mind is present these are sensed, otherwise they would not be.

I have now tried to explain why we are conscious of existence on earth. As there is another conscious existence apart from physical matter, it is reasonable and logical that analogous conditions will combine to make up our existence, when the time comes for us to change from being physical to etheric creatures at death.

In my previous books I have related etheric matter to physical matter, showing that as the latter is but vibrations between two fixed points, etheric matter is likewise vibrations above the ultra-violet waves. Etheric matter, like physical matter, is just vibrations. Its difference is in the greater frequency of its vibrations, which are too fast for our physical eyes to appreciate. Consequently it is quite reasonable and scientific to believe that substance exists beyond our physical sense perceptions, in which life and mind can function.

Now what do we lose at death? Only our physical body. Our etheric body, however, takes its place, and, instead of using physical eyes, we use etheric eyes which perform the same functions as our physical eyes. Our mind still functions through the etheric brain. We are told that Etheria is composed of substance too fine for us in the physical body to appreciate, and also that Etheria has light. The substance and also the light differ only in degree from our physical substance and light, but the chief characteristic of the substance is that it is more easily moulded by thought. It can be moulded by concentrated thought without the need of touch when the mind becomes developed enough thus to influence it. Light in Etheria is similarly produced as is our light, and affects etheric eyes by the same process as our light affects our eyes.

In Etheria, therefore, they have everything that we have here to make up our conscious existence: (1) Mind, (2) Brain, (3) Eyes, (4) Substance and (5) Light. I am told that their minds, brains and eyes function just as ours do, that their substance like ours is just vibration, and that their light like ours is likewise vibration. We are told that Etheria resembles our earth, and, bearing the foregoing in mind, we can accept this statement as reasonable, because we find that similar laws operate there as operate here.

Before I go further, however, let me summarise what I have been told about this unsensed but very real world to which I give the name Etheria. It is very like this world, the differences, where they occur, being due to the fact that its substance is finer than ours, that the bodies of Etherians are finer and that consequently mind is more influenced by, and has a greater influence on, etheric substance than has our mind on physical substance. Thus Etherians are more influenced by their surroundings on the one hand, and, on the other, can mould etheric substance by thought, which gives them greater opportunities and increased powers of expression.

The mentally developed Etherians have greater control over their minds than we have. Here on earth amongst certain orientals we find this faculty developed. The Yogis, after years of training, are able to project their etheric bodies to any desired place, and so we need not be surprised when we are told of the control Etherians have over their bodies. Besides this Etherians can travel at a great speed and, by concentrated thought, they can reach a given place without the effort and time we devote to travel. As their surrounding matter is finer than ours, and their minds have greater control over it, life is easier since desires can be more easily realised by thought.

Except for this, Etheria is similar to earth. Etheria, however, is a name for seven worlds, one within the other, and if we include the earth there are eight. These eight worlds or globes, one inside the other, resemble a wooden ball I have seen which can be unscrewed but only the outer ball or surface comes away from the rest, as underneath the outer ball is another, and so on till we come to a small one inside the rest. This last ball can be compared to our earth.

Each of these worlds has a surface, an atmosphere and light, so what I say of one refers to all. It must not, however, be assumed that the places where we have mountains and seas on earth have corresponding mountains and seas just above them in Etheria. The forces which made mountains, land and sea on earth, likewise made them in Etheria, but not necessarily in the self-same locality as they are on earth. I have also been told that there is a world of life lower in vibration than earth life, and that it is gross and crude. This lower world will not be considered under the heading of this chapter, as very little seems to be known about it.

First of all let us consider the surfaces of the various etheric worlds. On these there are land and water, trees, houses, fields, roads, vegetation of all kinds, rivers, mountains and valleys. Just what we experience on our surface is likewise found on the other surfaces, but the higher, or the farther away from the earth the surface is, so is the beauty increased, because each surface is composed of finer and finer substance, or vibrations. It seems to be a fact that the finer or faster the vibrations are, the more beautiful are the colours. My communicators tell me that I should not use the word beautiful but vivid, it being a more descriptive term. This vividness, I am told, increases as our minds develop. As a rose opens its petals to the light, so does the mind expand to its environment of finer and finer vibrations.

On these surfaces are men, women and animals, who live their lives much as we do on earth. As the food required for nourishment is easily obtained, and the essence is consumed instead of flesh and vegetables as with us, so life is easy—much easier than for us on earth. The passions engendered on earth, which are caused by the struggle for existence and by fear of danger, are lacking in Etheria. Damage to the etheric body does not take place, and sudden and violent death is unknown.

As the etheric body is differently and more easily nourished, and as clothing is also obtained easily by the effect of thought on etheric substance, the laws of the jungle, which even amongst civilised people on earth are so often in evidence, especially in war, and to a lesser degree in commerce, do not prevail. The power of thought makes it easy for the Etherians to house and clothe themselves, and all desires can there be satisfied in a way unknown on earth.

Just as the earth is made up of physical vibrations, so each globe surrounding the earth is also vibrating. The first globe enveloping the earth vibrates faster than the earth, and so on with each successive globe. Each globe receives its light and heat from an etheric sun concentric with our sun. Our sun is composed, just as our Greater World is composed, of globes, of which our sun is the one in the centre. The Greater Sun consists of eight suns including our sun. Our sun is a rotating globe surrounded by, and interpenetrated by, seven other rotating globes.

These different surfaces surrounding our sun are vibrating in tune with the surfaces surrounding our earth. The first etheric sun vibrates in harmony with the first etheric world, and so on. Just as the physical sun gives us our light and heat, so the first etheric sun gives light and heat to the surface of the first etheric world, commonly called the Astral World. Each surface in Etheria receives the light from the etheric sun's surface to which it is attuned.

In Etheria there are the equivalent to atoms, electrons and protons, which compose the substance on earth; it is all a question of degree or speed or frequency of vibration. The etheric suns vibrate by ether waves the etheric electrons on the different surfaces in Etheria, just as our sun vibrates the electrons on our surface. Each range of vibrations produced by the Greater Sun impinges on the electrons in tune with this range in the Greater World. Thus the sun to Etherians is as much to them as it is to us, and conditions their existence just as it conditions our existence.

It will now be seen that light and heat are produced in Etheria just as our light and heat are produced, and that light and heat vibrations are conveyed to the eyes and bodies of the Etherians by reflection just as they are on earth.

In Etheria there is an atmosphere surrounding each surface, and there are clouds and sky. Moisture ascends and descends there just as here. Climatic conditions prevail just as they do here, but they are more temperate. Seasonal changes occur. This, I am told, applies only to the first three surfaces above the earth. From the fourth surface onwards climatic changes practically disappear. On none of the surfaces in Etheria is there night as we understand it. Instead of night on the first three there is twilight, owing to the luminosity of their atmosphere.

In Etheria, as on earth, there is sky for the same reason that we have sky. Our sky is caused by the scattering and reflection of direct sunlight by fine particles floating in our atmosphere. For the same reason there is sky above each surface of Etheria. In

Etheria the colours are much more beautiful, varied and brilliant, and their scenery is consequently more beautiful than is ours, because their luminous atmosphere gives everything an iridescent appearance.

Such is the information I have received through different channels of communication between the two worlds, both in this country and abroad. The same questions always receive the same replies, and this confirmation everywhere leads me to believe that when I am told that Etheria is similar in many respects to this world it can be accepted as true.

Etheria in parts is more beautiful than the earth to those whose minds are attuned to beauty, just as it is uglier in places to minds of a lower order. There the mind conditions its surroundings. On earth our circumstances govern our surroundings, but in Etheria they are conditioned by minds being in harmony with other minds. Minds in harmony live together. There individual characters are transparent, and shame leads the bad to dark surroundings in the valleys. Consequently, in a world of finer matter, the mind conditions existence more than on earth. To the good it is a happier and more beautiful place than is this earth, but to others it is the reverse.

In Diagram No. 3 will be seen a representation of the Greater Sun and the Greater World. The large black circle represents the physical sun, and the small black circle the earth. Each etheric plane is numbered in the Greater Sun to correspond with the planes of the Greater World which are vibrating at the same speed. The outermost etheric sun plane is numbered 1 to correspond with the outermost greater world plane, also numbered 1. So we come down

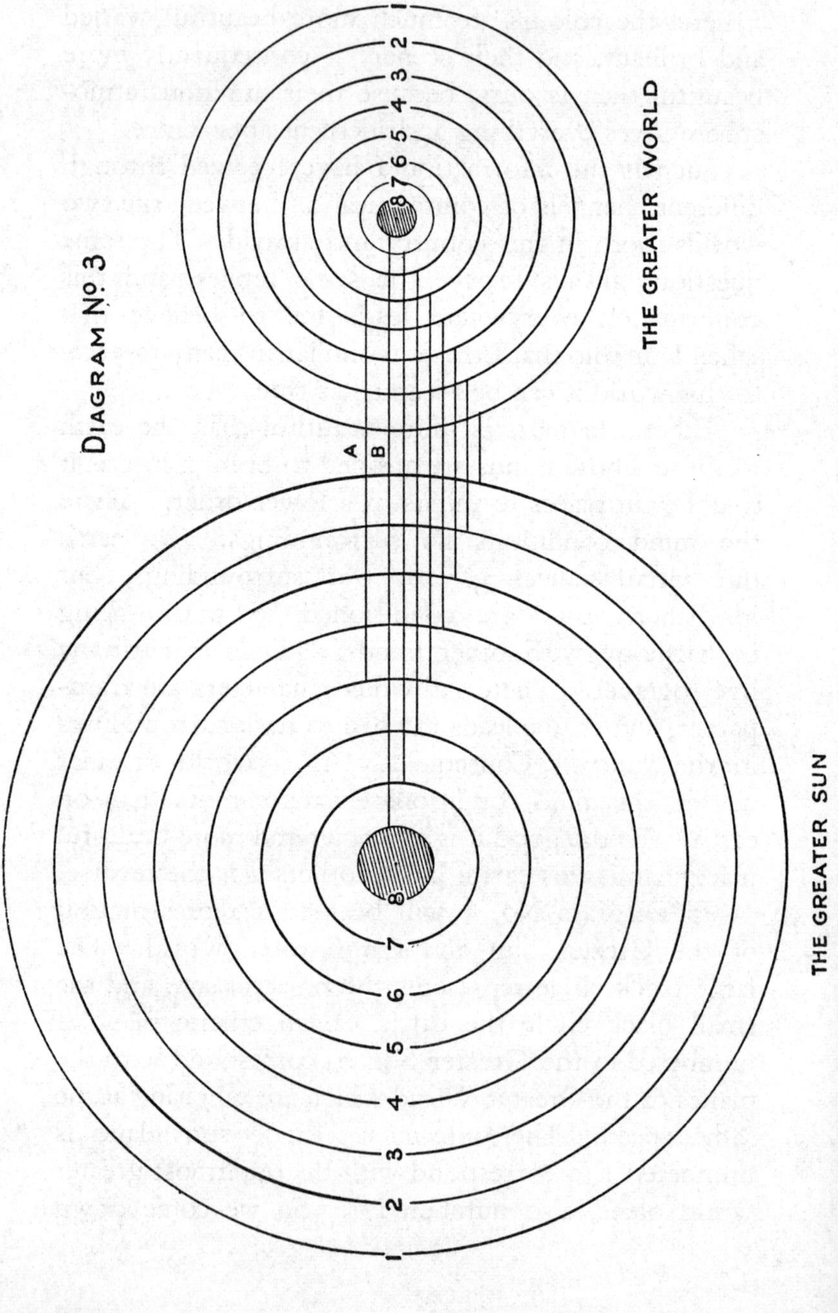

DIAGRAM N°. 3

THE GREATER WORLD

THE GREATER SUN

The Greater World

till we reach number 8, which is vibrating in tune with our earth.

The physical sun is constantly emitting radiation which pulsates the ether and produces ether waves. These reach the earth in eight minutes across a distance of just under 93,000,000 miles, a speed which is equivalent to 186,000 miles a second. These physical light waves make it possible for us physical beings, when our earth faces the sun, to appreciate surrounding physical substance by sight as already explained. The line marked B in Diagram No. 3 represents a beam of light from the sun to the earth. The line marked A represents a beam of light from what we might term the third sphere of the Greater Sun, and, this being in tune with the surface of the third sphere of the Greater World, is reflected to the eyes of those living on that surface and gives colour. The other parallel lines connect the surfaces of the Greater Sun and Greater World which are vibrating in harmony.

Here on earth we can experience daylight, even when the sun is not radiating light directly on to our surface. This time of day is termed dawn in the morning, and twilight in the evening. This comes about by the reflection to earth of the rays of light, by the molecules of the atmosphere. By this means a portion of the celestial vault is enlightened while the sun is invisible. This light is scattered or reflected by the atmosphere, due mainly to those fine dust particles which form the necessary nuclei for condensation of aqueous vapour. It is of course most brilliant in the quarter where the sun rises or sets, and in the case of a sunset it is called the after-glow. Both the morning glow and the evening glow are generally recognised as productive of the most beautiful effects to be seen in the sky.

In Etheria, as already mentioned, they do not experience night as we do, only twilight, owing to the luminosity of their atmosphere, which is more brilliant than is ours. Life in Etheria, I am told, is just one long day toned down at regular intervals by the light becoming more subdued, this twilight taking the place of our night. Just as our luminous sky shuts out from us the stars during the day and gives us the impression of a luminous vault, so does their sky operate in like manner and to such a degree that it appears to them also as a luminous vault, but of such brilliance that the etheric sun itself is unseen owing to the luminosity it creates.

Thus time is not calculated there as we calculate time, by the apparent movement of a luminous ball through the sky. This being so, time there is not divided into hours, days, weeks, months and years, and thus it ceases to be time as we understand this experience on earth. Just as our sun's light is broken up by the particles in our atmosphere, which distribute its different colours, the oranges and reds to the sunrise and sunset, the blue to the sky, the purple haze to the distance, the greens and pinks to the dawn and twilight, so are like effects produced in the atmosphere surrounding the various planes in Etheria.

On earth we experience light and colour in shadow, which means that, though there is an obstruction to the direct rays of the sun, yet they are indirectly reflected to our eyes. This is due to the reflection of sunlight by particles in our atmosphere. Thus in the room of a house which does not receive the direct rays of the sun there is light due to the luminosity of the atmosphere. In Etheria this condition is intensified, the luminosity of the atmosphere lighting the various surfaces even when they are turned away from the direct rays of the etheric sun. Consequently, from what we experience on earth, we can now understand that that which seems to be a contradiction—the fact that Etherians receive their light from the etheric sun and yet have no night—is not so, but can be explained in scientific terms.

Our sky acts as a mirror to the rays of the rising and the setting sun, and this prolongs our day. Otherwise our day would be shorter if we were dependent solely on the direct rays of our sun. It is all a question of the height of this atmospheric mirror above our surface. If our atmosphere extended to a much greater height than it does, the mirror would reflect the rays of light for a longer time, and our day would be lengthened and our night shortened. In Etheria, I am told, their atmospheric mirror is much higher above their surface than is ours, and thus the rays of the etheric sun are reflected for a longer time, enabling the surface turned away from the etheric sun to obtain light until it again receives the sun's direct rays.

We have an example of this on earth in our radio waves. These are of the same general nature as waves of light, except for the fact that they are thousands of millions of times longer. Being of a similar nature they have many properties in common with light waves. The early experimenters were greatly mystified when they found that they were picking up wireless stations at the opposite end of the earth without difficulty.

The reason for this is that as soon as radio waves reach a certain height they are bent back and return to earth. What the atmosphere does for us on earth by reflecting the sun's rays, and giving us dawn and twilight, a layer of ionised gas does to these radio waves.

One of these layers is known as the Kennelly-Heaviside layer and is found usually at a height of 65 to 70 miles above the earth's surface. Another layer, called the Appleton layer, is known to exist from 90 to 250 miles above the earth's surface. Moreover, experimenters have recently noticed echoes coming back from space after intervals of from three to thirty seconds, and, as radio waves travel at 186,000 miles a second, the same speed as light waves, it is easy to calculate that there must be reflecting layers at distances up to nearly three million miles from the earth. Our radio waves, therefore, which are sent off from London, do not go through the earth but upwards, and, striking one of these layers, return to earth, thus coming in contact with aerials in Australia.

When it is day here it is night in Australia, but if light rays were reflected, as are our radio rays, by the atmosphere at a much greater height than it extends at present from the earth's surface, then when it is light here it would also be light in Australia. Some of the sun's rays would strike us direct while others, going past the earth, would be caught by the atmospheric mirror surrounding the earth and reflected to Australia. Though Australia would not have the direct rays of the sun, and thus not have daylight, it would still be in reflected light which we would term twilight.

The moon has no atmosphere surrounding it.

Consequently there is neither dawn nor twilight. The rays from the sun strike the moon direct, and there is no reflection from a sky as on earth. No life can live on the moon's arid surface, but, if beings could exist, they would experience night coming suddenly to be followed by day coming equally suddenly. From black night they would experience brilliant sunshine as the sun became visible. At the end of the day they would be plunged into darkness without warning. If such beings were told that on earth we experienced light for one hour after the sun has gone below the horizon, and light for an hour before the sun was seen in the morning, they would find it difficult to believe. Yet we have this additional light because of our atmosphere, and, if it extended higher than it does, so would twilight and dawn be increased.

Little do we realise the importance to us of our atmosphere. Though unseen it is very real. If there were no atmosphere surrounding the earth the sky would look to us by day as jet black. The sun would be brighter and bluer, as its light would not have abstracted from it, by the atmosphere, a large part of its blue waves, and the stars would not twinkle but look like points of light. We can better realise the weight of the atmosphere above us by imagining that each one of us is covered over with 144 blankets of lead, each a quarter of an inch in thickness, and that the pressure from this weight is exerted equally on every part of the body.

Because of the atmosphere surrounding the earth we have seas, rivers and water. Likewise for the same reason these exist in Etheria. It is impossible for us to imagine life existing without atmosphere, and, if we were told from Etheria that none existed there, I could not relate conditions there to those of this earth. Etheria could not be understood by us. To be told, as I have been told, that conditions there are like conditions here would be incomprehensible to us if they had no atmosphere. My Etherian communicators, however, lay stress on the fact that the atmosphere plays as large a part in their lives as it does in ours, and that because of it they have moisture, water, rivers and seas. Besides this, their atmosphere, as previously explained, affects the light from their sun, just as it affects our light, only more so, in that it gives them more vivid colours and twilight. Consequently all they tell me can be related to our knowledge of conditions on earth. What they tell me appeals to my reason as scientific and rational.

My informants in Etheria always emphasise the fact that their atmosphere is more luminous than is ours, and that it extends to a greater height into space. It is, therefore, not impossible for us to imagine Etheria having light and twilight instead of light and darkness, as we have on earth. Etheria, they are always at pains to emphasise, is very similar to this earth, except that it is more vivid. There seems to be an iridescent sheen on things there that we have not here, and this is caused by the luminosity of their atmosphere. This discovery of Etheria about and around us, and the fact that conditions there are so like conditions here, is so contrary to past religious teaching that this fact in itself is significant and cannot have come from ideas latent in the minds of the mediums.

If, through mediumship, we had been told of another world far out in space, with conditions quite different from those existing on earth, we would have found it impossible to relate conditions there to those we understand. As it is we have discovered a new world, but, just as in the case of America, we find that the new world is very like the old world. Why should it be otherwise? It is part of the same world, its only difference being that it is composed of finer matter than we understand and appreciate. Similar laws to those we know on earth seem also to prevail.

As we are its future inhabitants it is only reasonable that conditions should be similar to conditions here. We know that nature makes all her changes slowly, and it would be unnatural if she ushered us into another order of existence entirely different from the one to which we are here accustomed. If this were so our preparation on earth would be of little or no value to us in our new condition. As it is, we find that we shall be easily able to adjust ourselves to what differences there are, much as we do in going from one house to another.

Keeping all this in mind I shall now summarise, from my carefully recorded notes taken down at the time, what I have been told about light in Etheria, by those speaking to me from Etheria on different occasions.

(A) We have no night here as you understand night.
(B) We have a sun and a greater sense of its invigorating power than you have of your sun. We should feel very lifeless without it. It is present

on every plane, and produces colours more varied and beautiful than are yours. Only a portion of the etheric sun's vibrations are reflected on each plane. We are conscious of those in harmony with the plane on which we live, just as you are of those which are reflected by your plane.

(C) We get our light from the source of all light, a great central force. Its brilliance depends on the distance the plane is from this source.

(D) We can get subdued light, but not so subdued as you experience.

(E) The flowers and trees are brighter on our hills than they are in the vales; it is a matter of light.

(F) Our light is soft, radiant, brilliant, beautiful and blending.

(G) We receive our light emanations from our etheric sun, concentric with your sun, whence comes light of great splendour and this is reflected to our eyes by the vibration of our substance, just as is your light by the vibration of earth substance. The reason for our not having darkness is because the rays of our sun are reflected by our atmosphere at a greater height than are the rays of your sun.

(H) Our atmosphere is naturally luminous, and extends much higher than does your atmosphere. On the first three planes there are shadows, but beyond these they get less and less definite as the atmosphere becomes more luminous. Just as there are shadows so there is shade.

(I) Our etheric sun sends rays through the ether and these are reflected to our eyes by substance. Consequently, like you, we experience colours but they are more brilliant and varied than are yours.

(J) We have day and twilight. Our atmosphere can reflect our sun's rays for a longer time than yours can, so we have twilight instead of night. We do not need sleep as you do, so we do not miss not having night.

(K) Our substance, like yours, is just vibration and so is our light. Our substance consists of what is equivalent to your electrons and protons. It is only a question of degree between us. Our substance is vibrating faster than is yours. Each surface reflects the vibrations from the etheric sun with which it is in harmony. Our progress from lower to higher planes is simply an experience of the world opening, as the result of our enlarging minds.

I am told, as will be seen in the foregoing summary, that etheric light waves function on etheric substance in a similar way as do physical light waves on physical substance, and are reflected to etheric eyes as are our light waves. This will be understood by a glance at Diagram No. 4. On the left is a segment of the Greater Sun, and on the right is a segment of the Greater World. This Greater World is made up of eight planes or surfaces, if we include the earth surface, and as we reach each our etheric bodies become more refined. Thus our etheric eyes can catch finer vibrations. The pyramid in the centre represents the different ranges of vibration. The largest represents the earth range. It harmonises with physical substance and affects the physical eye.

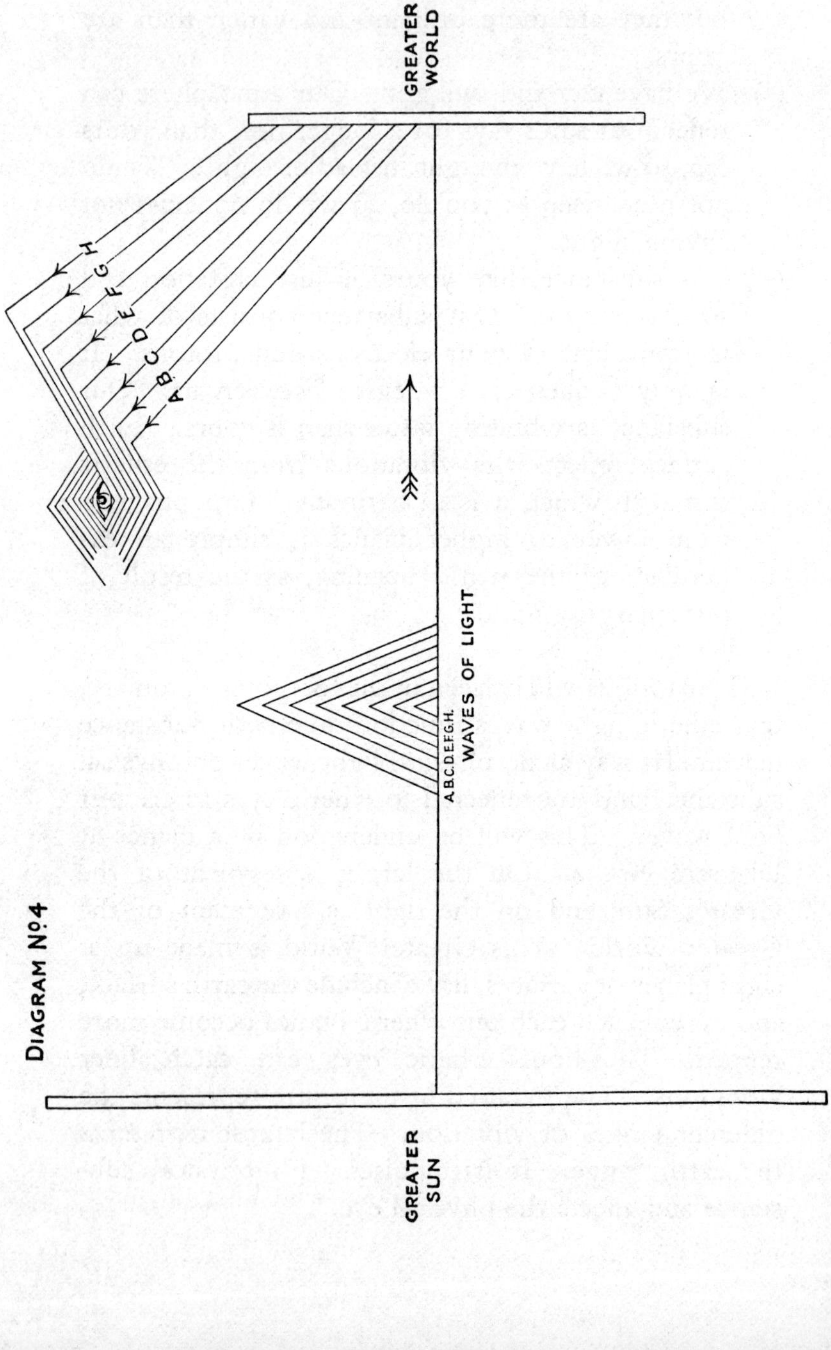

284 *The Unfolding Universe*

DIAGRAM No. 4

Each pyramid represents the range of vibrations in harmony with the different etheric planes, the smallest pyramid representing the light vibrations in harmony with the highest and finest etheric plane. The eye placed on the top of the diagram, just as it discards its various sheaths, and becomes attuned to finer vibrations, senses the reflection from the finer rays of the etheric sun. The different lines surrounding the eye represent what I might term the different etheric skins composing the eye, which are shed one by one as we rise through the planes.

Follow now the range which affects the physical eye, and is represented by a large pyramid marked A. It strikes the earth and is reflected to the physical eye with its heavy covering, as that is the wavelength to which the eye responds. So with each range on the plane to which it responds. Just as on earth certain wavelengths are spent when striking a substance to which they do not respond, so all the waves which find a response in Etheria are spent so far as we on earth are concerned, as we cannot respond to them. They exist all the same, just as the sun's rays are always with us in the day time, but we respond only to those the substance picks up and reflects to our eyes. All the rest are lost and might never be. Similarly all those light waves of the Greater Sun are lost to us because we have no substance on earth to respond to them. When we reach Etheria, the land of finer substance, then, in our finer bodies, we shall respond to the waves with which we are then in harmony. The waves to which earth substance responds will then be lost to us and be as if they never existed. Thus the earth will cease to exist to us, unless we lower our vibrations to be in harmony with earth vibrations, and so catch the physical sun's light vibrations.

It is quite impossible to get a grasp of the Greater World unless we think of it in terms of vibrations. On earth the same conditions exist as they do in Etheria, but, as we are in tune with them, we naturally accept these conditions. On the other hand, when visualising Etheria, we must do so in terms of vibrations, or otherwise we have nothing to build upon, no basis for our minds to erect a structure of ideas about those conditions beyond our sense of sight and touch. The universe is just vibrations and nothing more. It is a gigantic scale of vibrations of which our earth represents a minute fraction.

Physical bodies appeal to each of us on earth by their vibrations. We see those of our own body and of other bodies. At death the etheric body leaves the physical, and thus becomes apparent to Etherians who can see its faster vibrations, as their light waves are reflected by it to their eyes. We on earth see only the physical body but cannot see the etheric body because of its faster vibrations. In other words, on earth our bodies reflect physical light and in Etheria our etheric bodies reflect etheric light, and are consequently seen by Etherians.

This chapter has been considering vibrations so far as our Earth and Etheria, the Sun and the Greater Sun, are concerned, but these vibrations may be only part of a greater scale of vibrations which constitute the universe. The description I have given of the Greater World and the Greater Sun can doubtless be applied to other suns, stars, and planets of the universe. We are coming to realise that physical matter, vibrating from 34,000 to 64,000 waves to the inch, does not constitute the entire universe, and that space is filled with vibrations which make up other worlds quite beyond our physical range of sight. We are entering a new era of thought when all will think in terms of vibrations, and this will enable us to visualise the real universe in a way which is impossible for those who still live in the pre-vibration age of thought.

In this new era I foresee that everyone will think of the universe not only in terms of vibrations, but they will also talk of it in terms of vibrations. Gradually the mind of man will come to accept this method of expressing natural phenomena. It is only a matter of time; only a question of education. This is how everyone today would think if they applied logical thinking and our present-day knowledge to their lives.

Here I am a conscious entity, conscious of different sensations from the time I was born to the time I die. What am I, and what causes these sensations? There is no doubt that I am a conscious thinking entity, and that I experience pleasure and pain, happiness and unhappiness. Also there is no question that I can feel my surroundings by touch, and that these surroundings differ, some being hard, others soft. Besides this, I see. I see colours, I see that everything is coloured differently. I see what I term beautiful colours and I see ugly colours. I see things that give me pleasure and things that give me displeasure. I see things that make me happy, and things that make me unhappy.

Again, my consciousness is influenced by sound.

I can hear shrill sounds, and soft soothing sounds. I can hear sounds that give me pleasure or give me discomfort. I hear sounds which I term words, and these come from the mouths of others, contemporary inhabitants of this earth, who, from what they say, evidently experience something the same as I do. To them their surroundings on earth are evidently somewhat similar to what they are to me. Each sees the same colours, each hears the same sounds, but each interprets life's experiences differently, because each mind is different. The earth is really different to each individual. To some it means very much, to others very little, it being just a question of mental development.

In this way we go on from the cradle to the grave, thinking conscious entities, made happy or unhappy in accordance with our surroundings, and the condition of the bodies we inhabit and take along with us when we move. We are each in reality just a moving range of vibrations, living within numerous other ranges of vibrations, the vast majority of which we are not tuned to appreciate. We can move from place to place and experience different scenery, and different places, which constitute the small range to which we are attuned, and so our lives are made up by thus responding to our surroundings, the name given to these vibrations.

During at least one-third of our life on earth we are unconscious of our surroundings; this condition we term sleep. Then we dream, and at times we remember what it was about. We are just as happy asleep as awake. We do not fear to go to sleep nor to awaken, and so we live our lives, some happier than others, but to the great majority life is sufficiently tolerable and happy to make them regret the thought that it will come to an end on earth. The great majority are perfectly satisfied to accept their environment as they find it. Very few care to contemplate death, and the cessation of the sensations which they are daily and nightly experiencing. This, then, is life on earth.

It may be asked for what purpose am I here to experience these sensations. Why is all this so, and what does it all mean? Where am I making for? Am I really making for anywhere at all? If people could only realise that everything that thinks is guided by mind of various degrees. This unseen mind is to be found in everything that moves and grows, it is something that enters and leaves the material, a process which has been going on down the ages. Thought of every degree from that displayed by the developing flower and seed to that of the savant is the only reality and the only permanency. Thought brings the universe into being to each of us, and, when we became conscious, thinking individuals we became aware of a fraction of some great reality. Now that we have reached this stage we shall ever remain conscious beings.

Once we begin to think, we enter a state of consciousness which even death cannot annihilate. This thinking, picture-making mind, possessed by each individual, creates and remembers our experiences, because it pictures the universe for each of us and without these pictures, which we term thought, there would be no universe. Existence then does not extend merely over the short period between birth and death. Once we have established consciousness of our surroundings, this state of awareness never ceases to be, and we shall always remain conscious of them. All that happens is that our surroundings will change when we discard the physical body, and this change will affect our consciousness.

Just as there can be no universe without mind, so there can be no universe without surroundings to stimulate our consciousness. There must be these two states of vibration, and that which stimulates our consciousness we term matter. Matter, however, does not consist only of physical matter, as matter of all kinds exists in the universe, and our existence consists of our experiencing these different forms of substance. I do not limit the term matter to earth substance only, but to the substance of the entire universe, to all the vibrations which influence mind and make it produce images to which we give the term thought.

Now this may seem very mysterious, and cannot be understood unless thought of in terms of vibration. However, once we accept the fact that the universe is vibrations of different degrees, different wavelengths or different frequency, then everything becomes understandable. The fastest range of vibrations is mind. Down this scale we come until we reach physical matter, but below this there are still lower vibrations. We have instruments to detect some of these, and we name them radio waves, dark heat waves and long electric waves.

The highest vibrations of all, which constitute mind, in company with its etheric covering from which it is inseparable, encases itself for a time in the physical body, and through it becomes attuned to physical vibrations which impinge on it through the physical body. The physical body is, however, only the sheath, our body being held together by another structure which we term the etheric body. Possibly we have many sheaths. At death the etheric body leaves the physical body. It is an exact duplicate of the physical body, and functions like the physical body.

When we are out of the physical body we cease to sense physical vibrations, and sense the next range to the physical, which we term astral. After the astral we sense a higher range. Our existence consists of passing through various ranges of vibration, which we term planes, or surfaces, until the time comes when we leave entirely the etheric world surrounding this earth, and enter into a new order of existence which is meantime beyond our capacity to comprehend.

The physical body is an open network of electrons and protons. What is between these we term space. If this space were eliminated, and all the electrons and protons in the body were brought together, they would not occupy a greater space than does a dot made by the sharpest pencil. Our bodies, therefore, are mostly made up of space, just as is the universe to our physical eyes. What occupies this space which, together with the electrons and protons, composes the human body? An answer to the question would be difficult, but one thing is certain and that is that there is ample room for something besides what we term physical.

To our eyes the physical vibrations composing the physical body seem to take up all the space available, but we now know that each physical body is capable of accommodating numerous other ranges of vibration besides the physical. I am told that each physical cell has a duplicate etheric cell, and it is the radiation which these produce that causes the aura surrounding the body. Every living thing has an etheric body and an aura of different degrees. The etheric body, composed of these etheric cells, is consequently a counterpart of the physical body. When mind first begins to gather round it physical matter, it works through the etheric duplicate. It requires this link in order to make contact with the physical, the etheric being the structure on which the physical is built.

It is not the food we eat which determines the shape and size of our bodies. If we put a calf, a foal and a lamb in a grass field, after they leave their mothers, what do we find? Though they eat the same food and drink the same water, yet the body of each develops differently in size and shape. Besides this they are renewing their bodies each day. Throughout a lifetime the flesh and bones of animals, the same as those of humans, waste completely away, but we do not notice it because new flesh and bones take the place of the old. Each physical cell is renewed, but how is this possible without a structure to support the physical cell in its decay and renewal? It is, therefore, logical to accept the fact that there is an etheric duplicate structure, and that the physical is just the garment each living thing wears on earth, a covering made up from the food it consumes. Otherwise, if something permanent did not remain, our bodies would have no foundation or uniformity.

Dr. Raymond Pearl of Johns Hopkins University, U.S.A., has emphasised this vital fact by remarking recently:—

Probably there is not a single molecule in man at age 70 that was there at 20. In the intervening years the only thing about him that has survived is his pattern—a sort of transcendental or spiritual wraith through which has flowed a steady stream of matter and energy. It is the pattern that is the essence of the business. It alone survives.

How true this is, but how few realise that it is the first lesson man should learn when he starts to make enquiries about himself. Moreover, the etheric body is not just an inference or an hypothesis, as it has been seen by clairvoyants from time to time when leaving the body at death. This is how the famous medium Hudson Tuttle clairvoyantly witnessed a death. In his own words he tells us that:—

Slowly the spiritual form (spiritual body) withdrew from the extremities and concentrated in the brain. As it did so, a halo arose from the crown of the head which gradually increased. Soon it became clear and distinct, and I observed that it had the exact resemblance of the form it had left. Higher and higher it arose, until the beautiful spirit stood before us and the dead body reclined below. A slight cord connected the two, which, gradually diminishing, became in a few minutes absorbed and the spirit had forever quitted its earthly temple.

Along with the etheric body goes the mind, the picture maker, and all its memories. Though the brain on earth is constantly being renewed the mind remains unimpaired and remembers away back to childhood. Consequently the etheric brain, the duplicate structure which supports the physical brain, is the real seat of the mind, through which mind controls the physical. Besides this, the structure, which we term our etheric body on which the physical builds, is likewise permanent, in fact it is the real body. The mind of each of us is the real self, and the etheric body is its real home, whereas the physical body is a constantly decaying covering, for the purpose only of enabling the etheric structure to function for a time within the earth's range of vibrations. As we grow older the physical gradually loosens, thus enabling the mind and the etheric body to detach themselves quite naturally at death.

Thinking consists of image-making, and this constitutes conscious living. Our surroundings are constantly being imaged by our minds, and it is this image-making which makes us conscious of our surroundings. Consciousness is this image-making of our surroundings. When asleep we are termed unconscious, but the mind continues to make images from its experiences when awake. When we think of ourselves only as Mind, that our existence is made up only of mind images, and when we realise that mind never dies, but will always make images relating to its surroundings, then we have a basis on which we can build up the structure of our existence. By thinking like this we will understand why it is we are conscious beings, and how it is we never can lose this consciousness.

This earth is only a fraction of the real world. The world which comprises the earth and Etheria is composed of many ranges of vibration. Some are at a slower, and some at a greater, frequency than those which make up the earth. The earth is only one range. We sense only the earth, and that is the world to us when on earth. The real world is a vast range of vibrations, some lower than the earth but the majority higher. Imagine a cork having a certain specific gravity, and that it will float in something having the same relation to its gravity as has water. We can imagine the gravity of the cork, and the liquid in which it floats, being reduced over and over again on this basis, and the cork still floating.

If the cork were a living being, and had the capacity to die, that is to shed its covering, thus reducing the gravity which enabled it to float in water, and retain another body which responded to water of an equally reduced density, then it would still float in this less dense substance. This process can be imagined indefinitely. Just as the vibrations of the human body respond to those of the surface on which we live so the vibrations of the etheric body respond to the surface on which it lives in Etheria. Just as we on earth can sink in water by thought, so in Etheria they can sink by thought through the surface on which they dwell.

Imagine, instead of a cork, a range of vibrations which appeal to us as a cork, which is all a cork really is. Imagine again, instead of water, a range of vibrations which appeal to us as water, which is all that water really is. A cork will float in water. Call the cork C^1 and the Water W^1. These symbols represent two types of physical vibrations; one we call cork, and the other water. When you have something termed W^1 it will support something termed C^1.

The cork changes to C^2 and finds something W^2, which supports it just as water did, and so on *ad infinitum*. Let us think, instead of a cork, of ourselves, made up of mind the controlling substance, at the fastest known rate of vibration, which we shall call M. Besides this we have an etheric body at a slower rate of vibration, which we term E, and a physical body we term P, which is slower in vibration than E. We are thus made up of M + E + P. Each individual, then, consists of M + E + P, which is related to this earth. We live on a surface which supports M + E + P, as it is attuned to P, the body. Above the earth in space there is a surface made up of faster vibrations which in the physical we cannot sense. At death we shed P and become M + E, which is related to this higher surface. M + E therefore rises to it, and so becomes M + E in relation to this higher range of vibrations in tune with E which is our etheric body.

The universe, I repeat, is made up of countless ranges of vibrations. Where they begin and where they end we know not. All we know is the range which affects our consciousness through our physical body. These ranges all interpenetrate each other. Within the physical are numerous others we cannot sense.

Imagine again that we human beings have the capacity at death to attune ourselves to the next higher range. What then happens? We die physically, but can remain exactly where this event took place. Death is the shortest journey we shall ever take. We can thus remain erect in our etheric body while our physical body lies at our feet lifeless. We can stand on it, but would have no sensation that we were so doing. In our new body we experience another range of vibrations in tune with our new body, which latter is not really new, as we always had it but did not sense it. That new range makes up our new surroundings, but not all at once. Gradually our etheric body vibrates faster, and we enter the range which will make up our new world, but the surface of this new world, though parallel with the surface of this earth, is above it in space.

Imagine this earth surrounded by water, say ten miles in depth, and that there is another liquid less dense than water, also surrounding the earth, extending twenty miles from the earth's surface, and so on, one liquid after another interpenetrating the other, each lighter liquid extending ten miles beyond the other. We can thus picture, first the earth, and above it water in contact with the earth. Interpenetrating earth and water is a less dense liquid in contact with earth, which reaches higher in space than the water, and so on to the extent of seven different liquids, each lighter than the other, each in contact with earth, each interpenetrating the earth and each other, and all reaching to various heights above the surface of the earth.

Imagine a being who cannot sense water, living on the surface of the earth. He dies and becomes conscious of the water but loses consciousness of the earth. He does not remain on the earth surface or immersed in the water, but rises to its surface. There he lives for a time and dies again. This time he enters the less dense liquid, to again rise to its surface, and so on seven times, until he reaches the outermost surface of the least dense liquid. He is on the outermost surface of the Greater World, and is then fitted to leave this world to function in other surroundings apart from this world altogether.

K*

As each range of liquid is in contact with the earth, he could, while still remaining on the earth's surface, die seven times and each time enter a new environment, although he never moved from the earth surface. He would become unconscious, first of the earth, and then, at each successive death, of the liquid to which he had ceased to be attuned. He could thus enter a new environment at each death, but still be at a point in space on the earth's surface.

He, however, just like a man in water, naturally rises to the surface of his surroundings, but, like a man in water, he can sink back to the point in space termed the earth surface. This he can do in each environment, as each is in contact with the earth. He, however, would not appreciate the earth or the other surfaces he came through unless he attuned his vibrations into harmony with each. If he did not, he would go through the earth and not appreciate it. We human beings, at death, reverse this process and, by our etheric body becoming attuned to the first range of vibrations higher than the earth, we go through the experience of entering the astral range of vibrations at the earth's surface. Hence we rise to the surface of this range, where we live until fitted to experience something better.

Now this comparison of the different etheric spheres and surfaces, with liquid of lesser and lesser density, is reasonable, provided we also imagine that the different liquids interpenetrate the earth, and that when we enter the finer environment we can go through the earth and come out at the other side. It is just like the world being made up of eight separate globes. The smallest we call the earth. Around it and within it is the first globe of liquid we call water, but this forms a complete globe of water in itself, larger than the earth, with the earth in the centre.

So there are seven complete globes of these imaginary liquids, the densest being water, the others less dense, and each forming one globe within the other. Each is a separate entity in itself, and is only appreciated by the mind according to the density of the body it is inhabiting for the time being. It must be understood that I am using the words water and liquid only as symbols to make Etheria understandable.

In whatever environment we are, we can sink back to earth, but we cannot enter the environment we have not been in previously until our body becomes attuned to a higher environment or less dense liquid. This relates to each plane of consciousness. Dying is just the preliminary to an extension of our faculties, an experience we must go through to become more developed, just as we leave the nursery for the schoolroom. This is the best way I can explain the real world, and death. At each death we shed a sheath, to fit ourselves for a finer environment and extended faculties, but we can come back to earth from each. Earth death, however, is the only occasion on which we leave a body behind us, as on the other occasions the sheath is shed through dematerialisation.

Call these extensions of faculty "dimensions" if you like, and say that we pass from this three-dimensional environment into a four-dimensional environment and so on, each change adding to our faculties until time and space cease for us altogether. Then we shall have powers above and beyond anything we can possibly imagine as three-dimensional beings.

Thus at séances we experience Etherians communicating with us who are in different environments, and do not sense each other, but can make contact with earth. They have come down from their own separate surfaces and, after leaving us, rise to them again. They of course can make contact with the other surfaces below their normal environment at will, and thus get into touch with other planes besides the earth. Consequently we can have seven different orders of beings present at a séance, each unsensed by us, and, if we include ourselves, eight different orders, but only by means of a medium can they make contact with us.

I do not say that those in what we call the highest planes do come back to earth, as they have no earth memories, but what I mean is that all who have earth memories can come back to earth. Each can go through the world they live in, besides the other worlds of lower vibrations, and come out at the other side. That is a faculty one has when living on a substance I have likened to water and with a body the density of which can be altered at will, whereas we on earth cannot go through our surface, but only on it.

I was looking at an ant-heap the other day, which was alive with life, and later I looked up a book on natural history which gave a section in diagram of an ant-heap. It is honeycombed with galleries and shafts. So it occurred to me that this little world of life must resemble what the Greater World would look like to someone endowed with sight which embraced all the ranges of vibration of which the Greater World is composed.

If this being were situated, let us say, at some point

in space where he could see the entire Greater World, it would look something like an ant-heap, with life moving along the galleries, which correspond to the surfaces of the various planes, and passing up and down the shafts, which correspond to the "thought-ways" which exist between the various planes of the Greater World. There they move from plane to plane by desire, and this comes about by thought affecting the vibrations of the etheric body, to attune it into harmony with the vibrations of the surroundings desired.

Our imaginary being situated in space would see this constant stream of life moving in all directions within this mass of substance I call the Greater World. I give a diagram of this surging life as it would appear to this observer with full vision looking at the real world from without. To him we would seem just as microbes in a globule appear to us when looked at through a microscope, and yet how important each one of us feels! This state of mind comes about because we have the power of intelligent rational thought. We are individual beings but dependent on one another, each one co-operating towards the fulfilment of a great unceasing purpose.

In Diagram No. 5, I give the Greater World as it would look to a being possessed of this expanded vision, which could take in all the ranges of vibration. He would see the various galleries, the surfaces alive with life, and life moving upwards and downwards between them. The surfaces are indicated by the curved lines. I show the eight surfaces already referred to but there may be, and probably are, others containing different types of life. The small crosses represent life on earth. The dots represent etheric life, which it will be noticed is not confined to the surfaces, as the spaces between the surfaces are filled with life moving between the various surfaces.

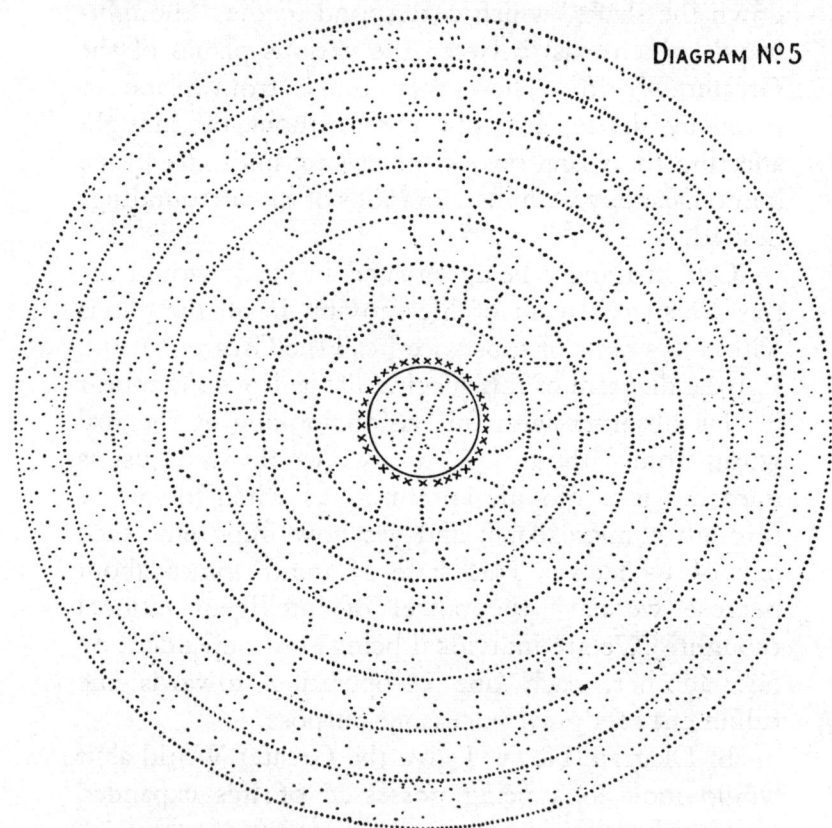

DIAGRAM No. 5

This, then, is the real world—not *on* which we live but *in* which we live—and, though it may seem fantastic to those who have never thought about it, it is no more so than our idea of the ant-heap would appear to an ant, which in its own order of life is just as intelligent as we are.

I shall try two pages further on to give an impression of how these different spheres really interpenetrate each other, and yet appear to their inhabitants as separate spheres, each having a surface which seems to those living on it to be the only surface, and to constitute the only world. It will be seen to resolve itself into a scheme of interacting vibrations to which different individuals are attuned to different ranges.

Our onlooker would, I think, come to the conclusion that the Greater World, this mass of vibrating substance, is just a combination of myriads of thoughts, conditioned by what we term substance. The thoughts influence the substance, and the substance the thoughts. It is just like an individual's brain and mind. The brain in this case is the substance of which the Greater World is composed, and the thoughts are the individual mind images. Each one of us is a cell in this Greater World, a cell composed of mind and substance. Our onlooker would thus see a live mass of pulsating energy, each living creature having its place in this mass of teeming life, according to the mental images each individual formed, these constituting to each its life and its world.

In this living mass nothing ever dies. Matter changes its form, and life changes its conditions, and the highest life of all, of which we are part, always retains its consciousness and memory. Life is moving slowly to higher states of consciousness which seem to have no end, and one by one each individual thinking mind or cell leaves this revolving mass of thinking substance, and seeks another habitation.

Individual life is going through a continuous evolutionary process so far as the Greater World is concerned. By degrees it attunes itself to a higher order of thought, becoming perhaps ultimately at one with the Infinite, its experience with substance at different frequencies of vibration having fitted it for this higher existence.

Beyond the Greater World we cannot go, because outside this limit there are none to tell us what the conditions are like. Yet, from the philosophic discourses I have received from those in Etheria who have given much thought to human destiny, I have been given suggestions which are significant enough to provide the basis for the deepest contemplation for ages to come, during our evolution towards this at-one-ment with the Divine Mind of the Universe. Darwin carried our knowledge of evolution only up to the man stage. Spiritualism carries it to the superman stage, and proves that though our bodies are related to the animals, our minds are related to the Infinite Mind of the Cosmos.

Diagram No. 6 is for the purpose of conveying to us on earth the compass of the vision of our imaginary onlooker, of his impression of eight worlds in one, but each distinct and separate. It is impossible for us physical beings to imagine matter interpenetrating. We can imagine one layer over the other, but we cannot imagine two layers of matter making one whole, yet entirely separate. The state in which such conditions obtain may be termed the fourth dimension, and, as the number of layers increases, so do the dimensions. However, this name, the fourth dimension, is used only to express something we cannot understand, but in imagination, by looking at this diagram, we can arrive at some kind of conception

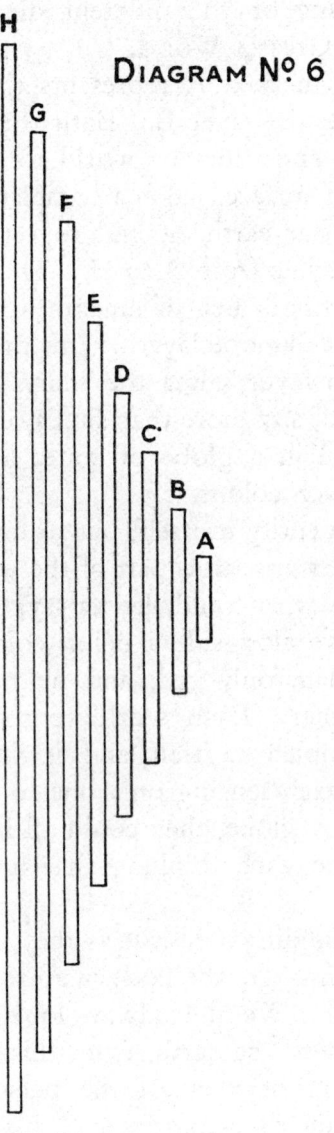

DIAGRAM N⁰ 6

of the meaning of the different dimensions which make up the Greater World.

The layer marked A represents the earth. This interpenetrates the layer B. Both these layers make up a distinct and different world to the inhabitants living on each surface. B is a complete world within and without our earth A, and so on right through the different layers from A to H. The diagram looks like a concertina. Let us imagine this pressed together to look like one layer. This pressing together must not, however, alter the individuality of each separate world, any more than fluids of eight different colours placed in a globe of water affects the individuality of each colour.

Each is an entity in itself, but to us when they are in solution they appear as part of the water. A being coloured blue who could, let us say, appreciate only blue could live alongside a being coloured red who could appreciate only red, and neither would ever notice the other. Each world to these individuals would be complete in itself, and, if there were eight such beings, each sensing only one of the colours we had put in the globe, they could all live together in the same place, each thinking that he was the only inhabitant.

Our surroundings are just as they appear to be to us mentally through the body we are inhabiting for the time being. We must always look on the Greater World, including the earth, from this point of view, from the point of view of the person who is experiencing only the sensations of his surroundings. The earth is our world to us in the physical body. It ceases to be the world to us when we leave the physical body and function in the etheric body, because we then sense our surroundings through etheric substance.

So we shall progress from one stage of experience to another in the ages to come, sensing these different orders of finer matter. It is possible to think of the real world only from this mental point of view. Mind is the only unchanging factor common to all eight planes of The Greater World. The substance of these different orders of existence change according to their vibrational frequency, but mind remains the same. We must always put mind first and life as the expression of mind. Each mind is oneself, and what clothes it, or what its surroundings are, depends on the place we have reached in the Greater World. This place is determined by the quality of the body which the mind inhabits for the time being.

Until each one of us can rise mentally to the high level of thought which will enable us always to put mind first, and all else last, the universe will never be understood. This matter is so important that I devote the next chapter entirely to its consideration. I have entitled it "Mind is King". We have now arrived at the steps leading up to the Infinite, and, by the time we have climbed them, we shall have reached the presence of the Ruler of the Universe.

CHAPTER VIII.

MIND IS KING.

The contemplation of the Ruler of the Universe, into whose presence we are approaching, raises thoughts profound and reverent. Under whatever name this over-ruling Presence is known—God, the Almighty, the Universal Mind, or the Cosmic Mind—it always stirs our emotions. Since man rose from the level of the beast, in all lands, he has reverently bowed himself in worship of the sovereign Ruler of the Universe. Let us now approach the Presence by giving serious thought to the subject which was to our ancestors, and is to many living today, the object of so much reverent worship.

We must always keep permanently before us the fact that Mind is everything, that Mind is the King of Kings and Lord of Lords, in other words that Mind is God and God is Mind. Only in terms of Mind can we possibly comprehend the universe. So let us start with a consideration of ourselves, in which we can appreciate mind in its highest state of development on earth, and then in thought rise to greater heights.

In the physical world we individuals are mind incased in physical bodies, surrounded by physical substance. After death we are mind incased in etheric bodies, surrounded by etheric substance. Thus this refining process goes on with mind always in control of the body, and the body becoming more refined as time passes. As it becomes more refined it functions in more refined matter. In the physical, mind is not sufficiently in control of the body to enable us to change the density of our bodies, and consequently we are confined to the surface of the earth. In the etheric body, however, mind has much more control, because the etheric body is a finer substance, and can be more easily controlled by the mind.

Therefore in the etheric body we live on a surface, having latitude and longitude, yet we are not conditioned by that surface. We can go through that surface, and penetrate it and its sphere, so that we can travel right through to come out at the surface at the opposite point to where we were. Our thoughts take us without effort to the surroundings we desire. If our desires are low and gross, we naturally gravitate to the grosser surface of the lower sphere with which they are in harmony. Some minds on earth are, however, already fitted for the conditions prevailing on the higher surfaces, and at death they pass through the lower surfaces of Etheria, as these are inhabited by minds which must develop further before they can rise to finer realms.

The man or woman of selfish and crude thinking, of evil thoughts, cannot live on the surface of the higher planes where dwell the finer minds. The finer minds adjust their bodies to these finer vibrations, and thus they are attuned to the more brilliant light of the higher planes. In Etheria everything must be in harmony, and this is reached naturally. There, character and thoughts are much more in evidence than here, where they can be hidden in a way they cannot be there. The evil, therefore, are miserable in the company of the good, and the good are equally so in the company of the evil. The evil-doers are ashamed of their misdeeds and their evil thoughts, and this leads them to seek shelter where they can be alone and brood over their past misdeeds.

The evil consequently keep to the lowest surface, and there etheric missionaries have sometimes great difficulty in finding them, because their thoughts put up a barrier which makes contact with them almost impossible. The suicide may hide himself from his fellows in shame because of his weakness, but sooner or later his self-respect returns. Such is not necessarily the case with those who have brought about their own deaths in consequence of disease or despair. I am told that insanity is due to abnormal physical conditions of the brain, which prevent the mind from functioning in a normal fashion. When freed from the physical, the mind is strong enough to assert itself and develop through its etheric brain in a way it cannot do through the physical brain. Here on earth we are in a suit of armour, namely the physical body, which does not always fit us. In the etheric world, we are in a suit of clothes which, as we develop, comes to fit us perfectly.

Just as low minds live in wretched surroundings on earth, so they produce the same conditions there. Many, however, on earth, through poverty, live in conditions with which they are not in harmony. In Etheria they will rise to the surface for which their minds are fitted and congregate with like minds, being drawn irresistibly to the conditions and surroundings for which their minds fit them.

The developed will be attracted by all that is

beautiful, and the undeveloped by that which is gross and crude—like to like in everything. The intellectual will be attracted by the intellectual, the kind by the kind, the loving by the loving, the noble by the noble, the wicked by the wicked. The good and the bad find their places, to which their individual character assigns them. Only by repentance, and wishing for something better, will the undeveloped and wicked minds advance and lead their owners to happier surroundings.

As the mind desires, so are our surroundings in Etheria. If after death we wish to make contact with the grosser mental conditions, we can do so by attuning our body by thought into harmony with their density. Many do so for the purpose of raising those living on the lower etheric surfaces.

At the most we can only visualise this Greater World. It cannot be a reality to us. All that is real is the earth, the first rung of the ladder. We take the next step and it in turn becomes real. What is, however, real now and ever will be is our mind, because this enables us to appreciate the earth and visualise Etheria.

We can obtain only a glimpse on earth of the next step. The steps beyond are a matter for our imagination, but the information we receive from Etheria enables us to make certain speculative deductions. The faint gleam we have of our next state gives us an idea of what the step beyond that has in store for us, and thus we can in imagination look up our ladder of life and visualise each rung on which it will some time be our destiny to stand. We can picture this ladder reaching beyond our gaze, but the glimpse we now have of the next rung enables us to turn faith into knowledge.

To our ancestors the view was so clouded as to be difficult to discern. Now that it has become clearer one thing stands out prominently, namely that the individual mind is indestructible and is in fact the only reality. Mind is ourselves and it only will be ourselves throughout all eternity. Mind is the only reality on earth and we find it occupying the same position in Etheria. When we put our foot on the next rung of the ladder of life it will enable us to appreciate Etheria, and the things of this earth which we are now experiencing will then become a memory.

When we come to realise the reality of mind we reach the conclusion naturally that the only thing in the universe that counts is mind. To each of us our mind constitutes the universe, as everything which, to each individual, makes up the universe is imaged by the mind. Mental images are therefore the universe to each conscious being. Without mind the universe would never be sensed. Consciousness would cease to exist, and if consciousness of our surroundings ceased there would be no universe, because something cannot exist to us if the thing that would make us conscious of it does not exist. If there is no consciousness then there can be nothing of which to be conscious.

Only that of which we each are conscious exists for the time being. Time is therefore this experiencing of ideas stimulated by our surroundings. When asleep, time ceases because we are not conscious of our surroundings. The mental images caused when awake by our surroundings, and regulated by those surroundings, are not regulated when we are asleep. Hence dreams, which are caused by our mind continuing to image without being under the control of substance. The difficulty in remembering our dreams is due to the speed of the sequences, a dream covering only a few seconds of time and yet embracing events which normally would occupy time and space of considerable duration and distance.

When awake our surroundings act as a regulator to our mind, whose image-making is governed by our environment. This we term normal consciousness, and the images produced are in consequence remembered. It is not difficult, however, to imagine that when our surroundings change, as they do in Etheria, and become composed of faster vibrations, our mind becomes regulated by these, and its image-making speed is increased. Therefore time, as we know it, is related to our surroundings on earth, and their time to their surroundings.

We are accustomed from birth to a certain time measurement, but in Etheria we shall become equally accustomed to another time measurement, and, as we reach finer and finer surroundings, time as we understand it now will cease to be. When mind can embrace all, then time will cease, but so long as we are confined here and hereafter to substance, and a sequence of ideas caused by substance, time exists.

Just as the idea of time changes until it vanishes altogether from our minds, so also will distance, height, depth and length, as we free ourselves more and more from substance, because the speed of the mind is the speed of thought, which is instantaneous. When our mind can move with its thoughts without being burdened by a cumbersome body to carry with it, then distance ceases to be.

Our bodies, as time goes on, get finer and are thus more easily moved by the mind. As they get finer, so distance decreases. When we reach the region of pure thought, and mind completely controls substance, then distance and all that it means to mind in substance will vanish.

Mind is the only reality. Without mind there is no matter. Existence means thinking. Thinking requires mind, but nothing can exist to the individual of which no thinking being is conscious. The universe to each is what each is thinking for the time being. We therefore get back every time to the fact that mind dominates the universe, it makes the universe to each thinking being, and consciousness consists of thought stimulated by surrounding substance. It is impossible, however, to imagine mind alone in the universe, without surrounding substance. They are inseparable, as without one you cannot have the other. What changes is the density of the substance.

What, then, is the object of life? A thing without life does not think. Life is the combination of mind and matter, and in consequence of this combination we have thought. To think, then, must be the purpose of conscious existence. Conscious existence can have no other purpose than the production of thought. Thought stimulated by environment produces reactions, in the form of movement, to which reaction we give the name life.

Can we now answer the age-long question—What is the object of existence? If we do not think, we cease to exist. So long as we think, we exist. For what purpose is this thinking? Is it for the purpose of developing better and greater thoughts? It would seem to be so, as part of the scheme of our evolution. We think better thoughts because we must, not otherwise. Our minds are developing because their vibrations are attaining a higher frequency, and this produces an improved mental standard. Humanity in the mass, in spite of temporary stagnation and setbacks, is being carried along this ever-widening stream of developing thought, which, some day, may carry us into the sea of full understanding when all will be understood.

On earth we can only dimly appreciate the power of thought, but as we go on in our career after death we shall realise more and more its potency and effect on our surroundings. Psychometry shows how mind and substance can interact, and it gives us a faint idea of the potential power of mind over matter. We are thinking out something which on earth is only dimly mirrored, but, as we go on, it becomes more and more clear until it becomes a great reality. We are each one of us a developing mind. It more and more controls our surroundings until they become just as we think. As we reach vibrations of greater frequency our thoughts mould our surroundings, until ultimately we reach the range of vibrations when our mind completely dominates its surroundings.

Then time will be no more. Then space will cease to be. Then we shall have reached the region of pure thought. Then we shall have reached harmony with the Divine Mind and become in tune with the Infinite. Then we shall have reached at-one-ment with the guiding Mind of the universe. This, through the ages, has been the desire of the mystic and the philosopher. This goal ahead, which so many instinctively feel to be there, is the cause of man's religious emotions, and the reason for the prayers, ritual and ceremony in all the world's religions. Moreover, it brought about philosophic reasoning and mystical contemplations.

By the time we reach the stage of pure thought, time and distance will have ceased to exist, as there cannot be time or distance to thought. Time will be the "all now" and distance will be the "all here". Time, as we at present understand it, is only a physical property. In Etheria it is an etheric property. In the mental world which is our destiny it is unknown.

Distance is likewise a physical property just as it is an etheric property, but in the region of pure thought distance ceases, as where we think or desire to be there we shall be. The real universe, being Mind, is therefore timeless and spaceless. It has no distance, it has no time, all is now and all is here. This timeless, spaceless world, where the universe will be comprehended, is our destiny, and all who have the desire to do so can eventually reach it. It is therefore futile to try to explain the universe on a physical basis, as mind is the universe, and the physical just a phase which mind is experiencing.

We on earth are looking at the universe upside down. Mentally, we realise that the earth circles round the sun, though physically the opposite seems to be the case. Likewise it seems to us that the physical is the universe, but such is not the case. Mind, the universe, has no boundaries. It is boundless, timeless and spaceless. Mind consists of substance quite different from physical or etheric substance. It is intangible and immaterial, but nevertheless very real. It is physical and etheric substance which gives dimensions to the mind. In the region of pure thought, mind conditions substance instead of substance conditioning mind.

When we reach that stage we shall have entered a different order of vibrations from those constituting the earth and the etheric planes, and there mind is king. Then we shall appreciate the universe as it really is, and not topsy-turvy as we do here, where the vibrations of substance, with which mind is in contact, are at a much slower frequency than mind itself. Mind, when all that comes about, will have become unchained and liberated, having worked its way out to freedom and control of its surroundings.

The universe is working out its own destiny, which is the ever greater perfection of mind, and all who try to enlarge and ennoble their thoughts are fellow-travellers on the road which is becoming clearer, broader, smoother and more pleasant to travel. This is why the claim can be made that we live in an unfolding universe, which will some day cease to be wrapped up and hidden from our minds, because the individual mind is unfolding and playing its part in an infinite drama which is eternally being enacted.

When we reach the end of the unfolding, time will have ceased, and in that condition there will be no beginning and no end. Consequently we shall never reach the end. To us there will be no end and no beginning, as time will have ceased to be. This being so, our destiny is to reach infinity with our individuality unimpaired, and there we shall no longer be finite beings. Our minds will then have returned home after their journey through matter.

As the individual mind never dies, so we are ever conscious of our own ego, of each being oneself. Such thoughts must have been in the mind of Socrates when he said, "Beyond question the soul is immortal and imperishable and our souls will truly exist in another world," and again the words attributed to Saint Paul on this subject are familiar to most people, "For this corruptible must put on incorruption, and this mortal must put on immortality."

Substance, to which mind reacts and which reacts to mind, can be likened to the human body through which mind is working. The universe comprises mind and body as does the individual. Mind penetrates all substance and is the cause behind all vibration. A tree thinks subconsciously and sends its roots to find water, while its leaves absorb oxygen. It comprises a lower range of mind than has an animal, and so we can descend the scale to the lowly fungus and seemingly inanimate life.

Everything vibrates and so thinks in different degrees, but conscious thought alone makes mental images which cause memory, to which instinct is closely related. Conscious thought consists of this mind image-making. Thought in substance has not this capacity; it is a lower form of thought, but it keeps the whirling electrons and protons in orderly motion in a stone.

We are here now as thinking units in one form or another. Each of us has always been a part of thinking units. Until we became individualised we were part of a pair of thinking units, and that pair the product of four thinking units, and so on. The further we go back the more diffused becomes the mind which is now unified. From the moment of conception of this thinking unit which each of us terms "myself", mind grows and develops. We build our bodies by subconscious thought and take substance from our surroundings to do so. Our subconscious thought constructs both our etheric and our physical bodies, and these are what we have subconsciously imaged.

Without our mind there would be no body, and without the body there would be no individual mind in our present state of consciousness. They are both complementary to each other. In this physical body our mind, which is ourselves, senses surrounding matter, but it will sense etheric substance through the etheric body when we function in that body after death. We do not sense the etheric body on earth, just as we do not sense etheric substance, but it is there nevertheless, just as Etheria is about us though we cannot see it or feel it.

Just as our bodies grow by absorbing physical and etheric nourishment, so our minds absorb mental nourishment from the mind substance of the universe. Why should this ever cease? If mind is a developing substance and draws its powers from the universal mind, there seems no reason why this development should ever end, because we shall ultimately cease to be conscious of time, and only of eternity, a state of consciousness apart from time. Thus we shall not be conscious of either beginning or end. We shall have BECOME. We shall be, and in this state we shall have reached Infinity and all this implies.

Our thoughts, when this state is reached, will encompass the universe, because mind will then be king in each of us and have conquered substance. Mind on earth is crucified by the flesh, but it is working out its own salvation and will in time experience resurrection from the flesh, and ascension to its throne, after passing through its experiences in earth and Etheria. We can think of existence only in terms of time and space. What the universe will mean to each one of us when all this vanishes, and we have entered our kingdom, no finite being can say. We shall only be able to comprehend infinity when we become infinite.

To mind there is no end. To mind in its own realm beginning and end have no meaning. To mind there is no distance, as in the Realm of Mind distance means nothing. When thinking about ourselves we should think of mind, and mind only. We have no end, because beginning and end refer to time. Where there is no time there is no beginning and no end. We always were mind, but we each of us had a conscious beginning at birth. What became conscious always was and always will be.

When we reach this timeless state we do not experience time, so what seems strange now will not be so then. Distance, which makes the universe incomprehensible to us in the physical, will mean nothing to us then. We shall then comprehend the universe and shall be able mentally to embrace it.

Mind is King

It is quite impossible to imagine ourselves a million years hence. Years mean something to us now. Then they will mean nothing. What will we be thinking and doing? We shall be responding to our conditions as we do now, though these will be vastly different from what we experience today. We shall not be thinking of this earth and the things of this earth. What we are experiencing at the moment will by then be completely forgotten, just as are our nursery days. Our individuality, however, can remain unimpaired, as our minds will still be ourselves. It is a question of memory. Memory, so to speak, trails after us like the smoke of a train, and the further it is from its source of origin the more dissipated it is. We live enveloped in memory, as a battleship in a smoke screen. It trails the smoke with it, but is always producing more, while at the same time that which has been previously produced becomes dissipated.

We are, on earth, conscious individuals in a time-space world. What it will be like to be conscious individuals in a timeless spaceless world is difficult to imagine. Because we are unable to do so, it does not follow that we shall not be just as much individuals then as we are now, though with vastly extended powers over those we have at the present time.

What concerns us, however, is this, that if we live aright and think aright and do the right, our happiness should increase and not decrease. The object of everyone is happiness, and the more unselfish each one is the greater is his happiness and content. When we reach the region of pure thought we shall have come to the state of absolute content and harmony

L

with the Cosmic Mind of the universe. When that stage is reached, all thought of whence and whither will have vanished from our minds. As there will be no such question, there will likewise be no answer. Then we shall not question our origin or our destiny. We shall accept what is, without wishing for more or less. We shall have reached at-one-ment with the divine. We shall have attained to a state of harmony with our surroundings, which means complete happiness.

This is the magnet which draws the mystic beyond the physical, and the philosopher beyond earth's troubles. It is the inspiration of religious belief from the savage worshipping his image to the Christian Eucharist, this desire for at-one-ment with the Infinite. It has been the cause of all forms, ceremonials, rites and rituals of all religions, of beliefs in crucified gods, who by death brought about this at-one-ment, the cause of sacrifice due to the belief that without the shedding of blood there is no forgiveness of sins or reconciliation with the Infinite.

Man's misconstruction and misinterpretation of reality has caused suffering, sorrow and cruelty. It has been and still is due to ignorance. On the other hand, these religious beliefs have conferred great comfort and solace to believers who instinctively felt that earth did not constitute their entire existence, that wrong and suffering on earth would be righted when they reached the place where harmony reigned, and where their desires, which earth could not meet, would be satisfied.

To most minds a material exhibition of the unknown, of the infinite, seems still necessary in spite of all our advance in knowledge. These material expressions, whether in the form of eating a victim's body and drinking his blood on the one hand, or in memory of a victim's death and suffering for humanity on the other, satisfy and give comfort to many.

To those minds, death means entering the presence of God, to be judged either at the time of death or on the resurrection day. They fail to realise that both here and always they are in the presence of God, as we are part of God, because God is just another name for Mind. We are our own judges and are passing judgment, and determining our future life, by our every thought and action. It is therefore incorrect to say of the dead that God has taken them to be with himself. What has happened is that a part of God, functioning through physical matter, has ceased doing so and, instead, is continuing to function through a finer substance in a new environment.

The aim of philosophy is to find unity in the universe, to find at-one-ment, to find harmony. Philosophy reaches reality by logic and reason, not by accepting appearances, which increased knowledge shows us to be only the shadow of reality. This mirage, which surrounds us, we find to be unreal the more the universe unfolds.

Just as our capacity enlarges, so are we enabled to visualise the extended panorama of reality and ignore the world of appearance, the physical universe, which deceives us on every occasion. The universe to some can now become understandable, though far from being understood. As the mind is, so is the universe. Just as more powerful telescopes reveal a greater material universe, so the greater the mind the more complete becomes the universe to that mind, and the nearer at-one-ment is reached with the Divine Mind which comprehends all and orders all.

An ordered and a guided universe unfolds before us, because it consists of that which thinks. The philosopher by reason, and the mystic by intuition, gain at-one-ment with the directive intelligence through contemplation, while the less developed seek to attain it by religious observations, forms and ceremonies. Thus religion and science are blended in one to those having the power of discernment, as both stand for increasing knowledge of the working of the Infinite Mind of the Universe.

Our reasoning leads us up through man to God. The mind in man, which is all that is man, is part of God, and God is Mind. Mind fashions us, it fashions our surroundings, it fashions the earth, Etheria, the planets and the entire universe. God, our maker and sustainer, is none other than Mind.

Behind all the forces of nature is mind. Every cause has mind the cause, and every effect is the reaction to the cause. The effect in turn becomes another cause, and so mind is behind both cause and effect which have been from all eternity and will last throughout eternity. Without mind the universe would be dead, lifeless, instead of pulsating with life. It is these pulsations that influence our minds and thus make the universe real. Without them it would cease to be, as there would be nothing to influence the individual mind to make its images. Without mind-images the universe would cease to be, as what is can only be if it is appreciated, and appreciation requires mind.

We have therefore reached the source of all the

phenomena in nature, and penetrated into the presence of Divinity. By realising that Mind occupies the throne of the Universe we have reached Reality, attained to the Ultimate, which is now, always has been and ever will be.

By Mind are all things made and fashioned, by Mind are all things moved, from the whirling electrons to the revolving planets. Mind pulsates substance. By Mind we live and move and have our being. As Mind we are all the sons and daughters of God, because we are all more or less developed parts of the Divine Mind. Each thinking thing throughout the wide domain of space and time is part of God, and in each is God revealed. Just as each one develops mentally, so is the universe better appreciated, and God, the Infinite Mind, becomes an ever greater reality as we attain closer affinity with this, the guiding force of the entire universe.

CHAPTER IX.

THE COMING WORLD RELIGION.

The preceding chapters make it clear for what Spiritualism stands, this attuning into harmony with the divine in nature. Speech with those who come and speak to us at séances is not religion, any more than conversation amongst the inhabitants of earth is religion.

Why Spiritualism is the coming world religion is because in place of philosophic, mystical and religious speculations on what happens at death, it gives facts. Facts conquer creeds. We now know for certain what is our destiny so far as the next step on the ladder is concerned, and thus we need not base our religion any longer on faith. Spiritualism is not a speculative religion as are all the other world religions, because it is a religion based on fact, on reason and on experience. When people become educated enough to understand the basis on which Spiritualism is built, their mental development will increase, and with it will also advance the feeling of greater at-one-ment with the guiding mind of the universe.

We now know that death is just the entrance gate to a more enlarged outlook on the universe, and our friends in Etheria tell us that we pass on from stage to stage, developing progressively, until we attain powers of understanding that are beyond our present capacity to imagine.

To achieve this development in an orderly and satisfactory way, our etheric friends make it clear that our lives should be governed by certain guiding principles which can be summarised in the one word love. Thus we must try to develop unselfishness in our lives, and live for others more than for ourselves. This giving out, instead of taking in, has the effect of refining our minds, with the result that those who give most really receive most. Thus they attain more quickly the innate desire latent in everyone, of becoming in tune with the Infinite, which is our destiny.

This, then, is the religion of Spiritualism, born of the knowledge that we do not die but are for ever destined to progress and develop, just as the divine mind of the universe, of which we are part, is progressing and developing. This religion requires no churches, priests, creeds, dogmas or doctrines. It has no exclusiveness, as it embraces the entire human race. It is not in conflict with science, as it is science. It is not conflicting with philosophy, because it is philosophy. It is not contrary to mysticism, because it is mysticism. Science and natural religion are one, and always have been one, as both stand for truth based on evidence and experience. Philosophy, mysticism and natural religion are one, and always have been one, as they likewise stand for truth and always have stood for truth based on experience.

Mrs. Rose Champion de Crespigny, in her recent book *This World and Beyond*, writes as follows: "Why in a country, professing to be Christian, contempt and hostility should be shown towards those who attempt to prove one of the chief tenets of Christianity to be true, is a mystery that must go unsolved until secrets are no longer hid."

The answer is contained in this book, so no one need wait for an answer to the mystery until secrets are no longer hid. The reason is obvious to all who get down to the bed-rock, as I have attempted to do. Christians worship Christ, a name for a theological doctrine, which teaches that only the Christian way leads to heaven.

If they put Jesus in place of Christ there would be no hostility to Spiritualism, as what Jesus taught, and what Spiritualism teaches, are much alike, though the Church has so mixed up his teaching with its own theology that a superficial reading of the Gospels and Epistles, as is done by most, gives such a conflicting range of opinions that few can find a way out of the maze. The entire "Quelle" gospel, given in this book, should help to clear away many of the difficulties experienced by seekers after truth at the present time, especially if they remember that on to this simple record of a simple life all those doctrines, which are difficult to believe and understand, were added over a long period of time.

Christians worship the symbolism of true religion, the drapings, the wrappings theology has wound round a central truth, and these wrappings almost obliterate what true religion stands for. These wrappings have a hidden meaning now forgotten by the priesthood, who teach doctrines relating only to the clothes put on to religion. These are so old and musty that it is difficult to identify the body beneath. Spiritualism stands for the central truth in religion, which it is well-nigh impossible for Christians, worshipping the drapings, to perceive. Hence the hostility of Christians towards Spiritualism.

Christianity is, as I have shown, just Paganism, and Paganism was once something else, and so back we go to the religion of the savage. All the orthodox religions are related to each other; they are cousins, more or less removed from each other, but as we go back so the ancestral tree narrows until we eventually reach the origin of them all.

In spite of the relationship existing between all world religions, they are not on speaking terms with each other, as each accuses the other of a bastard birth. The representatives of Christianity, for instance, recently refused to sit round a table with those of other world religions to discuss world religious problems, the reason given for the refusal being that Christianity was the only true religion, or, to continue our simile, it was the only legitimate child of God, all the others being born out of wedlock.

Each religion is based on an underlying truth, namely survival after death, and has for its object the reaching of at-one-ment with God. This has been bound up with the belief in Christs, in crucified saviours, in the eating of their bodies and the drinking of their blood, in forms and ceremonials, ritual, holy books, holy churches and holy men who claim to interpret God's message to man.

Little wonder that Christian people see no resemblance between Christianity and Spiritualism! Little wonder they are hostile to it, because Spiritualists discard the drapings Christians worship; they put them aside as things of use only to an uneducated age which they have now outgrown. Spiritualists are therefore trying to educate the people so that they may outgrow the superstitions of the past, and this Christians resent as they cannot yet see that what they worship is false, and that these false drapings are hiding them from the greatest truth nature has ever revealed to mankind.

What is needed today is a new interpretation of religion, not a reformed Christianity for which some are hoping. Christianity cannot be reformed, it must be abandoned, as it will be when the people develop intellectually. Christianity is based on the religion of the savage, and in this day of greater enlightenment we cannot profess a religion founded on the speculations of primitive man. The new revelation has come to us, and in spite of the hostility of Christendom it will gather more and more adherents. In time it will become accepted by all because it comes direct to us from Etheria, and has not been misinterpreted, mangled and distorted by the priests as have all the religions of the past.

Few as yet realise that one of the great events in world history occurred last century. Not that what happened was new any more than steam was new, because engineers only applied the expanding force in steam to the needs of industry.

Likewise, since 1848, messages from the world to which we are all travelling have been systematically recorded, and used for the needs of natural religion, they not now being kept hidden by the priesthood as happened in the past.

The reason this is such a great event in world history is because the people themselves had become intelligent enough to understand its meaning, and were no longer dependent on an organisation whose policy has always been to keep the problems of life and death a mystery. Education and freedom of thought had advanced sufficiently by 1848 for the people to think out for themselves the meaning of life and death, which had hitherto been considered a question too sacred and profound for any to ponder over except those divinely appointed for the purpose.

Another factor, which made it possible for the people to form their own views on this matter of life and death, was because a century previously public opinion had stopped the Church from burning mediums. As mediumship is a hereditary gift this obliterating of mediums had almost extinguished the psychic power latent in mankind, but by 1848 it had redeveloped sufficiently to enable Etherians to demonstrate their presence to us on earth. Slowly we began to grasp the great significance of their visits, and progress commenced in understanding the mystery of death. That is why what happened in 1848 is one of the great dates in the history of man. Looking back over the great events of history, there are few others of greater importance than the fact that we have discovered our dead, and where they live.

In the brief résumé given of the structure underlying all the world's religions, the following questions arose: Why did our ancestors worship one or more gods? Why did they write books which they considered holy and containing God's message to men? Why did they offer sacrifices to appease the gods? Why did they turn their wealth over to an organisation for the purpose of maintaining churches, priests and monasteries? Why, since man became a thinking being, has he devoted a great part of his energy, thought and labour, to making supplication to the gods, and to supporting those he believed to be their representatives on earth?

There is only one answer to these questions, and it is found to account for all the practices we have enumerated. All were due to one thing—man's fear of the unknown. If men had never feared death, the preceding chapters of this book would never have been written. If man had had definite evidence of his true position on earth, and that when death took place he would enter another world, as naturally as he entered this world, he would never have feared and his happiness would have been enormously increased.

Ignorance relating to this great event in nature, death, has been the cause of unimaginable misery and cruelty. It has sapped man's vital energy, and added to his labour through the feeling that it was necessary to employ others to act as intermediaries between him and the unknown. Consequently ignorance has maintained a black-coated army of men in the west and a yellow-cloaked army in the east. The fear of the unknown has been the cause of all this waste, misery and suffering, besides being such an obstacle to mankind's progress, welfare and happiness. Eradicate that fear, open the door of death, point out the land beyond, and you have once and for all removed the source of so many miseries and errors. You have once and for all removed from man's shoulders the burden he has been carrying since he first began to realise that he had a soul.

The inventors, the thinkers, the mechanics, the artists and all who have added to the world's happiness and well-being, have not been able to remove this aching dread. Taking all that these great ones have done for the good of humanity, the result of their labours will not give mankind such happiness as the definite knowledge that there is nothing to fear at death, and that all who live aright have a great future in store. Until recently the scientists, the inventors and the constructors have been condemned whenever they produced something new for the good of humanity. Much that has been produced for the good of the people has been condemned, and in many cases those who have produced it have been ill-treated, and often murdered.

The Spiritualists have now come forward and told humanity that they can give definite, reliable evidence that life continues after death, that communication has been opened up between this order of existence and the order we shall enter at death. They tell mankind that there is nothing to fear, that there is no God of vengeance awaiting to punish his creatures when they enter the door of death, but that we punish ourselves by remorse because there, more than here, our faults, failings and mistakes become clear, to be in consequence more regretted. Spiritualists show the reasonableness of nature's plan, and that what is termed death, for those unburdened by wrong-doing, is just the beginning of a conscious existence freed from all the misery, troubles and worries of mankind on earth. They tell the world that every individual can prove their assertions for himself or herself, just as conclusively as everyone can determine the fact that boiling water produces steam.

What we know of death and the after-life is as scientifically proved as any other fact in science, but the great majority of people in the world are still ignorant of this. Consequently the Spiritualist today is treated with contempt by many people, because of the fact that his knowledge of what takes place at death is considered by the ignorant to be the result of his wandering imaginations, and contrary to the will of God.

The Spiritualists nevertheless have brought to the world the one great thing humanity wanted. They can prove to the satisfaction of any intelligent individual, who cares to take the trouble to investigate, that the claims they make are true. Most people, however, do not believe that such is possible, and many continue to live their lives in fear of the unknown.

It was science that first relieved this fear, when it made clear to all thinking men that the claims put forward by the various world religions are false, that God is not a person, that there is neither a personal God nor a personal Devil, and that the heavens are not the abode of an unjust judge awaiting to sentence the great majority. Moreover the centre of the earth is not the abode of the devil and his angels, into whose company all unbelievers would be consigned. Science proved that this earth was but a speck in an immense cosmos, and not the centre of creation round which the stars revolved.

Copernicus was the first man to show the fallacy of this theory, and the first printed copy of his book, propounding what is now called the Copernican system, reached him as he was dying. This book was the first evidence our ancestors had that the Bible was not literally true, and it opened the first round between the thinkers and the Church. For seventy years the Church did its best to keep this knowledge from the world, but ultimately truth conquered and from the time of Copernicus, who died in 1543, ignorance has had to give place to knowledge.

Science has proved the immensity of the universe and the insignificance of the earth. Science has made man's life happier, healthier, cleaner and brighter. Science has pushed theology aside, and for that reason our happiness is vastly greater today than was that of our ancestors. Science has told us nothing about the after-life, because science until recently has never investigated the question. What science has done, however, is to show that the after-life envisaged by the theologians is a creation born in the days of ignorance.

Better the dreamless vacuity of eternal peace; better eternal sleep, and that death should land us on the shore of oblivion where the sea of life casts no wave, than that our naked souls should be clutched by the orthodox God. Better far that we and those we love should return to earth, and become part of the elemental wealth of earth again, that we should become unconscious dust, and that death should be the end of life, than that we should be the victims of the Christian God described so pithily by Robert Burns as a monster who "sends one to Heaven and ten to Hell all for his glory".

Science has shattered to pieces the claims and threats of the orthodox, and in consequence life is infinitely happier for those who put science before theology. Those who do not are still under this pall of terror and fear of the unknown. Even in this enlightened age I know men and women who are in misery and unhappiness because a loved one has died who was not a believer in the Christian creed. It is almost unthinkable that there can be people today so ignorant as to harbour in their minds the idea of such a savage God. Yet so it is, and millions of the human race still believe in the orthodox religion into which they were born, and suffer unnecessarily through ignorance of the facts of nature.

Fortunately, as a result of the findings of science, most intelligent people have thrown over many of the beliefs of orthodox religion. They have no use for the priesthood, and seldom or never enter a church. Consequently orthodox religion is steadily losing public support, and, at the present rate of secession from the Christian religion, orthodoxy will continue to reign supreme for some time yet only in the most ignorant of Catholic countries.

Just as one religion in the past grew out of another, and as Christianity developed out of Judaism, Mithraism and the theological thought of Alexandria, so today we are experiencing a new religion arising out of the ashes of the old, but for a different reason. Christianity owes its place today to the fact that it became the State religion of Rome. If this had not happened it would probably have died a natural death, as occurred to so many of the cults in existence at the time of its birth.

The semi-Pagan emperor Constantine, however, was more attracted by Christianity than by Mithraism. The old Roman religion fought hard to maintain its hold on the people, and, from time to time after the death of Constantine, it seemed as if it would regain its hold and that Christianity would be pushed aside Christianity, however, succeeded in maintaining the position established for it by Constantine, though for several centuries there was constant warfare between the two.

When Christianity obtained supremacy—when the Pope became supreme on the fall of the Roman Empire—all the Mithraic documents and writings were destroyed, so that future generations would not become conversant with the fact that much of what was called Christianity was really Mithraism under another name. The Christian priests realised all too well that in order to become established Christianity had to absorb Mithraism and all it stood for. That is one reason why Jesus, if he returned to earth today, would not recognise the religion which claims him as its founder.

The new religion, however, which is now giving light to mankind under the name of Spiritualism, owes its origin to very different circumstances. Only last century did its light dawn upon the world, and yet it has made far greater progress than did Christianity in the first hundred years of its existence. The Apostle Paul, according to a leading ecclesiastical authority, never at one time addressed audiences of more than a hundred or so, and fifty years after the death of Jesus it is estimated that there were no more than six thousand Christians in the world.

Spiritualism has quickly passed through the stages of childhood and youth, to be today in the full flush of vigorous manhood. In Britain alone there are three million people who accept its principles, 1,500 churches or centres, and the number of Spiritualists throughout the world runs into many millions. Spiritualism must become supreme because it is based on evidence. It must continue to progress until all the other religions are forgotten, for one reason and one only—it is based on natural law and the old religions are man-made things.

Spiritualism is the only revelation which, coming direct to mankind from Etheria, has not been intercepted by the priesthood, and interpreted as the clergy consider fitting to the needs of humanity. Whether it could have been understood in the days of ignorance is a question. The priests decided that the people were not fitted to receive it undiluted, and so they contaminated it with their own theories and dogmas. How much this was necessary, and how much this was done to preserve their power, is a question we need not labour here. What is certain is that as people become educated they are finding that they have been misled, and this discovery is now reacting on the organisation which has been responsible for propagating error.

The old religions are dead or dying because of the false teachings attached to them. What is not true cannot last; only truth will ultimately prevail. In accepting as true what Spiritualism stands for—an unbroken life and that death is but an incident, a stile to be climbed over, so to speak, on an endless journey—our mental outlook undergoes a complete change.

Our outlook on the universe, on our course of action, on our attitude to our neighbours, on war, on pain and suffering, assumes a new character. We claim that Spiritualism has added to our knowledge something that makes the cosmos more understandable than anything which has previously been within the knowledge of mankind. Between those who accept Spiritualism as religion and add nothing to it, and those who accept all that nature has to reveal, there is no disharmony of thought. To them Science and Religion are one. They just constitute mankind's experience of the unfolding universe

When Spiritualism is fully accepted it will satisfy our utmost longings and our intellectual desires. Mankind will find it to be Religion, Science and Philosophy combined. Our reason will never be ruffled, our inmost desires will be fully met, our mystic longings will be satisfied, and our philosophic reasoning expanded. History will be better understood, and humanity, mentally and morally, will rise to higher heights.

Disease will be better combated when it becomes known that man is a psychic being, and that many of his material ills can be cured by their being attacked from this standpoint. Those in sorrow will receive comfort denied to those who lean on faith and discard knowledge, and all the deeper longings of our race, which have been the cause behind the world's religious beliefs, will find satisfaction in this increased knowledge that is now coming to the human race.

Love and human affection have, down the ages, whispered that death was not the end of life, and that somewhere, sometime, somehow, friends and loved ones parted by death would meet again. It was all so vague, so shadowy, the whisper was so soft, the phenomenon of death so like that of a flame blown out, and the promises, attributed to Jesus, made so long ago, that it is hardly to be wondered at that faith often wavered and hope turned to despair.

Throughout the ages the hope of a life beyond

has battled with the doubts of what seemed so evident. No reply came from the lips of the body stilled in death, no smile, no recognition. Surely this was the end. Nature for some inscrutable reason had wantonly destroyed what she had so mysteriously created.

Thus the old, old story is repeated time and time again. The old, old story told since love was born, and for what purpose? Is our reason at war with nature, that we should resent her plans and acts which run counter to our notions of what should be?

Rather is it not that to us mortals the incidents of earth, which cause sorrow, pain and suffering, are in reality but waves we must all brave before we reach the shore where pain and suffering are no more? Why this schooling which some receive in harsher measure than others? Why have some to battle with the sea of life more than others? It is part of nature's plan to make us strong individually, to build our characters, to increase our capacity, and to strengthen our minds. Earth's school to some is unaccountably hard and rough. Why should some be born in luxury, comfort and wealth, free from pain and disease, and others be poor, sickly and live unhappy lives through no fault of their own? There are many whys in life, and, if this life be all, there is no sane or satisfactory answer.

Death can be compared to the struggle of the child towards the light at birth which to some is harder than to others. What we call death is really birth, the leaving of the womb of earth, with its struggles and its sorrows, for a life of happiness, in which we shall know what life really is. This being so, then compared to our eternal life how little does earth-life matter! The reward when it comes will obliterate from our memory all our past suffering and disappointments on earth.

Nature makes return in full measure in the after-life for all she demanded here, for life is but a weaving between the here and there. Both here and there are really one, but we on earth can see only the underside. There the pattern, woven by each on earth, will be seen in its true colours. If we weave well, and the threads, which make the warp and woof of character, are strong and truly woven, adequate reward will be ours.

Opportunity will again be given to everyone, and all neglected chances on earth will be repeated there. under happier and more favourable circumstances, The mistake we make is to think that the underside of the weaving, which is all we can see on earth, is the whole pattern. So much on earth conveys an impression which is different from what it is in reality. We think the sun circles the earth. We think the earth is solid and the sky is a dome. We think that death is the end of life until knowledge, based on facts, tells us that appearances are not reality. Appearances on earth are so often an illusion, that it is wiser to wait until we attain to the fuller life before passing judgment on the unfairness of earth-life, or on the injustice with which we are surrounded. When we know more, how different it all will be! We beings in the flesh can no more judge the meaning of existence, by our short life on earth, than can children in the nursery grasp the meaning of life on earth.

It is only by absorbing the new philosophy of life,

which Spiritualism teaches, that we can gain a clearer glimpse of reality. When this philosophy becomes religion to each one of us, what to many today, as to our ancestors in the past, has been dark and mysterious, will become understood through our increased mental development. "Now we see through a glass darkly but then face to face" (1 *Corinthians* xiii, 12) is quite a good way of putting it.

Though we are unable to experience the reality of Etheria until death, yet we can obtain the assurance we need from those who have come back to tell us that life on earth is like our time in the nursery. When this, our nursery stage, passes on earth we enjoy a larger, fuller life in Etheria, and understand better many things now mysterious. Then will many of our doubts and wonderings be explained.

When visualising the new religion, I must define what I mean by a Spiritualist. Many nowadays term themselves Spiritualists in error, thinking that they can be Spiritualists if they accept the seven principles of Spiritualism, and still retain all or many of the old orthodox beliefs.

This causes dissension and discussion where no such things should exist. A Spiritualist is one who accepts the seven principles of Spiritualism as they stand, and adds nothing to them from orthodox religion. The Christian Spiritualist, the Jewish Spiritualist, the Hindu Spiritualist and the Mohammedan Spiritualist accept the seven principles, and, in addition to these, much of the superstition attached to the religion into which they were born.

Spiritualism stands for knowledge, and its beliefs are based only on what is evidentially demonstrated. Its adherents accept survival and communication as being scientifically proved, and an order of conduct which reason tells us is right, quite irrespective of the fact that our ethical conduct is endorsed by our friends who communicate with us and who, moreover, give us good reasons why such conduct should be followed. Right is right and wrong is wrong. Mankind has lived long enough on earth to have learned what his attitude should be towards his neighbour and himself, though unfortunately he does not always act in accordance with this knowledge.

The acceptance of survival and communication opens up to the Spiritualists a new view and perspective of life, an enlarged panorama of the universe. He realises that thought produced by mind is the all-important reality in the universe. Because surrounding matter in Etheria can be moulded by thought in a way unimaginable here, our conditions there are more influenced by mind than here on earth. Consequently mind training is our objective in life, as what we think here we shall also think there. As we control our thoughts or minds here, so will our position be better or worse in so far as these are directed to good ends or bad, towards unselfish, pure and noble thoughts, or the reverse.

Moreover, finding Mind the all-ruling Sovereign of the universe, and that we are all endowed with part of that sovereign's attributes, we can understand and grasp the universe from a new angle. This different aspect is a mental one which relegates physical matter, hitherto accepted as forming the universe, to be one of various substances of ever finer quality which stimulate mind into action.

That, briefly, is as far as we have arrived for the present. That is the limit of our extended knowledge, no more and no less. This being so, I must term much accepted by Spiritualists with a prefix as unscientific and as unsupported by evidence. I do not deny, for instance, the doctrine of Reincarnation, as it may be true, though I cannot understand how it can be. That does not make it untrue, but I only insist that it is quite unproved and it rests on no scientific evidence. Spiritualism, therefore, does not include the belief in reincarnation. The evolution of the species can be explained by mind developing by means of its absorption of finer vibrations without recourse to the theory of reincarnation.

Spiritualism, again, does not embrace the belief held by some that throughout the ages, from time to time, what is termed the Christ Spirit, or the Cosmic Christ, incarnated in different men, and that these became Christs, Avatars, Messiahs or Buddhas. Much is made by Christian Spiritualists of what they term the Christ Spirit, but they might equally well emphasise the Buddha Spirit. They tell us that the Christ Spirit will conquer the world. If so why should the Buddha Spirit not also conquer the world? Christ is the Greek for the anointed one, as it was customary to anoint the victim before he was sacrificed, and Buddha is the Pali for the enlightened one.

It is wrong to use the word "Christ" in any connection, except as referring to the second member of the Christian Trinity, the Very God of Very God, who came to earth from heaven and suffered for the sins of the world on Calvary, so that all believers could be saved. To talk of the Christ Spirit, or the Cosmic Christ, means nothing to any thoughtful person. Such expressions are quite illogical and contrary, not only to usage, but to the meaning of the word. This being so, it is foolish to talk about the Christ Spirit as having manifested during different incarnations down the ages. The word Christ is definitely associated with a specific theological dogma, and the word Christian stands for a person who accepts this form of belief. When that dogma ceases to be accepted, the word Christ fails to have any meaning to humanity, and the name of Christian can be dropped.

The bishops made it quite clear at the 1934 Convocation at York that only those who accept the creeds of the Church are Christians. To talk in a vague kind of way about the Christ Spirit, as so many do who have given up orthodoxy, is foolish in the extreme. The word Christ means nothing apart from orthodoxy, and those who perpetuate this error confuse themselves as well as others. The word Christian should only be used by the orthodox, and they and they only are entitled to the name.

There is not an iota of evidence that down the ages what is termed the Christ Spirit manifested in human flesh. From first to last the Christ Spirit belief has grown out of the imagination of those who realise the resemblance in the stories told about Buddha, Krishna, Apollonius and others, which the realy fathers of the Christian Church made use of in constructing the life of Jesus called Christ by Paul. So these believers in the Christ Spirit manifesting down the ages have jumped to the conclusion that these men, all probably endowed with great psychic gifts, were incarnations of some divine spirit which they term the Cosmic Christ or Christ Spirit. The true explanation is of course that one religion copied from another, and told similar stories about their god-men, all of which had symbolic meanings now unrealised except by those who have delved deeply into the past.

That these stories were copied by one religion from another is just as well known as that the Jews copied most of the Pentateuch from Babylon, and yet various theologians have written books to try to prove that the Babylonians copied from the Jews. The Tibetans believe that the Dalai Lama is a god, and that at his death his spirit enters a child born at the moment of his death, and so the Divine Spirit persists in each incarnation. This is just as sensible as the idea of various incarnations of the Christ Spirit, but only a Buddhist would believe it.

Prejudice will distort truth on every occasion, and this latest attempt to distort facts to favour theories will go the way of all other such attempts, but before it does so many unthinking people will be led down the wrong road. It is impossible to read into the reported sayings of Jesus that he accepted such ideas about himself, and this should settle the matter for every unprejudiced and logically-minded person.

When those who make this claim grow in knowledge they will find that there are many others, besides the ones they thus honour, equally entitled to share the privilege. Under similar conditions, if Paul had been behind Apollonius he would have become the Christ instead of Jesus. The seventy odd years which intervened between their deaths was sufficient to establish the Christian cult in a way the Apollonian cult never was established. Round Apollonius grew the same legends as grew around Jesus. He was worshipped with divine honours for four centuries, and at Tyana a temple was erected in his memory. For propaganda purposes the Christian fathers doubtless borrowed some of the stories they told about Jesus from the life of this great psychic, as many Pagans believed what was told of Apollonius who is an historical character.

The term Christ Spirit is of recent birth, a new catch-phrase which perpetuates the ancient belief of a god-man coming to earth, but surely no one can be expected to believe that nineteen hundred years had to elapse before Christianity was correctly interpreted, as the advocates of this new Christianity assert. Unfortunately the term Christ Spirit is used regularly by those who fervently wish to see the world's religions united. They evidently cannot see that this bringing in of a name associated with a particular cult or religion, and interlocked with Christian dogma and tradition in such a way that it can never be separated, will act as a barrier against the adoption by mankind of a common religion which must be free from all the old superstitions.

I am in entire agreement with those who take the view that in the world's history great and good men have arisen to enlighten the darkness of their surroundings. Why, however, associate them with a theological dogma whose origin is well known? Why not believe that these great ones were highly endowed with psychic power, and in this way the etheric world became revealed from time to time to the ancients? Before we talk about the Christ Spirit we should have definite evidence as to what the Christ Spirit means. To some it means all that is good, but why associate good with a sectarian name?

We want to bring all the world religions into one, and to realise this ideal we must drop sectarian names. The terms "Christ Spirit" or "Cosmic Christ" just continue this old sectarian view of religion which all Spiritualists wish to see abandoned. We would not adopt the name "Krishna Spirit" or "Cosmic Krishna", and that being so we cannot expect the Hindus, Mohammedans or Jews to ever adopt the Christian terminology. Let us think in world terms and not be parochial in our religion.

Again, to hold up Jesus as a perfect man is as wrong as it is to imagine him as God. The intelligent people of today have ceased to look on him as a god, but some still consider him as a perfect man. There is no evidence for such a claim, in fact the record we have of his life shows that he was human like ourselves, and had our human failings. He said nothing, so far as we know, in favour of science, art, education, sanitation or social reform, and never spoke against cruelty to animals or slavery, which in his day, and throughout the Christian era, disgraced mankind. His limitations are obvious, but, as he was just a product of his time, no one thinks of criticising these. Attention is only drawn to them because of the claims Christians make about him which are as false as they are absurd.

Socrates, Plato and Confucius gave vastly more light to the ancient world than did Jesus. Buddha was undoubtedly the greatest religious teacher the world has known, and has attributed to him a code of ethics of a higher order than any before or after his time. He produced for the benefit of humanity his eight-fold way of right thinking and right acting. He was the first to declare the universal brotherhood of man, and his followers, though they have degraded much of his teaching and turned it into creeds and dogmas, have followed his precept of peace and love to all men. He insisted that reason based on evidence is our only guide to truth, and that only through knowledge can mankind attain happiness. Only then could Nirvana be attained, when the annihilation of greed, covetousness and all evil was achieved, and when only justice, mercy and goodness remained.

Buddhism, which is accepted by four hundred and fifty millions, can proudly claim that it has seldom been the cause of war and strife, and that its founder was the first to proclaim that knowledge and wisdom are the only two levers capable of raising humanity. Lao-Tsze, the founder of Taoism, occupies a place close to Buddha, and his teachings, though they have been debased just as have been those of Buddha and Jesus by those who followed, reveal an attempt to grasp the Infinite essayed by only the few. Confucius, a contemporary of Lao-Tsze, had more the philosophic than the mystical mind of his fellow countrymen. Mencius, who lived a century later, and other Chinese teachers emphasised the fatherhood of God and the brotherhood of man, the Chinese as individuals always having been the most unwarlike people. The name of Confucius is cherished by a third of the human race, and, like his contemporaries in Greece, Socrates,

Plato and Aristotle, he taught a philosophy which has profoundly influenced the thinking portion of the human race for 2,500 years.

Spiritualism consequently discards all the false claims made by Christians about Jesus being the first to bring light to the world, and in their place it gives the mystic evidence on which to base his mysticism, which is not done by any other world religion.

I am not a mystic, but in my opinion what Spiritualism reveals should be enough to give material for the mysticism of the most mystical, the philosophy of the most philosophical, and satisfy the longings and aspirations of every type of mind. That is why I believe that Spiritualism must become in time the only world religion.

The great and noble mystics of the past may have been highly developed psychically, and controlled perhaps by some advanced Etherians, but there can be no evidence for this, because we know so little about their lives. It can be assumed as true, but we have no witnesses or records of any value to support the claim. No one can be dogmatic on the subject, but I submit that it is possible that those who came to be called Christs, Saviours or Avators were strongly endowed with psychic power, were great healers, and taught the people by inspirational addresses. Their deification, however, came about by their being seen again after their deaths as priestly victims, and they were in consequence looked upon as having conquered death and appeased the anger of the gods towards mankind.

The theological opinions expressed by those Etherians who have recently left the earth are exactly what one might expect, considering their views when here. They find themselves in a world very much like this one, and mix with those of their own mental level. We would not accept an opinion on religion expressed by anyone and everyone on earth, but, if some religious opinion is uttered through a medium, it is looked upon by many as a divinely inspired utterance, which must be believed because it comes from Etheria.

All advanced Etherians are latitudinarian in their opinions. Let us consider these and ignore the sectarian views expressed by those who are still sectarians just as they were on earth. Opinions firmly held change slowly, and making the change called death does not alter these all at once. This earth's beliefs are often retained for a considerable time. The human mind is so conservative there in the lower planes, just as here on earth, that to many the old beliefs are a help. They have not reached God's throne to be judged, and this event some in Etheria still anticipate. It is all a question of mental development, and as this comes the old ideas are shed. The intelligent on earth are far in advance of the ignorant in Etheria. Displacement of the physical body does not involve the displacement of ignorance.

The denizens of Etheria who come back are mostly our own friends. They are the only ones we can recognise, and to accept their religious or philosophical opinions, just because they have entered another order of existence, is unreasonable, not to say foolish. They often refer to Christ when they mean Jesus.

The religious views expressed should be critically examined in the light of reason, but never taken seriously when they enter the controversial field of dogma or doctrine, on which everyone on earth has a different opinion, as is the case in the lower planes of Etheria. It is very noticeable that the most advanced minds which communicate with earth ignore all dogmas and doctrines, concentrate on the necessity of developing our characters on earth, and insist on the futility of accepting any of the world's creedal religions. Before, however, we can attract these advanced minds, our own thoughts must be in harmony with theirs, and not confined, as are those of most people, to just obtaining evidence of survival, and being quite indifferent to all matters of a scientific and philosophical nature. We get from Etheria only that for which we are mentally fitted, just as we do on earth.

It seems to be abundantly clear that when Etherians get beyond the influence of earthly ideas all this world's orthodox beliefs fade from the mind, and religion becomes philosophical contemplation of the divine in nature. Christian Spiritualists, and all others who claim to be Spiritualists with a prefix, who have joined forces with the Spiritualists in their belief in proved survival and communication, should therefore try to shed their sectarian opinions and develop along a line of thought more in accordance with the higher teaching which comes from Etheria. Until they do so they are not Spiritualists, and the religious contentions they bring into the ranks of Spiritualism are unfortunate, but seemingly inevitable.

I therefore put on record the extent and also the limit of our knowledge as Spiritualists, and repeat that there is no confirmation from advanced Etherians of the creeds, dogmas and doctrines of any religion, Christian or any other. Moreover there is no evidence for reincarnation, or in support of one or more Christ Spirits entering human flesh. In other words, each body is the habitation of the individual mind, and when the etheric body leaves this earthly tabernacle it never returns in any form to renew its association with earth, so far as our present knowledge extends.

Let us keep to what we know, which is sufficient to satisfy the longings and the desires of humanity. It is enough for the most profound philosophy and the most advanced mysticism, without burdening this great revelation with matters which have no bearing on our life or conduct. These additions to the revelation Spiritualism is giving to the world do not comfort the intelligent, they satisfy no longings, and meet no needs of the thoughtful mind. Why not therefore concentrate on, and profit by, what we know? It is surely enough to satisfy the most philosophical and mystical until our knowledge further increases.

Each individual and nation accepts the religion for which the mind is fitted. The ignorant cannot comprehend the religion of the philosopher, just as the Catholic, with his saints and images, cannot understand the religion of the Deist. The Deist in turn cannot comprehend the Christian Trinity. Orthodox religions are all man-made things, fitted for the needs of the mental development of their time. They satisfy the mentality which fears and dreads the unknown, and reveres and sanctifies everything mysterious in nature. They satisfy the uneducated in this life until the human mind advances. Until mental development occurs it is impossible to change ideas. The change comes naturally as the mind develops.

I can only point out the errors of the old, and the truth of the new, and leave it at that. Those whose beliefs are upset or changed by what I write are ready for the change and have no firm grasp of the old. These become converts to the new, but those not ready for the change remain wedded to the old against which no argument can prevail. The advanced views expressed in this book await them when they are ready for the change. Until then the teachings of the Church satisfy them. They are ministered to by the priests, whose policy is to enhance the old and denounce the new.

Stagnation means deterioration, and if the priesthood will not try to advance the people's knowledge, and thus add to their happiness and mental well-being, others must. Now that Spiritualists have the certain knowledge of the after-life they can press forward in their attack on the ramparts of ignorance. When faith could not be replaced by knowledge it comforted those who had it, and that sufficed. Now, however, knowledge can take the place of faith, and this will bring increased happiness and comfort to all. No organisation must be permitted to stand in the way of its advance, and we must forever be ready to help those whose moorings to the old faith are weakening. Spiritualists must keep the truth before the people and slowly they will absorb it. That is the duty of every Spiritualist, and that is the reason for this and my preceding books.

The mind of man hates the thought of annihilation, and dreads the idea of extinction. Every tribe and every nation has some form of religion, pure or impure, according as the minds which make up the tribe and nation are developed or undeveloped. Humanity spends a great part of its conscious existence in giving thought to the hereafter, however hazy that place may appear. Worship and prayer are inbred in humanity, but when the future life is revealed to the masses, in the way it has been to Spiritualists, worship and prayer will give place to contemplation.

The Western world probably gives less thought to these devotional exercises than do the Eastern nations and many primitive tribes, with whom religion is more closely connected with their every-day life. Nothing happens without a reason, and this instinct to worship can only be explained by the fact that the masses instinctively realise that their real selves, their souls, are at times more in tune with another order of existence than with the present order, and that through prayer and worship contact can be made with this unseen realm.

Religion, then, embraces much, and for this reason it is difficult to define. To some, religion means belief in a certain creed, to others (who should use the word ethics and not religion) it means a rule for our conduct in life, and again, to others, it is a mystical union with the unseen. The word, however, should certainly not apply to the belief in church creeds or the performing of church rites and ceremonies. True, many through these find comfort and help in their religious life, but the past history of creeds and dogmas, and those who believed in them, is such that it has made the name Religion hateful in the minds of those who are often the truly religious.

Many of the most wicked on earth have believed most firmly in God and the orthodox religion of their time. In Christendom the belief in the Trinity, and the creeds of the Church, have gone hand in hand with murder, torture and savagery. Nowadays we do not consider Torquemada, Alva, Cortes or Calvin men whom we would like to follow. In their days they were looked on as truly religious men, which shows that belief in creeds does not make for goodness. They were bigots of the worst type, who believed so earnestly in the Christian creeds and Bible that they went to any lengths to enforce their acceptance. To this end they persecuted, tortured, murdered and imprisoned all who disagreed with their opinions, and brought the name of orthodox religion into everlasting disrepute.

That was one reason for the orthodox persecuting those they considered unorthodox, but there was another potent influence which must not be overlooked. These orthodox fiends believed that Jesus said it was better to enter heaven halt and lame, bruised and bleeding, than to reach hell whole and strong. They therefore honestly considered that their duty lay in making all those who differed from them return to the path which they thought led to salvation, and all the force which lay at their command was used for this purpose. They were honest but mistaken, cruel but ignorant, and believed that, when persuasion failed, torture was justified in a matter of such vital importance as the salvation of the soul.

Quite the most amazing fact that strikes the student of history is that the greatest factor in man's life has been the subject of the most flagrant abuse.

Socially he has slowly asserted himself and risen from serfdom to independence. He will make still further progress when invention places within his reach, with the minimum of exertion and exaction, all his daily necessities and comforts. The evolution of man materially is easy to follow, a question solely of the improvement in the means of production, adaptation and distribution of the wealth wrung from nature's storehouse.

When, on the other hand, we study the other great factor in his life, namely religion, what do we find? In the first place he has never used his intelligence, as he has in politics and industry; he has never applied his reason to his religion. In every other walk of life man has progressed by applying reason and thought to his every-day life. In religion he has done exactly the opposite. He has never thought nor reasoned, and has always employed a class of men, set apart for the purpose, to tell him what he should believe, and what the future has in store for him. Being human, they found at an early date, and ever after retained the view, that it was not in their interests to enlighten him or to try to enlighten themselves. If man had used no more intelligence in his political and economic activities than he has done in religion, he would never have risen materially beyond the beasts.

Religion is a word which should be used to express a great reality to everyone. It is the instinctive, and very real feeling in each of us, that we individual thinking units are related in some mysterious manner to the guiding principle, the Divine Intelligence, which orders the universe. We prize our individuality beyond anything else in life, and detest the idea of its destruction. Everyone, from the materialist to the mystic, has an indefinable longing to be assured that death does not bring about this annihilation of the personality.

Religion is what I might call the urge to attain at-one-ness with the Cosmic Mind. We feel a relationship to the controlling, thinking substance of the universe, and that we are not mere creatures of flesh. This desire for at-one-ness is in each of us. In those in which it is developed the religious sense is strong. while in those in which it is undeveloped it is weak. Believing ancient superstitions, however it may help some, has nothing to do with real religion, because the religious sense may be developed in the agnostic and quite undeveloped in the believer in the supernatural,

Lastly, I must add what should now be considered as of as great importance in our lives as our religion, but which is so often lamentably lacking, though always emphasised by the teachers and philosophers of the past, namely our duty to each other. The belief in what is termed God has helped little in the past, as the cruel and wicked imagined a god just as cruel and wicked as themselves. The instinctive belief in an after-life has helped little, because the cruel and wicked just imagined it as conforming to their own desires. Today, however, with our greater knowledge, knowing as we do that the after-life is not only a place, but a condition of mind, we realise that our happiness there depends on our actions here, on the character we build up here, and not on believing the superstitions handed down from the past.

Consequently religion and ethics have this common bond, though their origin and history are quite different. Religion came into being when man found that he could make contact with another order of life which he believed intimately affected him. Instinctively he felt related to it, and thought that through it his dismay and wonderings could be explained. On the other hand ethics have come about from experience, as gradually mankind built up a moral code. As his intelligence increased he found that it was better to be happy than miserable, secure than insecure, and by using his memory and experience it was found that certain things should not be done, and other things should be done, if the greatest happiness is to be secured.

Since the time of primitive man we have gone far to advance our ethical behaviour and way of life one to another, and this should continue. When our minds become more developed, that is, more *en rapport* with the Cosmic Mind, each individual will find it impossible to act towards others in a way he would not wish himself to be treated. Telepathic contact, between mind and mind, is increasing and bringing each of us into closer touch with the feelings of our neighbours. Moreover this telepathic contact is expanding to include all mankind, who are now coming to be looked on as having feelings and aspirations like ourselves in contrast to the sad state of affairs up to within recent times.

Similarly, when the mind of man develops, all blood sports, with their accompanying cruelty, will pass away, and so will vivisection and its attendant suffering. Hunting the fox, hare or stag, as takes place in some countries, and torturing a bull to death, as happens in other lands, will be looked back upon by our descendants, with their more developed minds, as inadmissible and outrageous. They will wonder how any civilised people could have found pleasure and enjoyment at the expense of suffering. Just as we feel today towards the cruelties of our less developed ancestors, so will our descendants look back on the cruelties existing today. Against these the Church has never protested, while those responsible for them are often honoured and respected members of that institution.

As we are related to the guiding intelligence of the universe we should not cringe or bow the knee before it. We should not worship it, or prostrate ourselves before it, as the ignorant do to position and wealth on earth. Everyone, however, who has brought his mind into greater harmony with the Infinite can acknowledge that his life is guided and influenced by it, his intelligence enlarged, and his understanding of the universe increased.

To me, natural religion can best be defined in a few words as the Science of Living. These three words embrace our duty to ourselves, to our neighbours, and the directing aright of the urge in us to so develop that we fit ourselves to the best of our ability to occupy our place on earth. By so doing we are making our place in Etheria. As we are on earth so shall we be there.

The past is interesting only as history, but it does not concern true religion as we understand it. Therefore Spiritualists look forward not backward. It matters nothing under what name these ideals and aspirations are known, and consequently the name Spiritualism in itself is unimportant. It is like the name we give to a picture, but it is not the name but the picture that matters. What counts is the state of mind I have tried to visualise, and which I hope will some day guide humanity.

Religion therefore includes our being aware, some more, and others much less, that we are other than material creatures, that we are in reality etheric beings, inhabiting for a time physical matter, and that we are in some way related to the mind guiding the universe. To some this is a very real relationship, whilst to others it is not so, but in everyone the feeling exists. Natural religion includes conduct, because what we sow here we reap, if not here, then hereafter. If everyone would follow out as far as possible the golden rule that we should at all times do to others as we would that they do to us, that our lives should be unselfish, and that our first consideration should be for others, a firm basis would be laid on which to build our characters and our philosophy.

Spiritualism and natural religion stand for the same thing, and mean the same thing. Spiritualism is contained within the following seven principles, and these summarise all that I have already written:—

(1) The Universe is governed by Mind, commonly called God. All we have sensed, do sense, or will sense is Mind expressing itself in some form or another.
(2) The existence and identity of the individual continues after the change called death.
(3) Communication, under suitable conditions, takes place between us here on earth and the inhabitants of Etheria, into which we shall pass at death.

(4) Our conduct must be guided by the golden rule of doing to others what we would wish to be done to ourselves.
(5) Each individual is his own saviour, and he cannot look to someone else to bear his sins, and suffer for his mistakes.
(6) Each individual reaps as he sows, and he makes his happiness or unhappiness just as he harmonises with his surroundings. Each one gravitates naturally to the place in Etheria in harmony with his desires, as there desires are gratified more easily than here on earth.
(7) The path of progress is never closed, and there is no known end to the advancement of the individual.

Clause 3 cannot come under the definition of religion in quite the same way as do all the other clauses. It is, however, important, because communication establishes the fact that there is an after-life and that our beliefs here are built on a firm basis. Survival after death is the bed-rock of religion, and on this foundation our religious knowledge now rests.

These seven principles constitute what Spiritualism stands for, no more and no less, and from an ethical standpoint they are superior to and juster than the teachings of any orthodox religion. Those who add a prefix to the name Spiritualism confuse the issue and bring disharmony into Spiritualism. Spiritualists, on the other hand, are in complete harmony with each other, and regret the controversies caused by Christians, Jews and Hindus adopting the name

Spiritualist and still remaining wedded to their old beliefs.

These seven principles are not a creed which all must believe or perish everlastingly, which, we are told, is the fate of all who do not accept the orthodox creeds. These principles are just a statement of facts which Spiritualists have proved by evidence, and can be added to as our knowledge increases. It is impossible for Spiritualism to stand for something which is contrary to our reason and outside our knowledge. That is why Spiritualism does not include Christian Spiritualism or Jewish Spiritualism, or any Spiritualism with a prefix.

Spiritualism stands for what is true and proved by evidence. Consequently it is not intolerance on the part of Spiritualists which causes them to take their stand on evidence to support their principles, and say that what is unsupported by evidence cannot be added to their seven principles. Spiritualism is natural religion based on evidence, whereas all the world creedal religions are based on error, and devoid of evidence to support their tenets. Both science and history prove them to be false in their claims and assertions.

These seven principles need no label, and what they stand for will come to be accepted naturally as true and right in the years ahead, when the name Spiritualism is perhaps forgotten. Meantime let it be clearly understood that Spiritualism stands for entire freedom of thought and tolerance in religion. Its supporters, while claiming the right to put their case forward, acknowledge that those holding different opinions have an equal right to advocate their beliefs.

Spiritualism's seven principles are no more than a synopsis of its beliefs. Just as the medical profession has laid down certain regulations relating to healing, which it has found to be based on evidence and experience, and which every doctor must accept or cease to be a doctor, so Spiritualists defined their principles. Those who are Spiritualists naturally expect that all who call themselves Spiritualists should conform to those principles, and not add to them something which is quite contrary to their meaning. Christians, Hindus, Buddhists and Mohammedans are quite justified in thus standing for their own beliefs, and each would object to anyone professing to adopt their faith while holding contrary opinions.

Spiritualism is religion based on natural law. It is not designed for Christians any more than for Buddhists or Jews. Spiritualism holds fast to facts, and patiently awaits the followers of all the world religions to join its ranks, when they have discarded the beliefs they have outgrown. Spiritualists recognise the difficulty most people have all the world over in discarding in part, or in whole, the early teaching they received when their minds were plastic, and which they accepted without reasoning. All the same, truth cannot be changed to meet their wishes. Comparatively few can take the wide outlook, uninfluenced by the religion into which they were born. Truth is eternal, and patiently waits for the mind of man to unfold, when it will enter the open door with gladness.

What Spiritualism stands for is sufficient for the intelligent man and woman—for their guidance through life and their comfort at death. Moreover, those who accept its principles are enabled to enter the next state of existence well prepared for what awaits them. They will know where they are and what is expected of them, whereas those lacking this knowledge, or holding other beliefs, find conditions very different from what they imagined on earth, and are consequently out of harmony with their surroundings until their mental outlook changes.

When Spiritualism's seven principles, which are sane and just, become accepted, they will unify and raise humanity, and lead to peace, contentment and happiness amongst nations and individuals alike. Then humanity will become truly civilised, and we shall one and all become fitted on earth to take a higher place in Etheria, and pass more quickly through those planes in which our ancestors had to stay, because of their ignorance and debased mentality.

Having defined religion, as Spiritualists understand it, we can now obtain an answer as to why one of the greatest factors in man's life has been the subject of the most flagrant abuse and error. To say that it is all due to ignorance is true; but why, having progressed materially and morally, is he still the victim of ancient superstitions, which are much the same today as they were in the days of primitive man?

The answer is simply this, that the future life has only been definitely revealed to mankind within the past hundred years. The vast majority still know no more about the future than did primitive man, and all mankind's material discoveries on earth have taught him nothing of the hereafter. In a word, mankind generally knows no more about his destiny today than did his ancestors, in whose imaginings originated all the orthodox religious beliefs, which are the same today as they were thousands of years ago. Yet man retains the instinctive belief held by his ancestors, which is embraced in the word faith, that something is in store for him beyond the grave.

Until the age of science, which came into being in the 16th century, our material comforts had improved but little on those of primitive man, who knew how to build with stone and use the metals to a degree, but otherwise he was little better than the savage. Except for having stone houses in which to live, and metal implements to work with, our pre-science ancestors lived much the same life as primitive man. Their method of transport was the same, their means of communication was unchanged, reading and writing were unknown to all except the few, and their knowledge of disease and sickness was primitive. Until the age of science, mankind was only to a degree better than his primitive brother, thousands of years back in history.

With the advent of science all has changed, and in three hundred years we have made an advance in our comforts, in our methods of healing, in our relief of pain, in our happiness, in our means of communication, and in our methods of passing our thoughts from one to another, far and away greater than that made in all the ages prior to the 16th century. With this knowledge has come freedom of thought, and an enormous advance in our attitude towards each other as individuals, though much ground has still to be covered before cruelty, tyranny and intolerance cease to be.

Until within the last hundred years we knew nothing of our destiny, and so religion has stood still. Orthodox religious beliefs are consequently still those of early man. The knowledge a few possess today will some day be known by all. What has been hidden is now revealed, and religion will make as great a stride forward in the next three hundred years as has our material knowledge, our comfort, and our happiness during the past three hundred years.

Two great events in the history of man are the discovery of the scientific method of obtaining knowledge, and the discovery of his destiny. The first has revolutionised his social life, and the second will revolutionise his religious life and outlook. We are today at the beginning of this second great transition stage in man's history. Only a few so far realise it. The majority are still quite ignorant of it, just as a hundred years after the death of Copernicus only a few believed in the rotation of the planets and of our earth round the sun.

Then everyone believed in the universe as imagined by Ptolemy, the famous Egyptian-born Greek scientist, who conceived the earth as an immovable body poised in the centre of an immense solid sphere, in which the sun, moon and stars were fixed. Day and night, he believed, were caused by this sphere revolving completely round the earth every twenty-four hours. The sun, moon, planets and stars, he thought, were hung in the heavens for our benefit to give us light and heat.

Today nearly everyone believes more or less in the orthodox religions of the past. The light, however, is now breaking through, and this second step in human advancement is slowly becoming realised amongst the more intellectual and advanced of the human race. The past history of man is that of ignorance of his possibilities on earth, and of his destiny. Three hundred years ago he came to realise better what the earth had in store for him, as he used his intelligence and reason. Today he is just beginning to realise what death has in store for him, what his destiny really is, and the real meaning of existence.

As intelligence increases fear of the future will vanish, and the greatest enigma man has had to solve, namely death, will have been mastered. It is foolish to say "There is no death," because there is, just as there is birth. Death, however, is not a curse, something to fear, but the release of the individual into a fuller, happier and freer life than can be experienced on earth.

The belief that each of us is an immortal soul was not born in any church or temple, is not the result of any religion or of any creed, and is not confined to the pages of a single book. This hope, which has ebbed and flowed down the ages, is the giant oak round which have twined the crude and cruel weeds of all this world's superstitions, well-nigh strangling the tree itself. These cumbrous growths have not supported the tree but have been supported by it, and so long as men and women live and love and die this belief will never die. As knowledge grows, this age-long hope will become a certainty, love will cease turning to despair, and life will be shorn of its greatest sorrow.

Thus, as our knowledge increases, we shall face our life on earth with a greater certainty of happiness, if we live aright. We shall face our future after death with confidence, through the knowledge brought by those who have gone before, who tell us that what they now experience is a larger, fuller life, to which death is but the entrance gate.

CHAPTER X.

THE CHURCH—PAST AND FUTURE.

THE Christian Church is, and always has been, an exclusive organisation for the purpose of preserving and propagating doctrines decided upon by certain theologians at various councils in the 3rd and 4th centuries. We have already considered the various separations, estrangements and divisions which have taken place amongst its members throughout the Christian era, and these, it will be remembered, led to the formation of the Greek Orthodox Church and the Protestant Church. The original Catholic Church, centred in Rome, retained the loyalty of those Christians who did not break away from the parent organisation, and it still, as always, considers itself the one and only Church of Christ.

Those who called themselves Protestants accepted the decisions made by the theologians of the 16th and 17th centuries, who produced what they held was a reformed Christianity, but which was based nevertheless on the findings of those early councils. Both sections of the Church, moreover, held to the belief that they were the custodians of the same divine revelation which came to the world nineteen hundred years ago, and that it was their duty to propagate it to the exclusion of all others. This revelation, they held and still hold, is final and complete, and requires nothing to be added to it and nothing to be subtracted from it.

The attitude of what is termed the Roman Catholic section of the Christian Church is uncompromising, and as unwavering as it always was. Certain Protestant sections admit more toleration and greater latitude of thought, but by far the majority retain the exclusiveness which has been so pronounced in the history of Christianity throughout the Christian era. It is quite evident to anyone who follows the sayings and doings of the leaders of Protestantism in this country, that they intend to retain intact what they term the fundamentals of Christianity, without giving away one jot or tittle.

This has once more become clear by the attitude of the bishops at the Convocation of York in June 1934, at which was considered the attitude of the Bishop of Liverpool towards the Church of England's doctrines and regulations. The Bishop had allowed an eminent scholar to preach an evening address in Liverpool Cathedral. This leader of thought, Dr. L. P. Jacks, the Principal of Manchester College, Oxford, believed in only one God, whereas Christians believe in three gods, in spite of the fact that Jesus said there was only one God, Our Father in Heaven. Because Dr. Jacks believed what Jesus believed, the bishop who permitted him to speak was told that such a thing must never happen again. The resolution to this effect, which was adopted unanimously, ended as follows:—

> Accordingly this House is of the opinion that in the exercise of his discretion, approved in 1922, with regard to invitations to preachers at special services, the bishop should not extend such invitation to any person who does not hold, or who belongs to

a denomination which does not hold, the common Christian faith in Jesus as Very God of Very God, who for us men and our salvation came down from heaven and was made man.

The Bishop of Liverpool accepted this ruling by his brother bishops.

Dr. Jacks, be it noted, did not touch in his address on church doctrines or dogmas, but, taking as his subject "The Everlasting Life", stated his views as one who had deeply studied this question as a psychical researcher. The substance of the various opinions expressed by the bishops in their speeches of condemnation was, that the Church must not countenance in any church building any views expressed by one who did not accept completely and entirely the Christian creeds, dogmas and doctrines, even though these were not the subject of the address. The bishops affirmed that they would make no concession, and that the addresses to the faithful must be delivered in the churches only by those who professed the creeds of the Church.

I refer to this matter solely because it makes evident that the Christian Church intends to retain its out-of-date dogmas and doctrines. Those who believe that the Church is ripe to adopt the new revelation, and discard the old garments of ignorance, are, I am afraid, suffering from a delusion. I see no indication of this when I look out over the entire horizon of orthodoxy, though undoubtedly there is a strong undercurrent indicative of a desire for reform. This is slowly becoming very powerful, and some day will become strong enough to sweep away the present

Church teaching, but when this goes Christianity goes also and the clergy know this only too well.

Truly the universe unfolds very slowly, and in spite of all the advance in knowledge which has taken place over the last three hundred years, in spite of the knowledge which Spiritualism gives that our happiness in the next state depends, not on creeds, but on our life and character here, despite all these factors, the Christian Church retains and emphasises the fact that it stands for what it has always stood for, namely the opinions of the early Church fathers.

The speeches of the bishops at the Convocation of York show that the leaders of the Church have to-day the same theological minds as their predecessors in the early Church. The views they expressed, and which were endorsed by the Archbishops of Canterbury and York, were just as narrow as those held by Athanasius, and just as obscure, involved and contradictory in their meanings as those expressed by Augustine. The opinions of our bishops are just as foolish as those of Irenæus, and as partisan as those of Jerome. Sixteen hundred years have added nothing to the knowledge or wisdom of the Church leaders, who maintain the exclusiveness exhibited by its early founders. Need we wonder that the river of thought has flowed past this organisation, leaving it in an eddy wherein linger those to whom thinking is an effort, or who are so much the slaves of custom and tradition that they support the ancient edifice because it was maintained by their forefathers?

The Council of Nicaea was called because of the heresy of Arius, who could not accept the doctrine of the deity of Jesus. Sixteen hundred years have elapsed, the same controversy continues, and the same opinions are expressed today as were held by the early fathers of the Church, who are described by the Rev. Dr. Davidson, the eminent ecclesiastical authority, as "credulous, blundering, passionate and one-sided men".

Throughout this period the doctrine of the Trinity has been the cause of incalculable suffering and cruelty, because of the attempt by the Church authorities to force it on unwilling people. It has, moreover, excluded from the fellowship of the Church some of the greatest and noblest minds of the Christian era. The result has been that, since the Renaissance, fewer and fewer intelligent people have supported its doctrines, and those who have contributed most to the uplifting of mankind, socially, mentally and morally, have in many cases remained outside its walls, to receive its abuse and criticism. This is what history records from the days of Erasmus to the present time.

The irony of it all is that the Church of England is maintained and supported for the purpose of preaching and propagating superstition, receiving in exchange a tenth of all the produce of the land. This burden is borne by everyone because the tithe, as the tax is called, increases the price of all foodstuffs. Consequently the people in Britain are thus indirectly taxed to support an organisation which excludes from its precincts all who accept what Jesus said about himself, that he was not God, and that there is only one God.

The great majority believe that the Church is preaching the Gospel of Jesus, being quite unaware that it is doing the very opposite, and is in fact strongly anti-Jesus. Most people think that the Christian documents have divine authority, and are blissfully ignorant of the fact that, as these have come down to us, they express in many places only the opinions of the early Church fathers, who added to them, deleted portions of them, and altered the few simple stories about Jesus, so as to make them suit their decisions as to what Christianity was to be. Jerome, in 384, candidly admits that he did so, and it is on his Latin translation that the Christian Bible has been retranslated into English and hundreds of other languages.

Those early Church fathers were not men of high reputation. Eusebius,[1] who was Bishop of Caesarea, and is termed the Father of Ecclesiastical History, wrote, for instance, *The Life of Constantine*, which is an extravagant panegyric and quite unreliable. His history of the Church to the year 324 is impaired by his avowed resolution to record only what would reflect honour to the Church. It was Eusebius who prepared the first draft of the Nicene Creed, and only accepted the final draft at the command of Constantine, at whose right hand he sat during the council.

It is now well known by all scholars that the Christian documents, as we now have them, have come to us through the hands of scheming, unscrupulous, zealous priests. Until the 5th century the Gospels and Epistles were in a fluid state and were altered, added to, and withdrawn from, from time to time, by different priestly scribes and copyists to bring

---

[1] *The Encyclopædia Britannica* under "Eusebius" and under "Creeds", and Canon Robertson's *History of the Christian Church* give much interesting information on early Church history.

them into line with the Pagan beliefs which Christianity absorbed in the early centuries of its growth. Not until the Council of Carthage, in 397, was an attempt made to protect these writings from interference by zealous partisans, but it took a century before this effort partially succeeded. However, it was not until the 17th century that the clergy ceased to tamper with the Scriptures, for the purpose of bringing them into line with what they thought they should be.

Instead of Christianity being a divine revelation, it is in reality what the Church fathers at their various councils decided it was to be, and over them was the iron hand of Constantine, who made sure that their opinions coincided with his own. He was a murderer, as he killed his wife, son and nephew. He was an autocrat but, on the other hand, a more enlightened monarch than many who had preceded him. His policy on the whole was constructive, and he inaugurated many legislative reforms, which, however, did not extend to the peasant class, whose position became no better than that of serfs.

Constantine brought the persecution of the Christians to an end, and placed them on the same footing as those professing other religions. Christianity attracted him to an increasing degree, though it is doubtful how much it really meant to him personally and how much it just represented another trinity of gods under whom he had fought his battles and been victorious. To the end of his days he worshipped Christ and Apollo equally, considering Apollo and Christ as two names which stood for the same idea. It was not until he was on his death-bed that he sought baptism. To him Christianity seems to have been a mere cog in his wheel of government, and how it was put to the people mattered nothing so long as it was presented in a way that suited his policy.

Next to Saint Paul, Constantine did more to establish Christianity than any other man. He was the autocrat of the Roman world. No Senate or Council shared his schemes. His empire was shaking and he needed some form of unified belief to bring cohesion to his wide domains. The building of Constantinople was one of his schemes to secure this result. His decision to make Christianity the state religion of the Roman Empire was another, and this admirably suited the wishes of the Christian bishops who saw in this the opportunity for increased power.

Constantine, however, did not calculate on the fierce animosities, the hatred, jealousy and divergence of opinions which were grouped under this name. Much troubled by this bitterness, and in an endeavour to bring peace and harmony into the Christian community, he called together a conference of all the Christian churches throughout the Empire and this was held at Nicaea. He must have been bitterly disappointed at the results achieved when he discovered that his imperial edict, instructing all to accept and believe the Nicene Creed, was not observed. It was not until the time of Theodosius (379–395) that unity was established, when all the unorthodox meetings of the non-trinitarians were forbidden, and no one was permitted to express non-trinitarian opinions. By the 5th century Christianity had become so solidified that it wielded greater power than any emperor, and reached to the outermost limits of the Roman Empire.

After the transfer of the capital to Constantinople the Bishop of Rome took the title *Pontifex Maximus*, which had been held by the emperors, to become the most powerful influence in Christendom, thus realising for a time the dream of Saint Augustine of the Church being the ruler of the world, as then known, to which kings, emperors, princes and all mankind must bow in subjection. The history of Europe from this time onwards for a thousand years is largely the history of the failure of this grandiose political ideal, to which Constantine gave the priests the initial urge.

Constantine's decision to elevate the Christian cult to the status of a national religion had the effect of bringing to an end the last persecution of the Christians. The duration of this martyrdom was from 303 to 312 during the reign of Diocletian. Gibbon, basing his figures on statements made by Eusebius, estimates that the total number of Christian martyrs during the period of this persecution did not exceed a total of 2,000, and that this figure would not be much exceeded if it were used to include all the Christian victims of Roman persecution.

Gibbon contrasts this with the multitude who died as the result of Christian wars and persecution during the reign of Christianity, instancing the fact that over 100,000 victims perished in the Netherlands alone during the reign of the Holy Roman Emperor Charles V. Since Gibbon's time a detailed estimate has been made of the number who have suffered from persecution and from wars started by the Christian Church, the appalling total of 25,000,000 victims being reached. These slaughtered men and women suffered and died because they could not accept the creeds and dogmas of the section of the Christian Church under which they lived. Both Roman Catholic and Protestant churches, when they had the power, tortured and massacred all they called heretics, and between them they made Christendom a vast slave camp for some fourteen hundred years.

The Roman people were in reality not intolerant to other religions, in fact quite the reverse, and there seems no reason to believe that the persecution of Christians would ever have taken place had it not been for the fact that they refused to acknowledge the divinity of the Emperor, which eastern idea had been brought to Europe by Alexander the Great. Diocletian was the last to hold this opinion, as Constantine discarded it. The persecution of Christians therefore ceased when he became Emperor, and, with this change of policy, came his decision, as already recorded, to make Christianity the official religion of the Empire.

It was one thing to decide on unity and quite another to attain it. However, the first step had to be taken, and the Council of Nicaea was the result. There the wranglings of the bishops and priests, on the question of the correct definition of Christianity, became so heated that Constantine burned all their recommendations without reading them, and then proceeded to consider the question of a creed for all to believe. After much heated discussion, when blows were struck and papers and books thrown about the Council chamber, the amendment put forward by Arius was defeated. That meant the defeat of the Unitarians, the triumph of the Trinitarians, and the birth of the Nicene Creed which was afterwards altered and amended by someone unknown, at a place unknown and at a date unknown.

After Constantine had settled matters to his own satisfaction he commanded the creed to be signed by all present, but not all did so. Eusebius signed it but wrote afterwards a pastoral letter to his flock in which he said that the creed was more creditable to his ingenuity than to his candour. He was particularly anxious not to offend Constantine, who had a great opinion of his ability and saw in him the unscrupulous man he required to bring his policy to fruition.

Eusebius was the principal intermediary of Constantine in carrying through the reformation from the old order to the new, and played somewhat the same part as that taken by Thomas Cromwell, twelve centuries later, at the bidding of Henry VIII. Eusebius helped to produce a reformed Paganism under the name of Christianity, and Cromwell a reformed Christianity under the name of Protestantism, the same bitterness and persecution between Christians following after Constantine's days as followed after the reign of Henry VIII.

Eusebius was a courtier, who lived at the court, and his scheming mind managed to overcome the numerous difficulties which were continually occurring. His was a difficult role to fill and his policy was to pursue a moderate course. He had to contend with Athanasius, with his extreme trinitarian views, on the one hand, and Arius, with his anti-trinitarian views, on the other, while the voiceless people were helpless, their country's future religion being determined for them by an autocratic emperor.

It is only necessary to study early Church history

to realise that, like his master Constantine, Eusebius, and the other Church fathers, took advantage of the desire for something new, which was springing up in the minds of the people, just as Thomas Cromwell, and the other reformers at the Reformation, took the opportunity afforded by the same mental expansion to suppress the old and further the new. Both awakenings were due to Greek philosophy gaining in influence over the superstitions fostered by the priests.

At the time of Constantine the priests won, as, by effecting a compromise between the two in the form of Christianity, philosophy was buried for over a thousand years. The deadening hand of superstition laid its weight over the Western world, but fortunately it was not for ever. At the Renaissance, Greek philosophy again caused an upheaval in the religion of the people, and this time the compromise was Protestantism. Nevertheless the change was only partial, because half of Christendom preferred to retain the old superstitions of Paganism, its numerous gods being known as saints.

It seemed at first that the priests had won again. The Catholic section of the Christian Church was still secure, and the priests were still supreme. So, for a time, were the Protestant priests, but owing to the fact that Protestantism was not so centralised and organised as Catholicism, and each individual claimed the right to worship as his conscience dictated, numerous sects and divisions were the result. This led to discussion and debate, and all the time the Protestant mind was developing. For several centuries the Protestant priests kept control, though with a weakening grip, by forbidding their followers to read any works other than those they permitted, but gradually this tyranny passed, and with reading came more freedom of thought and expression.

As education increased the forces of superstition weakened, to the increasing alarm of its purveyors. Its battalions today are in disorderly retreat, or, to use the words of the Moderator of the General Assembly of the Church of Scotland, The Right Rev. Dr. Thomson, as reported in the *Glasgow Herald* of 30th October, 1934, "Today the forces of Christ were in retreat practically all along the line." In other words Paganism is being steadily displaced, as the result of increased knowledge.

The story of the past three hundred years is just the history of Protestant Europe shedding Paganism. At the time of Constantine, and for three centuries thereafter, Paganism continued in the Middle East disguised as Christianity. Mohammed caused the first split and took half of Christendom unto himself. Then came into being the Greek Orthodox Church in the 11th century, and this great event was the cause of that vast area, known today as Russia, being converted to Christianity. Then came Luther in the 16th century, to produce a diluted form of Paganism to be called by the queer name of Protestantism. This form of belief took half of what remained of Western Christendom, but its break from the authority of Rome eventually led to increased latitudinarian beliefs, to end in our day in numerous sects which have most of the essential beliefs in common, but adopt a more tolerant attitude than ever before in Church history towards each other and those holding heretical opinions.

Greek philosophy has been behind the reform movement, aided these last four hundred years by the discoveries of science, and the adoption of the scientific method of investigation. Philosophy has ebbed and flowed these last nineteen centuries, and, as the years pass, it is coming more and more into the lives of the people. Throughout it has been the enemy of Paganism, and the history of Europe, since the Greek philosophers gave their great thoughts to mankind, has been a record of the fight between the philosophic thinkers and the superstitious. Had philosophy won when it was first given to the world, what a different story history would have to tell! But it was not to be, as mankind was not ready for it.[1]

Today another mental revolution is taking place, and the cause behind this will carry mankind to a stage which he could not have reached by means of philosophy, since it lacked the evidence necessary to back up its assertions and deductions. However, the proof is now forthcoming, and, under the name of Spiritualism, we have philosophy combined with evidence. Consequently the forces of progress have been immensely strengthened, and those of reaction irreparably weakened.

The rising generation takes no interest in, and is quite indifferent to, ecclesiastical opinions about ancient dogmas and doctrines, and fully endorses the opinion recently expressed by Dean Inge that the only way to remain orthodox is by not thinking.

---

[1] The history of the early Christian Church will be found in *The Psychic Stream*, and the history of the Church throughout the Christian era is recorded in *The Curse of Ignorance*. Particulars of both books are given on page 3.

Thinking is killing orthodoxy. As a result a new Church is rising out of the ruins of the old, now steadily falling in public estimation.[1] The old still has its vast wealth, gorgeous buildings, cathedrals, theological colleges and churches. These, however, will not attract congregations unless the people feel that in the preaching which takes place in these buildings truth comes before tradition and custom.

Fortunately there are large halls where meetings are taking place, wherein the people hear the truth, as we now understand it in this age of greater knowledge, and with each year that passes more and more of these public halls are being used for the instruction and enlightenment of the people.

Spiritualism is a life to be lived and needs no church. It is, however, in the nature of humanity to meet together, and Spiritualists have their meetings just as those of other religions. This Church of the future must be capable of attracting the wise and the simple, the learned and the unlearned, the good and the true. It must not be based on doctrines, or on tradition, but on knowledge. Today we have the knowledge on which to base religion, and this our ancestors lacked. The new revelation rests on knowledge, and those who accept it are quite indifferent to tradition.

The future Church must be as broad as the bounds of science, and embrace the universe. The Church of today is as narrow as were men's views of the universe

---

[1] *The Church of England Newspaper*, in its issue of 26th October, 1934, drew attention to the steady decline in Church attendance in Greater London, whose churches have a seating capacity for two millions. In 1903 the average attendance on Sundays was 510,664. In 1933 it fell to 391,400, though the population had increased in the interval from $5\frac{1}{2}$ millions to $7\frac{1}{2}$ millions.

when the Church was founded. The new Church is based on evidence, investigation and knowledge. The old Church is based on ignorance and superstition. The new Church welcomes all shades of opinion which tend to elevate mankind, help him on his road through life, and reveal with greater clearness the life to come. The old Church refuses to glean further knowledge, as to it all truth is contained in its sacred documents, creeds, dogmas and doctrines.

The object of the new Church is to increase knowledge of the life here and hereafter, and what it stands for will become accepted in time by the orthodox Church of today. Those who are preachers today will become the teachers of tomorrow, and their pulpits will be occupied by those who can guide the people towards a higher standard of life and a closer relationship with the unseen. Worship and prayers will develop slowly into contemplation of the Infinite. A special place will be given to psychic healing, because many of the troubles to which man is heir can be cured by etheric doctors acting through human mediums on the etheric body, which reacts on the physical body and thus effects a cure.

As the aim of the Church of the future will be to increase knowledge and give health, it will receive the support and help of the great thinkers, the great healers, the wise and the learned, and become a powerful instrument for good. It must be tied to no tradition, creed or dogma, and discard unnecessary ceremonial which appeals nowadays only to the simple-minded. It must not be too sacred and so discourage discussion on all aspects of knowledge. Its pulpits must be the forum for the dissemination of all shades of opinion. They must not be reserved, as they are at present, for a special class of men trained to look on life from one narrow angle.

Its Bible will never be completed, as it will contain all the facts that man has won, and is winning every day, from nature. The real Bible is neither holy nor sacred. These are words which are used in connection with orthodox religion and its observances, but those who use them in this connection expose their lack of knowledge. What is unknown or mysterious too often receives the names of holy and sacred, but when the unknown and the mysterious become known and understood their holiness and sacredness disappear. So it has been from the beginning, and what is holy and sacred to the savage is not so to the educated. Consequently everything connected with orthodox religion ceases to be holy and sacred when understood.

When Etheria is known to be a world like this one, inhabited by people like this one, the sacredness of it all disappears. When it is realised that we are each one of us a part of God, and God is the over-ruling Mind of the Universe, the sacredness of the Infinite disappears. The universe then becomes natural. Only ignorance of the unknown makes it unnatural. Holy and sacred are words used by those who cannot think deeply. There are therefore no holy books, as all have been naturally produced. A few may have been written under partial inspiration from Etheria, by means of automatic writing, but when the source and mechanism of it all is known, they cease to be sacred. Some inspirational writings of the highest order will take their proper place in the Church of the future.

What is holy is love. What is sacred is the home.

The real Bible embraces all the ennobling literature of the world, and everyone who adds a fact to knowledge adds a text to the Book of Knowledge. So the past should be treated as history and not worshipped as it is today. The present and the future are ours, and the past is only of interest to us as the story of our ancestors, from which we can learn their achievements and mistakes, and try to profit by them. Nothing should be considered too sacred to be discussed. Everything in life is of interest. To reserve a certain tradition which has come to us from the past, as being the only material fit for religious consideration, is stupid and not fitted for the broader and wider minds of the coming generation.

Those who sit in the pew should have as much right to express an opinion, as occasion permits, as those who preach from the pulpit. Discussion leads to knowledge, and diversity of views leads to the truth. As intelligence grows the performing of rites and ceremonies will decline, so that the Church will gradually cease to be used for the purpose of following the ritual of Paganism as it is today. When people come to realise that the Eucharist, or Holy Communion, is a Pagan institution incorporated into Christianity, fewer and fewer people will wish to take part in this ancient ceremony.

Baptism, another Pagan ceremony, will gradually be abandoned when people appreciate that baptism does not lead to salvation. Custom dies hard, and baptism by many today is retained because it was believed in fervently by our forefathers. Today children are baptised for the most part because their parents consider it is a correct and seemly thing to do.

The Church of England baptism service is archaic, and fitted for an age when education did not exist. It cannot appeal today to men and women of intelligence. It emphasises that the child is born in sin, which is an insult to motherhood, and belongs to the time when everything to do with women was sinful. They were under a curse and the cause of all the evil in the world. The local registrar's office is the only place where future generations will register the fact that a child has been born, so that the state may keep its correct account of the population.

Any intelligent person who has been at a baptismal service in the Church of England, and witnessed the godfather and godmother solemnly taking the most inviolable vows as to how they will bring up the child, which does not belong to them, must feel that an institution which supports such humbug is a sham and utter fraud.

Instead of the parents taking the vows as to how they will bring up the child, these pledges are solemnly taken by the godparents. If the godparents tried in the least degree to carry these into effect, the parents would be the first to resent the uncalled-for interference. These pious promises are taken by the godparents, who have not the least intention of performing them. Never an attempt is made to do so by those who solemnly declare that they will bring up the child as a faithful member of the Church, and give it the prescribed religious instruction. The parents stand by as interested spectators, and quietly listen to their own responsibilities being transferred to those to whom they do not belong.

What is termed Confirmation in the Church of

England is ordained for the purpose of getting young people to support the doctrines of the Church at an age before their minds are sufficiently formed to realise the error they are expected to accept. What most people accept at Confirmation satisfies them throughout their lives. Joining the Church, and accepting its creed, the majority think is sufficient, and seldom thereafter do they give any intelligent thought to the subject.

The Churching of Women is derived from the idea that a woman is unclean after childbirth, and requires purification after being in contact with a child uncleansed from original sin by baptism. The idea came from Judaism and, like other Judaic laws which have been discarded, this ceremony will be abandoned in time.

Marriage needs no priest to perform the ceremony. The local registrar can do all that is required to make the marriage legal. A church is a very suitable building for the ceremony of marriage, and will doubtless continue to be used for this purpose. Words of wisdom and advice can also be given by some suitable person to the marrying couple, but they will be practical, useful and helpful, and not wrapped round with ancient garbage. The present marriage ceremony, which incorporates the superstitions of the past, must be abandoned some day.

The first sentence in the Church of England marriage service is false, and no sane person outside of a church would ever make such a remark. What a terrible example, this dishonesty, to give to a young couple starting married life! Marriage was not instituted by God at the time of man's innocency, as every intelligent person knows that the story of Adam and Eve is a fable. It is also untrue to say that matrimony signifies a mystical union between Christ and his Church, and is adorned and beautified because Christ attended a marriage service in Cana of Galilee.

The burial of the body should not be a function of the Church. The body should be conveyed quietly to the graveyard and interred with as little ceremony and display as possible. It is the discarded instrument of the soul and should be forgotten as quickly as possible. Future generations will pay less and less attention to the earthly body, and consequently the time will come when the grave will not receive so much thought as it does today. By many it is a shrine held sacred, and worshipped. To it pilgrimages are made. It is clothed with flowers, and on some graves flowers are continually renewed.

The worship of the dead body in Christian countries is ghoulish. Never an important man dies but crowds file past his dead body. It "lies in state" and is venerated. To Christians, according to the teaching of their Church, the dead body is the future habitation of the soul, which will reanimate it on the resurrection day. This mistaken idea gives no comfort, and keeps the mourner from realising that the etheric body has passed into Etheria and, with the personality intact, the released soul awaits reunion with its loved ones when their turn comes to pass on.

The dead body is not the person, and the thought that so often passes through the mind that we have seen the last of our friend is just another of nature's illusions. We must always remember the reality behind the appearance. We should never speak about having buried our friend, or that he is in his grave, or talk of where he was buried. These are all Christian expressions born in the belief that we lie in our graves until the resurrection.

Instead of grave-stones, the future church will have a place set apart for tablets on the walls in memory of the departed. On each will be the name, the date of death, and on some the date of the first communication to earth of the person in whose name it is erected. Instead of a service of mourning, one will be held expressing confidence to the mourners that the departed has entered into a happier and fuller life.

When death takes place, the thoughts of the people are more in harmony and attuned to the other life, and opportunity will be taken to emphasise that the departed has lived on earth for the allotted time, and passed on into a new and happier order of existence. A medium, on such occasions, in the days to come will doubtless be present, and will inform the friends gathered together of the safe arrival of the departed into the new life. Emphasis will always be laid on the reality of the continuation of life, and consequently the dead body will be looked on as something which is of the past.

The present materialistic burial service, which is as depressing as it is irrational, will be discarded as knowledge increases, and the form adopted by Spiritualists at their funeral services will take its place. We shall then have come to look on death as a door into a new life and not as a state of coma enduring until the resurrection day. A church will be used for the assembly of the friends of the departed who will be reminded that death, which seems to be the end of a personality, is not so, that life never ceases, and that what is experienced at death is just a change of conditions, a change from the physical to the etheric expression of life. Amongst Protestants it is not felt necessary to have a priest present at the bedside of the dying, and so the time will come when he will not be deemed necessary at the graveside.

Future generations will study the writings and communications which come through from Etheria, and, in consequence, our way of living and thinking will become better and happier. Conditions will therefore become more harmonious; the present-day constant threat of war will vanish as the result of the knowledge that man is an etheric being, and that all responsible for shortening his life—his time of preparation on earth—will suffer mentally for the crime both here and hereafter. As the mind becomes more refined, the very thought of war will become so repugnant to humanity that such an event will be impossible. Then armies on land, navies on sea, and aeroplanes in the air for fighting purposes will be disbanded, and humanity will make use of nature's storehouse for the purpose of construction only, and never for destruction.

I foresee the time coming when guns, grenades, tanks and bayonets will be looked on with as much repugnance and horror as medieval instruments of torture are regarded today. I anticipate the time when a battleship will be classed in the same category as the hateful slave galley of the past, and the fighting bomb-dropping aeroplane as a pestilence against which humanity will turn in loathing, and never tolerate. It is all a question of mental development, of a change in the mental outlook, which will come in time and bring with it its blessing.

The Church of the future will help people to live aright, educate them in all things pertaining to a more developed culture, will set its face resolutely against war, misery and cruelty, and tell all there is to know about our destiny. It will encourage the virtues, not as pertaining to a particular creed, but as part of the common knowledge of mankind. The medium will more and more take the place of the priest and minister, who have maintained their positions by claiming that they have an ancient revelation to expound to mankind. Consequently the reformed church will discard this delusion, realising that we have this divine revelation now, that it is not something that happened to a select few nineteen centuries ago, but that it is with us today in greater force than ever before.

This revelation comes through those gifted people termed mediums, and each church in the future will have attached to it a medium who will take the place of the ordained cleric. In trance, or by clairaudience and clairvoyance, the medium will direct the thoughts of the people to their destiny, and comfort those who have lost their loved ones by making real to them the fact that these still live in a world about and around this earth of ours. These resident mediums will be the future parish priests. They will conduct the healing circles and the funeral services, being supported from time to time by mediums who travel from church to church because of their special gifts.

As happened in the time of the early Apostolic Church, which was displaced by the Christian Church our descendants will come to look forward to hearing and honouring those who will be the great mediums of their time. All mediums cannot be equally gifted, but it will be arranged that the most developed will go from place to place, so that all will benefit by them, and will anticipate their coming with delight.

Today our great mediums are confined to the large cities, and the halls to which they go are crowded to the doors. As mediumship increases and improves it will come to be better appreciated, and the people will get more and more comfort from it, be encouraged and helped by it, and think more deeply of life and the things appertaining to life. Besides this, the information we obtain from the advanced minds in Etheria, through mediumship, may solve some of our present problems, and enlarge our scientific and philosophic knowledge in a way few today can imagine.

This vision of the future can only be realised slowly, just as mediumship increases, but that it will be realised eventually there is no doubt, now that mediums are allowed to exercise and develop their gifts. Since the burning of mediums ceased, mediumship has steadily increased, so much so that the next hundred years will, I believe, witness the realisation of part at least of my vision. Perhaps, some hundreds of years later, a much larger proportion of the people will have developed the gift of clairaudience and clairvoyance, as it is a potential faculty within each of us.

The reformed Church, which I visualise, will have a leader in charge of each individual church, whose duties will be similar to those of the President who directs each Spiritualist Church at the present time. He, and a duly elected committee, will be responsible for the management of the church. He will be a man of culture and education and will lead the services. The music will be provided by the musical talent of the district, and will be expressed, not only by an organ, but also by other musical instruments. The Spiritualist Hymn Book contains many beautiful hymns written in the light of modern knowledge, and also many of the old hymns altered so as to omit matters which Spiritualists discard. The leader will also conduct the reading, which will not be confined to the Bible as it is now in orthodox churches, but will embrace all the great ennobling literature of which we are the heirs.

The leader will also be responsible for giving an address which will be part of the service. He will invite others capable of this duty to help him from time to time. The addresses will be for the purpose of education and enlightenment, and will cover a wide ground. The future church will not be confined, as it is now, within the bounds of the Old and New Testaments. Its ideals and ideas will be derived from the great and the good of all times and all nations, and its heroes will be all those who have helped to raise mankind above the savage.

The Church of the future will be run mostly by voluntary help. The medium in most cases will be paid, and probably also the conductor of the music, as these duties are specialised, and those who perform them will doubtless require some payment. The clergyman will automatically disappear, as, with the advancement of education and knowledge, he will not be required. His place will be taken by one who has the capacity to teach and impart knowledge, and also by a medium who will keep us in touch with Etheria. The medium will be the instrument through which advanced Etherians will inform and instruct mankind with regard to our destiny, and how we should live aright here on earth.

The visiting of the sick, and others in sorrow or in special need of help, will be done by a band of voluntary workers whose special duty it will be to minister to those in trouble. This tendency is already in evidence. Numerous welfare, and other similar organisations, are now administered mostly by voluntary workers, and, as the hours of labour lessen, there will be more time available for this voluntary work. The amount of voluntary work now done is vastly greater than it was fifty years ago, and it will tend to increase.

The future Church will be the centre round which this work of mercy and uplifting will be performed. Its duties will be to increase the culture of its congregations, comfort the mourners by getting them into touch with their friends who have passed on, assist the needy, heal the sufferers, and help all those who are finding too heavy the cares and troubles of this world.

Each church will have a healing circle and a healing medium. When these mediums become numerous enough, this side of the church will co-operate with the medical men of the district, as some of the patients can be healed better by psychic methods than by those now practised.

Few people realise today how much is being done by psychic healing. True, the number of psychic healing mediums is limited, but those who have this gift are doing a great and noble work. Doubtless this side of mediumship will increase as the psychic art develops, and this means that ever more people will be found capable of being the human instruments. As a wire is to electricity, so the medium is to the healing ray which passes through his physical body and hands directed on the part of the patient's body the etheric doctor is attempting to heal. The rays stimulate the patient's etheric body which in turn affect his physical body.

A dozen names occur to me, as I write, of mediums I know personally who are carrying on this work of healing the body by psychic means. Most of the cases that are cured have been given up as incurable by the medical profession, but in spite of this the cures effected are remarkable and significant. These psychic healers have the power, by touch and by passes, to remove pain and effect recovery, a matter which is beyond the capacity of the physician. They generally do this in trance, under the control of someone on the other side who has been a doctor on earth, and has studied in Etheria the ways and means of giving health and relieving pain to sufferers on earth. This doctor control uses the medium as an instrument, through whom he passes those healing rays which are well known to all who are familiar with this method of healing.

These healing rays act on our etheric body, and stimulate it in such a way that it reacts on the physical body. This stimulation which the physical body thus receives brings about a cure, but there is much we do not know about this method of healing, and only gradually is a literature about it accumulating. We can appreciate the healing without knowing how it comes about, but what we find to be equally remarkable is the accurate diagnosis made by the healing medium when in trance. The doctor control, speaking through the medium, says that he can see clearly the human body both inside and outside, and, by the colour of the rays given off by the etheric body, which we call the aura, he knows what is wrong and the part which is not functioning properly. From my personal experience, when observing healing mediums at work, I can certainly testify that the diagnosis of the medium in trance is singularly accurate and to the point.

My duties as a magistrate have brought me into contact with those mentally afflicted, the insane, who are classed under the name of lunatics, our ancestors believing that such persons are unbalanced by the moon. I have had to certify them for confinement in what are now termed Mental Homes. I have visited them and talked with them, and my belief has grown that much could be done to help many of those unfortunates if we established the right conditions on earth to enable healers and others in Etheria to make contact with them. Some are probably suffering from the influence of low-minded Etherians who are earth-bound and find expression of earthly ideas through those we term insane, but who are in reality too sensitive to these influences, and are not strong enough mentally to resist them. The gross vibrations surrounding those earth-bound Etherians, keep those of finer vibrations in Etheria from making contact with them for the purpose of removing their influence from these sensitive earth people.

With the help of a good medium and sitters I believe something could be done to relieve insanity. Those afflicted could join these circles, one at a time, and thus enable the healers in Etheria to break the bad influence and effect a cure. Not all insanity is due to possession, but, whether this is the cause of the derangement or not, the mind can best be cured by those in Etheria who understand it in a way no earth doctor does. In the future we may find that through mediumship a new life will open up before some of these unfortunate people, who have now to live apart from their fellows because of their abnormal and unstable minds.

Spiritualism greatly needs a college devoted to the development of mediumship and the educational training of platform speakers. In this training college mediums would be developed according to their gifts. Those who developed healing power would be helped along those lines, and so on with all the branches of mediumship. Clairvoyants and Inspirational speakers in trance would be trained for platform work. Those again whose gifts lay in obtaining communications at séances by Direct Voice and in trance would have this form of mediumship developed.

Platform speakers would receive instruction and education in the various old-world religions, and in the literature of Spiritualism. They would be taught elocution and how best to hold an audience. The new knowledge which Spiritualism brings would be placed before them in all its aspects, and they would be trained in the right way of conveying this to the people, just as the various political parties today train students who wish to become political speakers.

This will all come gradually just as money becomes available and as the demand for greater knowledge increases amongst the people. This is but a forecast of what we may expect to develop, and it is the duty of Spiritualists to prepare the ground for this centralisation and control of the Spiritualist Church which is arising out of the ashes of the old. When the mentality of the people is ripe for the advance, Spiritualists must be ready to supply the mediums and the speakers, and to do this effectually a central organisation in, or near, London is essential.

At the present day most of the sermons delivered from Christian pulpits are so childish, and divorced from all scientific thought, that the time must come when those preached will not be only for the benefit of the lowest intelligences in the community. The time must come when the sermon will not violate our reason and intelligence. The shallowness of most present-day discourses, the absence of reason, of logical thought, of accuracy, and of any attempt to tell the truth, strikes the average educated man so much that he seldom if ever attends church services.

Nowadays fewer and fewer are interested in hearing discourses taken from texts in the Bible. In the old days when the clergy could frighten the people by threatening them with hell they obtained large congregations. This fear has now to a great extent passed, and they have nothing to put in its place. Nevertheless they are still bound by their creeds, dogmas and doctrines, and must trim their remarks to keep within this boundary. Few preachers have any knowledge of the after-life, about which people really want to know. Consequently they cannot touch on this subject, except in the vaguest of terms. The sermon of the future will be bounded only by our knowledge, and will encompass in its range the whole history of thought and action.

Spiritualists look forward to the dawn of reason some day entering the orthodox Church. They have ceased being slaves to tradition, or bowing in idolatrous worship to a fetish in the form of a theological dogma inherited from primitive man. To them worship consists of contemplation of the divine in nature, and can best be described as Natural Religion. Service means the uplifting and the enlightening of humanity. Honest thinking, loving sympathies and kindly services have replaced creeds and taken the place of prayers and ceremonials.

Spiritualists believe that nothing is too sacred to be investigated so long as the aim is to reach the truth. Their desire is to save humanity from ignorance and wrong-doing through knowledge and right thinking, and their atonement is at-one-ment with the Divine Mind of the Universe, which develops as the resul of the greater knowledge obtained through communication with Etheria. Faith changes to knowledge, and knowledge enhances and enlarges our mental outlook, bringing it more into harmony with nature's scheme for our unfoldment. Evolution is not confined to earth, as it is continuous mental development, to become more pronounced as we journey through the spheres. Here we can be in heaven just as much as in Etheria, as heaven is not a place but a condition of mind. It is a question of harmony and contentment, and where these reign is Heaven, the reverse condition being Hell.

If the priesthood were inspired by these ideas, and could discard all the dogmas and doctrines taught in theological colleges, how different would be the preaching in the churches today! The student life of the clergy is wasted in learning Greek, Hebrew and Latin, and being taught just enough to enable them to preserve and preach the old tradition, without devoting to the subject intelligent thought.

A study of comparative religion and pre-Christian religious history would be much more useful than the foregoing, but we cannot expect much change for the better until the people themselves develop mentally. Ultimately it is they who must determine what they are to believe and what they wish to receive in the way of religious nourishment and comfort. With improved education the tendency now is for the people to go where the truth is preached, and, for this reason, Spiritualist churches are filled to overflowing, and new ones are swelling their number each year.

I therefore foresee the Spiritualist Church leavening in time every other religious organisation. The vitality of religion can only be maintained by unbroken contact with the etheric world, and, whenever this is abandoned, organisations or individuals become stereotyped. When this comes about orthodoxy develops, and then religion consists of man-made beliefs, ritual and ceremony. Just as the Unitarian Church has exerted an influence towards a more rational outlook on old beliefs, so the Spiritualist Church of the future will help to bring the Christian Church back to the way from which it strayed in the

4th century when it abolished the medium from church services in the Apostolic Church. Then Christianity was born. When the medium ceased to be regarded as a divine oracle, and came to be called a servant of the devil, religion in the true meaning of the word ceased. However, the fortunate decline in the power of the Church made it possible for Spiritualists last century to bring religion back to the people as nature intended it to be, and this tendency will increase as the years pass on.

Orthodox religion today, having no natural basis on which to form a unified world-wide belief, finds itself at times in curious and tragic situations. Spiritualism appeals to all men and women throughout the world, because the basis of Spiritualism is everywhere the same, the same mediumship and teachings from Etheria being world-wide. On the other hand orthodoxy is parochial, and consequently today the leaders of the Christian Church would disdain the idea of sitting round a table and discussing religion with the leaders of Mohammedanism, or Buddhism, or any other religion, as they consider that only they have the truth. The Church of the future will have no section which considers itself superior to any other, because the same evidence of the after-life, and its teachings, will be available to everyone. Every human being has the same destiny and the same interest in the future life, and this vital fact should form a common bond which will cement all nations in mutual sympathy and friendship. Just as people born into the various world religions gather together at a Spiritualist service, because the barriers of creed have been broken down, so in time will this become possible with the entire human race.

I foresee the time coming when all intelligent and educated people are able to attend church services with pleasure and profit, without having their reason outraged as it is today. Then the preachers will have become teachers, to discourse on science, philosophy and history, and their relation to our way of living for the improvement of our characters. They will draw lessons from the mistakes of the past, and, at the same time, show how courage, endurance, fortitude and self-sacrifice have raised mankind to the position we now occupy. Congregations will then learn about the martyrdom, self-sacrifice, and noble lives of very many who lived outside the influence of the Christian Church.

Our descendants will be told about Socrates and his noble death, and how he of all the ancients gave more light to the world on the subject of the reality of the soul, and the after-life, than any of the gods or prophets of any orthodox religion. They will hear that the Greek and Roman philosophers added more to the human understanding of the universe than can be learned from all the pages of the Bible. They will learn that the story of Regulus, in his dealings with the Carthaginians, is one of the noblest epics of the Pagan world, inspiring to all who read it, as it reveals the heights to which man can rise in support of honour, truth and justice. Then those who come after us will appreciate that the virtues, and the great and noble thoughts of the pre-Christian world, were not confined to a small race living within the borders of Palestine.

Coming to more recent times, they will learn that Giordano Bruno was as great a saint as any of the martyrs on the Christian roll of fame, and that his example lit a beacon which has increased in brilliance since his foul torture and murder by the Church of Christ. Our descendants will discover that Thomas Huxley set a nobler example of a life fighting for the truth than that of many of the saints of Christendom, and that Charles Darwin told us more about the origin of man than is to be found in all the inspired sacred writings of the world. Moreover, Ingersoll, though a professed agnostic, lived a more noble unselfish ethical life than many of his orthodox traducers, and Voltaire, one of the greatest enemies of the Christian faith, did more for human liberty than all the priests of Christendom throughout the Christian era.

Future generations will have extolled to them one of the best and greatest of women, one of the saints of the Pagan calendar, the noblest example we have of intellectual womanhood, and one of the last representatives of the ancient culture of Greece. Her name was Hypatia, and she was foully murdered by one of the world's greatest criminals, Cyril, Bishop of Alexandria, because she protested against his slaughter of the Jews. This fiend was made a saint of the Christian Church in recognition of his services in promoting the Christian faith by exterminating 30,000 Jews. The real heroes, when the blight of orthodoxy is removed, will become known and take the place of many of those the Church has glorified and sanctified.

A great duty falls on all Spiritualists to lead the world on to this higher plane of thought. To do so the Spiritualist Church must take every opportunity to raise the level of intelligence of those who speak from its own platforms. This will become easier as more intellectual and better educated people become Spiritualists. The Spiritualist Church in the past has been supported largely by the poorer section of the community, as those of wealth and position have mostly ignored it and often bitterly attacked it. The orthodox Church has the financial and traditional support of the State, many of its members being wealthy and influential people, while the Spiritualist Church has been handicapped by its adherents having none of these advantages.

General education in this country commenced as recently as 1870, so one need not be surprised that this new Church, largely supported by deserters from the orthodox churches, was unable to command the services of many who had been fortunate enough to receive the wider education enjoyed by those who remained loyal to traditional religion. Spiritualism is not fashionable as a religion, its church buildings are simple, but, in spite of these drawbacks, it is more and more attracting the people, and, as this proceeds, a higher level of education and knowledge will become observable on the Spiritualist platform. Nevertheless it is remarkable how widely read many Spiritualists are, and their knowledge of philosophic thought is equally noticeable.

The intellectual level of the whole community is rising and, this being so, there will be no difficulty in the years to come for all the Spiritualist churches to have men and women on their platforms of a high standard of education. This opinion is strengthened when we consider the high level now attained by speakers in the many large halls in London where the very best that Spiritualism has to offer can be found. Let these great Sunday gatherings be a model for every Spiritualist church, as what can be reached in London can likewise be achieved throughout the country.

Most Spiritualist churches have a library, and this is something vital that is still lacking in orthodox churches. As mental development proceeds the neglect of mental culture will be rectified, and all future churches will some day be provided with a library of the best books on Spiritualism, Philosophy and Religion. Ever more time is being devoted by the community to reading, and, as the hours of work shorten, by more machines taking the place of manual labour, so will study and self-culture increase.

A Literary Club should be attached to each church, having for its object discussions, debates and other intellectual pursuits. The unfolding of the universe comes with the enlarging of the mind. As the mind enlarges so does the universe unfold before it. This process cannot be hurried, but, when the mind is ripe to assimilate new ideas, they will be there in plenty awaiting entrance. As the mind is so is the universe. Consequently it behoves everyone to give a prominent place in life to mind culture, and to encourage this will be one of the functions of the reformed church.

The study of psychic literature is today attracting far more people than is generally believed. Some of these belong to the old orthodox churches, and some to none at all. Many of these people wish to know more about the subject of survival after death, but have no wish to sing hymns and put up prayers in the process of learning. Consequently the Spiritualist Church does not attract them, and they receive greater knowledge and understanding by attending lectures given by the many able speakers attached to this new movement of psychic thought. This being so, most of our large cities have now Psychical Research societies, and many others will have them in the years to come. These societies are devoted entirely to the investigation and discussion of psychic phenomena from a scientific aspect, and the emotionalism connected with church services is entirely absent. In the years to come these societies may do as much as Spiritualist churches to spread the new knowledge, because they appeal to the intellectual and thinking people who are anxious to increase in knowledge without committing themselves to a religious organisation.

So far we have considered the Spiritualist Church only from the point of view of the adult, but we must not forget the children. Each church has attached to it a Lyceum, which is the name given to what the orthodox Church calls the Sunday School. The Lyceum is not confined to Sunday teaching, and its teachers interest themselves in the lives of the children throughout the week, in their games, their education, and their general well-being. So far there are very few books, suitable for a child, dealing with the new knowledge, and there is an opening here for someone to make it simple enough for a child to understand. There should be a great increase in this class of literature in the years to come, because even children have outgrown present-day religious literature for the young.

The child of the future will be taught in a simple way about the deeper problems of life, and not have his mind poisoned by superstition. He will be told the stories of the heroes of the past, who will not be confined to the pages of the Old and New Testaments. The child will be taught the truth about Jesus, who will not be presented, as he is today, clothed in theological garments. Children will be influenced to model their lives and characters on the lives of the good and noble of all ages and of all nations. The necessity of developing a high ethical outlook must ever be kept before them, and the importance of the virtues should be taught to a child in place of theology which has no elevating influence. Children, from an early age, must be taught the importance of truth and honesty, and that the kind, merciful and just are the men and women who are the most respected and generally the happiest.

When the child grows from childhood to youth he will be told of the continuance of life, and that as we live here so shall we be hereafter. He will not be frightened by death, but be taught that it is an incident in life which all must experience, and about which there is nothing to be afraid. He will be told of the lives and doings of the people in Etheria, and how life there is very much like life here. He will learn how in Etheria people can make themselves happy and unhappy just as they can here, and that to the good and true, the upright, the honest and the unselfish, it is a more beautiful world than this, but that to those who have the reverse of these qualities it is a more unhappy world to live in than this earth, until they mend their ways. Life on earth should be put forward as something to be lived to the best of our ability, that the good are the noble and the unselfish the righteous.

Children should be taught to do right for right's sake and not for fear of punishment hereafter, that unselfishness is the highest virtue, that the most loving and the most unselfish are the happiest. The more kindness they give the more they receive. Finally everyone must obey nature's laws or they will suffer and be unhappy, like disobedient children who go contrary to their parents' instructions.

As portions of the Bible are quite unfit for children, this book should be kept from them until they are grown up, and it should never be referred to as superior to every other book. When they are old enough, they should be told that the Old Testament is a record of an ancient primitive people, relating to their history and religious development. Jehovah should never be represented to a child as being different from the gods of other nations, who were all cruel and ignorant, because man makes his gods in the likeness of himself.

The myths and miracles in the Bible should be explained to a child as stories, such as are found in all ancient literature, and not be taken as literally true. A child should not be taught something which he must discard when he grows up. Consequently religion should be confined to facts only, and neither theology nor superstition should have a place in religious instruction. Natural religion, as is contained in the Seven Principles of Spiritualism, is sufficient as guide and comforter to all in their journey through life from the cradle to the grave.

Example is better than precept, and if parents set

their children a good example, are unselfish, and show kindness to each other, the child will be more influenced by this example than by lessons on ethics and stories of the heroes of the past. Let the parents be the heroes to the child, as what they are the child by imitation may become.

History in the years to come will be taught truthfully, and not distorted as it is today to support the state religion. The history of Christianity will be taught as impartially as that of other religions. Its cruelty, its opposition to, and its contempt for, all advance in thought and progress will be told to children at school, so that they need not find it out for themselves in later life. Many held up as saints to children today will have to come off their pedestals and give place to men like Giordano Bruno and women like Hypatia, who were the real heroes of the past, their noble example and work being ignored because they would not accept Christianity.

More attention should be given to the works of the philosophers and thinkers of Rome and Greece. Because they expressed nobler, and more humane, thoughts than does Christianity, they have been ignored by our religious authorities, as comparisons are sometimes dangerous. History in the future will not be influenced by the Church, as it has been so flagrantly in the past, and still is. Our schools in the future must be entirely free from ecclesiasticism and priest-craft, and then the truth will be taught, but only then.

Some people believe that the Christian Church will adopt Spiritualism "lock, stock and barrel", when there will be no need for lay people to perform what is really the Church's work. I have given very serious consideration to this question, and I am fully convinced that the Church never gives such an idea a moment's consideration. Its attitude has always been, and is now, one of disdain and contempt. This bearing it has adopted since the priesthood came into being in the time of Cyprian in the 3rd century. Then the Pagan priests, who had become Christians, put themselves in the place of the ministers and mediums of the Apostolic Church, the mediums being finally abolished from all part in the service by Pope Damasus, an immoral and unscrupulous pontiff, on the instigation of Jerome in the 4th century.[1]

Should the Church now adopt Spiritualism, the whole organisation, as it exists at present, would fall to pieces. Its power lies in keeping the people ignorant and in maintaining the mysteries. Once the people know the truth and realise that salvation and reaching heaven are not dependent on a belief, or the performing of some rite or ceremony, the whole orthodox Church organisation will fall apart like a house of cards. The bishops know this, and that is why they dare not give anything away. Once admit a crack in the Church's structure and the people will desert the shaking edifice.

If the clergy today, in every pulpit in the land, told the people the truth, that survival was scientifically proved, that we all entered the etheric world at death, that our place there would be determined by our characters and the way we live here and not by our

---

[1] For details of this important event see *The Curse of Ignorance*, Vol. I, and *The Psychic Stream*.

beliefs, the entire ecclesiastical organisation of the Christian Church would cease to function. Spiritualism is something quite apart from churches, clergymen, holy books, and the performing of rites or ceremonies. Spiritualism stands for a scientific fact which can be verified by anybody who makes the necessary investigation, and once the principles of Spiritualism are accepted by the people there will be no further need for parsons or churches as now constituted.

I do not mean by this that once the population of this country believes in survival there will never be any religious meetings. The large and increasing number of Spiritualist meetings and churches throughout the country, and the world, proves that Spiritualists like to meet together as do believers in other religions. To assemble ourselves together is a social human desire, which will continue, but what will change is the order of the service and the views expressed. Mediums will more and more command the platform, to become ever-increasing competitors with those who falsely claim to be the appointed representatives of God on earth, and the revealers of his only revelation to mankind.

I believe that, as at present organised, the Spiritualist Church will continue to grow and flourish, as there the medium takes the first place. That is how it should be, and that is how nature, as I see it, intends it to be in the future. In the Christian Church it is the priest who takes the first place, and the medium is ignored, but we do not want to have ignorant speculations about the other world. We want to hear about the other world, from the other world, through the medium.

To me it is inconceivable that, as at present organised, the Christian Church would agree to the medium taking the place of the cleric. It has not yet even reached the stage of the medium being employed to give clairaudience, and the organisation will fight this innovation to the last. So Spiritualism need expect no help, support or encouragement from Christianity, so long as Christianity remains Christianity. The priesthood started the fight in the 3rd century, have continued it bitterly since then, and will be for ever hostile to the truth which clearly reveals their spiritual nakedness.

The strength of Spiritualism lies in our Home Circles where mediums are being developed. As this happens they will come before the public and do the work which is now being performed by an ecclesiastical organisation. Today these Home Circles number many thousands in Protestant countries throughout the world, and, in the years to come, as mediumship increases, their numbers will likewise advance. As Catholic countries become liberated from the yoke of Rome, Home Circles will start there, just as they have done in Protestant countries, until the time comes when the people will communicate with Etheria in the home. Thus all sects of priest-craft will cease to be because their need will have passed away.

Rescue Circles, which already exist in all English-speaking countries, will spring up in increasing numbers all over the world, and souls in darkness, wandering in the lower plane of Etheria, will be enlightened and guided into the fuller life of the higher planes. This rescue work will increase in scope just as mediums become more plentiful. In fact the whole future of Spiritualism is bound up in the number and quality of mediums. If these increase in numbers, and if they be endowed with psychic gifts of high quality, nothing can prevent the spread of Spiritualism, but, if this development does not take place, Spiritualism will not grow and gather weight. It is the evidence that mediums produce which increases the Spiritualist ranks, and, this being so, we are in the hands of nature, the mother of us all, mediumship being an hereditary gift which is passed on from generation to generation.

Spiritualist Churches, as they are managed today, are not all perfect; nothing is, for that matter. Much work lies ahead in raising the intellectual level of the individual church leaders and their congregations. The system is right, the breadth of vision, the toleration, and the freedom from creeds and dogmas are all that can be desired. The basis of the Spiritualist Church organisation is sound. All views are welcomed from the Spiritualist platform, and I have spoken from time to time from such platforms on which were sitting people born into the various sects of Christendom, into Buddhism, Hinduism, Judaism and Mohammedanism. This shows how Spiritualism destroys all barriers, and how religious differences are caused only by the drapings hung round a central truth.

The intellectual level, however, of some of the speakers must be raised. What is termed clairaudience, and in the smaller churches is accepted as such, is sometimes nothing of the kind. It degenerates at times into vague descriptions of Etherians who could not be recognised by any stretch of imagination. This must be stopped; the leaders are well aware of this weakness and are endeavouring to correct it.

Until, however, the level of intelligence of the church leaders, and their congregations who tolerate this, rises, the Spiritualists' National Union can do little. Time and education alone will raise the level, and slowly clairvoyance and clairaudience will improve everywhere until they reach the wonderful heights they have attained in the leading Spiritualist churches.

I have had unique opportunities of studying this remarkable gift of clairaudience. I have spoken on Spiritualism in the largest halls of most of the cities and towns of Great Britain and Ireland. I do this as a duty, taking neither fee nor travelling expenses. My reward consists in knowing that my addresses give comfort and help to many. This about myself, however, is a digression and I only refer to these meetings for the purpose of emphasising this wonderful gift of clairaudience which some people have.

At some of my meetings my address is followed by clairaudience, and I think I can claim that I have heard and seen messages given to hundreds of people, and that these messages contained thousands of facts. I keep notes of these, and I am safe in saying that 95 per cent. of the facts given are accepted as correct. Of the remaining 5 per cent. I would judge that a certain number of non-recognitions is due to the incident referred to being forgotten by the recipient, and the rest to dourness on the part of the recipient, who is determined not to admit anything. After one of my meetings I overheard a man saying to another,

"It was all true enough but it was for me and me alone, and I wasn't going to let the audience know anything about my private affairs."

It is certainly impossible for the recognition of these messages to be arranged beforehand with members of the audience, and it is also quite impossible for the clairaudient to know normally the private details given to the people in the audience. The reason fraud is impossible to imagine is because clairaudients go from town to town, throughout the country, and arrive just before the meeting commences. The fees they are paid are so small that to suggest that they are able to afford to maintain an organisation of any kind for the purpose of obtaining family secrets is quite ridiculous. The only people who can know the details given are the members of the family, either on earth or in Etheria.

The evidence is now so voluminous in favour of clairaudience, that we must accept the explanation these clairaudients give that they hear voices which normal people do not hear. The character and integrity of our leading clairaudients are above reproach. I have experienced clairaudience given, not once but often, by Horace Leaf, Thomas Wyatt, Arthur Ford, Stella Hughes, Helen Hughes, Estelle Roberts, Annie Johnston and Helen Spiers. I know them personally and I can vouch for their integrity.

When they tell me that they can hear voices and see Etherians not heard or seen by normal people, I am bound to accept their statements as correct. As they give the clairaudience from the same platform from which I have been speaking, I can hear them talking in a low voice to the Etherians who are giving them messages to pass on to people in the audience. I hear what the clairaudients say to their friends in the etheric world, but I cannot hear what they hear, and it is by what the clairaudients say to their audience that they are judged. One thing certain is that the clairaudient is receiving a message from some unseen individual and passing on what is heard. That is a definite opinion I have reached after many years of close study and investigation of this fascinating phenomenon.

The accuracy of their messages, as I have already said, is remarkable. Full christian and surnames are given of those who are purporting to speak from Etheria. These generally come first, and then the full addresses are given of the places they lived at on earth. After the name and address are recognised and accepted by the person in the audience to whom the clairaudient points, intimate details of incidents follow which relate to the life on earth of the person communicating. Sitting as I do on the platform I can see clearly that what is given is accepted as true, as everyone spoken to is asked to say yes or no to each item of information.

Though, as I say, I have heard thousands of facts given in this way, I am still impressed by this great gift some people have of hearing voices and seeing forms which are unsensed by the ears and eyes of the vast majority. This gift of clairaudience and clairvoyance is increasing, and I believe that this supernormal faculty, which can be observed by such large numbers, and be at the same time so convincing, will, more than anything else, bring home to the people the reality of Etheria and its inhabitants.

As clairaudients develop in number, more and more

people will become witnesses to the truth of what Spiritualism stands for, and, in my opinion, there is no doubt whatever that clairaudients will take a leading part in the Church of the future. If there were one hundred men and women in this country with the gifts possessed by our leading clairaudients, it would only take a comparatively short time to convince the people of Great Britain that Spiritualism stands for the truth, and that the claims it makes can be supported by evidence.

Some people jeer at clairvoyance of an inferior type, and their scorn is sometimes rightly deserved, but they should remember that it was the Christian Church which burned or drowned all our mediums up to within the last two hundred years. Only slowly is this hereditary gift returning, and Spiritualists are doing their best to develop this rare gift which Christianity did its utmost to destroy when it had the power. In ignorance and fear the Christian Church, which should have protected and developed mediumship, destroyed the mediums and so kept back from humanity a great truth which, when understood and accepted by mankind, will revolutionise for the better the entire human race.

When the Church could no longer destroy the mediums, it denounced Spiritualists as servants of the devil, and today it prevents the B.B.C. from broadcasting Spiritualist services or talks on the subject. Well it knows that Spiritualism is the greatest force opposed to orthodox religion, and, for this reason, wherever it has the power, the Church will keep it under or use it for its own purposes. Orthodoxy will fight to the last to preserve its organisation, and only by receiving less and less support from the public will it ultimately be conquered.

The Church has had its use in the past, comforting the ignorant by myths and legends. The Church of the future will be of even greater service, but it must be a reformed institution. The Church of the past has had great powers which it abused on almost every occasion when it was supreme. Nevertheless it has been a source of help and comfort to many, and has kept alive the belief in survival, though its teachings of the after-life have been so crude and cruel that it is questionable if these have not caused as much misery as comfort. Those within its walls got the comfort, while its clergy denounced, imprisoned and persecuted all outside. Its influence, moreover, was always against the people obtaining greater knowledge and improving their social conditions.

Only now are our slums being demolished, and we are beginning to realise the evil in the traffic in weapons of destruction. Some day we shall realise the incongruity of having Armistice Day turned into a military parade, and practically the entire seating accommodation of Westminster Abbey reserved for representatives of the Army, Navy and Air Force, civilians being told that they can occupy any seats left vacant. This is the order of precedence throughout the land on this day devoted to prayers for peace. Churches on this day are decorated with banners and flags, martial music beats the air, and men wearing uniforms and medals meet one at every turn.

The Church, dishonest today as it ever has been, pays lip service to the Prince of Peace on the one hand, and on the other joins up with the God of Battles and the Lord of Hosts. Orthodoxy, folly and ignorance go together. That is why traditional Christianity and war are inseparable, because ignorance has been at the root of every war, and war will not stop until the time comes when knowledge takes the place of ignorance.

Today we are living in fast-changing times, and now that mediums are safe from destruction it is only a question of time till Spiritualism takes the place of Christianity, and mediums take the place of the priesthood. When the Church was forced by public opinion to cease burning witches, its power began to wane. It claimed, and still does, that it only is the medium between earth and heaven and that was the reason it gave for burning Joan of Arc and quarter of a million so-called witches. When it could no longer do so, mediumship revealed its false assertions and that only nature provides the connection between the two worlds.

The Spiritualists' National Union is an organisation for the purpose of protecting and encouraging mediumship. Such a body in the future will be the organisation through which religious teaching will be given to the people, and gradually it will take the place of the organisation of the present Christian church. The Church buildings will still be the property of the people, who will continue to use them, but what is taught in them will be changed. The Pantheon at Rome, once a Pagan temple, is now a Christian church. So Saint Paul's and Westminster Cathedrals, now Christian churches, may some day become Spiritualist churches.

The people themselves will force the change by failing to attend the orthodox Church services, and the time will come when the teachings of Spiritualism will be more widely accepted in proportion as orthodox teachings become discarded. This movement will increase and gather greater force, though from year to year the change will be little noticed. It will be a slow development, like the one which has reduced the power of the clergy over the last two hundred years. Let us hope that within another hundred years their power will have become quite negligible. This will be the consequence of education and the teachings of Spiritualism. Orthodoxy will, however, fight this innovation to the last, and, as I have already said, sink eventually into oblivion, because of fewer and fewer people supporting its doctrines.

When this happens everywhere mankind will have become mentally free of religious superstitions, and this will help the human family to live in greater harmony amongst themselves. When this much longed for time comes about, humanity will then worship in one cathedral with similar ideas and ideals. Religious sects and divisions will then cease to be, as everyone by then will be enlightened about his destiny. When this comes about the Church of the future will embrace the universe in its teachings, and its members will be all mankind. Its priests will be the mediums, the teachers and all the healers of humanity. Its altar will be dedicated to love and service, and within its precincts the two worlds will meet.

CHAPTER XI.

REALITY UNFOLDING.

THROUGHOUT this book I have tried to stress the fact that Mind is the great reality. History tells the story of how humanity has been led upwards by following the lead of those minds more developed than the rest. With the spread of education, the mental level has risen, but still some minds lead the multitude and this will probably always be so.

Education enlarges the vision. The uneducated person is like one dependent on his two eyes. Education is a telescope and, if turned backwards in history or forwards into the future, it gives an enlarged vision to the user. Without education we are without knowledge. Without knowledge we are parochial in our opinions and ideas. It is wiser to eat of the fruit of the Tree of Knowledge, and be banished from the Eden of Ignorance, than to leave it untouched. Better to err and learn than make no mistakes and no progress. Progress comes from making mistakes, and error rectified leads us to the road of truth.

To primitive man, without knowledge, the world was bounded by the limit of his vision. Education has slowly enlarged our vision. We see more, we see further, and we see better. Thus our mind enlarges, our ideas change, and our judgment improves. With our greater knowledge, our judgment of the past and the present differs from that of our parents or our grandparents. We have a wider perspective when we look back in time and forward in time, because we have more facts to guide our judgment. Who is it we have to thank, and to whom are we indebted for the unfolding of the universe which has already taken place?

Who is it we should thank for what we know and are today? We must thank the inventors, the discoverers, and the thinkers. These are the pioneers who led humanity up the rocky road of progress. They have gone before and cleared the way by removing the stones, over which their followers would have stumbled. On every hand was the mysterious and the sinister. The thinkers went before with the torch of knowledge, in the light of which the inexplicable and the perplexing faded away.

The priests followed with the multitude, seeking every nook and cranny in the hedges alongside the road on which humanity was travelling, and frightened the multitude by their mysterious warnings. They were for ever waving the red flag of danger. The thinkers carried the green flag of progress and urged the people forward. The priests lagged behind crying "Stop" while the thinkers called "Come on." The thinkers ahead were denounced and traduced by the multitude behind, and often persecuted and murdered. The thoughtful, however, have been proved right, and the priests and the mob have been wrong. The priests have retarded reality unfolding, while the thinkers lived in an unfolding universe, and, by their increased knowledge, have added greatly to the happiness of mankind. The rational thinkers have now an established reputation, which they have won for themselves by always being guided by the lamp of reason.

Who, then, have we to thank for the countless blessings we now enjoy? We must thank all the pioneers, the men and women who gave us their thoughts and example, and who have transformed our way of life beyond the dreams of by-gone kings. They sowed the seed for us to reap the harvest, and fought through the jungle of ignorance to the light. Living as we now do amidst the triumphs of genius, and in the liberty won for us by the martyrs of progress, let us look back and remember those who gave us the priceless inheritance of liberty and knowledge.

To early man the earth was a place circumscribed within his own means of locomotion. We must thank the Chinese for the invention of the compass, which was copied and improved by the Arabs, and finally perfected by Lord Kelvin. This led to navigation and navigation led to discovery. Columbus, with the help of some merchants of Palos in southern Spain, set out across the Atlantic with three ships to find Asia and its reputed vast wealth. He believed that the way to India could be reached by sailing west, being inspired by the discoveries of Marco Polo, the greatest traveller of his age, who discovered India, China and Japan. Columbus thought he had discovered India by sailing west, whereas he had found the islands of a new continent. Marco Polo was therefore the cause behind the discovery of America.

Cabot was really the first to discover the mainland of America, though he thought it was Asia, but we must not forget that five centuries earlier the Viking, Eric the Red, landed in the far north of the new world and that he was the grandfather of the first white child, a girl, to be born there. His deeds are recorded in Icelandic literature, the first country in Europe to have a literature of its own. Captain Cook put Australia and New Zealand on the map. The Magellan expedition was the first to circumnavigate the globe and prove it to be round. Drake was the first Englishman to see the Pacific Ocean, and Vasco da Gama discovered the sea route to India by the Cape of Good Hope. Livingstone helped as much as anyone to open up a large part of Africa. These are the representatives of many others who explored this earth, and the sum total of their discoveries has given us increased knowledge and greatly additional wealth.

To the scientists our thanks are also due. The Moslems, in the 10th century, were the first to build colleges and observatories throughout the wide territory, from Persia to Spain, over which they ruled. They introduced the ten numerals, studied mathematics, mapped the earth and the heavens, and gave the planets the names by which they are still known. Throughout Christendom, in the Dark Ages, no one thought deeply about anything. Roger Bacon was the first Englishman to think and investigate in a scientific way. He was the father of English Science, and, from fear of the knowledge he amassed, he was kept apart in a monastery by the Church authorities for eighteen years.

The scientists have proved to us how much is hidden in nature, and how little we learn of her wondrous treasure by superficial thought. By investigation, by experiment, by discovery, they have revealed to us a new world undreamed of by our ancestors. They have improved our standard of living, our comfort, our health and our means of locomotion. They have shaken the world's superstitions to their foundations, and made men think instead of just accept.

Copernicus published his book, *On the Revolutions of the Heavenly Bodies*, in 1543. Lippershey in 1608 so arranged lenses that objects were exaggerated, and he thus invented the telescope which enabled Galileo, on the night of 7th January, 1610, to prove the truth of what Copernicus had asserted. Later Galileo published the result of his discoveries in his book *The System of the World*, and with his telescope proved the insignificance of the earth, besides the immensity and greatness of the universe. Leonardo da Vinci, the greatest mind of the Renaissance, Copernicus, Galileo and Kepler were the fathers of present-day scientific thought, and they were followed by Herschel and Laplace. On the foundations these men laid, our modern science of astronomy has been built.

Lavoisier and Priestley discovered the basis of the laws of chemistry and so displaced the alchemist. Newton, the first mathematical physicist and a master of exposition, made comprehensible, a century later, Kepler's three laws by his discovery of the law of gravitation. Franklin tapped the lightning, which led to the age of electricity, and Lyell calculated the age of the earth from the story the rocks can tell us. Let us thank these pioneers, and many others, while also remembering Humboldt, Haeckel and Lamarck for all the bricks they added to the temple of knowledge.

Before the age of science, humanity knew

nothing of its ancestry. Darwin and Alfred Russel Wallace jointly contributed to give us the story of our origin. Faraday, the father of electricity, introduced the age of modern scientific thought. Clerk-Maxwell, Helmholtz and Hertz discovered the ether waves, which made it possible for us to hear the music and the voice transmitted by our wireless set. Likewise their discoveries enabled us to relate Etheria to the rest of the universe in terms of vibrations. Otherwise our future state could never have been understood or comprehended.

Within recent years great progress has been made in our understanding of the construction of matter, that which seems so solid but is in reality not so. Dalton, one hundred years ago, laid the foundation of this knowledge, Crookes continued the work, and Marie Curie discovered radium which greatly helped in the quest. J. J. Thomson revealed matter as composed of electrons and protons, Rutherford contributed much to our knowledge of the structure of the atom, and Einstein's theories and calculations enabled physicists to understand some unsolved problems. Millikan measured the electron. Soddy shed fresh light on radio-chemistry, and Richards added to our understanding of atomic weights. Aston, Ramsay, Rayleigh and Moseley further increased our acquaintance of the substance to which our minds react, and lastly, but not least, Langmuir, one of the most brilliant American scientists, has done much to explain chemical action.

These great experimental thinkers, and others like them, have made it possible for us to comprehend more clearly what physical substance really is. Now we are able to contemplate it as a range of vibrations within a fixed limit, and find a place in space for further ranges outside our ken. Thus we can envisage, on a strictly scientific basis, the etheric world which affects etheric minds, just as the range we term physical causes the images in the minds of the people on earth. These mind images we term thought, and thinking constitutes existence, which, as the result of our increased knowledge of matter, can now be related to another order of life besides the one we know on earth.

Inspired by the progress made by Science, inventors followed fast. Gurney discovered the incandescent light, and turned night into day. Arkwright, Cartwright, Lee and Crompton, by their inventions, made it possible for the poor to wear clothes that the rich would have been proud to possess two hundred years previously. Thimmonier gave us the sewing machine and all it means to every home. Gutenberg, by inventing the printing press, provided the means for the circulation of knowledge, because the Arabs by then had copied from the Chinese the way to make paper. Caxton was the first Englishman to set up a printing press in England and standardise the English language, thus preserving from further degradation the English of Chaucer. Braille made it possible for the blind to read.

The power of steam was known in the 2nd century B.C. when Heron, the Greek, was the first to turn it to practical use. From 1629 onwards various attempts were made to produce a serviceable steam engine, Branca, Somerset, Savery and Newcomen laying the foundation on which James Watt was to construct the first modern condensing steam engine which has conferred untold blessings on mankind. Nasmyth gave us the steam hammer which can just crack an egg, or forge a propeller shaft and so make possible the ships of today.

Roads up to the 18th century were just dirt tracks with no solid foundations, and it was McAdam who taught us how to make them, on which wheel traffic became easy. For these Trevithick produced the first steam locomotive, but it was soon superseded by the locomotive on rails. Brindley built canals, and was followed by Telford, the great canal, road and bridge builder, whose contemporary was the famous engineer John Rennie who also built many large bridges, buildings, docks and harbours.

George and Robert Stephenson were the pioneers of steam traction by rail and were our first builders of rail locomotives, rail-roads and railway bridges. Brunel built railways, viaducts, tunnels and docks, and produced boots by machinery so that today the world's population can be shod by machines occupying a comparatively small area of ground. Graham Bell gave us the telephone, Marconi the radio, and Karl Benz the motor car. Last, but not least, we must remember Archimedes the Greek, born 287 B.C., the father of all inventions and scientific discovery, and the greatest mathematician of his age.

Following the advent of science came the desire for greater human liberty. Throughout the pages of history we find that this desire came up against vested interests and authority, especially during the era of scientific thought, when man's mind began to expand its narrow bounds. Foremost stand out the names of Clarkson, Sharp, Wilberforce, Paine and Buxton, who roused Britain to the evils of slavery, and so also did Garrison in America, who did more than any American of his time to change opinion about the employment of slave labour. Wycliffe was one of the first to withstand the authority of pope and priest, and denounce the wickedness of the Church. Luther broke the power of the Holy See at Rome. Simon de Montfort laid the basis for our Parliamentary system of government in the 13th century, and this became, as the years passed, a government of the people for the people.

Throughout the Christian era, from the time the Church obtained its political power, many martyrs have suffered in their stand for liberty of thought and expression. This also took place in other lands professing other faiths, but it is particularly true of Christendom, in comparison with other places and other times, because here lived a virile people who became the leaders of mankind. These stalwarts for what they considered truth are so numerous, and all equally heroic, that no one name can be picked out from the others. This indeed was a great and noble army of suffering heretics who died in their fight to keep the torch of liberty burning.

During the 18th and 19th centuries outstanding men strove to free the people from the tyranny of the Church. Voltaire in France, by his writings, exposed the infamies of the Roman Catholic Church, the falsity of its doctrines, its abominable cruelties, and did much to break its power. Ingersoll, more than any other, helped to break the domination of Protestantism throughout the world. He, more than any other man, exposed the errors of the Christian religion in a way that people could understand. Voltaire and Ingersoll are representatives of outstanding minds which led the more educated section of Christendom away from the Church, and into the light of knowledge.

Thomas Paine, that stalwart of political and religious liberty, was the first to advocate the United States of the World. He, along with Jefferson and Franklin, drew up the Declaration of Independence of the United States of America, and in 1779 he introduced into the Assembly of Pennsylvania the first measure to abolish slavery. What Paine commenced, Lincoln completed. To Paine the world was his country, and Victor Hugo one hundred years later advocated the United States of Europe as a nucleus on which to build the ideal federation of nations, first envisaged by this far-seeing benevolent Anglo-American champion of liberty.

Throughout history we find outstanding men who fought and conquered tyrants. Miltiades at Marathon broke the power of Darius the Persian, the most powerful monarch of the east, and Themistocles defeated his son Xerxes at sea when he tried to repeat his father's experiment of bringing Europe under oriental domination. The victories of Gustavus Adolphus consolidated the work of the Reformation, by defeating the Roman Catholic forces which had gathered to bring Protestant Europe, by force, back to the Roman Catholic Church. This terrible religious war lasted for thirty years.

Howard and Drake shattered the power of Spain when she attempted to bring England again under the domination of the Pope. Aided by the forces of nature, by wind and storm, they defeated the Grand Armada when it seemed as if our doom was sealed.

Washington ended the tyranny of England by defeating her forces, and then was formed the United States of America which became an example of democracy and freedom to the people of Europe groaning under their tyrannical kings. Wellington, at Waterloo, ended Napoleon's dream of dictatorship, Bolivar freed Spanish America from the yoke of Spain, and we are all too well aware of those to whom our gratitude goes out for saving Europe from German tyranny in our own times.

With the development of intelligence, and the advance of knowledge, leaders arose who improved the law and government of the state and established justice. Throughout history we find men in authority who did their best to govern fairly and justly. Hammurabi (1792-1750 B.C.), King of Babylon, gave his country the wonderful code of laws from which those attributed to Moses were copied. Solon made the laws of ancient Greece. He repealed the cruel laws of Draco, which resembled those of England at the beginning of the 19th century, when scores of petty offences were punishable by death. Solon put just laws in their place, abolished injustice, and made the laws of Athens the pattern for the world. The laws made in Babylon, Athens and Rome form the basis of the legislation of all civilised countries. Julius Caesar made wise and good laws. He brought civilisation to barbarous Gaul, and a hundred years afterwards Agricola laid the foundation for good government in Britain.

The feeling, which has grown stronger as the years passed, that we must treat our neighbours as we ourselves wish to be treated, has grown much more definite within recent years. Consequently, with the help received from the public, men like Barnardo, Müller and Quarrier, took pity on the poor children and gave them homes which their parents could not provide. John Howard exposed the appalling conditions of our prisoners, herded together in dens of iniquity in this country and throughout Europe at the end of the 18th century. He was followed by Elizabeth Fry, who taught us that prisoners were still human beings and should be treated humanely. She exposed the horrible conditions in which they lived, and brought about the prison reform to which Howard had dedicated his life. Then it came to be realised that it was more sensible to build schools to educate the children as to the right way to live, than to build prisons to house the ignorant who became criminals.

Just as schools have increased, so in proportion has crime declined, but we have not yet learned that it is wrong to send criminals to Etheria by means of hanging, shooting or electrocution. The day will come when these unfortunate people will be confined, during which time efforts will be made to develop their minds. Their reformation must come sometime and it might as well start here.

Winstanley, because of the number of lives lost by wrecks on the Eddystone Rock, decided to build on it a lighthouse. For many years he fought the opposition of Trinity House, which was founded by Henry VIII for the purpose of accommodating the Trinity House brethren, whose duty it was to pray for the souls of all who were lost at sea. In return for this they were given the salvage of all the wrecks around our coasts. The more wrecks there were, the more they earned for saying prayers. Consequently they opposed Winstanley's scheme, but he won through in the end. He erected his lighthouse, built of wood, and perished in it during a great storm.

Samuel Plimsoll, appalled at what was known as coffin ships, a name given to overloaded ships, managed, after great opposition by vested interests, to get all vessels marked by what is known as the Plimsoll line, so that lawfully they could not be overloaded. Shaftesbury laboured throughout his entire life to reduce the time children had to work, and to improve their terrible conditions. His name will not be found on the Church's calendar of saints, but, by all who have the welfare of humanity at heart, he will ever be acknowledged as one of the greatest of this world's humanitarians. His entire life was devoted to this one object and, against the opposition of vested interests, he helped to free the poor and down-trodden from their oppressors.

What Shaftesbury did for the poor Richard Martin did for animals. He succeeded, after years of work and discouragement, in getting the first laws passed in this country for the purpose of protecting animals against cruelty, and was one of the founders of the Royal Society for the Prevention of Cruelty to Animals.

As our knowledge grew so our health improved. Much has been done to diminish pain and suffering, plagues and disease. Sanitation has enormously increased the standard of health and abolished the scourge of plague. Hippocrates, the father of medicine, practised his art 2,300 years ago and showed the Greeks how cures could be effected. Galen, in Rome, six centuries later, laid the foundation for our present methods of healing. The record of the lives of those early healers, and their sympathy for suffering humanity, show us to what heights those ancient Pagans rose in thought and action. Unfortunately Christianity suppressed their discoveries and, instead of attributing disease to natural causes, assigned it to devils. Now we know the power of the mind over our ailments. What the mind cannot cure here on earth it has the power to do in Etheria, as it has more control over the etheric body, which does not tire there as it does here and is not subject to the ills to which flesh is heir.

After the Renaissance we find men arising who began to study anew the writings of those pre-Christian doctors. Harvey and Servetus demonstrated the circulation of the blood. To Harvey belongs the credit of placing the science of medicine on a firm foundation. Hunter raised surgery to a science, but for a time it seemed as if his efforts would be fruitless, owing to the number of deaths which were due to blood poisoning and gangrene. That danger passed when Pasteur and Lister, who followed him, drew the sting from the invisible microbe and thus made operations safe. Jenner killed the scourge of smallpox, to become known as the father of preventive medicine, and Simpson, by the discovery of chloroform, stilled the throb of pain. Florence Nightingale, the mother of nursing, laid the foundation of the modern hospital and nursing home. These pioneers are representative of the men and women who have worked and laboured to improve the health of mankind. They were denounced in their day and generation, even by those who were working with the same ends in view.

Throughout the ages there have always been path-finders who tried to enlighten the human mind. Socrates, Plato and Aristotle, the supreme thinkers of their time, gave the world some mighty thoughts, and Cicero, Marcus Aurelius, Epictetus and Epicurus words of great wisdom. These master minds were amongst the first to put knowledge before superstition and thinking before faith and blind belief. Euclid taught men to think and reason, and Xenophon, by his writings, showed the danger of the power of Persia spreading across Europe. Thucydides and Herodotus told us all there was to know about the ancient world, and Tacitus and Livy recorded the story of Rome and its empire.

Within our own times Layard, Rawlinson and George Smith unearthed the story, inscribed on bricks, of the empire of Assyria. Vittorino da Feltre was the first European schoolmaster, and set the example, which was followed a hundred years later at the Renaissance, when people began to think instead of just believe. Spinoza and Kant relit the lamp of reason which had been extinguished since the closing of the schools of philosophy in the 6th century. Locke set men thinking deeply on the right way to live and govern themselves, and Berkeley looked behind appearances to find reality. Dr. Johnson, one of the greatest scholars of his age, fixed the meaning of words by producing the first English dictionary, and Gibbon, Hume and Macaulay gave us the history of Europe and England.

We must not forget to thank the artists and the architects, those who put their ideas on canvas and those who carved them into stone. Reynolds,

Gainsborough, Rembrandt, Constable, Turner and many others have all added to the happiness of the world by their beautiful pictures. Pericles rebuilt Athens and made it a city of art and beauty, the wonder of the age. Phidias built there the Parthenon and adorned it with five hundred of the most perfect statues ever carved. They were so beautiful that they were worshipped as heaven-made things. It is to the Greeks, and their literature and culture, our thoughts should turn rather than to Palestine if we wish to pay reverence to those who brought light to the world. Moreover it was to Greece that our thinkers went in the 16th and 17th centuries to rekindle the knowledge extinguished by Christianity.

In the time of Pericles and Phidias culture was at its zenith, when the thoughts of the people were directed towards learning, philosophy, art and poetry. If this had continued, and the schools had remained open in the years between then and now, how different would our condition be today! How much more advanced would be our culture, our knowledge, our art and our wisdom! Unfortunately the waves of ignorance swept over this golden shore of knowledge, and the Christian Church submerged it by its superstition and persecution. Creeds supplanted knowledge, and Europe sank beneath the waves, out of the light, into the night of the Dark Ages.

The rediscovery of the literature and art of ancient Greece, in the 16th century, brought about the Renaissance, when we find that men like Michael Angelo carved beauty out of the rugged stone. Then arose great master architects, such as Inigo Jones and Christopher Wren, who left their thoughts in stone for all London to see. In Europe eminent architects also built magnificent buildings to commemorate this age of mental development, but these men are too numerous to mention here by name.

The musicians and poets have gladdened humanity. We must thank Handel for his great compositions, and Mendelssohn, Beethoven and Wagner for music which has enraptured millions. Mozart has gladdened the world with his harmonies. Stradivarius brought the violin to the highest point of perfection by his genius for thoroughness and detail, and on this instrument Kreisler has thrilled multitudes. Shakespeare, the brightest literary star of the Renaissance, encompassed the earth with his ideas, and recorded in verse and story most of the knowledge of his time. Two hundred years later he was followed by Goethe, the master mind of his age, whose interests, like those of Shakespeare, were universal.

Our homes have been made happier, brighter and better by those who added to their beauty. Art decorates our walls and adorns our daily life. Chippendale and Sheraton gave us beautiful furniture, and Wedgwood used his genius as an artist to bring the production of pottery to a high art.

The name of Sir William Crookes stands out in this roll of fame, as, in his time, besides doing so much for physics, he did more than any other man to establish the fact that our religious instinct has a scientific basis, and that there is a reason for it which can be scientifically demonstrated. Attacked by his brother scientists, scoffed and jeered at, he pursued his purpose and demonstrated to the satisfaction of any unbiased and intelligent-thinking individual that life continues after death, and that the men and women of Etheria can come back to earth whenever a suitable medium is available. The veil between the two worlds was pulled apart during the course of his wonderful experiences and experiments. He represents a large number of men and women who, by patient research, have placed psychic science on a firm basis, and proved to all who care to study the results of their labours that we are psychic beings, and that communication takes place between us on earth who wear the physical garment and those who have discarded it.

The leaders of the human race, of which the foregoing are amongst its most outstanding representatives, have helped in the unfolding of reality. We speak of them as dead but in truth they did not die, and, with numerous others whom they represent, they did not pass away into oblivion. Their minds are still active, still working, and still pursuing the path of progress. As they led humanity on earth, they are leading humanity in Etheria, and some day we can meet them if we have the wish to do so. There, just as here, are great leaders to whom mankind will always look for guidance and try to follow.

The master minds of the human race have brought us to the position we are in today, and to them we record our thanks. If it had not been for such pioneers, humanity would still be pursuing the life of the savage. The race has been raised to what it is today by our ancestors following the gleam those pione rracersied on ahead. They brought knowledge to mankind, and this great mental asset has immensely increased human happiness. Knowledge is strength, because it helps us through life, and the more we have of it the more the universe unfolds before us.

We cannot have too much knowledge, as it comes from a universal sea which increases instead of diminishes, the more we draw from it. There is no selfishness in obtaining knowledge, and it is one of the greatest things worth having. The more you have of it the more you can give away, and the more you can help those who lack it. The more we give the more we receive. Let us therefore all strive after knowledge, but always remember to combine with it wisdom, as without wisdom we are unable to use our knowledge aright.

Let us thank all the good and the noble in whatever situation in life they lived. Let us thank all who have done what was in their power to live lives of usefulness by helping others, by endeavouring to raise the fallen, and to help the helpless. Our gratitude goes out to all martyrs who fell before the tyrant for the sake of honour and freedom of thought, to those who put truth, kindness and justice before all else, and to all who were persecuted because they brought increased mental light to the world. Our thoughts turn to them in thankfulness, as, by their example, we enjoy the comfort, happiness and liberty which are ours today.

Those sensitive people, our mediums, deserve our lasting gratitude. Most of them in the past have suffered from persecution, suspicion and, in some cases, impaired health because of the lack of knowledge of those who sat with them. Bravely they persevered and carried on, the consequence being that now our leading mediums are becoming respected and honoured by the very people who only a few years ago jeered at them and doubted their honesty.

The foregoing men and women, whose names I have mentioned, and thousands of others, are the heroes of the human race, and to them our thanks are due for their example and for what they have accomplished. In this land of the free we can now imagine all they suffered, and remember their courage, fortitude and endurance, so that honest thinking might prevail. Never should we forget the pioneers of the past, all the good men and women, who helped to turn the night of mental ignorance into the day of knowledge and increased understanding. Let us be grateful to those who brought about the dethronement of false gods and extinguished hell's eternal fire. Let us venerate the breakers of chains, the destroyers of dungeons, the healers of disease, the relievers of pain, the founders of free states, the champions of free thought, the makers of just laws, and all who worked for the increase of human happiness. What they have done has turned their dungeons into shrines, and made their scaffolds sacred.

History is just the story of the activities of the mind in its contact with the physical. Each mind plays its part in navigating its own ship, which we term the body. Each individual can be likened to a ship in sail on the ocean of life, moved by the winds of different ideas, and guided by the compass of reason. The more accurate the compass the straighter the course we sail. The more skilfully the sails are set the more we can take advantage of the winds of knowledge which carry us on our course. Each one of us is a unit in himself or herself, and, like ships, we can exchange signals with each other.

Some minds, like well navigated ships, can catch the breeze of knowledge in advance of others, and forge ahead, while others lag behind with their sails fluttering in the wind. All, however, are sailing for a destination where life will be easier for those who have set their course to the best of their ability. Just as each one makes the most of the opportunities offered by the breeze of knowledge, the sooner will he reach the haven of understanding where the unfolding of the universe will be completed.

Looking back on history we see humanity ever struggling upwards towards the light. Owing to the lack of knowledge its course has been too often one of mistakes and failures. Fortunately each mistake and each failure has taught its lesson, which the generation that followed has not always forgotten. Nature is not our enemy, and if we use our intelligence she will become our friend. Why she seems sometimes to be against us is because we are ignorant of her laws, and so become her servant instead of being her master. When we have learned her laws aright, as we shall some day, we shall take a wider outlook, when that which is not now understood will become clear.

The mind of man can be either a garden or a desert. If it is watered by the rain of liberty, and wooed by the sun of freedom, it grows and flourishes, but if liberty and freedom are absent it becomes a desert. What we are today is due to the fact that our ancestors won this liberty for us, and our minds can now grow unrestrained by the tyrant's lash. When men and women were uneducated they were slaves to their masters who ruled both Church and State. Gradually the change has come, and today in English-speaking countries we can proudly assert that there is complete liberty of thought and action, provided we concede to others what we claim for ourselves.

In this land of the free the only infidel is the man or woman who does not live up to his or her highest ideals, and the only blasphemy is to be untrue to truth and to deny facts which are supported by evidence. This definition of these two words now finds acceptance amongst the educated, whose minds have expanded because liberty of thought has enabled us to develop in intelligence. Bradlaugh was the last public victim of Christian intolerance, and, as he died in 1891 worn out by his fight for freedom of thought, it may be said that intellectual liberty, for which the pioneers fought, is but two generations old. Young though it is, its strengthening beams of light are opening up for us a wonderful vista, which is becoming clearer and more vivid every day.

Liberty lubricates thought, which tyranny clogs. As the mechanism of the mind moves faster, our thoughts produce those wondrous changes in surrounding substance which add to our comfort, pleasure and happiness. We are in reality following after Etheria. We have, however, more difficulties than Etherians have, as our minds work on a grosser material which makes it more difficult for us to accomplish our desires. In Etheria different laws operate, because there surrounding matter is less gross, it is finer, and the minds of Etherians can mould it to their desires without the physical labour necessary with us on earth.

Nevertheless we are obtaining control over our surroundings to an increasing degree, and are thus approaching to a greater similarity between our conditions here and the conditions there. The gross matter of earth necessitates an intermediary of some kind to enable us to mould it to our desires. This accessory is either our hands or feet, and when we are limited to these life is primitive. The next device is a tool of some kind or another, and when this is used our conditions are less primitive. Now we have learned how to make machines which do the work of hands and tools, and consequently we can extract from nature's storehouse more of what we desire, our life thus becoming fuller, happier and easier.

In Etheria they are as much farther on in their capacity to mould substance as we are in advance of the savage. The savage cannot comprehend, for instance, how machines can produce, by the work of two hundred men, all the iron framework required for all the motor-cars in the United States which only a few years ago needed twenty thousand men to produce. Likewise it is difficult for us to understand how it is that in Etheria they can change the shape of their substance by concentrated thought, without the intermediary of hands, tools or machines.

One thing we know is that the mental process both here and in Etheria is the same. The mind first images its desires, and, as the result of these mind pictures, substance is altered in shape. We on earth require the help of an intermediary. Though we cannot employ so direct a method in achieving our plans as they can, still we can claim that our thoughts, or mind images, precede all the changes we make in substance. In Etheria other laws prevail, of which we know nothing, but from what we are told it is evident that mind, if directed on substance intensely, can change the shape and form of etheric substance. This direct method of obtaining one's desires simplifies life enormously and eliminates the labour and toil required on earth to obtain our desires.

This moulding of substance on earth into the likeness of our mind images requires effort, but looking back over the pages of history we notice that the effort is becoming less and less, and the results achieved are becoming greater. Our primitive ancestors used as much effort to cut down a tree, slice it up and burn or carve it into the shape of a boat, as we expend in producing a motor-launch. When the difference in the results obtained is considered, it is evident that mind is getting more control of its surroundings.

As in the case of the motor-launch, so likewise in the matter of all our means of locomotion and travel, distance is being overcome by speed. Other comparisons indicate the same progress. Compare, for instance, the modern dwelling-house with the mud hut or cave of the savage, and test any of man's present achievements with those of the past. Then we realise how mind is dominating its surroundings to an ever greater degree. Thus, by invention, we shall reach the age of leisure when nature will perform for us much of what has been toil in the past, and we shall then have more time for mental culture and amusement. Consequently we are entering a new age, we are at the beginning of a new order, and every day its presence is slowly making itself felt.

Everything is tending to make life easier and fuller, and, just as our desires become more and more easily supplied, so will more time be devoted to enjoyment and the pursuit of knowledge. Considering how short the time is since only a part of humanity learned to read and write, to what degree will the evolution of the human race have reached some centuries hence, when the countless blessings knowledge gives to mankind will have borne fruit? Two hundred years hence our descendants will find it difficult to realise how we lived, just as we find it difficult to understand the lives of our ancestors. Moreover our descendants will have this further advantage, namely they will have behind them several hundred years of compulsory organised education, whereas the majority today are the products of only some sixty years, and that of a very elementary type.

Increased knowledge is enabling us evermore to dominate matter and mould it as our minds desire. Consequently we can appreciate what Etherians mean when they tell us that they can mould their surroundings more easily than we can. This greater power of thought which they possess makes life easier for them, just as our machines, which are created by thought, make life easier for us. Here on earth we obtain only a glimmer of reality, and what I am trying to do is to show how this flicker can direct our thoughts to the reality we shall some day reach in Etheria, when mind is in greater control and we shall be more as we think.

This being so there is nothing greater and nothing wiser for us to do than to develop our minds and characters on earth, so as to fit ourselves more thoroughly for the greater command our minds will have on their surroundings. Let us put reason always first. Let us form our opinions and beliefs only on evidence, and in this way we shall develop an intelligent mind. Ignorance is lack of knowledge, or the absence of mental images born from experience. The more intelligently we can create, and the more reasonably we relate images to each other, the wiser we are. Wisdom comes from experience, and making use of our memory for the purpose of living sensibly. Wisdom is the memory of the past put to a correct use. Mistakes are caused by making wrong mental pictures, or incorrectly relating them to one another. A well-balanced mind, a man or woman of good judgment, can always attune their mental pictures so as to arrive at correct decisions. They act wisely, and they live wisely, because of this well-balanced control over their actions.

Self-control maintains the harmony of the mind, whereas anger extinguishes the light of reason. All the honours that kings, princes and rulers can give, all the material wealth individuals can acquire during their time on earth, are as nothing to be compared to strength of character, wisdom and intellectual development. Mental control and mental development are greater assets than titles, and knowledge is a great possession. These mental values will for ever remain with us, whereas material possessions, either in the form of wealth or honours, are only of a temporary nature. They pass from us at death, but our mind and character will be for ever with us; they are ourselves.

Here on earth, whatever are our thoughts, we

are destined to live until our minds decide that they can no longer occupy this earthly vehicle. In Etheria, however, it is different, as there, the more our minds progress, the higher is the state they reach. Death on earth is caused by mind being unable to stay any longer in the physical, but in Etheria our mind so refines our body that it rises naturally to the range of vibrations of the surface higher up. We on earth are refining, or not refining as the case may be, our etheric bodies by our thoughts, and so fitting ourselves naturally for the place we shall occupy in Etheria. We cannot notice this refining process of our etheric bodies, but it is nevertheless progressing day by day, and life, to those who guide their lives wisely, consists of this unsensed development.

The great difference between death in Etheria and death here is that there it comes gradually. We reach a state of mental and bodily refinement which makes the transition easy. Here we have violent deaths, and injury to the body, but there these are not experienced. What is deformed on earth is only the physical body. The etheric body, which is a replica of the physical, may be thought of as deformed like the physical, but in Etheria the mind has power to make the body as it desires, and naturally it will, by thought, mould it to normal.

Thus the hunchback, the armless, the legless, the deformed, the lame and the halt will be trained in Etheria to straighten their mis-shapen bodies and limbs by concentrated thought. By this means they will obtain the perfect bodies denied them on earth because the physical was too gross to be properly controlled by their minds. Their minds, when the deformity arose, were either not sufficiently strong, or circumstances prevailed which were abnormal, and thus their minds did not build up the perfect normal body. So with the blind and deaf. Though thus afflicted physically they have their etheric sight and hearing, and when they function after death in their etheric bodies they will not lack what was denied them on earth through some physical deformity. The armless and legless never lost their etheric arms or legs and consequently will be able to use them when out of the physical body.

Our minds in Etheria establish equilibrium with their surroundings in a way they cannot do here. As the thoughts are, so are our surroundings. If our thoughts are low and evil, they affect our surroundings in Etheria because they influence us to keep apart from the good from very shame because of our wickedness. Our etheric bodies reflect our characters, so much so that they are revealed for all to see. In Etheria our thoughts become things. The bad mix with the bad because they think alike. They gravitate naturally to grosser substance which can influence their minds. They do not wish to be seen; they prefer the shade to the light, because in the light their wickedness and grossness is revealed.

In times past this place of gloom was the next abode for most after death, but fortunately the more developed now miss it. Nature has a place for all, and in the old days each step from the lower to the higher realms had to be taken, and few missed a rung of the ladder, but now it is different because in the case of the most advanced their ideals and ideas have developed and become more refined.

The good experience just the opposite to what befalls the bad. These wise and righteous people prefer to dwell in the light, and, as they advance in knowledge, wisdom, goodness and righteousness, their bodies become more refined. They consequently rise beyond the astral plane, which can be better described as the place where Etherians dwell when they first reach Etheria. It is the first surface upon which they live. There the good and the bad separate themselves quite naturally by mental desire. The backward remain there for an indefinite time. The evil, because of their grosser vibrations remain hidden, to become almost forgotten except by the missionaries who devote their lives to showing them their errors, and endeavour to raise them in their own estimation, so that they can feel that they are fit companions for those of higher mentality.

Slowly the astral plane clears itself of its old inhabitants who fit themselves to live on a higher surface of finer matter. As the earth produces fewer and fewer of a low mentality, so the population of the astral plane decreases. Most average educated intelligent good people pass quickly through the astral on to the surface above, and it is from this plane that most of our friends come when we meet them in the séance room.

The plane above the astral world is one of great charm and delight. The colours especially are much more beautiful than those we know, having a softness, delicacy and charm which we do not experience on earth. I have explained in a previous chapter how colour means almost everything to us in life, and that is equally true of Etheria. There, however, it stimulates the mind more than it does on earth, because of the finer vibrations which reflect it to the etheric eye, and these vibrations pass through the finer etheric brain to the mind. Here on earth our colour vibrations are slower, and they reach our mind through the slower vibrations of our brain.

The mind being much more highly stimulated in Etheria by colour, means that greater pleasure and delight are found by Etherians in their surroundings than we can obtain from ours on earth. Thus their happiness is greatly increased, they tell us, because of the gorgeous colouring given off by etheric substance. Consequently they live in more beautiful surroundings, according to the development of their minds. The mind is responsible for the degree of refinement of the etheric body, and the more refined the body is the more exquisite are the surroundings in which it lives.

This growing knowledge of Etheria, and how we should live to reach its highest realms, may in time stop war and dissension on earth. Gradually the mind of man on earth will desire peace for contemplation and mental development, and more and more resent disharmony. Those who say that war is necessary for the evolution of the race are guided in this view by a materialistic outlook on life. Certainly war brings out in many the qualities of courage, self-sacrifice and patience, but, on the other hand, it develops and intensifies all that is evil in human nature. Until we knew what our destiny really is, it seemed as if the laws of the jungle should prevail between man and man, just as between beast and beast. Our ancestors argued that it was the duty of each one to acquire as many possessions as possible during the short span of conscious existence on earth. Might was therefore logrified at the expense of right, and war, which is only a form of mass thieving, pillage and cruelty, was thus honoured and worshipped.

Now that we know that we are in reality mental creatures, and not just material creatures, we begin to look at things differently, and realise that the control and cultivation of the mind leads to greater happiness than by allowing our carnal lusts to prevail. We shall some day reach the stage of mental development when all will realise the wisdom and necessity of placing a higher value than we now do on these nobler mental conceptions. This mental development is so necessary in the world today to preserve peace and promote happiness and harmony. Some day fear will depart, and mankind, instead of wasting his energies, either in preparing for destruction, or in arming against destruction, will devote them to securing increased comfort, culture and happiness for the race.

War must be selfish, and it promotes selfish desires and grosser mental vibrations. On the other hand mental development can overcome baser desires and in their place put knowledge, wisdom, understanding, unselfishness, kindness and charity towards all. War is nothing less than larceny accompanied by murder and violence. It has come down to us from the days of the jungle, when mind was so undeveloped that it had to obtain its desires by force. With mental development we shall know better how to obtain our desires by intelligent thought, and consequently we must develop our thoughts and not be guided by the unthinking unreasoning mind of primitive life which prevails even in our times. War does not advance humanity, and the invention of those things we need for our comfort and happiness do not come from conflict.

Consider the thousand separate wars which have been fought in Europe within the past 2,500 years. Have these conflicts advanced man's comfort and happiness? Have they increased his speed of travel, or improved his mode of living? Not in the slightest degree. These improvements came about only when science developed, and the more man has thought and reasoned, the more his comforts and happiness have increased. Peace does not bring about the degeneracy of the human race. Nature provides us with quite enough to fight against without our entering into combat with our neighbour.

In the days of old, war was an every-day event in life; more or less all men fought each other. Neither mentally nor physically did our ancestors improve, but rather their minds were stunted as compared with the minds of the present day. Their bodies were smaller and weaker than our bodies now are. Since we began to apply our minds in an intelligent way to our daily lives our bodies have been healthier, stronger and better. Our health and physique have improved, and we are taller, stronger and better shaped than were our ancestors.

This is the result of mental development, of law and order within the individual nations, and what we have yet to learn is the application of this state of affairs internationally throughout the world. Just as duelling, and the general taking of life, have ceased, so war will end some day, but this will come to pass by humanity realising that it is mind, and its development, that counts on earth, and nothing else. When the physical is set in its proper place, and mind is enthroned as king, peace, contentment, harmony and happiness will reign on earth, and war will be no more. This much longed for state of affairs will come about only by mental development, but the improvement must take place everywhere, as undeveloped nations endanger the peace of the world which can only be maintained when all are determined that war shall cease.

The League of Nations, lacking force behind its decisions, is not yet strong enough to stop war, but at least in Geneva peace occupies the throne and is recognised by many as the king who should be obeyed. The trouble is that those who wish to live under the reign of peace are helpless when one or more backward nations desire war. When the peace-lovers dominate every nation, and the reign of righteousness is acknowledged, then the League of Nations, or some other similar organisation which may take its place in the years to come, will function properly as a court of arbitration for disputes, provided always that it has force behind it to enforce its decisions.

The League of Nations stands for the peace, prosperity and well-being of mankind, and, with education increasing and knowledge growing, this aim must conquer and ultimately supersede the low conceptions of life of which ignorance is the parent. In religion, just as knowledge increases, fear departs. Likewise in politics, as knowledge increases, fear will likewise depart. Change the ideas of the people by true and honest education, and as these change it will be found that there is no cause for fear. Uproot greed and the lust for power; make it to be realised that mind is king, and that force is the weapon of the savage, of the one who worships matter and ignores mind, and the strong and the weak will live together in happiness and contentment.

This sane way of living has been accomplished in many countries to such good effect that in time it may become an international and not only a national achievement. Mutual trust and respect between the different nations may some day succeed the present tension caused by fear and distrust, though more conflicts and waste of wealth may take place before all mankind learns the right way to live.

Early man gradually became more merciful and kinder, and instead of eating his enemy he left him to die. Progress continued, and, instead of leaving him to die, he made him his slave. At a later date, instead of making him his slave, he made him a prisoner of war to be released after the fighting was over. The stage we have now reached is that of inflicting death, pain and wounds on our adversaries in war, and, immediately after doing so, we succour them and try to cure our wounded enemies who become prisoners, and relieve their pain. We have still to reach the stage when we cease to inflict death, wounds and suffering on each other in war, and, if our mental evolution is to continue, the time must come when nations will abhor war as much as they detest murder.

CHAPTER XII.

THE WIDER OUTLOOK.

THE universe is slowly unfolding itself before us, and these thoughts I have expressed show that this is because of developing mind. Throughout the pages of this book we have travelled from the age of darkness and superstition to the more enlightened times in which we now live. We have seen that the human race has evolved on earth by mental development. On the higher steps of the ladder leading to the Infinite similar evolution is taking place, and the history of Etheria will show that there, just as here, as the mind advances and develops, so happiness increases and desires are more easily gratified.

Just as the earth has gone through the stage from barbarism to civilisation so also has Etheria, because the minds which earth developed made up Etheria. Developing mind is written across the pages of the history of the Greater World, though we on earth are aware only to some extent of our own small share in this growing consciousness. This growth of ideas, this increase in wisdom, comprises the history of the inhabitants of both Etheria and the earth.

As our minds unfold, they become capable of embracing an extended and enlarged view of life, its meaning and its destiny. This new knowledge gives us encouragement to think aright and live aright. It turns faith and hope into experience. Besides this it explains history; it explains the doings of our ancestors and their thoughts. The glimmer of Etheria has always been present in the minds of our ancestors throughout the past ages, and has dominated their thoughts and actions. Death has always had a powerful influence on the thoughts and deeds of mankind. Etheria, though unseen, has helped to make the history of the human race, as, apart from man's desire to clothe and nourish his body to meet his desires, and to live happily, his instinctive knowledge that Etheria was his real home has influenced his life here on earth, between the cradle and the grave.

Politics comprised man's activities to meet his bodily needs, and religion his mental needs, this being so today as of old. Moreover, all events are related to current or earlier happenings. Every idea prevailing today has a long ancestral tree with its branches and roots going back into the dim and distant past. Every cause produces an effect which in turn produces a cause, and, if we knew enough, we could trace an event right back but never complete the chain of which we at the moment hold the last link, because all our knowledge leads us to believe that never was there a time when cause and effect did not exist. They are the attributes of eternal Mind.

The Bible contains constant reference to an unseen world and the contact of its inhabitants with our earth. Likewise we find similar events recorded in the literature of other nations. History cannot be divided up into two sections, sacred and profane, as man's religious ideas run right through the story of the human race. Heraclitus, 2,500 years ago, taught that all men were part of the Divine Mind. Marcus Aurelius, termed the noblest of the Pagans, writes of the universal mind of which we are all a part. In Greek and Roman literature we find expressions and thoughts about the divine in nature which have never been surpassed by any Christian theologian, and, when we come to the belief in a life after death, we find the same assured confidence in another and happier existence hereafter.

Consequently when reading Homer we find stories of those who have died returning and talking to men and women on earth. Hesiod also tells similar tales and in the records of Egypt, Babylon, India and China the same kind of stories were told. In these ancient days the inhabitants of the other world were at times recognised and conversed with as they are at the present time. Spiritualism, and what it stands for, is not new, in fact it is the oldest religion in the world, and all that is new about it is that we recognise the communicators as the men and women they were on earth and do not call them gods or attribute to them supernatural power. Moreover, with printing and paper now at our disposal, we are able to record these experiences and conversations accurately, and thus prevent them from becoming exaggerated myths and legends as happened in the days gone by.

Many men and women in the past lived in close contact with Etheria, and those who were martyred because of their psychic gifts became at times historical characters, besides being allotted a high place in the other world. Socrates, Krishna, Jesus, Apollonius, Plotinus, Mohammed and Joan of Arc lived in close contact with Etheria. Cicero also had psychic experiences, and this brilliant man of affairs writes of our being able at times to leave the body and converse with Etherians whose appearances are so frequent that he considered all who doubted this fact to be bereft of reason.

Out of the darkness of the past glow these psychic lights, besides many others whose lives have not been recorded. Down the ages mankind has been in touch with Etheria, and the two worlds have never been entirely apart. Our education in the future must include a knowledge of both worlds, now that the feeble glimmer, perceived in the days of old, has grown to be a shining light. Etheria, as our knowledge grows, will become more and more a reality to be anticipated with pleasure. Knowledge will cast out all fear of death, which is but the portal through which we pass into this hitherto little-known country. Though Etheria has just glimmered to past generations, and the light to our ignorant ancestors has been feeble, it has nevertheless persisted and never been altogether extinguished. Now that mediums are safe from destruction, mediumship, which is an hereditary gift, is increasing at a rapid rate and each year the light is burning brighter.

Some say that the Christian Church preserved this glimmer, and that for this we should be thankful. All the orthodox religions of the world doubtless did preserve it, but they wrapped it up so much that one can scarcely trace the glow on the pages of history. The Church in every land, under whatever name it flourished, was supreme, and all came within its authority. Doubtless many who were attached to the organisation perceived the light beneath the coverings better than did the organisation itself, which gave more thought to worldly matters than to the

The Wider Outlook

affairs of the mind. In the Dark Ages the monasteries and convents produced some enlightened minds, and, until those places of retreat became corrupt, many did what they could to help the poor and relieve suffering. They also preserved the art of reading and writing which, but for them, might have been forgotten throughout Christendom.

This much is true, but the student looks on the matter rather differently, because he realises that, so far as the Christian Church is concerned, it extinguished a much greater light. If Christianity had never come into being there is no reason, so far as one can see, why this torch of knowledge would not have increased in brilliancy and illumined the whole world.

We cannot feel much gratitude to Christianity for extinguishing Greek philosophy, and putting in its place its own superstitions, developed from savagery. That which was borrowed from Greece, after passing through the crucible of Christian theology, was distorted beyond recognition. Much better would it have been to have had Greek thought, pure and undefiled, than the impure and defiled which Christianity represents, the outcome of the speculations of the Church theologians, men whose ignorance is now generally recognised. On the other hand, the ideals and noble thoughts of the illustrious Greeks illumine the mind and lead to harmony in thought and action.

Those, therefore, who are grateful to the Christian Church for preserving the glow would not be so thankful to it if they realised that it extinguished a flame, and preserved only the glowing embers. The belief in immortality and in the other world did not come with Christianity, as has always been claimed. What it invented was that entrance to Heaven could only be obtained by belief in Jesus Christ as the saviour of all believers. This has always been claimed, and still is, in every Christian Church and at every Christian funeral. Christianity, by this arrogant and false claim, well-nigh extinguished all mankind's philosophical reasonings, and substituted creeds and dogmas which brought hatred, misery and unhappiness in their train.

Its destruction of mediums, so as to prevent the glow from turning into a flame, is one of the most outstanding facts in history. It denied to the people the greater light for the sake of its own preservation. When, however, its power was broken last century, and the people refused to bow any longer to its authority, the black pall Christianity had held over the light, and through which only the glow could be seen, was lifted. Then the light burned into a flame.

What nature intends to be must be, and nature means humanity to know about its future after death. This knowledge will become a beacon of light to humanity, which no one will be able to dim, now that the people have come into their own. Today, the light Spiritualism has given to humanity burns like a flame. Tomorrow it will burn as a bright light, and some day as a brilliant arc. In the past, humanity groped by the aid of a feeble flicker, but now we see more clearly as the light is brighter, fanned as it has been by the people Christians excluded from their churches.

Thus it will be seen that Christianity was responsible for extinguishing the light of Greek and Latin philosophy, their art and culture. By its wholesale destruction of mediums it kept from Christendom the definite knowledge of the other world, and the comfort this knowledge brings. It kept prosperity from the people by glorifying ignorance and denouncing intelligence. It withheld from humanity the art of healing by attributing all disease to devils, and consigning to oblivion the works on medicine and healing produced by the Greeks, Romans and Arabs. It kept Europe in misery and poverty, and, had it not been for the scientists, and the thinkers, whom the Church persecuted, so long as it had the power to do so, we would still be in the same miserable plight today as Christendom was in for fifteen hundred years. Nevertheless its followers claim that we should be grateful for all the comfort and help Christianity has given to humanity!

Any comfort it has given has been counterbalanced by the misery occasioned by its doctrine of eternal punishment, and any social good it is now doing is by following the example of men and women of the past who worked for the good of humanity, with no encouragement or assistance from the Christian Church. Did the Church hold out a helping hand to Lancaster, Barnardo, Lord Shaftesbury, General Booth, and many others, when, amidst the criticism of orthodoxy, they pursued for long a lone path by themselves in their effort to raise humanity? It was not Christianity which prompted these men to do what they did, but their humanity.

History does not tell us that the bishops in the

House of Lords championed Lord Shaftesbury, and helped him to carry through his legislation for helping and raising the poor, or that the bishops supported Wilberforce in his fight against slavery. History does not mention that the bishops took any part last century in helping and encouraging legislation for the raising of the standard of living and the education of the people in this country. Instead, history tells of their determined opposition to all reforms introduced into the House of Lords.

I can find no record of the Church opposing cruelty to animals; in fact, the reverse is the case. The Church has supported fox-hunting, stag-hunting, otter-hunting and hare and rabbit coursing, and all their accompanying cruelties. Many of its country priests have joined in these so-called sports, and some of its most devoted members are enthusiastic supporters of these blood sports, but dutifully refrain from them on certain holy days throughout the year! Those who partake of this form of enjoyment bring their minds down to the level of the hounds, which have only one thought, that of killing and drawing the victim's blood.

The leaders of a religion of creeds and dogmas, history tells us, consider these and these only, and their efforts and exertions are directed only to maintaining the edifice of tradition, and keeping from the people any facts that would upset belief in their teaching. Unfortunately the history of the Christian Church is black indeed, and its record over the past nineteen hundred years, when written by an impartial historian, as it will be some day, will disclose facts which will show that the claims its followers make today are unjustifiable, and directly opposite to what is the truth.

Slowly the people are adjusting their ideas to encompass the wider range which now stretches before our vision. Within the memory of most of us is the family circle joining together in family worship, when the family Bible was brought out and its pages reverently turned over and read. Those days are past and never will return, but the Home Circle has come to stay, and it will take the place of family worship. Mediumship is a natural gift, and many of us can develop it, more or less. Home Circles, more than any other method, will bring the two worlds together, and make Etheria a great reality. There is a large band working on the other side, and taking every opportunity to get messages through to us. As time goes on we shall respond more and more to their efforts, and every new Home Circle makes wider the bridge spanning the two worlds.

What this book records are facts based on evidence, so far as they relate to this earth. The statements made with regard to the next state of consciousness, which I have termed Etheria, are based on communications which I consider I have received from that world. They have not been put down hastily or accepted casually. I have taken pains to verify them in every possible way. For five years I sat regularly with John C. Sloan, one of the most powerful direct voice mediums in this country, and during those sittings my secretary took down in shorthand verbatim what was said. I was not, however, content with this, and, after those sittings with Sloan terminated, I devoted much time and painstaking effort to have what was told to me confirmed through other mediums.

This I have done over the past years, and I can claim that I have received, through our leading mediums, information about Etheria which confirms in every detail all that I was previously told. The beliefs expressed regarding what happens beyond the state of consciousness in which my communicators were, are the result of their own philosophic reasonings based on what they have been told from higher planes. Just as we on earth cannot see much beyond the next step, so they are similarly situated. Their destiny is as much a matter of speculation with them as it is with us. However, they have this great advantage over us on earth, that they have made the first step, and are in touch with those who have taken further steps. Consequently they are better able than we are to base their philosophy on something more tangible than we have to guide us.

I, therefore, claim for this book that it takes one as far as one dare go, with our present knowledge. As this increases, as communication improves, our destiny should become clearer. Now that we have come to realise that death is without a doubt only a step into another order of consciousness, and that existence is made up of such steps, each one of which is leading us up to a realm where the individual mind becomes supreme in itself, a sound basis is established for a philosophy which is none other than a science. Philosophy has therefore become less speculative and more scientific. As it is now able to base its reasonings on the ascertained fact of survival, and all that this implies, its pronouncements have the same authority as those of the other sciences. Philosophy, Religion and Science have thus become one, with the same ideals and aspirations.

In this, and my two preceding books, I have attempted to direct the gaze of those who read them to the larger panorama comprising the Greater World, and to focus what we now know about our life on earth and in Etheria. This greater vista, in turn, enables us to understand the true meaning of religion and discard much that has become mere accretions down the ages because of ignorance.

With greater knowledge life should be happier. To obtain happiness is the aim and endeavour of everyone. Happiness increases as our minds develop, and this development further unfolds the universe. If we live and think aright we grow in wisdom and understanding to the increase of happiness, because unhappiness is caused by ignorance of nature's laws. Living in harmony with these laws, and not contrary to them, comes from knowledge, and the more we apply this understanding to our daily life the wiser we are, because it brings about increased happiness.

This being so we can assert with confidence that knowledge shows us that to strive after right living, or righteousness, is the height of wisdom. Moreover the nearer we reach to perfection the more beautiful will be the place in which we shall dwell in Etheria. The vibrations of our etheric body on earth, though encased in the physical garment, become more refined as we attune ourselves more closely to nature's plan, and, as we are here, so shall we be there. Our desires and ideals here we shall be able to realise there.

We are either carrying out this refining process on earth, or we are not. The wise are doing so, the foolish are not, though the latter may have to wait until they reach Etheria before they realise their lost opportunities on earth. There they will see things more clearly, and, as they do so, the urge to rectify their mistakes will strengthen. There is a mental gulf in Etheria, deeper far than any on earth, between the good and the bad which is impossible to bridge so long as the bad remain bad and the good remain good. The barrier ceases to be when the mentality changes. The bad cannot live with the good, but the bad can become good, and, when they do so, they leave their evil companions and evil surroundings and live with the good. It is all a question of harmony of thoughts and ideals.

Ignorance and misery are twin brothers. Knowledge and happiness are likewise related. Ignorance produces hate, intolerance, misery, disharmony and discontent. On the other hand knowledge casts out fear and brings love, tolerance, joy, peace and contentment. Ignorance produces fear and breeds cruelty, revenge, discouragement and worry. Knowledge cultivates kindness, forgiveness, hope and trut Ignorance stands for dread, dejection, strife and selfishness. Knowledge brings courage, elation, compassion and generosity. Ignorance causes distrust and suspicion, while knowledge produces good-will and confidence. We can choose the one or the other, but, as we know more, so do we choose those qualities which lead to happiness. Ignorance is painted on the sign leading to the path of human misery. The road to happiness is indicated by the sign-post of knowledge.

Spiritualism, which stands for knowledge, helps to lift the tragedy from life. Those who view life as a drama, consisting only of acts between the cradle and the grave, should give serious thought to the meaning of all that Spiritualism stands for. Judging life wrongly, they live it wrongly. To consider that it is but a short journey, interspersed by some eighty odd milestones for the few, and less for the many, surely gives those who do so a warped perspective. If the child thought that the nursery stage was the beginning and end of its career it would not grow and develop normally.

Spiritualism, when accepted, creates as great a mental revolution as did the acceptance of the Copernican system. Faith is such a feeble flicker when compared with the full blaze of knowledge. Few can see more than the gleam of the flickering stars to lead them through the valley of death. Hope has held aloft what little light there was, but it was not much better than that of a candle. Today the hill-tops have been illumined by the rays of the rising morning sun, but only those on the heights can appreciate the meaning of the coming day. The vast majority are still in the valley and see only the stars.

Knowledge makes life understood, is indifferent to old age, and turns life from being a mystery into a great reality. Once it is realised that mind in man never dies, old age is appreciated as but the preparation for a great awakening to an existence, greater and fuller than earth-life can ever give. We are never too old to learn, and knowledge, combined with wisdom, brings mental satisfaction, which is the desire of all. Once it is accepted that mind never dies, but only changes its environment, then death on earth, no matter at what age, is understood to be merely a bend in the road of life, round which humanity is for ever turning.

Conceived of love and ecstasy, and born in pain, cherished in loving arms and nursed in infancy, the infant becomes a child, looking with wondering eyes on all around, thinking and pondering. Beguiled by mimicry it utters speech, and thus releases the thoughts moulded by the mind. So this creation of two loving souls grows from childhood to be a man or woman, when once again the union of twin souls begets another, and the same mysterious process begins anew.

So, as man and wife, whose union thus adds again to life, they live and hope and love, touched at times by sorrow, pain and disappointment. Then, growing old amidst the love of children, and children's children, their grip on this world's things loosens, and slowly they journey on towards the horizon, like the setting sun. With locks of grey they live prepared to meet the twilight which precedes a glorious dawn.

Surrounded by love and care, amidst all that toil and thought has brought together, first one goes round the bend of the road alone, and love, nursed by knowledge, says "Till we meet again." Then the other follows, bidding a last farewell to all this earth contains. What gives sorrow here gives joy there. Though the family circle has been reduced on earth, it has been increased in Etheria.

Love is the greatest force in the universe, and love, in all its phases, is the magnet which draws mind to mind and makes us live together within the human family. This great force is not severed by death, and love for friends on earth, by friends in Etheria, is just as great as it was when these Etherians lived on earth. Consequently those who loved each other most on earth, when separated for a time by death, can most easily make contact with each other through mediumship. Where the love tie is strong there is seldom disappointment.

Love inspires the artist, the poet, the musician, the patriot and the philosopher; it is the force that draws us to each other and is drawing us each slowly back to the Infinite. The happiest home on earth is the one where love comes first, because then home life becomes a melody, discords having ceased to produce discontentment and disharmony. Let us therefore cultivate this greatest of all the forces of nature. To do so brings happiness. Where love and honest reasoned thinking live side by side, contentment reigns.

All the good and evil in this world are the result of right or wrong thinking. Each is master of himself or herself. No king or government, no one can make us think other than we wish to think. Our thoughts can give us happiness or unhappiness, and we must choose which to have for ourselves. Each individual mind sits on its own throne. No one can ever dethrone it, or make it think and act other than it wishes to think. It is supreme. Failure and disappointment are words we use to denote a state of mind, but we can make them mean nothing to us if we wish to do so.

If each mind is firmly enthroned all life's troubles can be ignored, and our thoughts concentrated instead on the good, the beautiful and the true. Each can choose. If we have thought our way into trouble we

can equally well think our way out. If we are held
down by sorrow or worry, we are holding ourselves
down. We can, if our mind is strong enough, un-
shackle these thoughts which make us unhappy, and
dwell instead on those which make us happy. Each
mind sets its own margin of happiness or unhappiness,
and expands or contracts its kingdom of contentment.
Acting honestly and thinking truly bring content,
which leads to happiness.

Let us all be bearers of what we feel to be the truth,
whose light comes only from the torch of evidence,
illuminating for mankind the road to knowledge.
Let us realise how truth can be reached only by
fixing intently our gaze on this torch of evidence, and
being guided by it. We must not linger by the way-
side trying to find truth in the shadows, as there we
shall lose our bearings and miss our guide.

To arrive at truth we must seek knowledge, and
to obtain knowledge we must seek evidence. We
must discard prejudice, and not be misled by ancient
tradition, or religious revivals which are the order of
the present day, and are the result of loose thinking
on the deeper things of life. What we have been
taught to believe in youth should be carefully sifted
to make sure that there is evidence for our beliefs.
If no evidence exists for these, they should be discarded, as they are lumber and hamper us on our way.

At all times place reason first, as only through
it can we obtain evidence, which is our only guide
to truth. Whatever this earth and Etheria have in
store for us, to whatever heights we reach, on whatever shore of consciousness our minds may some day
touch, it will be by our being guided by our reason

and understanding, nurtured in liberty, that greatest of all blessings, won for us by our forefathers, who by their exertions made it possible for our minds to unfold in peace. Thus our minds are enabled to develop more and finer images, the sum total of which to each individual is the universe, a word which represents myriads of endless ideas or thoughts produced by each individual mind.

Our eternal home is in reality our own mind, and it became so with our first conscious thought. Throughout this earth-life the individual mind expands and develops and, as it does so, our outlook embraces an enlarged aspect. Our minds make up our life. Our minds are ourselves. On earth our minds are greatly conditioned by our surroundings, and are largely dominated by them, but in Etheria the mind controls its surroundings to a greater and greater degree, as its bodily habitation becomes more refined. The history of each individual mind is just the story of it becoming more the monarch and less the slave of its surroundings.

When the mind becomes supreme, by being in complete control of surrounding substance, it becomes all-powerful. Time and space cease to be, and its refinement, owing to purification throughout the ages, enables it to appreciate reality in the region of pure thought where it will eternally dwell. Then will the universe have unfolded. Then will the universe be understood.

Consequently, life is developing and expanding mind. As it expands it becomes less centred in itself, and reaches out in sympathy and understanding to other minds, thus amplifying its experiences and understanding. Though our development does not proceed unchecked, progress nevertheless is continuous. However spiral it may seem to be it is always onwards and upwards. Ultimately we reach attunement with the Infinite, and, by the experience gained on our journey through the spheres, we are fitted to live and work in harmony with the Divine Mind of the Universe.

Mind is the only reality, the only permanency, its successive habitations and abodes being temporary and transient. Unfolding mind unfolds the universe until time and space cease to be. Thus to each and all there can be no end. Our destiny is to live and develop. Life is the emerging of the individual mind from bondage to freedom, from ignorance to knowledge, from selfishness to unselfishness, from error to truth, from the temporal to the eternal, and from the finite to the infinite.

This state of becoming constitutes eternal life, as in the realm of mind there is no beginning and no end to either space or time. This is our destiny; it is for this each one is living, and it is for this each one is developing. This is the reason why we became conscious beings, and it is for this our earth is the nursery, and Etheria, in its various aspects of finer matter, both school and college. After learning the lessons each stage has to teach us, we shall then be prepared for the part which will become ours naturally in our eternal home.

Let us therefore be followers of the light of knowledge, and be guided by the lamp of reason. If we are, then, when we turn the bend in the road of life, its brightness will increase, and so likewise will our happiness. In our progress through the spheres of Etheria, alighting and lingering as we shall for a time on each surface, the bends will become fewer and less pronounced, our surroundings will become more beautiful, and our knowledge and wisdom will attain to greater heights.

Ultimately, when time and space cease to be, we shall reach at-one-ment with the Infinite, and then to each the universe will have unfolded because the individual mind will have attained the capacity of appreciating reality.

This concludes the Trilogy on Spiritualism, comprising *On the Edge of the Etheric*, *The Rock of Truth*, and *The Unfolding Universe*.

INDEX

INDEX

A

AAPEP (the devil), 96
Achilles, 96
Adam and Eve story, 390
Adolphus, Gustavus, 432
Adonis (deity), 174
Advanced minds in Etheria, 352
After-life, a condition of mind, 358
    belief is older than Christianity, 189
    Humanity always thinking about, 355
    Instinctive belief has helped little, 358
    Leading clergy doubtful, 23-4
    Religious systems cannot supply knowledge of, 24
    Spiritualist acceptance of, 32
Age, Mankind entering new, 446
Age of Thought, The New, 215-47
Agnostic and religious sense, 358
Agricola (Roman), 433
Agrippa (king), 123
Alexander the Great, 379
Alexandria, 127, 160
    centre of early Christianity, 117
    Prelates of, 99
    seat of Christendom, 182
    Theological thought of, 336
Alexandrian thought attributed to Jesus, 129
Allen, Grant, 53 *fn.*, 60
Altars, 101
    built for gods, 91
    Dying victims lying on, 104
    of sacrifice, 57
    Origin of, 55-6
Alva, Duke of, 356
Ananias and Sapphira, 83
Ancestor worship, grew out of belief in apparitions, 54
Ancient Egypt, 78*fn.*
Ancient literature, 218
Ancients and belief in contact with spirits of the dead, 199
    had a place for gods in science and philosophy, 199
Angelo, Michael (sculptor), 438
Anger puts out light of reason, 448
Animal sacrifice, 78
    sacrifice supplants that of humans, 78
    prevention of cruelty to, 193
Ant-heap resembled Greater World, 300-1
Anthropologists and development of life, 205
Anthropomorphic God, Belief in, 35
    Origin of, 54
Anti-Jesus, the Church is strongly, 374-5
Antioch, seat of Christendom, 182
Anu the illustrious, 93, 105
Apollonian cult and Christianity, 346-7

Apollonius, an historical character, 345, 347
    lived in contact with Etheria, 459
    Same legends told about as of Jesus, 347
Apostolic Church, 403
    and mediums, 61, 412
    replaced by the Christian Church, 393
Apparition of Jesus, 137, 181
    seen by Paul, 123
Apparitions are understood by Spiritualists, 126
    Belief in, 54, 237
    Origin and basis of supernatural religion, 219
    primitive man termed them gods, 219
Appleton layer, 278
Apports, 237
Arab literature on medicine and healing, 463
Arabs copied and improved the compass, 425
    copied from the Chinese, 429
Aramaic language mistranslated, 121
Archimedes (Greek), 430
Arians become outcasts, 172, 173
Aristarchus (astronomer), 26*fn.*
Aristotle (Greek philosopher), 43, 65, 159, 350, 437
Arius (Presbyter), 155, 158, 373, 379 380
Arkwright, Sir Richard, 429
Armada defeated, 432
Armistice Day. Incongruity of, 420
Armless and legless possess their etheric limbs, 450
Art. Rediscovery of, 438
Asia Minor established first Christian churches, 182
    Mediums attached to temples in, 220
Assyria and religious worship, 58, 104
Assyrians, 93, 105
Assyriologists, and the deluge, 94
Aston (physicist), 428
Astral plane, the, 97, 271, 291, 298
    Educated good people pass quickly through, 451
    Higher surfaces than the, 451
    or Hades, 222
    the place where Etherians first dwell, 281-6, 451
Astrology, 38
Astronomers and the universe, 203
Astronomical clock and time, 254-5
Astronomy, 38, 202, 203
Athanasian Creed, 128, 151, 180
Athanasius, Bishop, 158, 160, 373, 380
Athena (deity), 105
Athens, 438
    laws of, a pattern for the world, 433
Atmosphere and Etheria, 280, 281-6
    importance of, to us, 279

Atmosphere is more luminous in Etheria, 280, 282
weight of, 279
Atom, structure of the, 262, 428
Atomic weights, 428
Atonement, Belief in sacrificial meals, 135
  incorporated into Christianity, 75
  Origin of, 73
  story told before the Bible was written, 75
At-one-ment and philosophy, 323
  established between gods and worshippers, 134
  gained through contemplation, 324
  with God, basis of all religions, 329
  with the Divine Mind, 304, 316, 322, 324, 326, 358, 401, 475
Augustine, Saint, 177, 373, 378
Aura and doctor controls, 398
Aura and its causes, 292
Aurelius, Marcus, 437, 458–9
Automatic writing, 237
Avatars, probably psychic, 344, 350

B

BAAL (see Bel)
Babylonian Legends of the Creation, the, 98fn.
Babylonian records and Spiritualism, 459
Babylonian Story of the Deluge, the, 98fn.
Babylonian tablets, 93, 94
  tablets older than Bible, 95
Babylonians, 93
Bacchus (deity), 105
Bacon, Roger (scientist), 426
Baptism adopted by Christianity from Paganism, 81, 387–8
  Belief that child goes to hell if unbaptised, 81
  is an insult to motherhood, 388
Barnabas, 136
Barnardo, Dr., 434, 463
Become, We shall have, 320
Becoming, state of, constitutes, eternal life, 474
Beethoven, Ludwig van (composer), 439
Beginnings, The, 78fn.
Bel (deity), 105, 119fn., 128, 156
  denounced by Jehovah, 129
Belief in gods will fade away, 110
Beliefs should be based on evidence, 448
Bell, Graham (inventor), 430
Benz, Karl (engineer), 430
Berkeley, George (philosopher), 437
Bible, the, 35, 183, 217, 404
  accepted literally by Orthodox Christians, 177
  and an unseen world, 458
  and favourite texts, 110
  belief that Jehovah wrote it, 36, embraces ennobling literature, 387
  gives a different meaning to words, 219
  is not holy or sacred, 386
  Its authority, 37

Bible myths, 410
  not literally true, 334
  passages used to suit opinions, 161–2
  reading in Spiritualist churches, 395
  repeats ancient literature, 219
  Science is more reliable than, 41
  should be kept from children, 410
  supports war, slavery and wrongdoing, 36
  Why it is called the Word of God and the Holy Scriptures, 36
Biologists proclaim life has existed millions of years, 205
Biology. Study of, 205
Bishops and lay preachers, 371, 372
  and salvation, 412
  and slavery, 464
  at Convocation of York (1934) and their attitude to belief in the Trinity, 371–3
Blind and deaf. Education of, 192
Blind will have etheric sight, 450
Blood, Discovery of circulation, 436
  shedding in religion comes from savagery, 179
  sports and cruelty, 359
  sports, Church has never protested against, 360
  sports, Clergy often supporters of, 360
Boddington, Harry (author), 397fn.
Body becomes more refined, 308–9, 314
  Burial of, 390
  No individual mind without 319
Bolivar, Simon (liberator), 433
Book of the Dead, the, 95, 96, 98
Booth, General, 463
Bradlaugh, Charles (reformer), 444
Brahe, Tycho (scientist), 197
Brahma (deity), 92, 105
Braille, Louis (inventor), 429
Brain, Development of, 229–30
  Physical and Etheric duplicate, 228
  substance is dual, 259
  when diseased prevents mind from functioning, 211
Branca, Giovanni (engineer), 429
Brindley, James (engineer), 430
Bristol, Bishop of, 70
British Broadcasting Corporation, 40–1
  and Christian propaganda, 179
  ban Spiritualism, 179, 419
  Museum, 93, 98fn., 113
Bronze Age, 206
Bruno, Giordano (philospher), 26, 87, 161, 197, 404–5, 411
Buddha, 106, 345
  his teaching debased, 349
  left no writings, 106
  meaning of the name, 344
  Story of, 153
  was the greatest religious teacher, 348–9
Buddhism xvii, 191, 241, 349, 403, 415
Buddhists are atheists, 54
  disbelieve in divine sacrifice, 77
  zeal for converts, 195
Bull-fights, 359
Bultmann (historian), 119fn.

Burial service depressing and irrational, 391
Burkitt (theologian), 119*fn*., 141
Burns, Robert (poet), 335-6
Buxton, Sir Thomas Fowell (emancipationist), 430

C

CABOT (explorer), 425
Caesar, Julius, 433
Calvary culminates mysteries of antiquity, 176
　story originated in sun-worship, 78-9
Calvin, John (reformer), 161, 356
Cannibalism, attributed to the gods, 73
Canterbury, Archbishop of, 373
Cape of Good Hope, 426
Carlile, Richard, 192
Carpenter, Mary, 192
Carthage, 182
　Council of, 376
Carthaginians, 404
Cartwright, Edmund, 429
Catacombs of Rome, 111
　contain shrines and altars, 56
Catholics (see Roman Catholics)
Cause and effect, 200, 204, 324, 458
Caxton, William, 429
Cells composed of mind and substance, 303
　physical and etheric, 291
Ceremonials, 25
Cicero (Rome), 54, 132, 134, 159, 217, 437
　had psychic experiences, 459-60
Circles, Home, 414
　Rescue, 414-5
Chaldeans and psychic phenomena, 102
Chambers' Encyclopaedia, 101-2
Character, Development of, 38
　and our etheric body, 450
　Nothing wiser than to develop, 447
　Strength of, 448
Charlemagne (Emperor), 194
Charles V (Emperor), 378
Chaucer (author), 429
Chemical action, 428
Child of the future, teaching of, 409
Children and Seven Principles of Spiritualism, 410
　and the myths and miracles of Bible, 410
　What they should be taught, 409, 410, 411
Children's Spiritualist Lyceums, 408
Chinese literature and Spiritualism, 459
　records copied by the Arabs, 429
Chippendale, Thomas, 439
Chloroform, discovery of, 436
Christ, 118
　a name for a theological doctrine, 328
　a name substituted for Osiris, 176
　and Jesus. What these names stand for, 163, 166-71
　and Jesus cannot both be worshipped, 164, 165
　and matrimony, 390

Christ and Paul's influence on mankind, 125
　as God, Temples to, 106
　Barbarities and atrocities under flag of, 183
　crucified, theme of Paul, 132
　dethroned earlier gods, 175
　erroneously worshipped by Christians, 328
　Forces of, in retreat, 382
　is a name to denote a theological dogma, 125
　is Paul's creation, 164
　Meaning of, 76, 344
　No Christianity without, 118
　of Paul, not the son of David, 139
　replaced other saviours, 157
　should never be associated with Jesus, 76
　The theological, is repellent, 185
　The word's association and meaning, 345
　What the word stands for, 76
Christendom, its dark night of superstition, 159
　retains superstitions of Paganism, 381
　upheld and practised slavery, 86
Christos, Belief in, 127
　Speculations about, 128
　or "Chrestos" worshipped in Christian times, 140
Christs, Belief in, 329
　Earlier, 129, 135
　were probably endowed with psychic powers, 350
"Christ Spirit", Belief in originated in sun-worship, 130
　continues old sectarian differences, 348
　incarnations of the, 346
　its meaning, 348
　No evidence of it entering human flesh, 345, 353
　of recent birth, 347
　or Cosmic Christ means nothing, 344-5, 346
　Re-appearance of religious teachers after death, 130
Christian and other religions will someday be forgotten, 338
　beliefs derived from savage ancestors, 105
　bishops and increased power, 377
　masscres, 25,000,000 victims, 86
　people accept ancient superstitions, 31
Christian Church:
　a word misapplied, 183
　an exclusive organisation, 370
　and Etheria, 460
　and mediums, 412
　beliefs brought into disrepute, 356
　believes life and death must remain a mystery, 331
　Both sections of, hold same beliefs, 370
　burned or drowned all mediums, 226, 419
　cannot abandon the creeds, 116
　charity dead for centuries, 191
　claims about Jesus discarded by Spiritualists, 350
　comforted ignorant by myths and legends, 420

Q

Christian Church contributed no new knowledge, 373
  denounced Spiritualists, 419
  discourages psychic knowledge, 63
  disdains discussion with other religious leaders, 403
  dishonesty of, 420-1
  doctrines decided by theologians, 370
  dogma and tradition can never be separated, 347
  emphasises its creeds, dogmas, and doctrines, 372
  ethical claims are false, 43
  extinguished a great light, 461
  foundations are crumbling, 44
  has abused its powers, 420
  has been help and comfort to many, 420
  has nothing to replace fear, 400
  has supported war, 36-7
  history is black, 464
  hostility to Spiritualism, 328-9
  illogical teaching, 328
  is organisation of superstition, 185
  is rich and powerful, 106
  its creeds, dogmas, and doctrines, 372
  opposes enquiry into the life beyond, 68
  retains its out-of-date dogmas and doctrines, 372
  sermons are childish, 400
  split by Mohammed, 382
  submerged knowledge by superstition and persecution, 438
  teachings of the after-life crude and cruel, 420
  treats Spiritualism with disdain and contempt, 411-2
  What it stands for, 167
  When its power began to wane, 421
  worked Jesus into the new religion, 180
  would fall to pieces if it accepted Spiritualism, 412, 413
Christian cult, Commencement of, 120
  doctrines, Origin of, 118-40
  documents have no divine authority, 375
  faith, Basis of, 117-37
  faith developed by slow degrees, 138
  faith examined, 117
  faith, origin and growth of, ix, 75
  god an unjust tyrant, 85
  martyrs, 378
  Nothing to be proud about the name of, 190
  persecution, commencement of, 155
  philanthropists, 193
  priesthood opposed knowledge, 157
  religion cannot be associated with ethics, 183
  religion, Contradictions of, 174-76
  religion not the religion of Jesus, 76, 337
  representatives refuse discussion, 329
  Christian Spiritualists are not Spiritualists, 187, 195-6
  Spiritualists should shed sectarian opinions, 352
  superstition, 42, 44
  Trinity, 93, 353, 344
  wars and persecution, 378-9
  worship based on fear of the unknown, 90
Christianity xvii (*see also* Orthodox religion)
  a combination of five earlier religions, 99
  a reformed Paganism, 380
  a tangled mass of contradictions, 153-4
  advocates both good and bad, 183-4
  an accumulation of ancient beliefs, 117
  an assembly of illogical ideas, 36
  and belief in immortality, 462
  and its revolting history, 182
  and Jesuism diametrically opposite, 184
  and learning could not live together, 66
Christianity and Mythology, 78*fn*.
Christianity and Spiritualism have no possible connection, 187, 189
  and the Athanasian Creed, 180
  and the future verdict of its eclipse, 162
  and war go together, 37, 421
  banished philosophical reasonings, 462, 463
  based on vicarious atonement, 105
  Basis of, 115, 155
  became officially established, 377
  borrowed ancient mythology, 38
  broken up by the Reformation, 161
  cannot be reformed, 330
  caused by Paul's vision, 171
  caused destruction of mediums, 462
  caused ignorance and illiteracy, 159
  Central theme is shedding of blood, 179
  changed the name of the gods, 156
  decreased as education increased, 62
  Definition of, caused dissent, 379
  denied people the greater light, 462
  denounced by Mohammed, 182
  developed from other religions, 158, 336
  distorted history, 67
  Doctrine of hell the blackest spot, 39-40
  does not aspire to greater heights, 37
  does not fit into age of scientific thought, 37
  Early history of, 156
  Effect of wholesale destruction of mediums, 463
  Evolution of, 115-63
  extinguished Greek philosophy 461
  founded by Paul, 76, 160

Index

Christianity, growth caused by becoming state religion of Rome, 336
image-worshipping lost many followers, 182
in pre-Christian days, 156
inflow of ideas from other religions, 127
is based on ancient mystical conception of union with deity through sacrifice, 176
is based on religion of the savage, 57, 179, 219, 330
is not a divine revelation, 376
is Mithraism, 337
is Paganism, 42, 153, 178, 329, 382
its assertions and beliefs, 115–40
its corruption great, 181–2
its fundamentals, 116
last of the saviour-god religions, 74
materialised the immaterial, 38
must give way to Spiritualism, 37
No support for supernatural claims, 153
No valuable teachings about the other world, 38
not fitted for present-day civilisation, 44
not unique, 176
nurtured at Alexandria, 99
opposes investigation, 37
Origin traced to psychic phenomena, 102, 171–2
planted in an age of ignorance, 181
reformed by Thomas Cromwell, 380
ritual cannot be explained by clergy, 225
stands by its creeds, 188
stands for what Christ stands for, 171
stands for what is untrue, 189
state religion of the Roman Empire, 377
summed up by Paul, 188
supported every form of evil, 183
suppressed discoveries, 436
traced to sun-worship, 176
trail of cruelty and misery, 40
unknown before Paul, 140
What it stands for, 188
Where it was conceived, born and cradled, 160
will be replaced by Spiritualism, 196
worships the dead past, 36
Christians, a privileged group, 216
agree all other religions are based on superstition, 115
and Jesuians at variance, 155, 164–5
attributed disease to devils, 436
believe in three Gods, 54, 371
cannot serve both Jesus and Christ, 164
cause controversies by adding name Spiritualist, 362
employ men to propagate lies about Jesus, 186
erroneously worship Christ, 328
Mystical, and their beliefs, 174

Christians, persecution of, 378
resent idea of outgrowing superstitions, 329–30
treated prisoners like beasts, 190–1
veneration of their dead, 56
Why they see no resemblance in Spiritualism, 329
will become Spiritualists if they think, 47
worship symbolism and drapings of true religion, 328
Church, A new one arising out of the old, 384
abolished learning, 66
acquisition of wealth, 84
and future use of its buildings, 421
and State still dominate individual consciences, 246
as a divine institution is untenable, 177
at Jerusalem was Ebionitish, 139
attendance in London declining, 384fn.
beliefs contrary to natural law, 172
disrupted by opposing views, 154–5
distorts the truth, 69
domineered over the individual and state, 191
fathers decided the new religion, 158
held the people in an iron grip, 201
influence declining, 69
is based on superstition and ignorance, 385
is fighting a losing battle against nature, 63–4
is strongly anti-Jesus, 374–5
launched crusades against heretics, 194
schools. Origin of and reason for, 62
stops burning mediums, 331
Church of England and confirmation, 388–9
baptism service is archaic, 388
beliefs, 162
its numbers dwindling, 44
maintained to propagate superstition, 374
marriage service not instituted by God, 389–90
receive a tenth of the land's produce, 374
Church of England Newspaper, The, 384fn.
Church of the future, 385, 393
and mediums, 422
based on evidence, 384–5
enlightenment about destiny, 422
forum for dissemination of opinions, 385–6
its altar will be dedicated to love, 427
its duties, 396
its leaders, 394–6
its teaching, 404
not confined within Bible bounds, 395
will assist in earthly ills and troubles, 397

Church will be attended with pleasure and profit, 404
  will become healing centre, 422
  will have no sects, 403
  will increase knowledge of life here and hereafter, 385
  will not be tied to dogma, 385
Churching of Women is a Judaic institution, 389
Clairaudience, 393
  and survival, 234
  Development of, 394
  Gift of, 416
  is increasing, 418-9
  is sometimes nothing of the kind, 415-6
  Majority of facts accepted as correct, 416-7
Clairaudients, 227
  hear Ethereans, 417-8
Clairvoyance, 393, 416
  and survival, 234
  Development of, 394
  Gift of, is increasing, 418-9
  sometimes jeered at, 419
Clairvoyants, 126, 227
  and etheric bodies, 126, 219
  frequently see spirits, 217
  revealed many spirits, each in turn deified, 220
  see etheric bodies at time of death, 293
  training for platform work, 399
Clarkson (emancipationist), 430
Clay tablets found in Nineveh, 93, 94
Clement, of Alexandria, 158, 159, 177
Clergy (*see also* Priests)
  and Spiritualism, 47
  and the learned professions, 70
  Attitude of, makes sorry history, 67-8
  beginning to wonder about their future, 71
  find it undesirable for people to know about the hereafter, 69
  What they are being trained for, 70
Clerk-Maxwell (physicist), 198, 428
Cobbe, Frances (humanist), 192-3
Codex-Sinaiticus, 112-3
Cogan, Thomas (philanthropist), 192
Colours, 262, 263, 264
  and the Greater World, 306
  in Etheria are vivid and beautiful, 270, 451
  vibrations on earth and in Etheria, 452
Columbus (explorer), 425
Comforter, the, 222
Compass, Invention of, 425
  proved the earth round, 199
  use of, helped to create a mental revolution, 202
Confirmation, doctrine of Church, 81-2
  in the Church of England, 388-9
Confucius gave more light than Jesus, 348
  had philosophic mind, 349
  is cherished by a third of humanity, 349
  left no writing, 119
Conscious existence, 267
  existence, five things required, 259

Consciousness and our surroundings, 287, 312
  is image-making, 294
  is not annihilated by death, 289-90
  Normal, 313
  Planes of, 299
  Why we never lose it, 294
Consecrated bread, eating of, 80-1
  When the belief arose, 80
Constable, John (painter), 438
Constantine the Great, 58, 99, 155, 157, 158, 160, 172, 336, 337, 375, 377, 379, 380, 381, 382
  elevated Christian cult, 378
  ended persecution of the Christians, 376
  was a murderer, 376
Constantinople. Building of, 377
  first Christian city, 182
  Transfer of capital to, 378
Contemplation will supersede worship and prayer, 90, 355
Convents corrupt in the Middle Ages, 191
Convocation of York (1934) and the creeds, 345
Conybeare, F. Cornwallis, 119*fn.*, 141, 143*fn.*
Cook, Captain (explorer), 426
Co-operative movement, 193
Copernicus (astronomer), 26, 27, 30, 87, 197, 202, 203, 258, 259, 334, 335, 367, 427
Cortes (explorer), brought orthodox religion into disrepute, 356
Cosmic Christ, or Christ Spirit, means nothing, 344-5 346
  terms continue old sectarian view of religion, 348
Cosmic Krishna, 348
Cosmic Mind, 107, 308, 322
  Our minds *en rapport* with the, 359
  Urge to attain at-one-ment with, 358
Cosmos, 250, 334, 338
Crandon, Margery and Walter, 236
Creeds, 25
  a mystical conception, 176
  and dogmas, maintenance of tradition, 464
  and orthodox religions will fade away, 38
  and persecution, 356
  are conquered by facts, 326
  are not required by Spiritualists, 327
  belief in, is for the ignorant only, 38
  belief in, not necessary for human progress, 193
  Christians must accept, 345
  supplanted knowledge, 438
Crespigny, Mrs. Champion de, 327-8
Crime has declined through education, 434
Critical Analysis of the Four Chief Pauline Epistles, A, 139
Crompton, Samuel (inventor), 429
Cromwell, Thomas, produced a reformed Christianity, 380, 381
Crookes, Sir William (scientist), 428, 439
Cross, the, a symbol older than Christianity, 59

Index

Cross, occupied prominent place in religious worship, 58
symbol of life and sacrifice, 58
Crucifixion, a relic of sun-worship, 223
an ancient religious drama, 223
Human victims sacrificed in Mexico, 80
of Jesus. Source of story, 79
Stories of the, 78
Cruelty, man's history of, 28
to animals supported by the Church, 464
Crusades, the, 191
a black spot in Christian history, 182–3
Culture increases as education advances, 191
Curie, Marie (scientist), 428
Curse of Ignorance, The, ix, x, xxi, 86*fn.*, 249*fn.*, 383 *fn.*, 412*fn.*
Cyprian Bishop, 412
Cyril, Bishop (of Alexandria), 405

D

DALAI Lama considered a god, 346
Dalton, John (scientist), 428
Damasus, Pope, 412
Darius (Persia), 432
Dark, Ages, the, 84, 181, 438
Christendom in, 191, 426
Commencement of, 66
Some enlightened minds during, 461
Darwin, Charles (naturalist), 26, 198, 207, 208, 304, 405, 428
Davidson, Rev. Dr. (theologian), 374
Deaf will hear in Etheria, 450
and blind, education of, 192
Dead discovered and where they live, 331
physical body of Jesus never rose from grave, 181
Worship of, 56
Worship of, in Christian countries is ghoulish, 390
Death, 222, 341
a preliminary to further development, 299
After-life faced with confidence, 368–9
and the after-life. Ignorance of, 332–33
by torture and massacre at hands of Catholics and Protestants, 86
cannot annihilate consciousness, 289–90
Despair through ignorance of, 339–40
does not change existence and identity, 361
Enigma of, answered, 368
Etheric body leaves the physical, 291
Few care to contemplate it, 289 here and in Etheria, 449
is a bend in the road of life, 470
is entrance to enlarged outlook, 326
is a change from physical to etheric life, 392
is a door into a new life, 391
is a natural event, 46

Death is a release to fuller, freer and happier life, 368
is man's shortest journey, 296
is not a curse, 46, 368
is not the end, 222
is really birth to a life of happiness, 340
its mystery solved helps explain existence, 23
Love for friends on earth is not severed by, 470–1
need not be feared, 332, 333
Only physical body is lost, 268
opens new environment, 298
Physical resurrection borrowed from the Egyptians, 38
presents us with a new range of thought, 250
Spiritualism is a comfort at, 364
Survival of, basis of each religion, 329
symbolised by experiences attributed to god-men, 222
Why it is caused, 449
Deaths, Seven different, 298, 299
Declaration of Independence, U.S.A., 432
Decline and Fall of the Roman Empire, 67*fn.*
Deformed body is only the physical body, 449
Deformities moulded to normal in Etheria, 449–50
Deification of Jesus. Beginning of, 137
Deities found prominent place in man's thoughts, 50
Deity divided up into a Trinity, 221
represented as three persons but one God, 221
symbolised in the likeness of man, 222
Deist, Religion of the, 353
Delphic oracle, the, 220–1
Deluge, the, 94
Destiny of mankind, 474
and our ancestors, 249
Communication with Etheria makes it clearer, 466
Every human being has the same, 403
explained by Spiritualism, 34
is now known to us, 326
is to live and develop, 474
Man's discovery of, 367
Master of our own, 41–2
to become in tune with the Infinite, 326
Whence? and Whither? 23, 24
Devaki, mother of Krishna, 92
Devil. No personal, 334
Devils and gods were considered rulers of the earth, 201
Devils were superior to the gods, 100
were cause of disease, 201
were evil gods, 241
Dimensions of Greater World, 304–6
Diocletian (Emperor), 378, 379
Dionysus (deity), 76, 156, 174
and Paul's beliefs, 124–5
Direct Voice and séances, 399
broadcast over the wireless, 236
phenomenon proves survival, 235
Directive force, or mind, 248
Disciples of Jesus believed Pau preached heresy, 136

Q*

Disciples resented the teaching of Paul, 136
Discoverers enlarged our knowledge, 424 *et seq.*
Discoveries banish superstition, 199
   caused consternation, 202
Discussion leads to knowledge, 387
Disease and psychic healing, 339
Diseases considered as caused by devils, 201
Distance and time, 316
   decreases as our bodies get finer, 314
   in the realm of mind, 320
   will be the "all here", 316
District Nursing Associations founded, 192
Dives and Lazarus story, 83
Divine in nature and its contemplation, 110
   Intelligence, man is related to, 357
   Mind. At-one-ment with the, 324, 401
   Mind. In harmony with, 315–6, 474
   Mind. Mankind is part of, 325, 458
   Mind of the Universe, 107
   Mind of which we each are a part, 89
   Mind survives death, 226
   spirit, belief in Tibet, 346
   spirits in pre-Christian times, 80
Dix, Dorothea (humanist), 192
Doctor controls in Etheria, 398
Doctrines and dogmas are not required by Spiritualists, 327
Dogmas, 25
   a mystical conception, 176
   and creeds have made religion hateful, 355
Domestic Missions for the Poor, 192
Dominic, Saint, slaughtered thousands, 194
Draco (Athenian law-giver), 433
Drake, Francis (explorer), 426, 432
Draper, John William (historian), 67*fn.*
Drapings are no longer required, 224
   had hidden meanings, 220, 225
   of religion, 224
   what they mean, 220–25
Dreams. Why they are caused, 313
Druidism and Christianity, 190
Dualism in relation to man, 229, 230
Durham, Bishop of, 44

E

Ea liest Sources for the Life of Jesus, The, 119*fn.*
Earth, appearanc s often an illusion, 341
   is a fraction of the real world, 294
   is a nursery, 474
   is different to each individual, 288
   is not the real world, 302
   is only one range of vibrations, 294
   in size no more than a grain of sand, 203, 255
   Same conditions exist in Etheria, 286
Earth, We get only what we are mentally fitted for, 352
   will become a memory, 312
Eastern nations and religion, 355
   Orthodox Church despises the West, 172
   Orthodox Church ex-communicated, 172
Ectoplasm. The link between the two worlds, 231–2, 236
Eddystone lighthouse, 434
Education enlarges vision, 423
   its effect on mankind, 423–42
   of the future, 460
   of the people, Bishops' attitude to, 464
   The advantages for our descendants, 447
Edwards, Passmore (philanthropist), 193
Effect and cause, 200, 204
   produces cause, 458
Egypt and religious worship, 58
   Origin of doctrine of Trinity, 182
   Theology of, 99
Egyptian art, 98*fn.*
   gods overruled other deities, 99
   gods, Stories of, 95–6
   mystical trinity of gods, 128
   priests and magic, 103
   records and Spiritualism, 459
   religion similar to the Christian, 97
Eight worlds in one. Impression of, 302–6
Einstein (physicist), 428
Electricity. Discovery of, 198
Electron measured, 428
Electrons and protons, 319
   Belief in, 31
   in Etheria, 272
   of physical body, 291
   What they are, 262–6
Elisha, his cruelty to children, 84–5
Elohim means the gods, 95, 218
Empty tomb symbolises death conquered by released spirit, 222
Encyclopaedia Britannica, 53*fn.,* 140–1, 180*fn.,* 375*fn.*
Endless future appears before us, 226
English language standardised, 429
Enjoyment. More time will be devoted to, 447
Enlil (deity), 93
Ennugi (deity), 93
Enurta (deity), 93
Environment, changes as we progress, 298–9
Environments, Etherians communicate from different, 300
Epictetus (philosopher), 43, 437
Epicurus (philosopher), 43, 55, 159, 437
Epimetheus (the Greek Adam), 75
Episcopalians in Scotland persecuted and murdered, 87
Epistles altered and added to, 375–6
Erasmus (theologian), 118, 374
Eric the Red, 425
Essenism. Teaching of Jesus came from, 181
Eternal home is our own mind, 473
   punishment. Doctrine of, 463
Eternity, a state of consciousness, 319
Ether waves. Discovery of, 428
   waves penetrate matter, 30

Index

Ether waves unknown fifty years ago, 230
Etheria, 272 (*see also* Astral plane and Greater World)
  a pleasant abode, 246–7, 273, 460
  A description of, 281–2
  a timeless, spaceless world, 321
  Advanced minds in, 394, 352
  and atmosphere, 280, 282
  and its inhabitants, reality of, 418
  and philosophical contemplation, 352
  and the insane, 310
  and those who lived in poverty, 310
  As on earth so we shall be there, 360
  is as the mind desires, 311, 446, 449, 473, 450
  Bad cannot live with the good, 468
  Belief in, based on communications, 362, 465, 466
  bends in the road become fewer, 474–5
  Blind and deaf will see and hear, 450
  Books written under inspiration, 386
  can be a lonely place, 246
  Colours in, 282–3, 451–2
  Communication with, 361, 392, 414
  Conditions above astral plane, 451
  Conscious existence as here on earth, 268
  Definition of, xix, 28
  Desires and ideals on earth will be realised there, 467
  Differences between death here and there, 449
  Different laws operate in, 444
  Doctor controls in, 398
  Earthly deformities will be moulded to normal, 449–50
  Effect of thoughts in, 247, 309, 450
  Etheric bodies reflect etheric light in, 286
  Everything is in harmony, 309
  experiences day and twilight, 281
  Experiences of the good, 451
  Faith changes to knowledge, 401
  Family circle increased in, 470
  fashioned by mind, 324
  flowers and trees are brighter, 282
  food required for nourishment, 270
  Gleams of our next state, 311–2
  Grosser mental conditions, 309, 311, 352
  Happiness there depends on actions here, 246, 358
  has many ranges of vibrations, 294
  Healers can help the mentally afflicted, 398
  Higher teaching from, 352
  Home Circles are making it a reality, 465
  Image-making speed of mind is increased, 313

Etheria, individuality unimpaired 321
  Information received by mediums, 466
  Informants in, 250
  in terms of vibrations, 286, 428
  is a name for seven worlds, 269–270
  is about us, 319
  is composed of fine substance, 268
  is our real home, 107
  is similar to earth, 268, 269, 279, 280, 281, 286, 386
  Its inhabitants visit this earth, 126
  Its sun has greater invigorating powers, 241–2
  Knowledge of, 401, 452–3, 475
  Leaders of human race will still lead in, 440
  Life in, 271, 272, 273, 276, 277, 439–40
  Light in, 268, 281–6, 282
  Like will attract like, 311
  made up of minds developed on earth, 457
  matter moulded by thought, 343
  Mediums will keep us in touch with, 351, 396
  Memory in, 321
  Mental process same as here, 445
  Name for Spirit World, xix
  Orthodox beliefs fade, 352
  Other laws prevail in, 446
  People in the home will communicate with, 414
  Progress through the spheres, 326, 475
  Proof of life in, 439–40
  Reality of, 342
  Refining process for, 467–8
  Revelation from, 63, 330
  Sending of criminals to, 434
  Spiritualism helps to fit us for, 195
  Substance in, 283
  Surroundings those for which we are mentally fitted, 247, 352
  The bad mix with the bad, 450
  There we have mind, brain, eyes, substance and light, 268
  Those who come back are mostly friends, 351
  Time and space in, 253–4, 320, 321, 475
  Time measurement in, 313
  Transition to higher surfaces, 449
  Without it history of man would not have been, 249
Etherians, 350
  Advanced, will instruct mankind, 396
  are breaking down dividing wall, 196
  are getting messages through to us, 465
  are in a world somewhat like ours, 351
  are influenced by their surroundings, 269
  are latitudinarian in opinions, 351
  are solid, not vaporous beings, 217

Etherians can live in beautiful surroundings, 452
 can read, 255
 can travel at great speed, 269
 communicate from different environments, 300
 demonstrate their presence to us, 29, 38, 331
 encouraged to communicate with us, xx
 get beyond influence of earthly ideas, 352
 have control over their bodies, 269
 have love for friends on earth, 471
 have not reached God's throne to be judged, 351
 in touch with other planes, 300, 301
 live in other ranges of vibrations, 256
 mould their surroundings by thought, 447
 possess the same minds as they had on earth, 256
 progress to higher planes, 283
 seen and heard, 126, 217, 417
 sometimes use name Christ when Jesus is meant, 351
 Theological opinions of, 350–1
 Vibrations surrounding the earthbound, 398
 with earth memories come back, 300
Etheric beings in physical bodies. We are, 38
 body at death, 286, 291, 296, 390
 body composed of etheric cells, 291
 body. Conscious existence continues, 29
 body does not renew its earthly associations, 353
 body holds the physical together, 291
 body is a replica of the physical, 449
 body is not an inference, 293
 body is permanent, 293–4
 body. Mind has more control of, 309
 body of Jesus seen by Paul, 123–4
 body symbolised, 222
 body survives death, 56, 268
 bodies are finer, 231, 268–9
 bodies, complete in Etheria, 450
 bodies live on a surface, 309
 bodies refined by thought, 449
 bodies reflect character, 450
 bodies seen at death, 293
 bodies seen by clairvoyants, 219
 brain is real seat of the mind, 293
 doctors cure many ills of mankind, 385, 397
 duplicate brain passes from the body, 228
 duplicate of human victims believed eaten by gods, 73
 eye. Finer vibrations reflect colour to, 452
 life. Diagram of surfaces, 302
 light waves, 283
 matter, like physical, is vibrations, 267

Etheric minds affected by etheric world, 429
 planes, 285
 spheres and surfaces, 270–86, 286–307
 substance, 308, 319, 452
 substance is expression of mind, 238
 substance produced by vibrations, 238
 sun, 277
 surroundings, 307
 world, 217, 222, 310
 world envisaged on a scientific basis, 429
 world revealed to the ancients, 348
Ethical behaviour, 359
Ethics and religion, 358
 and the materialist, 211
 have come about from experience, 359
Eucharist, the, 170
 and the Roman Catholics, 223
 copied by Matthew, Mark and Luke, 133, 134
 copied from Pagans by Paul, 132, 134, 135, 387
 Institution of the, 79
 Origin of, 223
 was not instituted by Jesus, 133, 135
Eucharistic ceremony in early times, 134
Euclid (mathematician), 437
Europe kept in poverty by Christianity, 463
Eusebius (Bishop), 158, 160, 177, 375, 381
 and Christian martyrs, 378
 helped to produce a reformed Paganism, 380
Evil doers in Etheria, 309, 310
Evolution towards the Infinite, 304
 is not confined to earth, 401
Evolution, Last Words on, 209
Evolution of Man, 208
Evolution of the Idea of God, The, 53fn, 60
Existence is a range of vibrations, 291
 means thinking, 314
 Mystery of, 23
 Object of, 315
Exodus on religious sacrifice, 73
Experiences come from our surroundings, 252

F

FACTS distorted to favour theories, 346
 are based on evidence, 465
Faith and knowledge, 24, 354, 469
Family worship, 465
Famine brought about by gods, 100
Faraday, Michael (scientist), 198, 428
Father-god. Its meaning, 222
 Principal god of trinity, 221
 represented mind in man, 221
Father-gods were savage tyrants, 35
Fear made man afraid to think, 245
 will some day depart, 453
Fielden, John (humanist), 192
Filioque. Meaning of, 172
Fire became symbol of life, 58

Firmin, Thomas (philanthropist), 192
Force is indestructible and eternal, 206
Ford, Arthur (clairaudient), 417
Four Gospels. The, a study of origins, 119*fn*.
Fox, Catherine (medium), 27-8
   Margaretta (medium), 27-8
Fox-hunting. Cruelty of, 359
Franklin, Benjamin, 198, 427, 432
Frazer, Sir James, 53*fn*., 57*fn*., 75, 78*fn*.
Free libraries and institutes founded, 193
   thought making inroads everywhere, xvii
Friuli, Council of, 180
Fry, Elizabeth (reformer), 434
Funeral services and the Church, 390-2
   services. Form adopted by Spiritualists, 391-2

G

GAINSBOROUGH, Thomas (painter), 438
Galen (physician), 435-6
Galileo (astronomer), 26, 87, 197, 227, 230, 427
Gamaliel (rabbi), 127
Garrett, Mrs. (medium), 232
Garrison, William Lloyd (emancipationist), 431
Gautama worshipped as Buddha, 106
Genesis on religious sacrifice, 73
Gentiles, adherence to the Christ idea, 155
Gentiles, Paul's message to resented by disciples, 136
Geologists applied observation, experience and experiment, 204-5
Geology. Progress of, 203-5
Gibbon, Edward (historian), 67*fn*., 378, 437
Gladstone (statesman), 35
Globes, eight separate, 298-9
Gnosis, 128
Gnosticism before Christian era, 139
Gnostics, their beliefs perpetuated, 174
God, according to Philo, 130
   as a Trinity, 221
   and belief, 219, 358
   and revelation, 71, 216
   as mind, 325
   Buddhists worship no, 241
   demands obedience and flattery, 106
   Early man's ideas very crude, 107
   Fire worshipped as a, 58
   idea abandoned, 199
   is another name for Mind, 323, 324, 386
   is not a person, 334
   is revealed in each, 325
   Jesus did not know that he was, 181
   Jesus said he was not, 374
   Man is always in presence of, 323
   Mankind is a part of, 386
   Many very wicked believe in, 355

God, meaning "Infinite Intelligence", 218
   Misconception of the word, 216, 218, 225
   Mohammedans worship one, 241
   of vengeance, 333
   Only one according to Jesus, 374
   in the Bible should read "spirit" or "spirits", 216-18
   Origin of the belief in a, 54-5
   Reason of, 131
   Relation of, to the Universe, 50
   should be read as "the gods", 73
   son of, represented flesh of man, 221, 222
   symbolised as a trinity, 221
   symbolised in the form of godman, 221
   the Infinite Mind, 325
Goddesses, or "other-world" women, 217
   once lived on earth, 219
God-man. Belief in his coming to earth, 347
   looked upon as one of a trinity, 221
   revealed God to man, 221
God-men. Similar stories told, 346
   were sun gods, 91
God-Mind behind all phenomena, 240-1
Godparents and baptism, 388
Gods, 52-3
   Altar to the twelve, 54
   and devils were considered rulers of the earth, 201
   appeared at séances, 220
   are not divine potentates, 216
   banished from universe through science, 207
   Belief in, in the image of man, 53
   Belief in, will fade away, 110
   believed to be in touch with human beings, 132
   brought about famine and war, 100
   communicated through mediums, 221
   cruel and treacherous, 92
   Effort to placate, 88
   held to be cause of all good or ill, 241
   invented by man, 25
   Man was a slave of the, 199
   materialised in presence of mediums, 220
   No crime omitted to placate the, 242
   of the Africans, 101
   of the Chinese, 101
   of the earth, 91
   of the Egyptians, 100-1
   of the heavens, 91
   omnipotent and omniscient, 91
   or "other-world" men, 217
   Phenomena of nature attributed to the, 201
   Power of the, 201
   Sacrificial ritual to the, 54
   superseded by law and order, 200
   Three Christian, 64, 92-3, 241
   We have all the attributes of, 226
   were all very ignorant, 93
   were once men who lived on earth, 219

God's Word in the Old Testament is a mistranslation, 218
   Worship of, caused untold cruelties and misery, 34
   Worship of, led to degradation of women, 34
Goethe, Johann, 209, 439
Golden Bough, The, 53*fn.*, 57*fn.*, 78*fn.*
Golden rule of living, 361, 362
Gospel records are not historical, 120
Gospels. Synoptic, are copies of earlier documents, 121
   put together bit by bit, 142
   were altered and added to, 375–6
Gravestones will be replaced by tablets, 391
Greater Sun, 273–5, 283–4
   can be applied to other suns, 286
   light waves lost on earth, 285
Greater World (*see also* Etheria)
   a continuous evolutionary process, 303–4
   a mass of pulsating energy, 303
   a mass of vibrating substance, 303
   as seen from a distance, 303
   and colours, 300
   Communication with, 251
   Consciousness and memory retained in, 303
   Developing mind written across history of, 457
   Diagram of eight surfaces, 283, 301–2
   explains history, 457–8
   has great wonders to unfold, 257
   Impressions of, 304–5
   in terms of vibrations, 286
   is as we are capable of visualising, 259, 311
   its comprehensibility, 250
   life changes its conditions, 303
   Panorama comprising the, 467
   ranges of vibration, 300
   scientifically discovered, 249
   Structure of, 250
   sun consists of globes, 271
Greece, Great thinkers of, 42, 55
   Mediums attached to temples, 220
Greek and Roman writings. Civilising influence of, 43
   ideals and noble thoughts, 461
   literature and culture, 438
   literature on medicine and healing, 463
   Orthodox Church, 382
   Orthodox Church excommunicated, 160
   Orthodox Church. Origin of, 370
   Philosophy, 383
   thought brought culture to Europe, 438
Greeks and psychic phenomena, 102
   were first with schools of learning, 66
Grissel Jaffray, a broadcast, 40–1
Gurney (inventor), 429
Gutenberg (printer), 429

H

HADES, or the astral plane, 222
Haeckel, Ernest (naturalist), 208, 209, 427

Hammurabi (King of Babylon), 433
Handel (musician), 439
Happiness and knowledge are twin brothers, 468
   is aim of everyone, 467
Harnack, Professor, 142, 143
Harvey (physician), 198, 436
Healing circles, 393, 396
   mediums, 396
   rays act on our etheric body, 397
Heat from etheric sun, 271
Heaven is a condition of mind, 401
   New Testament and difficulty of rich entering, 83
   of the Christians came from ignorant imaginings, 41
Hebrews, mental development of, 103
Helena, Saint, 160
Hell developed out of ignorant imaginings, 41
   Doctrine of, blackest spot in Christianity, 39–40
Helmholtz, Hermann (physicist), 198, 428
Henry VIII, 380, 434
Heraclitus (philosopher), 26*fn.*, 458
Hercules (deity), 134
Heretics. A noble army of suffering, 431
Herod, King, 119
Herodotus (historian), 437
Heroes of the human race, 430–37, 442
Heron (engineer), 429
Herschel, Sir John (astronomer), 427
Hertz (scientist), 428
Hesiod (poet), 75, 459
Higher Criticism, School of, 118
   surfaces than astral plane, 451
Hindu Gods, 92
   cannot adopt Christian terminology, 348
   controversies caused by adopting name Spiritualist, 362
Hinduism, 415
Hippocrates (father of medicine), 435
Historical Christ, The, 119*fn.*
Historical events caused by religion, x
History cannot be divided into two sections, 458
   Comparative religion and pre-Christian, 402
   in the future—no church influence, 411
History of the Christian Church, 375*fn.*
History of the Conflict between Religion and Science, The, 67*fn.*
History of the Intellectual Development of Europe, 67*fn.*
History would be different had Paul known Jesus, 137
Holy Communion is a Pagan institution, 387
   days of the Church, 82
   Ghost, the, 36, 222
   Love is, 386
   of Holies, 57
   Roman Empire founded, 194
   See power broken, 431
   Spirit, how belief developed, 80
   Spirit or Holy Ghost returned to earth, 222
   Spirit symbolical of man's etheric body, 222
Holyoake, George Jacob (reformer), 193
Home is sacred, 386

Index

Home Circles are making Etheria a reality, 465
  have come to stay, 465
  in Protestant countries, 414
Homer (poet), 96, 459
Horus (deity), 92, 93
Hospitals and nursing homes founded, 436
"Host", its meaning, 79
House of Lords, 464
Howard, John (reformer), 434
Howard of Effingham, 432
Howe, S. G. (educationalist), 192
Hughes, Helen (clairaudient), 417
  Stella (clairaudient), 417
Hugo, Victor (author), 432
Human liberty. Desire for, 430
Humanity divided by Christians, 194
  been raised by believers and non-believers in Christianity, 192-3
  has civilised religion, 245
  Its ignorance, 50
  Pioneers of, 424 et seq.
Humboldt (naturalist), 198, 427
Hume, David (philosopher), 437
Hunter, John (surgeon), 436
Huxley, Thomas (scientist), 405, 210
Hydesville (U.S.A.) xx, 27, 258, 330, 331
Hypatia (philosopher), 405, 411

I

IDEAS have a long ancestry, 458
Idolatry. Origin of, 57
Ignorance, 106
  and misery are twin brothers, 468
  enemy of mankind, xv
  honoured through fear, 245
  is better than knowledge from clergy's viewpoint, 69
  is parent of low conceptions, 455
  keeps science and religion apart, 216
  lives by night, 50-1
  Man's history of, 28
  No darkness but, 25
  of death and after-life, 333-4, 354
  of humanity, 50
  of orthodox in Etheria, 351
  relating to death causes misery and cruelty, 332
  Results of, 468
Ignorant cannot comprehend religion of the philosopher, 353
  think of God in the form of man, 106
  worship the past, 112
Image-making in Etheria, 313
Image worship, its origin and practice, 55, 111-12
Immortal soul. Belief in, 368
Immortality and the Christian Church, 224, 462
Incandescent light discovered, 429
India, its depraved religion, 104
Indian records of dead returning, 459
Individuality and personality at conception, 229
Individuals accept religion for which the mind is fitted, 353
Infidel. Its true meaning, 444
Infidels were responsible for starting march of progress, 77-8
Infinite, the, 89, 103
  Attunement with, 474
  Basis of religion is reaching out after, 178
  Contemplation of, 385
  Influence of, 360
  intelligence. Cruel teaching attributed to, 218, 219
  In tune with, 316, 326
  is beyond understanding, 50
  mind. Knowledge of, 324
  Our reaching at-one-ment with, 322-3
  Steps leading to, 451
Infinity and its comprehension, 320
Inge, Dean, 383
Ingersoll, Robert Green (reformer), 405, 431-2
Inquisition, the, 168
  in France, 193
  in Spain, 86
Insanity and Etheria, 310
  healers in Etheria, 399
Inspirational writings, 386
Institutes and free libraries founded, 193
Intellectual light through Spiritualism, 196
Intelligence causes fear to depart, 52
  Development of, 405, 433
  helping to discard superstitions, 26
  Increased, answers enigma of death, 368
  increasing in strength, 114
  will banish fear of the future, 368
  will cause Church to decline, 387
Intelligent on earth in advance of ignorant in Etheria, 351
Intolerance is fast disappearing, 46
Invention of telescope feared by Christian Church, 199
  will enable us to reach age of leisure, 446
Inventors, 429
  enlarged our knowledge, 424 et seq.
Investigation, scientific method of, 198
Ireland. History of, 169
Irenæus (Church father), 373
Iron Age, 205
Isis (Deity), 92, 129, 174
Islam, 172
  barbarities and atrocities during the Crusades, 183

J

JACKS, Professor (physical researcher), 371, 372
James, Saint, and Paul at variance, 136
Jeans, Sir James, 254, 255, 257
Jehovah, 94, 105
  a cruel god, 36, 100
  a god of war, 36
  a savage tyrant, 35
  an ignorant god, 93
  and Jewish priesthood, 84
  and sacrificial rites, 57
  and what is taught to children, 410-11

Jehovah, Christians endeavour to ignore him, 35
denounced trinity of gods, 129
denounces Baal, 129
god of Great Britain, 36
must remain the Christian god, 36
one of two gods in the Old Testament, 95
worship and adoration, 36
Jenner, Edward, 436
Jephtha, Story of, 73
Jerome, Saint, 158, 373, 375, 412
Jeshuah, the Hebrew name of Jesus, 185
Jesuians, 154, 183
believed Jesus used holy spirit as medium's control, 80
Jesuism, Account of early, 150*fn*.
and Christianity diametrically opposite, 184
Jesus, 36, 55, 74, 91, 118, 119*fn*.
a man, raised to a god through an apparition, 137, 154
acted to truths of Spiritualism, 184
added to pantheon of saviour gods, 176
admired, but not worshipped by spiritualists, 32, 184
and Christ cannot both be worshipped, 164, 165
and Christ, what they stand for, 163, 167–71
and legends surrounding sun worship, 180
as Christ or Logos, 127
as god, used as incitement for cruelty, 138
as recorded in the gospels, 141–3
as the son of man, 166–7
as Very God of Very God, 372
asserted there is only one God, 371, 374
associated with Christs of Paganism, 154
Beginning of the deification of, 137
Belief that the Divine Spirit was his medium's control, 80
believed by Unitarians to be a prophet, healer and teacher, 180
called Christ. Paul's construction, 345
Children will in the future be taught truth about, 409
Claim to be "The Light of the World" unfair, 42
considered a god by Paul, 132
considered a supernatural being, 139
contributed nothing to Christianity, 180
contributed nothing to knowledge of the after-life, 42
did not accept ideas about himself, 346
did not condemn cruelty of Jehovah, 36
did not know that he was God, 181
Documents relating to his life non-existent, 120
dragged into Christian superstition, 187

Jesus equal to Jehovah by a vote, 155
Followers of should be called Jesuins, 154
founded no Church or religion, 169
had human failings, 348
his crucifixion, 79
his earth life, 122
his moralisings found in leading world religions, 156, 165
his natural life taken from various sources, 181
his physical body never rose from the dead, 181
his teachings debased, 349
Historical, means nothing to mystical Christians, 174
idea of being virgin-born an afterthought, 166
ignored by Paul, 164
is not an historical character, 120, 153, 167
left no writings, 119
Legends and myths surrounding his life, 176
lies propagated concerning him, 186
lived in contact with Etheria, 459
Miraculous stories copied from Paganism, 181
never referred to his virgin birth, 181
No evidence he was a perfect man, 348
Nothing in common with Christianity, 153
one of many Christs, 135, 166
or Christ?, 164–96
Paul never referred to his ethical and moral teaching, 124, 136, 137
Paul's belief in his reappearance, 132
pictured as teacher, healer and man, 153
preached to Jews only, 136
psychic healer and teacher, 132
Quest for the historical, 118–9
represented as saviour of all believers, 462
second only to Jehovah in Paul's opinion, 132
seen in his etheric body, 123
should never be associated with Christ, 76
Spiritualists endeavour to bring Christians back to him, 171
Superstition accumulated round, 158
taught what Spiritualists teach, 328
Temptation in the desert, mythical element, 153
The real, can he be found?, 140
Vital problems he was silent about, 348
was behind Paul, 118
was born in a natural way, 181, 348
was never a Christian, 154, 184
was not responsible for Christianity, 184
was seen after death as an apparition, 181
was silent on Paul's doctrine, 137

Jesus was unorthodox towards Judaism, 184
 when on earth not known as Christ, 76
 worshipped as the god-man Christ, 106
 worshipped the god Jehovah, 35-6
 would not recognise the Christian religion 337
Jesus Christ, an Historical Outline, 119*fn.*, 141
Jesus Christ, appellation is entirely wrong, 184-5
Jews imagined Jehovah cruel because they were, 100
 believe in one God, 54
 cannot adopt Christian terminology, 348
 Controversies caused by adopting name Spiritualist, 362
 copied Pentateuch from Babylon, 346
 disbelieve in divine sacrifice, 77
 financiers of Europe, 83-4
Joan of Arc lived in contact with Etheria, 459
 Reason for burning of, 421
John Gospel of, not taken seriously, 140, 141
John, Saint, 134
Johnson, Samuel (author), 153, 437
Johns Hopkins University, U.S.A., 233, 292
Johnston, Annie (clairaudient), 417
Jones, Inigo (architect), 438
Judaic-Hellenic philosophy, 128
Judaism, 336, 415
 and Jesus, 184
 and Paganism used by Paul to found Christianity, 136
Judgment improves with education, 423-4
Julian (Emperor), 160
Jungle, Laws of the, 452, 453
Jupiter (deity), 100, 105, 111, 162
 Temptation of by Pan, the pagan devil, 153
Justinian I (Emperor), 66

K

KANT, Immanuel (philosopher), 437
Keith, Sir Arthur, 210
Kelvin, Lord, 198, 425
Kennelly-Heaviside layer, 278
Kepler, John (astronomer), 26, 87, 197, 198, 427
King of Kings is Mind, 308
Knowledge and happiness are twin brothers, 468
 and what it has brought us, 203, 468
 Attainments through, 467, 450
 brings happiness and comfort, 354, 474
 causes fear to depart, 455
 causes intellectual contentment, 25
 denounced through fear, 245
 Discussion leads to, 387
 enables us to dominate matter, 447
 enhances and enlarges mental outlook, 401

Knowledge enlarged on a scientific basis, 251
 Faith changes to, 354, 401
 Faith is feeble compared with, 469
 Foundations of, 198
 has brought freedom of thought, 366
 helps life's burdens, 89
 increased by remembering mistakes, 25
 increases as culture and education advances, 191
 is strength, 440-1
 Its effect on mankind, 423-42
 Limit of Spiritualists extended knowledge, 344
 Makes life understood, 468
 More time will be devoted to, 447
 of Spiritualism helps mankind, 469
 produces strong characters, 245
 replaces faith, 25
 Scientific method of obtaining, 202, 367
 set in motion by Copernicus, 203
 Spiritualism an addition to, 32
 will cast out fear of death, 460
 will discard materialistic burial services, 391
Kreisler, Fritz (musician), 439
Krishna (deity), 92, 345
 left no writings, 119
 lived in contact with Etheria, 459
Krishna Spirit, 348

L

LAING, Samuel (author), 211
Lamarck (naturalist), 198, 427
Lamsa, George (Aramaic scholar), 120-1
Lancaster, Joseph (schoolmaster), 62, 463
Langmuir (physicist), 428
Lao-Tsze, 349
Laplace, Pierre (scientist), 207, 427
Last Supper, the, 132-4
Last Words on Evolution, 209
Lavoisier, Antoine (chemist), 198, 427
Law-givers in pre-Christian days, 220
Layard (Assyriologist), 93, 437
Leaf, Horace (clairaudient), 417
League of Nations stands for peace, 455
Lee, William (inventor), 429
Leo IX (Pope), 172
Leonardo da Vinci, 26, 197, 427
Leviticus on sacrifice, 73
Liberty lubricates thoughts, 444
Libraries in Spiritualist churches, 407
Life changes its conditions, 303
 Continuation of emphasised, 391
 continues after death, 44-5, 392
 Desires more easily supplied, 447
 emerging of, and its results, 474
 Enlarged view as minds unfold, 457
 Everything is of interest in, 387
 here and in Etheria, 341
 is a series of experiences, 252
 is developing and expanding mind, 473-4

Life is easier in Etheria, 447
 is largely being conscious of colour, 266
 moving to higher states of consciousness, 303
 Object of, 314, 315
 on earth fits us for Etheria, 449
 on earth is a nursery, 342
 understood through knowledge, 469
 viewed as a drama, 469
 Youth to be taught continuance of, 409
Life of Constantine, The, 375
Life, The Wonders of, 209
Light, Humanity ever struggling towards, 443
 and consciousness, 259
 in Etheria, 281–6
 on earth, 285
 waves, reflected by electrons, 262
 waves, speed of, 261
Lippershey (inventor), 427
Lister, Lord, 436
Litany of the Church written from fear, 90
Literature Rediscovery of, 438
Liverpool, Bishop of, and Church doctrines, 371, 372
 Cathedral, Sermon by a layman, 371
Living, Joy of, 41
Livingstone (explorer), 426
Locke, John (philosopher), 437
Logos, 140
 highest mediator between God and the world, 131
 Meaning of, 76
 Speculations about, 128
Lord of all is Mind, 308
Lord of Hosts and Armistice day, 420
 worshipped by Christians, 421
Lord, The, should read "the gods", 73
Love by friends in Etheria for those on earth, 471
 draws mind to mind, 470
 for humanity is not confined to Christians, 192
 and those it inspires, 471
 is greatest force in the universe, 470
 is not severed by death, 470–1
Luke, Comparisons with other gospels, 141–3
 and "Quelle", 140–3
Luke, Saint, copied Paul's words, 133–4
Lunatics, Better treatment for, 192
Luther, Martin, 161, 431
 did not produce a new religion, 136
 his new interpretation of religion, 135–6
 produced a diluted form of Paganism, 382
Lyceums attached to Spiritualist churches, 408
Lyell, Sir Charles, 208, 427

M

MACAULAY (historian), 437
Magellan expedition, 426
Magic and Moses, 103
 developed from psychic phenomena, 103

Magic often practised by priests, 60, 101–2
 origin of, psychic phenomena, 103
Magicians and priests have much in common, 244
Man, a mental etheric being, 31, 32
 always thinking about the hereafter, 243, 355, 366
 and his attitude to religion, 357
 and his neighbour, 343
 beginning to realise his destiny, 368
 Belief in being an immortal soul, 243–4
 composed of mind and matter substances, 238
 detests idea of destruction, 354, 358–9
 developed from mammal ancestors, 207, 243
 Development of mentality, 103
 endowed with part of Mind, 343
 endowed with psychic powers, 339, 347
 Evolution of, 357
 Existence and identity continue after death, 361
 has advanced by remembering mistakes, 25
 has misconstrued and misinterpreted reality, 322
 His gods improved as he developed, 245
 his liberty due to past reformers, 443
 His mind can now grow unrestrained, 443–4
 History of, 25–9, 243
 Ignorance of, 32
 ignorance of his possibilities on earth, 368
 is a conscious thinking entity, 287, 288, 315
 is a thinking unit, 319
 is a trinity, 221, 238–9
 is a twofold being, 131
 is an etheric being, 107, 361
 is an individual but dependent on others, 301
 is for ever seeking truth, 196
 is his own saviour, 362, 471–2
 is improved through intelligence, 29, 359, 454
 is made up of two bodies and mind, 238, 324
 is other than a material creature, 361
 is part of God, 323, 386
 is related to Divine Intelligence, 357
 is viewing the universe upside down, 316
 makes God in his own likeness, 410
 must help himself and others, 246
 not brought into being by one creative act, 207
 prizes his individuality, 357
 questioned authority of king and priest, 245–6
 relied on gods, 28
 sees physical body but not the etheric, 286
 showed himself superior to beasts, 242–3

Index

Man the only known personal god, 226
  was afraid to think through fear, 245
  will progress still further, 357
Man's destiny if he helps himself, 310, 318
  happiness hereafter, 246, 445
  religious emotions, 316
  soul from the Materialist viewpoint, 227–8
Mankind, Advancement of, 105
  and ethical progress, 456
  and the unfolding universe, 317–318.
  are mental not material creatures, 453
  Death a powerful influence on, 458
  discoveries of, and the hereafter, 365
  discovering they have been misled, 338
  expected by Church to accept, 64
  fit themselves for place in Etheria, 449
  helped by knowledge of Spiritualism, 469
  is encased in physical bodies, 308
  knows little about destiny, 365–6
  material ills can be cured, 339, 385
  No end to advancement, 362
  not privileged to think, 64
  Religious beliefs of, 33
  requires an intermediary, 445–6
  second transition stage, 367
  still victims of superstition, 201, 365, 422
  Thinkers, increased happiness of, 424
  worships and prays through fear, 88
Marcion (Gnostic), 138*fn.*, 177
Marconi (inventor), 430
Mark gospel and "Quelle", 140–3, 153
  full of Aramaic phrases and idioms, 142
Mark, Saint, 133
  copied Eucharist from Paul, 133–4
Marriage an ancient contract, 82
  ceremony incorporates superstitions, 389
  and claims of Church, 390
Martin, Richard (humanitarian), 435
Martyrdom of Man, The, 67*fn.*
Martyrs at hands of Christians, 87–8, 431
Massey (historian), 78*fn.*
Materialisations under scientific tests, 236
Materialism, Age of, 27, 32, 50, 63, 197–214
  based on unevidential assertions, 238
  consequence of superstition, 201
  Cause of, 204, 244
  is passing, 33, 200
Materialists, 200, 211–12
  and spiritualists, 210, 213–4
  arguments against survival, 229, 232, 238
  assertion that no soul exists, 237
  Basis of their negative attitude, 227

Materialists, Claims of the, 29, 32, 33, 208
  had answers for everything, 208
  have only part of the truth, 213
  refuse to attend séances, 227
Matter, A universe of, 200
  and etheric substance, 238
  and force, 207
  and Mind two different substances, 253
  appeals by effect of electrons and protons, 267, 428
  consists of other than physical substance, 290
  is composed of atoms, 262
  is indestructible and eternal, 206
  is less gross in Etheria, 444
  is not solid, 30
  is only one expression of reality, 214, 290
  will be dominated by increased knowledge, 447
  without mind is non-existent, 314
Matthew, comparisons with other gospels, 140–3
  and "Quelle", 140–3
Matthew copied Eucharist from Paul, 133
Mediators, man's belief in, 25
Medicine, Science of, 436
Mediums, 33, 41, 56, 60, 61, 195, 220, 230, 280, 385, 403, 440
  accused of all ills, 244–5
  act as a nexus, 45
  and materialisations, 236
  and psychic healing, 396–8
  and the healing ray, 397
  are not equally gifted, 394
  are now safe from destruction, 460
  are rivals to the priests, 63, 226
  as future parish priests, 393
  at present confined to great cities, 394
  at séances, 300
  Belief that Jesus returned and used divine spirit, 80
  deserve lasting gratitude, 441
  destroyed by the Church, 64, 226, 331, 419
  elevated by the Roman Catholic Church, 63
  enable discarnate mind to express itself, 231
  externalise a force, 231
  formerly called witches, 64
  help loved ones to make contact, 471
  Idea they were possessed of devils, 244
  in trance, 397–8
  Information about Etheria, 466
  Investigation and development of, 113
  not accepted by the Christian Church, 412
  present at funerals, 391
  Religious opinion uttered through a, 351
  will be attached to each church, 393, 395
  will be honoured, 394
  will co-operate with doctors, 399
Mediumship a natural development, 244
  growing rapidly, 394, 460

Mediumship has for long existed, 245
  is a natural and hereditary gift, 331, 465
  made use of by priests, 244
  may open new life for the insane, 399
Memory, 321
Mencius (Meng-tse), a Chinese teacher, 349
Mendelssohn, Felix (composer), 439
Mental control a greater asset than titles, 448
  development, 229–30, 448
  development and desires, 453
  development and evolution, 401
  development and its results, 114, 454
  development can overcome base desires, 453
  development required to change ideas, 353
  development, Surroundings in Etheria and, 247
  development will make wars impossible, 392
  homes, 398
  images are the individual's universe, 312
  images cause memory, 318
  pictures if wrong cause mistakes, 448
  process here and in Etheria, 445
  revolution created by Spiritualism, 383, 469
  values will remain for ever, 448
Mentally afflicted helped by Etherians, 398
  afflicted often suffer from lowminded, 398
Messages spelt out by a tilting table, 237
Messiah, a Hebrew word meaning Christ, 76, 126
  not referred to in Old Testament as one with God, 128
  Paul's belief in, 132
  Speculations about, 128
Messiahs 344
Mexico and religious worship, 58
  human victims crucified, 80
  savage ancestors, 104
Meyers, Adolph (psychical researcher) 233
Might glorified over right, 453
Mill, John Stuart (philosopher), 192
Miltiades (general), 432
Millikan (physicist), 428
Mind, Activities of, 442
  and its powers, 247
  and matter two different substances, 253, 317
  and personality exist after death, 237
  and substance inseparable, 314
  and the brain, 211
  and the Materialist, 210, 228
  and the universe, 308
  As it is so is the universe, 252, 312, 315–6, 323, 407
  as the directing force, 214, 239, 240, 314
  Cosmic, The, 308
  culture, importance of, 407
  Development of, xviii, 315
  Development of, in Etheria, 452
  Discarnate, 231

Mind Divine, at-one-ment with, 324
  does not die, 253, 294, 320
  dominates physical substance, 230, 253
  Each is an individual universe, 256, 307, 312, 443
  encased in Etheric bodies, 308
  encompasses the universe as it develops, 252, 255
  eternal, Attributes of, 458
  Etheric body is its real home, 294
  expresses itself in different ways, 238, 361
  functions through etheric brain, 268
  goes with the etheric body, 293
  governs the universe, 239, 248, 361
  has more control in etheric body, 309
  has moulding power in Etheria, 446
  Harmony of, through self-control, 448
  History of each individual, 473
  in contact with matter, means life, 230–1
  Individual, is indestructible, 312, 318, 293
  Individual, is unfolding, 317
  Individual, will attain reality, 475
  in Etheria stimulated by colour, 451–2
  is behind all forces of nature, 324
  is fastest range of vibrations, 290–1
  is God, 308, 323, 324, 361
  is King, 230, 238, 308–25, 343, 427, 456
  is not part of the brain, 228
  is omnipresent, omnipotent and omniscient, 239, 473
  is ourselves and never dies, 256, 294, 312, 448, 469, 473
  is something apart from the physical organism, 232
  is super-physical and superetheric, 239
  is the only reality, 312, 314, 423, 474
  made and fashioned all things, 325
  Nothing wiser than to develop our, 447
  of man for ever seeks truth, 196
  of the universe, At-one-ment with, 316
  on earth conditioned by surroundings, 473
  penetrates all substance, 318, 325
  Physical and etheric substance give dimensions to, 317
  Refining process goes on, 308
  represented by Father-God, 221
  Speed of, is the speed of thought, 313
    he image maker, 254, 259
  The physical body a medium for expression of, 230
  the producer of thought, 207, 314
  There is no matter without, 314
  training is life's objective, 343
  Universal, 308
  Universe has no boundaries to, 317

Index

Mind unfolding, unfolds the universe, 474
  uses physical vibrations, 240
  Well-balanced and correct decisions, 448
  working out its own salvation, 320
Mind-God behind all phenomena, 240–1,
Mind-images, The universe would cease to be without, 324
Mind-substance is of different degrees, 253
Minds, finer ones attuned to higher planes, 309, 449
  in Etheria establish equilibrium, 450
  which earth developed make up Etheria, 457
Miracles, a mockery of nature's revelation, 38
Misery and ignorance are twin brothers, 468
Mistakes, Man's history of, 28
Mithra (deity), 92, 174
  Eucharistic service, 134
Mithraism, 336
  copied by the Church, 168
  its documents destroyed, 337
Modern Knowledge and Old Beliefs, 211
Modern Science and Modern Thought, 211
Mohammed, 54
  lived in contact with Etheria, 459
  split the Christian Church, 182, 382
Mohammedanism, xvii, 195, 403, 415
  retained one god only, 241
Mohammedans cannot accept Christian terminology, 348
  disbelieve in divine sacrifice, 77
Monasteries became corrupt, 191
Monism, 208, 209
Montford, Simon de, 431
Moon, a god of evil, 91
  has no atmosphere, 278
  has no life, 279
Moseley (scientist), 428
Moses and psychic phenomena, 103
  his code of laws copied, 433
Moslems believe in one God, 54
  first to build colleges and observatories, 426
  introduced the numerals, 426
  encouraged science during dark ages of Christianity, 191
Motherhood, Baptism is an insult to, 388
Motion and its laws, 206
Mourning will give place to confidence, 391
Mozart, Wolfgang (composer), 439
Müller (philanthropist), 434
Murderers, Fate of, 4343
Mutual trust must replace fear and distrust, 456
Mystery temples, 174–5
Mystical Christians, their beliefs, 174, 219–20
  contemplations, 316, 324
Mysticism, 243, 327
  and Spiritualism, 327
  Philosophy and natural religion are one, 327

Mystics and Christianity, 178
  of the past, 350
Myth, Magic and Morals, 119*fn.*, 143*fn.*
Mythology and religion, 92
  and saviour gods, 92
  borrowed by Christianity, 92

N

NAPOLEON, 86, 207, 433
Nasmyth, James (engineer), 430
Natural religion (*see* Religion, natural)
  obscured by the super-natural, 220
Nature and death, 340
  has a place for all, 450
  intends mankind to know its future, 462
  is the mother of us all, 70
  laws misunderstood, 28
  makes her changes slowly, 280
  Phenomena studied by man, 206
  returns full-measure in after-life, 341
Nature of the Gods, The, 134
Neo-Platonist, accepted three gods, 128
Netherlands, Persecution of Christians in the, 378
Newcomen (engineer), 429
New English Dictionary, The, 212
New Testament, added to or curtailed, 83
  and rich entering heaven, 83
  contains diametrically opposite opinions, 164
  Documents comprising the, 118, 156
Newton, Sir Isaac, 26, 87, 197, 206, 264, 427
Nicaea, Council of, 98, 99, 117, 137, 154, 155, 158, 159, 160, 161, 166, 190, 373, 377, 379
Nice, Council of, 58
Nicene Creed, 155, 158
  altered and amended, 379–80
  Belief in, 377
  Birth of, 379–80
  First draft of, 375
  Uncalled for addition to, 172
Nightingale, Florence, 193, 436
Nineveh, tablets discovered, 93, 94
Ninigiku Ea (deity), 93
Nirvana, Attainment of, 349

O

OBERAMMERGAU, Ancient religious drama re-enacted, 76, 223
Old Testament and the Hebrews, 103
  words "God" or "the Lord" are mistranslations, 217–8
On the Edge of the Etheric, vii, xiii, xix, 235, 250, 251, 475
On the Revolutions of the Heavenly Bodies, 427
Opinions based on facts bring knowledge, xv
  formed on evidence only, 448
Oracles, The, 175
Origen (early Christian), 159, 177
Origin of Species, 207

Ormuzd (deity), 92
Orpheus (musician), 174
Orthodox, only entitled to name Christian, 345
  Christians believe too much, 227
  Christians, Claims shattered, 335–6
  Christians still worship drapings, 224, 225
  Christians take sacred writings literally, 218–9
  fiends justified their cruelty and torture, 356
  religions are based on the supernatural, 213
  religions are man-made things, 353
  religions are related, 329
  religions cause unnecessary suffering, 336
  religions doomed to die, 38, 196
  religions engender folly, intolerance and ignorance, 215
  religions losing public support, xvii–xviii, 336
  religions not for the cultured and educated, xviii–xix
  religions of the past, 367
  religions, Origin of, 329
  religions, Spiritualism the greatest danger to, 63
  religious beliefs are those of early man, 366
  scientists and super-physical intelligences, 251
Orthodoxy not suitable for thinkers, xviii, 384
Osiris (deity), 92, 96, 98, 156, 174, 175, 176, 189
  his etheric body reappears, 74
  his sufferings, death and resurrection, 97
  god of truth and justice, 97
  the Christ of the Egyptians, 97
Osty (psychical researcher), 231–2
Other-world man or woman, 217
Our Dead, Where are They?, 23

P

Pagan Christs, 78*fn.*
Pagan priesthood opposed Greek philosophy, 157
  statues worshipped, 111
  superstitions retained by Christians, 381
Paganism, Luther produced a diluted form of, 382
  and Christian superstition, 187
  and Judaism, basis of Paul's teaching, 136
  disguised as Christianity, 382
  Few Pagans neglected eucharist, 155
  Philosophy has been its enemy, 383
Pagans and Jews, speculations about the Messiah, 128
Paine, Thomas (reformer), 193, 430, 432
Palestine, Sacred associations of, 182
Pandora, the Greek Eve, 75
Pantheon once a Pagan temple, 421
Paper, A mental revolution caused by its discovery, 202

Parables, Reason for, 223
Parson, The, still a priest in mental outlook, 67
Parsons (*see* Priests)
Parthenon (Athens), 438
Passion play performed before Christian era, 76
Past should not be worshipped, 387
Pasteur, Louis, 436
Paul, Saint, 74, 130, 377
  and a supernormal occurrence, 123
  and his audiences, 337
  and the etheric body, 318
  and the theological Christ, 154
  Basis for Christianity was Judaism and Paganism, 76, 135–6
  belief in Jesus as crucified saviour, 122
  believed his revelation was to him alone, 137
  chosen as an exponent of Christ, 132
  claimed he had seen the living Christ, 136
  claimed he was in regular rapport with Jesus, 136
  did not bother about earth-life of Jesus, 124
  Effect of his preaching, 137–8
  father of Christianity, 76, 117 118, 160
  founded a religion whose God is a monster, 183
  his experiences not unique, 125
  his mystical ideas are pre-Christian, 156
  his opinion of Jesus, 121–3
  his psychic experience, 132
  History would be different had he known Jesus, 137
  ignored Jesus, 164
  instituted the Christian Eucharist, 132, 133, 135
  intertwined the theological Christ with the human Jesus, 122
  Jesus as Messiah advanced to Jesus as Christ, 132
  Jesus was silent on Paul's doctrine, 137
  longed for the anticipated Messiah, 132
  never referred to moral and ethical teaching of Jesus, 136
  not interested in what Jesus said or did, 124
  refused to consort with other disciples, 133
  started idea of Jesus being saviour, 138
  supplanted Jesus for other gods, 134
  was strongly psychic and clairvoyant, 123, 171
  teaching different to disciples, 136
  used speculations of Alexandria, 129–131
  writings tampered with, 138
Pauline Christianity was Gnostic, 140
Pearl, Raymond (scientist) 292–3
Pericles (statesman), 438
Persecution by Christians, 378–9
Personality and individuality established at conception, 229
Pestilence brought about by gods, 100

Peter, Saint, his footprints and tomb, 111
  his teaching at variance with Paul, 136
Phelips, Vivian (rationalist), 211
Phenomena is never invented by science, 230
  natural, 31
  natural, believed to be expression of the gods, 201
  of nature, Men began to study, 206
  that occurs in presence of mediums, 232
Phidias (sculptor), 438
Philo (theologian), 127, 129, 130–1, 177
Philosopher gains at-one-ment through contemplation, 324
Philosophic reasoning, 316
Philosophy, 243, 248
  Aim of, 323
  and Spiritualism, 327
  Basis of, xviii
  has ebbed and flowed, 383
  is now more scientific, 466–7
  mysticism and natural religion are one, 327
  sacrificed for superstition, 159
  science and religion are one in ideals and aspirations, 467
  stands for truth, 327
  the enemy of Paganism, 383
  will supersede supernatural religion, 104
Physical body held together by etheric body, 38, 291
  and psychic science applied to way of life, xix
  body is medium for expression of mind, 230
  bodies appeal by their vibrations, 286
  ills cured by healing rays, 397–8
  matter and etheric substance are vibrations, 267, 290
  matter does not constitute entire universe, 287
  matter is not the sovereign power, 238
  science and psychic science joined together, 251, 258
  substance, What it really is, 428
  vibrations, 271
Pioneers of medicine denounced, 436
Pioneers of the past, 425–30, 442
Planes, or surfaces of Greater World, 248–307
  Evil people cannot live on the higher, 309, 310
Plasm and the scientist, 237
  Monism of, 239
Plato (philosopher), 43, 54, 65, 75, 130, 131, 132, 153, 159, 350, 437
  gave more light than Jesus, 348
Plimsoll, Samuel (humanitarian), 435
Plotinus lived in contact with Etheria, 459
Plutarch asserts no fraud by medium at Delphi, 220–1
Political labels came to have a meaning, 202–3
Politics, 455, 458
Polo, Marco (explorer), 425
Pope (poet), 198

Pope, The, 201
  became supreme, 337
  veneration of the, 112
Porphyry (Neo-platonist), 134
Pounds, John (humanitarian), 192
Prayer comes naturally, 90
  influenced by fear, 90
  Origin of, 88–9, 90
  what it should be, 89
  will be superseded by contemplation, 355
Prayers and the Christian Church, 90
Preachers will become teachers, 385, 404
Prejudice distorts truth, 346
Presbyterians adopt the Pagan Lord's Table, 134
Priestcraft will someday cease, 414
  greatest force against progress, 72
  unnecessary to Spiritualism, 34, 327
Priesthood obstructed psychic knowledge, 62
  elevated superstition in name of Jesus, 186
  retards people's knowledge, 354
  Rise in the power of, 59–60
Priestley, Joseph (chemist), 198, 427
Priests and magicians had much in common, 244
  against intellectual development, 61–2, 65
  and cruelty to animals, 464
  and marriage, 82
  are not required by Spiritualists, 34, 327
  are rivals to mediums, 226
  as intermediaries, 60
  cannot explain Christian ritual, 225
  cannot now plead ignorance, 224
  claimed their instructions came from the gods, 72
  consulted now by ignorant and uneducated only, 69
  Deceptions and follies of, uncovered, 61
  Difficult to believe their honesty, 224
  do not consider themselves as teachers, 64
  enhance old religion and denounce the new, 354
  frightened humanity by mysterious warnings, 424
  have their minds twisted in theological colleges, 402
  misrepresent Spiritualism, 64
  never taught facts, only superstition, 71
  ordered the lives of everyone, 81
  Origin of, 59–60
  placed themselves above the law, 85
  pretended to be mediums, 60
  tampered with the scriptures, 375–6
  were often magicians, 101–2
  were regarded as scientists and doctors, 201
  will be replaced by mediums, 393
  will be unnecessary at the graveside, 392
  wishes, if not carried out, incurred wrath of the gods, 85

Primitive man termed an apparition a god, 219
Prince of Peace and Armistice day parades, 420
Principles of Sociology, The, 53*fn.*
Printing brought about the Renaissance, 161
   press invented, 429
Prison reform, advocates of, 434
Prisoners, their conditions exposed by Howard, 434
Progress, meant less to our ancestors, 202
   and its victims, 245-6
   comes from making mistakes, 423
   Desire for, caused cruel persecution, 202
   was very halting, 203
Prometheus (deity), 76, 133
Protestant Christians and their Church's teachings, 162
   Church condemns mediumship, 63
   Church, Origin of, 370
   Church, Persecution and torture by, 379
   Europe is shedding Paganism, 382
Protestantism, 381-2
   a reformed Christianity, 370, 380
   accepted Paganism, 173
   and fundamentals of Christianity, 371
   drawing away from Christendom, 162
   limits those to be saved, 116
   when in power persecuted and murdered, 87
Protons and electrons, 319
Protons, Function of, 266-7
Psychic Healing, its great power and future, 396-9
Psychic healing, 385, 396-8, 397
   knowledge discouraged by Christian Church, 63
   knowledge obstructed by priesthood, 62
   literature, 407
   photographic mediums, 234
   photography alone does not prove survival, 234
   phenomena in various temples, 102
   phenomena is natural, 38
   phenomena, Reality of, 103
   phenomena was ignored and forgotten, 204
   power and 1848, 331
   power and obliteration of mediums, 331
   power of outstanding men, 347
   powers of Christs, Saviours and Avators, 350
Psychic Stream, The, ix, x, 75, 119*fn*., 383*fn*., 412*fn*.
Psychical Research societies, 408
   science, discoveries made by, 200
   science joined together with physical science, 251, 258
   science on a firm basis, 440
   science, Study of, 232
   thought era now beginning, 257, 285
Psychometry shows how mind and substance can interact, 315
Ptolemy (scientist), 367

Public wash-houses and baths, 192
Pythagoras (philosopher), 130

Q

QUARRIER (humanitarian), 434
"Quelle" document, 142
   gospel, 156, 328
   gospel, the most accurate, 143
   reconstructed manuscript, 143-53

R

RĀ (deity), 96, 97, 105
Radio waves, 278
Radium, Discovery of, 428
Ragged Schools founded, 192
Railway pioneers, 430
Ramsay (physicist), 428
Rappings at Hydesville, 27-8
Rathbone, William (humanitarian), 192
Rationalism, Meaning of, 212
Rationalist, Advantage of being a, 213
   need not be a materialist, 212
   uses his reason, 212
Rationalist Press Association, 143*fn*.
Rawlinson, Sir Henry (Assyriologist), 94, 437
Rayleigh, Lord (physicist), 428
Reade, Winwood, 67*fn*.
"Real Presence" adopted in 9th century, 79
   traced to a séance, 80
Reality is only a glimmer at present, 447
   and Mind, 325
   Capacity of appreciating, 475
   in Etheria, 447
   Mind is the great, 423
   Science will never discover by concentrating on physical universe, 256
   Unfolding of, 440
Reason is the only guide, 213
   Lamp of, 437, 448, 474
   must be placed first, 472-3
Red Cloud (an etherian), 53
Redeemers, Mankind's belief in, 25
Reformation, The, 67, 160
   Cause of, 161, 173
   could have been averted, 172
   consolidated by Gustavus Adolphus, 432
   Unitarians considered not complete, 173
Reformed Church (see Church of the future)
Regulus, Story of, 404
Reincarnation, Doctrine of, 344
   No evidence for, 352-3
Religion, 243, 248 (see also Supernatural religion)
   and at-one-ness with the Cosmic mind, 358
   and ethics, 358
   and its mistakes about creation, 205
   a mystical union with the divine, 174-5
   A new, required to inspire us, 37
   and science can be blended, 324

Religion and science kept apart by ignorance, 216
  cause of half the events of history, x
  comprised men's mental needs, 458
  developed from sun worship, 241
  Each has its own particular gods, 241
  entwined with supernatural words, symbols and rites, 220
  Errors which crept into, 216
  has not civilised humanity, 245
  is difficult to define, 355
  is not church rites and ceremonies, 355
  is not speech at séances, 326
  its garments of superstition, 215
  Man fails to use his intelligence in, 357
  Natural, and science are one, 327
  Natural, and Spiritualists, 401
  Natural, defined as science of living, 360
  Natural, includes conduct, 361
  Natural, is based on evidence, 363
  Natural, philosophy and mysticism are one, 327, 467
  Natural, stands for truth, 327
  Natural, will make forward strides, 367
  now raised to realm of science, xi
  One copied from another, 346
  One natural, will be universal, 38
  Scientific attitude to, 215
  should be confined to facts, 410–11
  should be great reality to all, 357
  Supernatural, unnecessary to hold society together, 245
  to the materialist is a question of ethics, 211
  What it stands for, 216
  When it came into being, 359
Religions all claim to have been revealed by God, 244
  are based on superstition, 219
  can be traced to psychic phenomena, 102
  Creedal, are based on error, 363
  Creedal, devoid of evidence, 363
  Meaning of forms and ceremonies of, 224
  of the past historically false, 107
  Old, are dead or dying, 338
  People worshipped many gods, 220
  Trinity symbol found in many, 221
Religious creeds, rituals and ceremonials are mystical conceptions, 176
  beliefs a crutch for the ignorant, 44
  beliefs and ceremonials, Their origin, 57
  beliefs are many and varied, 248
  beliefs comfort and solace, 322
  creeds, antagonistic to science, 34
  creeds have never raised humanity ethically, 38
  leaders keep facts from the people, 464
  opinions uttered through a medium, 351

Religious sects and divisions will cease, 422
Rembrandt (painter), 438
Renaissance, 26, 381
  Aftermath of the, 87
  brought about by printing, 161
  Effect of, 374
  Great men of the, 427
  Ignorance prior to the, 224
Rennie, John (engineer), 430
Rescue Circles, 414–5
Resurrection, Erroneous belief in, 390–1
  Stories of the, 78
  story borrowed from the Egyptians, 38, 98
  story of Jesus superimposed, 181
Reynolds, Sir Joshua, 437
Richards (physicist), 428
Riddle of the Universe, The, 209
Rimmon (deity), 105
Roberts, Estelle (clairaudient), 417
Robertson (historian), 78*fn*., 375*fn*.
Rock of Truth, The, vii, xiii, xix, xxi, 46*fn*., 99, 117, 119*fn*., 250, 475
Roman and Greek writings were the civilising influence, 43
  Catholic beliefs, 162
  Catholic Church, asserts it is the only Church of Christ, 370
  Catholic Church elevated eminent mediums, 63
  Catholic Church, Infamies exposed, 431
  Catholic Church insists on *Semper idem*, 188
  Catholic Church, Persecution and torture by, 379
  Catholic Church uncompromising, 371
  Catholic churches and worship of images, 58
  Catholicism and Luther, 136
  Catholics and the Eucharist, 223
  Catholics cannot understand Deist's religion, 353
  Catholics limit those to be saved, 116
  literature on mediums and healing, 463
Rome, Bishop of, took title *Pontifex Maximus*, 378
Rome, Noble thinkers of, 42
  seat of Christendom, 182
  State religion of, 336
Royal Humane Society founded, 192
Society for the Prevention of Cruelty to Animals, 435
Ruler of the Universe is Mind, 308
Running Water (an etherian), 53
Russia converted to Christianity, 382
Rutherford, Lord, 428
Rylands, L. Gordon (author), 139–40

S

SABATU, the Babylonian Sabbath, 94
Sacrifice for sins in pre-Christian times, 77
  of human victims, 72–73
  not a divine institution, 216
  Origin of, 73
Sacrificial doctrine encouraged sin, 77

Sages in pre-Christian days made contact with the gods, 220
St. Paul's Cathedral will become a Spiritualist Church, 421
St. Peter's, Rome, and the claims Roman Catholics make, 111
St. Thomas's Hospital, London, 192
Sallust (author), 175
Salvation is not dependent on a belief, 412
Savery (engineer), 429
Saviour-god, Origin of the belief, 74
Saviour-gods and mythology, 92
   before Jesus' time, 78
   Christ's name added, 176
   The sixteen, 78
Saviours probably had psychic powers, 350
Scandinavia and religious worship, 58
Schneider, Rudi (medium), 231, 232
Schools, Reason for building of, 434
Science, Age of, 30–1, 366
   and natural religion are one, 324, 327, 339, 467
   and religion kept apart by ignorance, 216
   and Spiritualism, 33, 257, 327
   discovered our physical origin, xviii
   discoveries banished the gods, 207
   Enquiry and investigation denounced by priests, 71
   findings accepted, 32
   has neglected unseen universe, 255
   has proved creedal religions to be false, 334, 363
   more reliable than the Bible, 41
   never invents phenomena, 230
   of living and our place in Etheria, 360
   of living, Definition of natural religion, 361
   outlook on the universe, 334
   Progress made by, 429–30
   Religious creeds antagonistic to, 34
   What it has done and neglected, 215, 335
Scientists persecuted by the Church, 463
   should investigate what Spiritualism stands for, 257
   threw over everything outside the material, 204
   What we owe to them, 426–9
Scottish Shorter Catechism, 216
Séances, 214, 227, 251
   and Direct Voice, 399
   and religion, 326
   and what happens, 300
   are places for education and mental development, xix–xx
   recorded in Greek literature, 220
   Supernormal phenomena take place at, 251
Sectarian views in Etheria, 351
Seneca (philosopher), 159
Sermons of the future, 401
Servetus (anatomist), 161, 436
Set (Egyptian devil), 97
Seven Principles of Spiritualism (see under Spiritualism)
Sewing machines invented, 429

Shaftesbury, Lord (philanthropist), 435, 464
   received no encouragement from the Church, 463–4
Shakespeare, William, 439
Sharp, James (emancipationist), 430–431
Shepherd of Hermas, The, 150*fn*.
Sheraton (furniture maker), 439
Sick healed by mediums, 396
Sight, Process of seeing on earth, 259
Simplicius (schoolmaster), 66
Simpson, William (author), 56
Sin, Beginning of the orthodox idea of, 73
Sir James Young (physician), 436
Siva (deity), 92
Slavery, abolition of, 193, 431–2
   and bishops, 464
   upheld and practised by Christians, 86
Sleep, 288–9
Sloan, John C. (medium), 465–6
Smallpox, Scourge of, killed, 436
Smith, George (Assyriologist), 94, 437
Social order, a new, 33
Socrates (philosopher), 43, 65, 132, 153, 318, 349, 437
   and his teaching, 404
   gave more light than Jesus, 348
   left no writings, 119
   lived in contact with Etheria, 459
Soddy (physicist), 428
Solar system, 198
Solon (Athenian legislator), 433
Somerset, Edward (Marquis of Worcester), 429
Space, Our bodies mostly, 291
   Physical vibrations and, 291
   will cease to be, 315
Spanish America freed, 433
Spectrum of the spectroscope, 264
Spencer, Herbert, 53*fn*.
Spheres, separate, 303, 306
Spiers, Helen (clairaudient), 417
Spinoza (philosopher), 209, 437
Spirit should be read for "God" or "the Lord", 218
   world is tangible, 28
   world known as Etheria, xix
Spirits of the dead, Ancients believed they were in contact with, 218
   were known as messengers of God, 130
Spiritualism, xvi, xviii, xix, xx, 33, 64, 114
   A college needed for, 399
   a life to be lived, 384
   a world-wide philosophic religion, 34
   accepts finding of science, 29, 34
   Addition of a prefix causes disharmony, 362
   Advance of, 44–5
   an addition to knowledge, 32
   and Christianity are poles apart, 187, 189
   and natural religion stand for same thing, 361
   as a new revelation, 330
   as a philsosophy, xiii
   as a religion, xiii
   as a science, xiii
   based on evidence, must become supreme, 337

Index

Spiritualism based on scientific evidence, 29
Basis of, 326, 403
Birth of modern, 28
broadcasting forbidden, 179
burns like a flame to give light, 462
cannot be changed to meet other religious ideas, 364
Claims of, accepted throughout the world, 29, 327
destroys all barriers, 415
discards all false Christian claims, 350
does not conflict with philosophy, 327
does not include belief in reincarnation, 344
enables mankind to enter Etheria well prepared, 365
ethical basis is right conduct, 38
experiences recorded accurately, 459
explains our origin and destiny, xviii, 34
explains phenomena of the universe, 34
Findings of, 32
Future of, 415
gives comfort in sorrow, 34
gives facts, 326
has created mental revolution, 469
has no exclusiveness, 327
has no holy dogmas and doctrines, 34, 384
has no need for priests, 226
holds fast to facts, 364
Hostility to, 328
is a comfort at death, 364
is a great danger to orthodox religion, 63
is based on natural law, 364
is drawing the people, 406
is gaining strength, xvi
is independent of holy books, 34
is mythology rationalised, 38
is natural religion based on evidence, 363
is not a new sect, 34
is not a speculative religion, 326
is not fashionable as a religion, 406
is not in conflict with mysticism, 327
is oldest religion in the world, 459
is philosophy combined with evidence, 383
is Religion, not A religion, 38
is religion not designed for other religious bodies, 364
is science, not in conflict with, 327
is science of the universe, 31
is sufficient guidance through life, 364
Its claims, 29
Jesus acted up to the truth of, 184
makes cosmos more understandable, 338
must supplant all other world religions, 34
name in itself is unimportant, 360-1
need expect no help from Christianity, 412

Spiritualism only understood by intelligent people, 223
progresses faster than early Christianity, 337
proves we are etheric beings, 38
proves we are gods, 226
Religion of, 326-7
requires no priests, creeds, dogmas or doctrines, 327
rests on a solid scientific basis, 227
reveals what happens after death, 195
Seven principles of, 361-4
shows that happiness hereafter depends on life and character on earth, 373
stands for a scientific fact, 412
stands for central truth, 328
stands for freedom of thought and tolerance, 363
stands for knowledge, 343, 469
stands for overthrow of superstition, 195
stands for truth and proved by evidence, 189, 196, 363
stands for what Jesus stands for, 171
still illegal in Great Britain, 41
stresses that only character counts, 38
studied by scientists, 232-3
Survival and communication, 343
teaches new philosophy of life, 341-2
teaches us our physical origin and destiny, xviii, 34
The best way to spread the truths of, 47
training of mediums, 399-400
truths becoming known, x
What it does not include, 344
What it stands for, 171, 189, 195, 196, 328, 338, 343, 363, 469
Why Christians see no resemblance in, 329
Why it does not include any prefix, 363
Why it is hated by priests, 225-6
will change humanity's outlook, xvi
will enter all departments of life, xv
will give intellectual and spiritual light, 196
will grow and gather in strength, 196, 415
will satisfy all intellectual desires, 196, 339, 350
will take the place of Christianity, xvii-xviii, 37-8, 421
Spiritualist belief of life after death, 229
Church arising out of the ashes of the old, 400
Church handicapped financially, 406
Church is raising level of intelligence, 405-6
Church, Lyceums for children, 408
Church organisation is sound, 415

Spiritualist Church, the President, 394
  Church will bring Christians back to where they strayed from in the 4th century, 402–3
  churches filled to overflowing, 403
  Hymn Book, 395
  journals, 189–90
  platform, all views welcomed, 415
  platform raising level of education and knowledge, 406–7
  principles proved by evidence, 362
  religion is based on facts, 326
  services attended by people of various religious beliefs, 403
  teachings will cause orthodox teaching to become discarded, 422
Spiritualistic beliefs, 343, 362
  strength lies in its Home Circles, 414
  teaching and that of Jesus are alike, 328
Spiritualists and Bible reading, 395
  accept apparitions, 126
  and funeral services, 391
  are not replacing one superstition by another, 47
  believe nothing is too sacred to be investigated, 401
  cannot be Christians, 189
  contemplate the divine in nature, 401
  Definition of a, 342
  do not worship Jesus but admire him, 184
  have evidence that life continues, 333
  hold the leadership of human thought, 257
  in search for truth, 401
  limit of knowledge, 352–3
  literary clubs, 407
  look forward not backward, 360
  National Union, 416, 421
  not intolerant, 363
  number many millions, 337
  outgrow superstitions, 330
  outlook on life, 31
  perceives what the Materialists lack, 213
  prove their claims, 334
  reach Etheria with knowledge, 365
  show reasonableness of nature's plan, 333
  show what caused Christianity, 171
  teach the world that man is his own saviour, 68–9
  The gulf between them and the Materialists, 210, 213–4
  their duty to lead the world, 405
  trying to bring Christians back to Jesus, 171
  Why they are treated with contempt, 334
Steam, discovery of its power, 429
  hammer invented, 430
  locomotive invented, 430
Stephenson, George (engineer), 430
  Robert (engineer), 430
Stag-hunting, Cruelty of, 359
Stars and planets, 203

Stoics, Philosophy of, 130
Stone Age, 205
Stradivarius (violinist), 439
Streeter (author), 119*fn*.
Subconscious idea of a future life, 248
Substance and time here and hereafter, 313
  and mind reactions, 318
  Etheric, 428, 446
  exists beyond physical sense perceptions, 267
  in Etheria too fine for perception in physical body, 268, 283
  influences thoughts, 303
  is penetrated by mind, 318
  Nature of, comprehended, 199
  on earth, Moulding of, 446
  on earth vibrates in harmony with sun waves, 261
  Physical, dominated by the mind, 253, 325
  produces vibrations which create mental image, 259
  vibrates faster in Etheria, 283
Suicide, The, 310
Sumerians, The, 93
Sun, The, 259–307
  a grain of sand in the universe, 254
  composed of globes, 271
  Etheric, its light and heat, 271
  gods, 91
  its size, etc., 261
  worship, 59, 130
  Worship, ceremonials and rites originated in, 117
  worship, forerunner of Christianity, 176
  worship, Saviour-god stories traced back to, 78
  worshipped as a god of goodness, 91
Sunday, borrowed from Mithraism, 180
Supernatural and natural intertwined, 124
  and belief in God, 358
  Believers in, 29, 33
  gods have disappeared from the sky, 197
  obscured the natural, 220
  religion has same beliefs as primitive man, 105
  religion is dying, 196
  religion unnecessary to keep society together, 245
  religion, What it stands for, 104
Supernormal, Ample evidence for, 213
  occurrence experienced by Paul, 123
  occurrences and scientists, 233
  phenomena take place at séances, 251
Superstition, Age of, 25–6, 32, 50–114, 197
  Age of, followed by materialism, 197
  All religions based on, 115
  banished by discoveries, 199
  Church of England maintained to propagate, 374
  Edifice of, blown up, 87
  elevated by priesthood in name of Jesus, 186
  its early beliefs, 57

Superstition retarded mental advance, 201
  supplants philosophy, 159
  taught by priests, 71
  termed Christianity, 181
  upheld by Pagan priests, 157
  will be overthrown by Spiritualism, 195
Superstitions, 29, 103
  accepted by Christendom, 31
  act as barrier to a common religion, 347
  Belief in, 358
  have nothing to do with real religion, 358
  incorporated in the marriage service, 389
  Mankind still victim of ancient, 365
  Mankind will become mentally free of, 422
  of the past, 30, 32
Survival after death, 229
  after death is bedrock of religion, 362
  after death, Study of, 407
  and communication, 343
  Belief in, 215
  Proof of, 234-7
  proved by six classes of phenomena, 236-7
Symbolic beliefs and rituals, 219-20, 346
Symbolism accepted literally, 221
Synoptic gospels vary in doctrine, 127
System of the World, 427

T

TAOISM teaching debased, 349
Tarsus, a seat of learning, 126
Teachings of thinkers obliterated by Christianity, 42
Telepathic contact, 359
Telephone invented, 430
Telescope created a mental revolution, 202
  called instrument of the devil, 199
Telford (engineer), 430
Temple, Archbishop, opposes enquiry into after-life, 68
Temples, 101
Ten Hours' Bill, 192
Themistocles, Admiral, 432
Theodosius I (Emperor), 377
Theological literature lacks scientific basis, xi
  picture shattered beyond repair, 205
Theology preaches religion of the savage, 105
Thimmonier, Barthelemy, 429
Thinkers enlarged our knowledge, 424 *et seq.*
  often denounced and traduced, 424
  persecuted by the Church, 463
Thinking consists of image-making, 294
  is killing orthodoxy, 384
  logically for future happiness, xv
  requires mind, 314

Thinking wrongly causes unhappiness and misery, xv
Thirty Years' War, 432
This World and Beyond, 327-8
Thomson (physicist), 428
  Right Reverend, 382
Thoth (deity), 96
Thought and matter inseparable, 207
  brings the universe into being, 289
  Conscious, consists of mind image-making, 303, 318
  Developing, is ever-widening, 315
  Freedom of, 246
  is lubricated by liberty, 444
  Mind images termed, 429
  New age of, 30
  produces movement, 314
  Speed of, is the speed of mind, 313
  Sub-conscious, constructs our bodies, 319
  when content and harmony reign, 321
  when time and space cease, 315, 316
  where mind conditions substance, 317
Thoughts control our destiny, 343
  in Etheria become things, 450
  influence substance, 303
  Intelligent, will cease the desire of force, 453
  refine our etheric bodies, 449
Thucydides (historian), 437
Tibetans believe Dalai Lama is a god, 346
Time and distance in Etheria, 253-4, 316, 320-1
  ceases when we sleep, 312
  is related to surroundings, 313
  will exist until mind embraces all, 313
Times, The, 44, 68, 70
Torquemada brought orthodox religion into disrepute, 356
Tower of Babel, 94-5
Tradition, and orthodox religion, 387
Trance, normal, does not alone prove survival, 233-4
  phenomena deserves to be taken seriously, 237
Tree of Knowledge, Wise to eat from, 423
Trevithick (engineer), 430
Trinitarians, The, 172
  responsible for murder and savagery, 356
  Triumph of, 379
Trinity conceived in Alexandria, 128
  Definition of the, 180
  Doctrine of, 180, 374
  doctrine taken over by Protestants, 173
  God symbolised as a, 221
  God-man looked upon as a member of, 221
  gods, 221-2
  House brethren opposed saving of life at sea, 434-5
  in Egypt was represented by equilateral triangle, 221
  of gods denounced by Jehovah, 129
  Symbol of, found in many religions, 221

The Unfolding Universe

Trinity symbol represented man, who is body, soul and spirit, 221
Truth, All should be bearers of, 472
  Diversity of views lead to, 387
  Errors rectified lead us to, 423
  How it can be reached, 472
  is eternal, 364
  must prevail, 34, 338
Tuckerman, Joseph (philanthropist), 192
Turner, Joseph (painter), 438
Tuttle, Hudson (medium), 293

U

ULTIMATE, Attainment of, 325
Ultra-violet rays, 267
Unitarian Church, 402
Unitarians, an influence for good, 173
  become outcasts, 172, 173
  believe in one personal god, 177, 180
  defeated at Nicaea, 379
  held Reformation was not thorough enough, 173
United States of America founded, 433
  States of Europe, Advocacy of, 432
  States of the World, first advocated, 432
Universal Mind, The, 308
Universe becomes an enlarged panorama, 343
  and our consciousness, 290
  as it really is, 317
  as mind, 238, 239
  as the mind is so is the, 252, 407
  boundless and timeless, 255
  brought into being by individual thought, 289
  compared to mind and body, 318
  Conception of, changing, 258
  Divine Mind of the, 304, 474
  dominated by Mind, 240
  explained in material terms, 204
  God is over-ruling Mind of the, 386
  Gods placed outside, in error, 240
  governed and ordered by mind, 248, 361
  governed by law and order, 30, 41
  Greatness and vastness of, 200
  Guiding intelligence of, 360
  has unfolded during our time, 249
  Immensity of, is overwhelming, 250
  includes unsensed forces, 238
  Infinite Mind of the, 324
  in terms of physics and chemistry, 210-11
  is a gigantic scale of vibrations, 240
  is a machine, 200
  is an assembly of developing thoughts, 253
  is greater than physical senses can comprehend, 238
  is slowly unfolding itself, 457
  is vibrations of different degrees, 290
  is what each thinks, 252, 314

Universe, Knowledge of vibrations will enable us to visualize the real, 287
  Matter is one expression of reality in the, 214
  Mind constitutes the, 312
  Mind the ruler of the, 308
  not sensed without mind, 312
  Outlook on the, 338
  Physical and material, 31
  Spiritualism is the science of the entire, 31
  The sun compared to the, 254
  Thinkers lived in an unfolding, 424 et seq.
  Throne of, occupied by Mind, 325
  unfolding comes from enlarging mind, 407, 467, 474
  will be comprehended when time and space cease to be, 320
  Without mind no, 290, 324
  Without vibrations there would be no, 240
  working out its own destiny, 317
Universe, The Riddle of the, 209
Unseen and unknown, had profound influence on our ancestors, 245
  force termed Mind, 238
  forces, The universe includes, 238
Uta-Napishtim, the Babylonian Noah, 94

V

VALENTINUS (theologian), 158-9
Vatican Palace, Rome, 112
Vasco da Gama (explorer), 426
Vedic mysteries of India came from psychic phenomena, 102
Vestal virgins, and their duties, 58
Vibration ranges of, in the Greater World, 300
Vibrations 239-40, 250, 290, 295, 428
  and the physical body, 290
  Astral range of, 298
  Colour, 452
  Each person is a moving range of, 288
  Earth is only one range of, 294
  Fastest range of, is mind, 290
  in tune with new body in Etheria, 296-7
  influenced by thought, 315
  Many ranges in Etheria, 294
  of body become related to higher surfaces in Etheria, 295, 449
  of Greater World as seen from outside, 303
  on earth and Etheria, 286
  produce matter and etheric substance, 238
  tangible to Etherians, 28
  The cause behind all, 318
  There must be two states of, 290
  We and Etherians live within different ranges of vibrations, 256
  which cause substance, 259
  will enable us to visualise real universe, 287
  Without them there would be no universe, 240

Index

Virgil foretold coming of the Christ, 128
Virgin birth never referred to by Jesus, 181
    adoration and sanctification derived from earlier sources, 129
    birth stories, 78
Virgins chosen as mothers of gods, 92
Virtues of pre-Christian philosophers, 404
    Importance of the, 393
Vishnu (deity), 92, 105
Vittorino da Feltre (schoolmaster), 437
Vohu Mano (deity), 92
Voltaire (author), 193, 405, 431-2

W

WAGNER (composer), 439
Wallace, Alfred Russel, 428
War brought about by gods, 100
    does not advance humanity, 453-4
    will some day end through developing mind, 393, 454-5
Wars intensify all that is evil, 452
    may cease through knowledge of Etheria, 452-3
Washington, George, 433
Waterloo, Battle of, 433
Watt, James (engineer), 429
Wealth, material and mental, 448
Weapons of destruction, Evil in the traffic of, 420
Wedgwood, Josiah (potter), 439
Wesley, John (priest), 28
Westminster Abbey and Armistice Day, 420
    Abbey will someday be a Spiritualist Church, 421
Wilberforce (emancipationist), 430, 464
Wilkinson, Catherine (philanthropist), 192
William of Orange, viii
Winstanley (lighthouse builder), 434-5
Wisdom (Sophia), 128
    from experience, 448
    is memory put to correct use, 448
Witchcraft laws still in force, 41
Witch-burning ceases, 28
Witches burned by the Christian Church, 421
    now known as mediums, were not allowed to live, 64
Women, Churching of, is a Judaic institution, 389
    degraded by worship of gods, 34
Wonders of Life, The, 209
World (*see also* Greater World)
    and life on it has existed millions of years, 205

World, Creation of in six days a fallacy, 204
    lower in vibrations than earth, 270
    Physical, ceases to us at death, 306-7
    religions, 23
    religions are speculative, 326
    religions cannot become united, 347
    religions extend back to sun worship, 104
    religions lead as far as the grave only, 24
    religions proved false by science, 334
    religions, Reason for, 316
    religions, relationship to each other, 329
    religions, study of by eminent men, 53
    religions, Their superstitions will be uncoiled, 189
    religions will be supplanted by Spiritualism, 34, 326-9, 350
    The greater, or Etheria, 248-307
    timeless and spaceless, is our destiny, 316
Worlds, Etheria and earth are not entirely equal, 460
    Etheria comprises seven, 269-70
World-saviours, episodes mutilated in their telling, 222
Worship of Death, The, 56
Worship, Origin of, 88
    will be superseded by contemplation of divine in nature, 110, 355
Wren, Christopher (architect), 438
Wyatt, Thomas (clairaudient), 417
Wycliffe, John (reformer), 431

X

XENOPHON (historian), 153, 437
Xerxes (emperor), 432

Y

YAHVEH stands for one God, 218
Yogis able to project their etheric bodies, 269
York, Archbishop of, 373
York, Convocation of (1934), 371, 372, 373
Youth to be taught continuance of life will not be frightened by death, 409

Z

ZENO (philosopher), 159
Zeus (deity), 75, 76, 95, 105, 125
Zoroaster (religious teacher), 92